CASES AND MATERIALS

PRODUCTS LIABILITY AND SAFETY

FIFTH EDITION

STATUTORY SUPPLEMENT

by

DAVID G. OWEN
Carolina Distinguished Professor of Law
University of South Carolina

JOHN E. MONTGOMERY
Dean Emeritus and Professor of Law
University of South Carolina

MARY J. DAVIS
Stites & Harbison Professor of Law
University of Kentucky

FOUNDATION PRESS

2007

THOMSON

WEST

© 1980, 1983, 1985, 1989, 1993, 1996– 2006 FOUNDATION PRESS

————————

© 2007 By FOUNDATION PRESS
395 Hudson Street
New York, NY 10014
Phone Toll Free 1–877–888–1330
Fax (212) 367–6799
foundation–press.com

ISBN 978–1–59941–302–0

[No claim of copyright is made for official U.S. government statutes, rules or regulations.]

 *TEXT IS PRINTED ON 10% POST CONSUMER RECYCLED PAPER*

PREFACE

This Statutory Supplement accompanies the Fifth Edition of Products Liability and Safety: Cases and Materials. This Supplement retains and updates the statutory material from the 2006 Supplement. Because of the publication of the Restatement Third of Torts: Products Liability, which is included, we have retained only the most critical portions of the Second Restatement. The Uniform Commercial Code and the various legislative materials included therein continue to be included. State legislatures continue to enact products liability "reform" acts of various types, and a comprehensive set of those statutes is included. The federal reform efforts of the past ten years seem to have subsided so those statutory materials have been deleted from this Supplement. The new federal legislation addressing liability of handgun manufacturers is included.

In order to maximize the materials available to teachers and students, we have erred on the side of over-inclusion, particularly in the selected state statutes. We expect teachers will be selective in their assignments from this supplement and intend that the supplement complement the individual teaching styles and topic preferences of our users.

From time to time we receive comments and suggestions for improvement from users of the book. We consider this information valuable in our ongoing effort to present teachers and students with the most useful and up-to-date materials on the law of products liability. To that end, as in the past, we invite comments and criticisms on the materials in the casebook and the Supplement alike.

DAVID G. OWEN
JOHN E. MONTGOMERY
MARY J. DAVIS

July 2007

*

ACKNOWLEDGEMENTS

We are grateful to Karen Miller, University of South Carolina School of Law Class of 2007, for her excellent research assistance in updating the state statutory material.

We would like to acknowledge the following publishers who permitted us to use the materials noted:

American Law Institute, Restatement of the Law (Second) of Torts, selected sections. Copyright 1965 by the American Law Institute. American Law Institute, Restatement of the Law (Third) of Torts: Products Liability, selected sections. Copyright 1998 by the American Law Institute. Reprinted with permission of the American Law Institute.

Uniform Commercial Code, Official Text and Comments, selected sections. Copyright 1987 by the American Law Institute and the National Conference of Commissioners on the Uniform State Laws. Reprinted with permission. All rights are reserved.

*

SUMMARY OF CONTENTS

*

TABLE OF CONTENTS

STATUTORY SUPPLEMENT

CASES AND MATERIALS

PRODUCTS LIABILITY AND SAFETY

*

RESTATEMENT (SECOND) OF TORTS

Selected Sections*

Chapter 14

LIABILITY OF PERSONS SUPPLYING CHATTELS FOR THE USE OF OTHERS

TOPIC 1. RULES APPLICABLE TO ALL SUPPLIERS

Scope Note: This Topic states the rules which are equally applicable to all persons who in any way or for any purpose supply chattels for the use of others or permit others to use their chattels. There are other rules which impose upon the suppliers of chattels additional duties because of the purpose for which or the manner in which the chattels are supplied or because the chattel has been made by them or put out as their product. These rules are stated hereafter. The peculiar rules which determine the liability of one who supplies a chattel or permits its use for purposes in which he himself has a business interest are stated in §§ 391–393. The peculiar rules applicable to those who manufacture the chattels which they supply are stated in §§ 394–398. The rules which determine the peculiar liability of vendors of chattels manufactured by others are stated in §§ 399–402. A special rule of strict liability applicable to sellers of articles for consumption is stated in § 402 A, and a special rule as to liability for misrepresentations made by a seller of goods to the consumer is stated in § 402 B.

The peculiar rules applicable to independent contractors and repairmen are stated in §§ 403 and 404. The peculiar rules applicable to donors, lenders, and lessors of chattels are stated in §§ 405–408.

In many instances the rules stated in the Sections in this Chapter may overlap, and the plaintiff may recover under the rules stated in two or more Sections. No attempt has been made to indicate, by way of cross-reference under any one Section, the other Sections upon which recovery may possibly be based.

§ 388. Chattel Known to Be Dangerous for Intended Use

One who supplies directly or through a third person a chattel for another to use is subject to liability to those whom the supplier should expect to use the chattel with the consent of the other or to be endangered by its probable use, for physical harm caused by the use of the chattel in the manner for which and by a person for whose use it is supplied, if the supplier

(a) knows or has reason to know that the chattel is or is likely to be dangerous for the use for which it is supplied, and

(b) has no reason to believe that those for whose use the chattel is supplied will realize its dangerous condition, and

(c) fails to exercise reasonable care to inform them of its dangerous condition or of the facts which make it likely to be dangerous.

Comment:

a. The words "those whom the supplier should expect to use the chattel" and the words "a person for whose use it is supplied" include not only the person to whom the chattel is turned over by the supplier, but also all those who are members of a class whom the supplier should expect to use it or occupy it or share in its use with the consent of such person, irrespective of whether the supplier has any particular person in mind. Thus, one who lends an automobile to a friend and who fails to disclose a defect of which he himself knows and which he should recognize as making it unreasonably dangerous for use, is subject to liability not only to his friend, but also to anyone whom his friend permits to drive the car or chooses to receive in it as passenger or guest, if it is understood between them that the car may be so used. So too, one entrusting a chattel to a common carrier for transportation must expect that the chattel will be handled by the carrier's employees.

In the cases thus far decided, the rule stated in this Section has been applied only in favor of those who are injured while the chattel is being used by the person to whom it is supplied, or with his consent. In all probability the rule stated would not apply in favor of a thief of the chattel, or one injured while the thief is using it. Nor would it apply, for example, in favor of a trespasser who entered an automobile and was injured by its condition. On the other hand, no reason is apparent for limiting the rule to exclude persons who are for any reason privileged to use the chattel without the consent of the person to whom it is supplied, as in the case of a police officer who commandeers an automobile to pursue a criminal, or moves it in order to avoid danger to the public safety.

b. This Section states that one who supplies a chattel for another to use for any purpose is subject to liability for physical harm caused by his failure to exercise reasonable care to give to those whom he may expect to use the chattel any information as to the character and condition of the chattel which he possesses, and which he should recognize as necessary to enable them to realize the danger of using it. A fortiori, one so supplying a chattel is subject to liability if by word or deed he leads those who are to use the chattel to believe it to be of a character or in a condition safer for use than he knows it to be or to be likely to be.

Illustration:

1. A sells to B a shotgun, knowing that B intends to give it to his son C as a birthday present. A knows, but does not tell B, that the trigger mechanism of the gun is so defective that it is likely to be discharged by a slight jolt. B gives the gun to C. While C is using the

gun it is discharged, and C is injured, by reason of the defective mechanism. A is subject to liability to C.

c. Persons included as "suppliers." The rules stated in this Section and throughout this Topic apply to determine the liability of any person who for any purpose or in any manner gives possession of a chattel for another's use, or who permits another to use or occupy it while it is in his own possession or control, without disclosing his knowledge that the chattel is dangerous for the use for which it is supplied or for which it is permitted to be used. These rules, therefore, apply to sellers, lessors, donors, or lenders, irrespective of whether the chattel is made by them or by a third person. They apply to all kinds of bailors, irrespective of whether the bailment is for a reward or gratuitous, and irrespective of whether the bailment is for use, transportation, safekeeping, or repair. They also apply to one who undertakes the repair of a chattel and who delivers it back with knowledge that it is defective because of the work which he is employed to do upon it. (See § 403.)

d. One supplying a chattel to be used or dealt with by others is subject to liability under the rule stated in this Section, not only to those for whose use the chattel is supplied but also to third persons whom the supplier should expect to be endangered by its use.

e. Ambit of liability. The liability stated in this Section exists only if physical harm is caused by the use of the chattel by those for whose use the chattel is supplied, and in the manner for which it is supplied. Except possibly where there is a privilege to use the chattel, the one who supplies a chattel for another's use is not subject to liability for bodily harm caused by its use by a third person without the consent of him for whose use it is supplied. This is true although the chattel is one of a sort notoriously likely to be so used. So too, the supplier is not subject to liability for bodily harm caused by its use by a third person who uses it even with the consent of him for whom it is supplied, if the supplier has no reason to expect that such a third person may be permitted to use it.

In order that the supplier of a chattel may be subject to liability under the rule stated in this Section, not only must the person who uses the chattel be one whom the supplier should expect to use it with the consent of him to whom it is supplied, but the chattel must also be put to a use to which the supplier has reason to expect it to be put. Thus, one who lends a chattel to another to be put to a particular use for which, though defective, it is safe, is not required to give warning of the defect, although he knows of its existence and knows that it makes the chattel dangerous for other uses, unless he has reason to expect such other uses.

f. As pointed out in § 5, the phrase "subject to liability" is used to indicate that the person whose conduct is in question is liable if, but only if, there also exist the other conditions necessary to liability. The person using the chattel may disable himself from bringing an action either by his contributory negligence in voluntarily using the chattel with knowledge of its dangerous condition, or by his contributory negligence in failing to make a proper inspection which would have disclosed the defect, or in failing to use the precautions obviously necessary to the safe use of the chattel.

Comment on Clause (a):

  g. The duty which the rule stated in this Section imposes upon the supplier of a chattel for another's use is to exercise reasonable care to give to those who are to use the chattel the information which the supplier possesses, and which he should realize to be necessary to make its use safe for them and those in whose vicinity it is to be used. This information enables those for whom the chattel is supplied to determine whether they shall accept and use it. Save in exceptional circumstances, as where the chattel, no matter how carefully dealt with, is incapable of any safe use, or where the person to whom it is supplied is obviously likely to misuse it, the supplier of a chattel who has given such information is entitled to assume that it will not be used for purposes for which the information given by him shows it to be unfit and, therefore, is relieved of liability for harm done by its misuse to those in the vicinity of its probable use.

  A chattel may be so imperfect that it is unlikely to be safe for use for any purpose, no matter how great the care which is exercised in using it. As to the rule which determines liability in such case, see § 389.

  There are many chattels which, even though perfect, are unsafe for any use or for the particular use for which they are supplied unless their properties and capabilities are known to those who use them. If such a chattel is supplied to another whom the supplier should realize to be unlikely to know its properties and capabilities, the supplier is required to exercise reasonable care to give to the other such information thereof as he himself possesses.

Illustration:

  2. A is a guest in B's house. A is taken suddenly ill. B gives him a drug which B knows can only be safely used if taken in certain doses and under certain conditions. B gives the drug to A, but forgets to instruct him as to the manner in which it is to be used. A takes it in a larger dose than is proper, or fails to take the precautions which are necessary to make it safe. In consequence A's illness is increased. B is subject to liability to A.

Comment:

  h. There are many articles which are so defective as to be incapable of safe use for any of the purposes for which they are normally fit or for use in the manner in which such articles are normally capable of safe use, but which are safe for limited uses or if used with particular precautions. If the appearance of such a chattel does not disclose its defective condition, the supplier is under a duty to exercise reasonable care to disclose its condition, in so far as it is known to him, to those who are to use it, or to inform them that it is fit only for these limited uses, or if used with the particular precautions.

The supplier of a defective chattel may have had peculiar experience with such chattels, and he may, therefore, be required to realize that a disclosure of the actual condition of the chattel will not be enough to inform the user of the danger of using it except for limited purposes or with particular precautions. If such is the case, it is not enough for the supplier to inform those who are to use the chattel of its actual condition. He must exercise reasonable care to apprise them of the danger of using it otherwise than for the particular purposes for which he should know it to be fit or with the particular precautions which he should realize to be necessary to make its use safe.

i. Where lot of chattels contains a few defective ones. It is not necessary in order that a supplier of a chattel for another's use be liable under the rule stated in this Section that he should know that the particular chattel is dangerous for the use for which it is supplied. It is enough that he knows of facts which make it likely that the particular chattel may be dangerous, as where he knows that it is part of a lot, some of which he has discovered to be so imperfect as to be dangerous. If so, he is required to exercise reasonable care to acquaint those for whose use the chattel is supplied of these facts, in order that they may realize the risk they will run in using the chattel and may make an intelligent choice as to the advisability of doing so.

Illustration:

3. A sells or gives to B a can of baking powder. A knows that several, though not all, of the lot of cans of which this can is a part have exploded when opened. He does not inform B of this fact. While C, B's cook, is attempting to open the can, it explodes, causing harm to C's eyes and also the eyes of D, B's kitchen maid, who is standing nearby. A is subject to liability to C and D.

j. So too, one may put into a stock of chattels which he intends subsequently to supply for the use of others, articles which he then knows to be, or to be likely to be, dangerous for the use for which they are to be supplied. It may, however, subsequently be impossible to tell which of the chattels are of this character, and, therefore, at the time the particular article is supplied the supplier may not know that it is dangerous. He is, however, subject to liability, since he knows that it may be one of the chattels which is dangerous. This situation usually arises where the supplier is a manufacturer whose business is divided into different departments. In such a case the operative department may discover a defect in a particular chattel which the subsequent processes of manufacture may make it difficult or impossible to detect. So too, defective material may be knowingly used in the manufacture of a lot of chattels so that it is obvious that some, though not all, of these must be defective. Here again the process of manufacture may make it impossible to tell, at the time the particular chattel is supplied, which of the lot are dangerous and which safe.

Illustration:

4. The A Manufacturing Company makes a lot of ladders out of a shipment of wood of which some is knotted. It is impossible to see the knots after the ladders have been painted. One of the ladders is sold to B. While C, B's servant, is using the ladder, it breaks because of the knots in the wood of which it is made. The A Company is subject to liability to C, although at the time the ladder was sold it appeared perfectly sound and the sales department which sold the ladder had not been informed that defective material had been used in the construction of this lot of ladders.

Comment on Clause (b):

k. *When warning of defects unnecessary.* One who supplies a chattel to others to use for any purpose is under a duty to exercise reasonable care to inform them of its dangerous character in so far as it is known to him, or of facts which to his knowledge make it likely to be dangerous, if, but only if, he has no reason to expect that those for whose use the chattel is supplied will discover its condition and realize the danger involved. It is not necessary for the supplier to inform those for whose use the chattel is supplied of a condition which a mere casual looking over will disclose, unless the circumstances under which the chattel is supplied are such as to make it likely that even so casual an inspection will not be made. However, the condition, although readily observable, may be one which only persons of special experience would realize to be dangerous. In such case, if the supplier, having such special experience, knows that the condition involves danger and has no reason to believe that those who use it will have such special experience as will enable them to perceive the danger, he is required to inform them of the risk of which he himself knows and which he has no reason to suppose that they will realize.

Comment on Clause (c):

l. The supplier's duty is to exercise reasonable care to inform those for whose use the article is supplied of dangers which are peculiarly within his knowledge. If he has done so, he is not subject to liability, even though the information never reaches those for whose use the chattel is supplied. The factors which determine whether the supplier exercises reasonable care by giving this information to third persons through whom the chattel is supplied for the use of others, are stated in Comment *n*.

m. *Inspection.* The fact that a chattel is supplied for the use of others does not of itself impose upon the supplier a duty to make an inspection of the chattel, no matter how cursory, in order to discover whether it is fit for the use for which it is supplied. Such a duty may be imposed because of the purpose for which the chattel is to be used by those to whom it is supplied. (See § 392.) A manufacturer of a chattel may be under a duty to inspect the materials and parts out of which it is made and to subject the finished article to such an inspection as the danger involved in an imperfect article makes reasonable. (See § 395 and Comment *e* under that Section.) Under certain conditions, stated in §§ 403, 404, and 408, an independent contractor or lessor may be under a similar duty of inspection.

n. Warnings given to third person. Chattels are often supplied for the use of others, although the chattels or the permission to use them are not given directly to those for whose use they are supplied, as when a wholesale dealer sells to a retailer goods which are obviously to be used by the persons purchasing them from him, or when a contractor furnishes the scaffoldings or other appliances which his subcontractor and the latter's servants are to use, or when an automobile is lent for the borrower to use for the conveyance of his family and friends. In all such cases the question may arise as to whether the person supplying the chattel is exercising that reasonable care, which he owes to those who are to use it, by informing the third person through whom the chattel is supplied of its actual character.

Giving to the third person through whom the chattel is supplied all the information necessary to its safe use is not in all cases sufficient to relieve the supplier from liability. It is merely a means by which this information is to be conveyed to those who are to use the chattel. The question remains whether this method gives a reasonable assurance that the information will reach those whose safety depends upon their having it. All sorts of chattels may be supplied for the use of others, through all sorts of third persons and under an infinite variety of circumstances. This being true, it is obviously impossible to state in advance any set of rules which will automatically determine in all cases whether one supplying a chattel for the use of others through a third person has satisfied his duty to those who are to use the chattel by informing the third person of the dangerous character of the chattel, or of the precautions which must be exercised in using it in order to make its use safe. There are, however, certain factors which are important in determining this question. There is necessarily some chance that information given to the third person will not be communicated by him to those who are to use the chattel. This chance varies with the circumstances existing at the time the chattel is turned over to the third person, or permission is given to him to allow others to use it. These circumstances include the known or knowable character of the third person and may also include the purpose for which the chattel is given. Modern life would be intolerable unless one were permitted to rely to a certain extent on others' doing what they normally do, particularly if it is their duty to do so. If the chattel is one which if ignorantly used contains no great chance of causing anything more than some comparatively trivial harm, it is reasonable to permit the one who supplies the chattel through a third person to rely upon the fact that the third person is an ordinary normal man to whose discredit the supplier knows nothing, as a sufficient assurance that information given to him will be passed on to those who are to use the chattel.

If, however, the third person is known to be careless or inconsiderate or if the purpose for which the chattel is to be used is to his advantage and knowledge of the true character of the chattel is likely to prevent its being used and so to deprive him of this advantage—as when goods so defective as to be unsalable are sold by a wholesaler to a retailer—the supplier of the chattel has reason to expect, or at least suspect, that the information will fail to reach those who are to use the chattel and whose safety depends upon their knowledge of its true character. In such a case, the supplier may well be required to go further than to tell such a third person of the dangerous character of the article, or, if he fails to do so, to take the risk of being subjected to liability if the information is not brought home to those whom the supplier should expect to use the chattel. In many cases the burden of doing so is slight, as when the chattel is to be used in the presence or vicinity of the person supplying it, so that he could easily give a personal warning to those who are to use the chattel. Even though the supplier has no practicable opportunity to give this information directly and in person to those who are to use the chattel or share in its use, it is not unreasonable to require him to make good any harm which is caused by his using so unreliable a method of giving the information which is obviously necessary to make the chattel safe for those who use it and those in the vicinity of its use.

Here, as in every case which involves the determination of the precautions which must be taken to satisfy the requirements of reasonable care, the magnitude of the risk involved must be compared with the burden which would be imposed by requiring them (see § 291), and the magnitude of the risk is determined not only by the chance that some harm may result but also the serious or trivial character of the harm which is likely to result (see § 293). Since the care which must be taken always increases with the danger involved, it may be reasonable to require those who supply through others chattels which if ignorantly used involve grave risk of serious harm to those who use them and those in the vicinity of their use, to take precautions to bring the information home to the users of such chattels which it would be unreasonable to demand were the chattels of a less dangerous character.

Thus, while it may be proper to permit a supplier to assume that one through whom he supplies a chattel which is only slightly dangerous will communicate the information given him to those who are to use it unless he knows that the other is careless, it may be improper to permit him to trust the conveyance of the necessary information of the actual character of a highly dangerous article to a third person of whose character he knows nothing. It may well be that he should take the risk that this information may not be communicated, unless he exercises reasonable care to ascertain the character of the third person, or unless from previous experience with him or from the excellence of his reputation the supplier has positive reason to believe that he is careful. In addition to this, if the danger involved in the ignorant use of a particular chattel is very great, it may be that the supplier does not exercise reasonable care in entrusting the communication of the necessary information even to a person whom he has good reason to believe to be careful. Many such articles can be made to carry their own message to the understanding of those who are likely to use them by the form in which they are put out, by the container in which they are supplied, or by a label or other device, indicating with a substantial sufficiency their dangerous character. Where the danger involved in the ignorant use of their true quality is great and such means of disclosure are practicable and not unduly burdensome, it may well be that the supplier should be required to adopt them. There are many statutes which require that articles which are highly dangerous if used in ignorance of their character, such as poisons, explosives, and inflammables, shall be put out in such a form as to bear on their face notice of their dangerous character, either by the additional coloring matter, the form or color of the containers, or by labels. Such statutes are customarily construed as making one who supplies such articles not so marked liable, even though he has disclosed their actual character to the person to whom he directly gives them for the use of others, and even though the statute contains no express provisions on the subject.

o.   Under the rule stated in this Section one who supplies a chattel to a third person for use is subject to the liability stated in this Section if he fails to exercise reasonable care to inform those for whose use the chattel is supplied of its dangerous condition. It follows that the supplier is equally liable if he actually conceals a defect in the chattel by painting it over or by a pretense of repair, or if by express words he represents it to be safe, knowing that it is not so.

TOPIC 3.   MANUFACTURER OF CHATTELS

§ 395. Negligent Manufacture of Chattel Dangerous Unless Carefully Made

A manufacturer who fails to exercise reasonable care in the manufacture of a chattel which, unless carefully made, he should recognize as involving an unreasonable risk of causing physical harm to those who use it for a purpose for which the manufacturer should expect it to be used and to those whom he should expect to be endangered by its probable use, is subject to liability for physical harm caused to them by its lawful use in a manner and for a purpose for which it is supplied.

Comment:

a.   *History*. The original common law rule was contrary to that stated in this Section. The case of Winterbottom v. Wright, 10 M. & W. 109, 152

Eng.Rep. 402 (1842), in which a seller who contracted with the buyer to keep a stagecoach in repair after the sale was held not to be liable to a passenger injured when he failed to do so, was for a long time misconstrued to mean that the original seller of a chattel could not be liable, in tort or in contract, to one other than his immediate buyer. To this rule various exceptions developed, the first of which involved the rule stated in §§ 388, 390, and 394, that a manufacturer who knew that the chattel was dangerous for its expected use and failed to disclose the danger became liable to a third person injured by the defect.

The most important of these exceptions, however, made the seller liable to a third person for negligence in the manufacture or sale of an article classified as "inherently" or "imminently" dangerous to human safety. By degrees this category was redefined to include articles "intended to preserve, destroy, or affect human life or health." For more than half a century, however, the category remained vague and imperfectly defined. It was held to include food, drugs, firearms, and explosives, but there was much rather pointless dispute in the decisions as to other articles, and as to whether, for example, such a product as chewing tobacco was to be classified as a food.

In 1916 the leading modern case of MacPherson v. Buick Motor Co., 217 N.Y. 382, 111 N.E. 1050, L.R.A. 1916F, 696, Am.Ann.Cas. 1916C, 440, 13 N.C.C.A. 1029 (1916), discarded the general rule of non-liability, by holding that "inherently dangerous" articles included any article which would be dangerous to human safety if negligently made. After the passage of more than forty years, this decision is now all but universally accepted by the American courts. Although some decisions continue to speak the language of "inherent danger," it has very largely been superseded by a recognition that what is involved is merely the ordinary duty of reasonable care imposed upon the manufacturer, as to any product which he can reasonably expect to be dangerous if he is negligent in its manufacture or sale.

b. This Section states the rule thus generally adopted. The justification for it rests upon the responsibility assumed by the manufacturer toward the consuming public, which arises, not out of contract, but out of the relation resulting from the purchase of the product by the consumer; upon the foreseeability of harm if proper care is not used; upon the representation of safety implied in the act of putting the product on the market; and upon the economic benefit derived by the manufacturer from the sale and subsequent use of the chattel.

c. *Not necessary that chattel be intended to affect, preserve, or destroy human life.* In order that the manufacturer of a chattel shall be subject to liability under the rule stated in this Section, it is not necessary that the chattel be one the use of which is intended to affect, preserve, or destroy human life. The purpose which the article, if perfect, is intended to accomplish is immaterial. The important thing is the harm which it is likely to do if it is imperfect.

d. *Not necessary that chattel be inherently dangerous*. In order that the manufacturer shall be subject to liability under the rule stated in this Section, it is not necessary that the chattel be "inherently dangerous," in the sense of involving any degree of risk of harm to those who use it even if it is properly made. It is enough that the chattel, if not carefully made, will involve such a risk of harm. It is not necessary that the risk be a great one, or that it be a risk of death or serious bodily harm. A risk of harm to property, as in the case of defective animal food, is enough. All that is necessary is that the risk be an unreasonable one, as stated in § 291. The inherent danger, or the high degree of danger, is merely a factor to be considered, as in other negligence cases, as bearing upon the extent of the precautions required.

Illustration:

> 1.   A manufactures a mattress. Through the carelessness of one of A's employees a spring inside of the mattress is not properly tied down. A sells the mattress to B, a dealer, who resells it to C. C sleeps on the mattress, and is wounded in the back by the sharp point of the spring. The wound becomes infected, and C suffers serious illness. A is subject to liability to C.

e. *When inspections and tests necessary*. As heretofore pointed out (§ 298, Comment *b*), the precaution necessary to comply with the standard of reasonable care varies with the danger involved. Consequently the character of harm likely to result from the failure to exercise care in manufacture affects the question as to what is reasonable care. It is reasonable to require those who make or assemble automobiles to subject the raw material, or parts, procured from even reputable manufacturers, to inspections and tests which it would be obviously unreasonable to require of a product which, although defective, is unlikely to cause more than some comparatively slight, though still substantial, harm to those who use it. A garment maker is not required to subject the finished garment to anything like so minute an inspection for the purpose of discovering whether a basting needle has not been left in a seam as is required of the maker of an automobile or of high speed machinery or of electrical devices, in which the slightest inaccuracy may involve danger of death.

f. *Particulars which require care*. A manufacturer is required to exercise reasonable care in manufacturing any article which, if carelessly manufactured, is likely to cause harm to those who use it in the manner for which it is manufactured. The particulars in which reasonable care is usually necessary for protection of those whose safety depends upon the character of chattels are (1) the adoption of a formula or plan which, if properly followed, will produce an article safe for the use for which it is sold, (2) the selection of material and parts to be incorporated in the finished article, (3) the fabrication of the article by every member of the operative staff no matter how high or low his position, (4) the making of such inspections and tests during the course of manufacture and after the article is completed as the manufacturer should recognize as reasonably necessary to secure the production of a safe article, and (5) the packing of the article so as to be safe for those who must be expected to unpack it.

Illustrations:

2. The A Motor Company incorporates in its car wheels manufactured by the B Wheel Company. These wheels are constructed of defective material, as an inspection made by the A Company before putting them on its car would disclose. The car is sold to C through the D Company, an independent distributor. While C is driving the car the defective wheel collapses and the car swerves and collides with that of E, causing harm to C and E, and also to F and G, who are guests in the cars of C and E respectively. The A Motor Company is subject to liability to C, E, F, and G.

g. The exercise of reasonable care in selecting raw material and parts to be incorporated in the finished article usually requires something more than a mere inspection of the material and parts. A manufacturer should have sufficient technical knowledge to select such a type of material that its use will secure a safe finished product. So too, a manufacturer who incorporates a part made by another manufacturer into his finished product should exercise reasonable care to ascertain not only the material out of which the part is made but also the plan under which it is made. He must have sufficient technical knowledge to form a reasonably accurate judgment as to whether a part made under such a plan and of such material is or is not such as to secure a safe finished product. The part is of his own selection, and it is reasonable for the users of the product to rely not only upon a careful inspection but also sufficient technical knowledge to make a careful inspection valuable in securing an article safe for use. In all of these particulars the amount of care which the manufacturer must exercise is proportionate to the extent of the risk involved in using the article if manufactured without the exercise of these precautions. Where, as in the case of an automobile or high speed machinery or high voltage electrical devices, there is danger of serious bodily harm or death unless the article is substantially perfect, it is reasonable to require the manufacturer to exercise almost meticulous precautions in all of these particulars in order to secure substantial perfection. On the other hand, it would be ridiculous to demand equal care of the manufacturer of an article which, no matter how imperfect, is unlikely to do more than some comparatively trivial harm to those who use it.

h. Persons protected. The words "those who use the chattel" include not only the vendee but also all persons whose right or privilege to use the article is derived from him, unless the nature of the article or the conditions of the sale make it improbable that the article will be resold by the vendee or that he will permit others to use it or to share in its use. Unless the article is made to special order for the peculiar use of a particular person, the manufacturer must realize the chance that it may be sold. This becomes a substantial certainty where the article is sold to a jobber, wholesaler, or retailer. So too, many articles are obviously made for the use of several persons or are sold under conditions which make it certain that they will be used by persons other than the purchaser. Thus the manufacturer of a seven-seated automobile which is obviously intended to carry persons other than the purchaser and his chauffeur should recognize it as likely to be used by any persons whom, as members of his family, guests, or pedestrians picked up on the road, the purchaser chooses to receive in his car. A threshing machine sold to the owner of a large farm is obviously intended for the use of his employees.

The words "those who use the chattel" include, therefore, all persons whom the vendee or his subvendee or donee permits to use the article irrespective of whether they do so as his servants, as passengers for hire or otherwise, to serve his business purposes, or as licensees permitted to use a car purely for their own benefit. They also include any person to whom the vendee sells or gives the chattel, or to whom such subvendee or donee sells or gives the chattel ad infinitum, and also all persons whom such subvendee or subdonee permits to use the chattel or to share in its use. Thus they include a person to whom an improperly prepared drug is hypodermically administered by a physician who has bought it from a drugstore which has purchased it from a wholesaler or jobber.

i. Persons endangered by use. The words "those whom he should expect to be endangered by its probable use" may likewise include a large group of persons who have no connection with the ownership or use of the chattel itself. Thus the manufacturer of an automobile, intended to be driven on the public highway, should reasonably expect that, if the automobile is dangerously defective, harm will result to any person on the highway, including pedestrians and drivers of other vehicles and their passengers and guests; and he should also expect danger to those upon land immediately abutting on the highway. Likewise the manufacturer of a cable to be used in the transmission of high voltage electric current should reasonably anticipate that if its insulation is defective its use may endanger even persons miles away from the cable itself.

j. Unforeseeable use or manner of use. The liability stated in this Section is limited to persons who are endangered and the risks which are created in the course of uses of the chattel which the manufacturer should reasonably anticipate. In the absence of special reason to expect otherwise, the maker is entitled to assume that his product will be put to a normal use, for which the product is intended or appropriate; and he is not subject to liability when it is safe for all such uses, and harm results only because it is mishandled in a way which he has no reason to expect, or is used in some unusual and unforeseeable manner. Thus a shoemaker is not liable to an obstinate lady who suffers harm because she insists on wearing a size too small for her, and the manufacturer of a bottle of cleaning fluid is not liable when the purchaser splashes it into his eye.

Illustration:

3. A manufactures and sells to a dealer an automobile tire, which is in all respects safe for normal automobile driving. B, an automobile racer, buys the tire from the dealer and installs it on his racing car. In the course of the race the tire blows out because of the excessive speed, and B is injured. A is not liable to B.

k. Foreseeable uses and risks. The manufacturer may, however, reasonably anticipate other uses than the one for which the chattel is primarily intended. The maker of a chair, for example, may reasonably expect that some one will stand on it; and the maker of an inflammable cocktail robe may expect that it will be worn in the kitchen in close proximity to a fire. Likewise the manufacturer may know, or may be under a duty to discover, that some possible users of the product are especially susceptible to harm from it, if it contains an ingredient to which any substantial percentage of the population are allergic or otherwise sensitive, and he fails to take reasonable precautions, by giving warning or otherwise, against harm to such persons.

l. The fact that the article is leased, given, or loaned to the user rather than sold or leased does not affect the liability of the manufacturer for his negligence in making the article.

m. Manufacturer of raw material or parts of article to be assembled by third person. It is not necessary that the manufacturer should expect his product to be used in the form in which it is delivered to his immediate buyer. A manufacturer of parts to be incorporated in the product of his buyer or others is subject to liability under the rule stated in this Section, if they are so negligently made as to render the products in which they are incorporated unreasonably dangerous for use. So too, a manufacturer of raw material made and sold to be used in the fabrication of particular articles which will be dangerous for use unless the material is carefully made, is subject to liability if he fails to exercise reasonable care in its manufacture. As to the effect to be given to the fact that the defect could have been discovered before the part or material was incorporated in the finished article, see § 396.

Illustration:

4. Under the facts stated in Illustration 2, the B Wheel Company is subject to liability to C, E, F, and G.

n. The rule stated in this Section applies where the only harm which results from the manufacturer's failure to exercise reasonable care is to the manufactured chattel itself.

Illustration:

5. A manufactures and sells to a dealer an automobile, which is purchased from the dealer by B. Because of A's failure to exercise reasonable care in manufacture the car has a defective steering gear. While B is driving the steering gear gives way, and the car goes into the ditch and is damaged. B is not injured, and there is no other damage of any kind. A is subject to liability to B for the damage to the automobile.

§ 398.   Chattel Made Under Dangerous Plan or Design

A manufacturer of a chattel made under a plan or design which makes it dangerous for the uses for which it is manufactured is subject to liability to others whom he should expect to use the chattel or to be endangered by its probable use for physical harm caused by his failure to exercise reasonable care in the adoption of a safe plan or design.

Comment:

a. The rule stated in this Section, like that stated in § 397, is a special application of the rule stated in § 395.

b. *When dangerous plan or design known to user.* If the dangerous character of the plan or design is known to the user of the chattel, he may be in contributory fault if the risk involved in using it is unreasonably great or if he fails to take those special precautions which the known dangerous character of the chattel requires.

Illustration:

1. The A Stove Company makes a gas stove under a design which places the aperture through which it is lighted in dangerous proximity to the gas outlet. As a result of this B, a cook employed by C, who has bought one of these stoves from a dealer to whom A has sold it, while attempting to light the stove is hurt by an explosion of gas. The A Stove Company is subject to liability to B.

TOPIC 4.   SELLERS OF CHATTELS MANUFACTURED BY THIRD PERSONS

§ 400.   Selling as Own Product Chattel Made by Another

One who puts out as his own product a chattel manufactured by another is subject to the same liability as though he were its manufacturer.

Comment:

a. The words "one who puts out a chattel" include anyone who supplies it to others for their own use or for the use of third persons, either by sale or lease or by gift or loan.

b. The rules which determine the liability of a manufacturer of a chattel are stated in §§ 394–398.

c. One who puts out as his own product chattels made by others is under a duty to exercise care, proportionate to the danger involved in the use of the chattels if improperly made, to secure the adoption of a proper formula or plan and the use of safe materials and to inspect the chattel when made. But he does not escape liability by so doing. He is liable if, because of some negligence in its fabrication or through lack of proper inspection during the process of manufacture, the article is in a dangerously defective condition which the seller could not discover after it was delivered to him.

d. The rule stated in this Section applies only where the actor puts out the chattel as his own product. The actor puts out a chattel as his own product in two types of cases. The first is where the actor appears to be the manufacturer of the chattel. The second is where the chattel appears to have been made particularly for the actor. In the first type of case the actor frequently causes the chattel to be used in reliance upon his care in making it; in the second, he frequently causes the chattel to be used in reliance upon a belief that he has required it to be made properly for him and that the actor's reputation is an assurance to the user of the quality of the product. On the other hand, where it is clear that the actor's only connection with the chattel is that of a distributor of it (for example, as a wholesale or retail seller), he does not put it out as his own product and the rule stated in this section is inapplicable. Thus, one puts out a chattel as his own product when he puts it out under his name or affixes to it his trade name or trademark. When such identification is referred to on the label as an indication of the quality or wholesomeness of the chattel, there is an added emphasis that the user can rely upon the reputation of the person so identified. The mere fact that the goods are marked with such additional words as "made for" the seller, or describe him as a distributor, particularly in the absence of a clear and distinctive designation of the real manufacturer or packer, is not sufficient to make inapplicable the rule stated in this Section. The casual reader of a label is likely to rely upon the featured name, trade name, or trademark, and overlook the qualification of the description of source. So too, the fact that the seller is known to carry on only a retail business does not prevent him from putting out as his own product a chattel which is marked in such a way as to indicate clearly it is put out as his product. However, where the real manufacturer or packer is clearly and accurately identified on the label or other markings on the goods, and it is also clearly stated that another who is also named has nothing to do with the goods except to distribute or sell them, the latter does not put out such goods as his own. That the goods are not the product of him who puts them out may also be indicated clearly in other ways.

Illustrations:

1.   A puts out under his own name a floor stain which is manufactured under a secret formula by B, to whom A entrusts the selection of the formula. The stain made under this formula is inflammable, as a competent maker of such articles would have known. Of this both A and B are ignorant, and neither the advertisements nor the directions contain any warning against using it near unguarded lights. C purchases from a retail dealer a supply of this stain and while D, C's wife, is applying it to the floor of the kitchen, C strikes a match to light the gas. An explosion follows, causing harm to D and to E, a friend who is watching D stain the floor. A is subject to liability to D and E.

2.   A, a wholesale distributor, sells canned corned beef labeled with A's widely known trademark and also labeled "Packed for A" and "A, distributor". The beef was negligently packed by B and is unwholesome. C buys a can of it from D, a retail grocer, and serves it to her guest, E, who is made ill. A is liable to E.

TOPIC 5.   STRICT LIABILITY

§ 402A. Special Liability of Seller of Product for Physical Harm to User or Consumer

(1) One who sells any product in a defective condition unreasonably dangerous to the user or consumer or to his property is subject to liability for physical harm thereby caused to the ultimate user or consumer, or to his property, if

(a) the seller is engaged in the business of selling such a product, and

(b) it is expected to and does reach the user or consumer without substantial change in the condition in which it is sold.

(2) The rule stated in Subsection (1) applies although

(a) the seller has exercised all possible care in the preparation and sale of his product, and

(b) the user or consumer has not bought the product from or entered into any contractual relation with the seller.

Caveat:

The Institute expresses no opinion as to whether the rules stated in this Section may not apply

(1) to harm to persons other than users or consumers;

(2) to the seller of a product expected to be processed or otherwise substantially changed before it reaches the user or consumer; or

(3) to the seller of a component part of a product to be assembled.

Comment:

a. This Section states a special rule applicable to sellers of products. The rule is one of strict liability, making the seller subject to liability to the user or consumer even though he has exercised all possible care in the preparation and sale of the product. The Section is inserted in the Chapter dealing with the negligence liability of suppliers of chattels, for convenience of reference and comparison with other Sections dealing with negligence. The rule stated here is not exclusive, and does not preclude liability based upon the alternative ground of negligence of the seller, where such negligence can be proved.

b. *History.* Since the early days of the common law those engaged in the business of selling food intended for human consumption have been held to a high degree of responsibility for their products. As long ago as 1266 there were enacted special criminal statutes imposing penalties upon victualers, vintners, brewers, butchers, cooks, and other persons who supplied "corrupt" food and drink. In the earlier part of this century this ancient attitude was reflected in a series of decisions in which the courts of a number of states sought to find some method of holding the seller of food liable to the ultimate consumer even though there was no showing of negligence on the part of the seller. These decisions represented a departure from, and an exception to, the general rule that a supplier of chattels was not liable to third persons in the absence of negligence or privity of contract. In the beginning, these decisions displayed considerable ingenuity in evolving more or less fictitious theories of liability to fit the case. The various devices included an agency of the intermediate dealer or another to purchase for the consumer, or to sell for the seller; a theoretical assignment of the seller's warranty to the intermediate dealer; a third party beneficiary contract; and an implied representation that the food was fit for consumption because it was placed on the market, as well as numerous others. In later years the courts have become more or less agreed upon the theory of a "warranty" from the seller to the consumer, either "running with the goods" by analogy to a covenant running with the land, or made directly to the consumer. Other decisions have indicated that the basis is merely one of strict liability in tort, which is not dependent upon either contract or negligence.

Recent decisions, since 1950, have extended this special rule of strict liability beyond the seller of food for human consumption. The first extension was into the closely analogous cases of other products intended for intimate bodily use, where, for example, as in the case of cosmetics, the application to the body of the consumer is external rather than internal.

Beginning in 1958 with a Michigan case involving cinder building blocks, a number of recent decisions have discarded any limitation to intimate association with the body, and have extended the rule of strict liability to cover the sale of any product which, if it should prove to be defective, may be expected to cause physical harm to the consumer or his property.

c. On whatever theory, the justification for the strict liability has been said to be that the seller, by marketing his product for use and consumption, has undertaken and assumed a special responsibility toward any member of the consuming public who may be injured by it; that the public has the right to and does expect, in the case of products which it needs and for which it is forced to rely upon the seller, that reputable sellers will stand behind their goods; that public policy demands that the burden of accidental injuries caused by products intended for consumption be placed upon those who market them, and be treated as a cost of production against which liability insurance can be obtained; and that the consumer of such products is entitled to the maximum of protection at the hands of someone, and the proper persons to afford it are those who market the products.

d. The rule stated in this Section is not limited to the sale of food for human consumption, or other products for intimate bodily use, although it will obviously include them. It extends to any product sold in the condition, or substantially the same condition, in which it is expected to reach the ultimate user or consumer. Thus the rule stated applies to an automobile, a tire, an airplane, a grinding wheel, a water heater, a gas stove, a power tool, a riveting machine, a chair, and an insecticide. It applies also to products which, if they are defective, may be expected to and do cause only "physical harm" in the form of damage to the user's land or chattels, as in the case of animal food or a herbicide.

e. Normally the rule stated in this Section will be applied to articles which already have undergone some processing before sale, since there is today little in the way of consumer products which will reach the consumer without such processing. The rule is not, however, so limited, and the supplier of poisonous mushrooms which are neither cooked, canned, packaged, nor otherwise treated is subject to the liability here stated.

f. Business of selling. The rule stated in this Section applies to any person engaged in the business of selling products for use or consumption. It therefore applies to any manufacturer of such a product, to any wholesale or retail dealer or distributor, and to the operator of a restaurant. It is not necessary that the seller be engaged solely in the business of selling such products. Thus the rule applies to the owner of a motion picture theatre who sells popcorn or ice cream, either for consumption on the premises or in packages to be taken home.

The rule does not, however, apply to the occasional seller of food or other such products who is not engaged in that activity as a part of his business. Thus it does not apply to the housewife who, on one occasion, sells to her neighbor a jar of jam or a pound of sugar. Nor does it apply to the owner of an automobile who, on one occasion, sells it to his neighbor, or even sells it to a dealer in used cars, and this even though he is fully aware that the dealer plans to resell it. The basis for the rule is the ancient one of the special responsibility for the safety of the public undertaken by one who enters into the business of supplying human beings with products which may endanger the safety of their persons and property, and the forced reliance upon that undertaking on the part of those who purchase such goods. This basis is lacking in the case of the ordinary individual who makes the isolated sale, and he is not liable to a third person, or even to his buyer, in the absence of his negligence. An analogy may be found in the provision of the Uniform Sales Act, § 15, which limits the implied warranty of merchantable quality to sellers who deal in such goods; and in the similar limitation of the Uniform Commercial Code, § 2–314, to a seller who is a merchant. This Section is also not intended to apply to sales of the stock of merchants out of the usual course of business, such as execution sales, bankruptcy sales, bulk sales, and the like.

g. Defective condition. The rule stated in this Section applies only where the product is, at the time it leaves the seller's hands, in a condition not contemplated by the ultimate consumer, which will be unreasonably dangerous to him. The seller is not liable when he delivers the product in a safe condition, and subsequent mishandling or other causes make it harmful by the time it is consumed. The burden of proof that the product was in a defective condition at the time that it left the hands of the particular seller is upon the injured plaintiff; and unless evidence can be produced which will support the conclusion that it was then defective, the burden is not sustained.

Safe condition at the time of delivery by the seller will, however, include proper packaging, necessary sterilization, and other precautions required to permit the product to remain safe for a normal length of time when handled in a normal manner.

h. A product is not in a defective condition when it is safe for normal handling and consumption. If the injury results from abnormal handling, as where a bottled beverage is knocked against a radiator to remove the cap, or from abnormal preparation for use, as where too much salt is added to food, or from abnormal consumption, as where a child eats too much candy and is made ill, the seller is not liable. Where, however, he has reason to anticipate that danger may result from a particular use, as where a drug is sold which is safe only in limited doses, he may be required to give adequate warning of the danger (see Comment *j*), and a product sold without such warning is in a defective condition.

The defective condition may arise not only from harmful ingredients, not characteristic of the product itself either as to presence or quantity, but also from foreign objects contained in the product, from decay or deterioration before sale, or from the way in which the product is prepared or packed. No reason is apparent for distinguishing between the product itself and the container in which it is supplied; and the two are purchased by the user or consumer as an integrated whole. Where the container is itself dangerous, the product is sold in a defective condition. Thus a carbonated beverage in a bottle which is so weak, or cracked, or jagged at the edges, or bottled under such excessive pressure that it may explode or otherwise cause harm to the person who handles it, is in a defective and dangerous condition. The container cannot logically be separated from the contents when the two are sold as a unit, and the liability stated in this Section arises not only when the consumer drinks the beverage and is poisoned by it, but also when he is injured by the bottle while he is handling it preparatory to consumption.

i. Unreasonably dangerous. The rule stated in this Section applies only where the defective condition of the product makes it unreasonably dangerous to the user or consumer. Many products cannot possibly be made entirely safe for all consumption, and any food or drug necessarily involves some risk of harm, if only from over-consumption. Ordinary sugar is a deadly poison to diabetics, and castor oil found use under Mussolini as an instrument of torture. That is not what is meant by "unreasonably dangerous" in this Section. The article sold must be dangerous to an extent beyond that which would be contemplated by the ordinary consumer who purchases it, with the ordinary knowledge common to the community as to its characteristics. Good whiskey is not unreasonably dangerous merely because it will make some people drunk, and is especially dangerous to alcoholics; but bad whiskey, containing a dangerous amount of fusel oil, is unreasonably dangerous. Good tobacco is not unreasonably dangerous merely because the effects of smoking may be harmful; but tobacco containing something like marijuana may be unreasonably dangerous. Good butter is not unreasonably dangerous merely because, if such be the case, it deposits cholesterol in the arteries and leads to heart attacks; but bad butter, contaminated with poisonous fish oil, is unreasonably dangerous.

j. Directions or warning. In order to prevent the product from being unreasonably dangerous, the seller may be required to give directions or warning, on the container, as to its use. The seller may reasonably assume that those with common allergies, as for example to eggs or strawberries, will be aware of them, and he is not required to warn against them. Where, however, the product contains an ingredient to which a substantial number of the population are allergic, and the ingredient is one whose danger is not generally known, or if known is one which the consumer would reasonably not expect to find in the product, the seller is required to give warning against it, if he has knowledge, or by the application of reasonable, developed human skill and foresight should have knowledge, of the presence of the ingredient and the danger. Likewise in the case of poisonous drugs, or those unduly dangerous for other reasons, warning as to use may be required.

But a seller is not required to warn with respect to products, or ingredients in them, which are only dangerous, or potentially so, when consumed in excessive quantity, or over a long period of time, when the danger, or potentiality of danger, is generally known and recognized. Again the dangers of alcoholic beverages are an example, as are also those of foods containing such substances as saturated fats, which may over a period of time have a deleterious effect upon the human heart.

Where warning is given, the seller may reasonably assume that it will be read and heeded; and a product bearing such a warning, which is safe for use if it is followed, is not in defective condition, nor is it unreasonably dangerous.

k. Unavoidably unsafe products. There are some products which, in the present state of human knowledge, are quite incapable of being made safe for their intended and ordinary use. These are especially common in the field of drugs. An outstanding example is the vaccine for the Pasteur treatment of rabies, which not uncommonly leads to very serious and damaging consequences when it is injected. Since the disease itself invariably leads to a dreadful death, both the marketing and the use of the vaccine are fully justified, notwithstanding the unavoidable high degree of risk which they involve. Such a product, properly prepared, and accompanied by proper directions and warning, is not defective, nor is it *unreasonably* dangerous. The same is true of many other drugs, vaccines, and the like, many of which for this very reason cannot legally be sold except to physicians, or under the prescription of a physician. It is also true in particular of many new or experimental drugs as to which, because of lack of time and opportunity for sufficient medical experience, there can be no assurance of safety, or perhaps even of purity of ingredients, but such experience as there is justifies the marketing and use of the drug notwithstanding a medically recognizable risk. The seller of such products, again with the qualification that they are properly prepared and marketed, and proper warning is given, where the situation calls for it, is not to be held to strict liability for unfortunate consequences attending their use, merely because he has undertaken to supply the public with an apparently useful and desirable product, attended with a known but apparently reasonable risk.

l. User or consumer. In order for the rule stated in this Section to apply, it is not necessary that the ultimate user or consumer have acquired the product directly from the seller, although the rule applies equally if he does so. He may have acquired it through one or more intermediate dealers. It is not even necessary that the consumer have purchased the product at all. He may be a member of the family of the final purchaser, or his employee, or a guest at his table, or a mere donee from the purchaser. The liability stated is one in tort, and does not require any contractual relation, or privity of contract, between the plaintiff and the defendant.

"Consumers" include not only those who in fact consume the product, but also those who prepare it for consumption; and the housewife who contracts tularemia while cooking rabbits for her husband is included within the rule stated in this Section, as is also the husband who is opening a bottle of beer for his wife to drink. Consumption includes all ultimate uses for which the product is intended, and the customer in a beauty shop to whose hair a permanent wave solution is applied by the shop is a consumer. "User" includes those who are passively enjoying the benefit of the product, as in the case of passengers in automobiles or airplanes, as well as those who are utilizing it for the purpose of doing work upon it, as in the case of an employee of the ultimate buyer who is making repairs upon the automobile which he has purchased.

Illustration:

1. A manufactures and packs a can of beans, which he sells to B, a wholesaler. B sells the beans to C, a jobber, who resells it to D, a retail grocer. E buys the can of beans from D, and gives it to F. F serves the beans at lunch to G, his guest. While eating the beans, G breaks a tooth, on a pebble of the size, shape, and color of a bean, which no reasonable inspection could possibly have discovered. There is satisfactory evidence that the pebble was in the can of beans when it was opened. Although there is no negligence on the part of A, B, C, or D, each of them is subject to liability to G. On the other hand E and F, who have not sold the beans, are not liable to G in the absence of some negligence on their part.

m. *"Warranty."* The liability stated in this Section does not rest upon negligence. It is strict liability, similar in its nature to that covered by Chapters 20 and 21. The basis of liability is purely one of tort.

A number of courts, seeking a theoretical basis for the liability, have resorted to a "warranty," either running with the goods sold, by analogy to covenants running with the land, or made directly to the consumer without contract. In some instances this theory has proved to be an unfortunate one. Although warranty was in its origin a matter of tort liability, and it is generally agreed that a tort action will still lie for its breach, it has become so identified in practice with a contract of sale between the plaintiff and the defendant that the warranty theory has become something of an obstacle to the recognition of the strict liability where there is no such contract. There is nothing in this Section which would prevent any court from treating the rule stated as a matter of "warranty" to the user or consumer. But if this is done, it should be recognized and understood that the "warranty" is a very different kind of warranty from those usually found in the sale of goods, and that it is not subject to the various contract rules which have grown up to surround such sales.

The rule stated in this Section does not require any reliance on the part of the consumer upon the reputation, skill, or judgment of the seller who is to be held liable, nor any representation or undertaking on the part of that seller. The seller is strictly liable although, as is frequently the case, the consumer does not even know who he is at the time of consumption. The rule stated in this Section is not governed by the provisions of the Uniform Sales Act, or those of the Uniform Commercial Code, as to warranties; and it is not affected by limitations on the scope and content of warranties, or by limitation to "buyer" and "seller" in those statutes. Nor is the consumer required to give notice to the seller of his injury within a reasonable time after it occurs, as is provided by the Uniform Act. The consumer's cause of action does not depend upon the validity of his contract with the person from whom he acquires the product, and it is not affected by any disclaimer or other agreement, whether it be between the seller and his immediate buyer, or attached to and accompanying the product into the consumer's hands. In short, "warranty" must be given a new and different meaning if it is used in connection with this Section. It is much simpler to regard the liability here stated as merely one of strict liability in tort.

n. Contributory negligence. Since the liability with which this Section deals is not based upon negligence of the seller, but is strict liability, the rule applied to strict liability cases (see § 524) applies. Contributory negligence of the plaintiff is not a defense when such negligence consists merely in a failure to discover the defect in the product, or to guard against the possibility of its existence. On the other hand the form of contributory negligence which consists in voluntarily and unreasonably proceeding to encounter a known danger, and commonly passes under the name of assumption of risk, is a defense under this Section as in other cases of strict liability. If the user or consumer discovers the defect and is aware of the danger, and nevertheless proceeds unreasonably to make use of the product and is injured by it, he is barred from recovery.

Comment on Caveat:

o. Injuries to non-users and non-consumers. Thus far the courts, in applying the rule stated in this Section, have not gone beyond allowing recovery to users and consumers, as those terms are defined in Comment *l.* Casual bystanders, and others who may come in contact with the product, as in the case of employees of the retailer, or a passer-by injured by an exploding bottle, or a pedestrian hit by an automobile, have been denied recovery. There may be no essential reason why such plaintiffs should not be brought within the scope of the protection afforded, other than that they do not have the same reasons for expecting such protection as the consumer who buys a marketed product; but the social pressure which has been largely responsible for the development of the rule stated has been a consumers' pressure, and there is not the same demand for the protection of casual strangers. The Institute expresses neither approval nor disapproval of expansion of the rule to permit recovery by such persons.

p. Further processing or substantial change. Thus far the decisions applying the rule stated have not gone beyond products which are sold in the condition, or in substantially the same condition, in which they are expected to reach the hands of the ultimate user or consumer. In the absence of decisions providing a clue to the rules which are likely to develop, the Institute has refrained from taking any position as to the possible liability of the seller where the product is expected to, and does, undergo further processing or other substantial change after it leaves his hands and before it reaches those of the ultimate user or consumer.

It seems reasonably clear that the mere fact that the product is to undergo processing, or other substantial change, will not in all cases relieve the seller of liability under the rule stated in this Section. If, for example, raw coffee beans are sold to a buyer who roasts and packs them for sale to the ultimate consumer, it cannot be supposed that the seller will be relieved of all liability when the raw beans are contaminated with arsenic, or some other poison. Likewise the seller of an automobile with a defective steering gear which breaks and injures the driver, can scarcely expect to be relieved of the responsibility by reason of the fact that the car is sold to a dealer who is expected to "service" it, adjust the brakes, mount and inflate the tires, and the like, before it is ready for use. On the other hand, the manufacturer of pig iron, which is capable of a wide variety of uses, is not so likely to be held to strict liability when it turns out to be unsuitable for the child's tricycle into which it is finally made by a remote buyer. The question is essentially one of whether the responsibility for discovery and prevention of the dangerous defect is shifted to the intermediate party who is to make the changes. No doubt there will be some situations, and some defects, as to which the responsibility will be shifted, and others in which it will not. The existing decisions as yet throw no light upon the questions, and the Institute therefore expresses neither approval nor disapproval of the seller's strict liability in such a case.

q. Component parts. The same problem arises in cases of the sale of a component part of a product to be assembled by another, as for example a tire to be placed on a new automobile, a brake cylinder for the same purpose, or an instrument for the panel of an airplane. Again the question arises, whether the responsibility is not shifted to the assembler. It is no doubt to be expected that where there is no change in the component part itself, but it is merely incorporated into something larger, the strict liability will be found to carry through to the ultimate user or consumer. But in the absence of a sufficient number of decisions on the matter to justify a conclusion, the Institute expresses no opinion on the matter.

§ 402B. Misrepresentation by Seller of Chattels to Consumer

One engaged in the business of selling chattels who, by advertising, labels, or otherwise, makes to the public a misrepresentation of a material fact concerning the char-

acter or quality of a chattel sold by him is subject to liability for physical harm to a consumer of the chattel caused by justifiable reliance upon the misrepresentation, even though

    (a) it is not made fraudulently or negligently, and

    (b) the consumer has not bought the chattel from or entered into any contractual relation with the seller.

Caveat:

The Institute expresses no opinion as to whether the rule stated in this Section may apply

    (1) where the representation is not made to the public, but to an individual, or

    (2) where physical harm is caused to one who is not a consumer of the chattel.

Comment:

a. The rule stated in this Section is one of strict liability for physical harm to the consumer, resulting from a misrepresentation of the character or quality of the chattel sold, even though the misrepresentation is an innocent one, and not made fraudulently or negligently. Although the Section deals with misrepresentation, it is inserted here in order to complete the rules dealing with the liability of suppliers of chattels for physical harm caused by the chattel. A parallel rule, as to strict liability for pecuniary loss resulting from such a misrepresentation, is stated in § 552 D.*

b. The rule stated in this Section differs from the rule of strict liability stated in § 402 A, which is a special rule applicable only to sellers of products for consumption and does not depend upon misrepresentation. The rule here stated applies to one engaged in the business of selling any type of chattel, and is limited to misrepresentations of their character or quality.

c. History. The early rule was that a seller of chattels incurred no liability for physical harm resulting from the use of the chattel to anyone other than his immediate buyer, unless there was privity of contract between them. (See § 395, Comment *a.*) Beginning with Langridge v. Levy, 2 M. & W. 519, 150 Eng.Rep. 863 (1837), an exception was developed in cases where the seller made fraudulent misrepresentations to the immediate buyer, concerning the character or quality of the chattel sold, and because of the fact misrepresented harm resulted to a third person who was

---

* Section 552D, in tentative form at the time § 402B was adopted, was ultimately rejected by The American Law Institute.—Eds.

using the chattel. The remedy lay in an action for deceit, and the rule which resulted is now stated in § 557 A.

Shortly after 1930, a number of the American courts began, more or less independently, to work out a further extension of liability for physical harm to the consumer of the chattel, in cases where the seller made misrepresentations to the public concerning its character or quality, and the consumer, as a member of the public, purchased the chattel in reliance upon the misrepresentation and suffered physical harm because of the fact misrepresented. In such cases the seller was held to strict liability for the misrepresentation, even though it was not made fraudulently or negligently. The leading case is Baxter v. Ford Motor Co., 168 Wash. 456, 12 P.2d 409, 88 A.L.R. 521 (1932), adhered to on rehearing, 168 Wash. 456, 15 P.2d 1118, 88 A.L.R. 521, second appeal, 179 Wash. 123, 35 P.2d 1090 (1934), in which the manufacturer of an automobile advertised to the public that the windshield glass was "shatterproof," and the purchaser was injured when a stone struck the glass and it shattered. In the beginning various theories of liability were suggested, including strict liability in deceit, and a contract resulting from an offer made to the consumer to be bound by the representation, accepted by his purchase.

d. "Warranty." The theory finally adopted by most of the decisions, however, has been that of a non-contractual "express warranty" made to the consumer in the form of the representation to the public upon which he relies. The difficulties attending the use of the word "warranty" are the same as those involved under § 402 A, and Comment m under that Section is equally applicable here so far as it is pertinent. The liability stated in this Section is liability in tort, and not in contract; and if it is to be called one of "warranty," it is at least a different kind of warranty from that involved in the ordinary sale of goods from the immediate seller to the immediate buyer, and is subject to different rules.

e. Sellers included. The rule stated in this Section applies to any person engaged in the business of selling any type of chattel. It is not limited to sellers of food or products for intimate bodily use, as was until lately the rule stated in § 402 A. It is not limited to manufacturers of the chattel, and it includes wholesalers, retailers, and other distributors who sell it.

The rule stated applies, however, only to those who are engaged in the business of selling such chattels. It has no application to anyone who is not so engaged in business. It does not apply, for example, to a newspaper advertisement published by a private owner of a single automobile who offers it for sale.

f. Misrepresentation of character or quality. The rule stated applies to any misrepresentation of a material fact concerning the character or quality of the chattel sold which is made to the public by one so engaged in the business of selling such chattels. The fact misrepresented must be a material one, upon which the consumer may be expected to rely in making his purchase, and he must justifiably rely upon it. (See Comment *j.*) If he does so, and suffers physical harm by reason of the fact misrepresented, there is strict liability to him.

Illustration:

1. A manufactures automobiles. He advertises in newspapers and magazines that the glass in his cars is "shatterproof." B reads this advertising, and in reliance upon it purchases from a retail dealer an automobile manufactured by A. While B is driving the car, a stone thrown up by a passing truck strikes the windshield and shatters it, injuring B. A is subject to strict liability to B.

g. Material fact. The rule stated in this Section applies only to misrepresentations of material facts concerning the character or quality of the chattel in question. It does not apply to statements of opinion, and in particular it does not apply to the kind of loose general praise of wares sold which, on the part of the seller, is considered to be "sales talk," and is commonly called "puffing"—as, for example, a statement that an automobile is the best on the market for the price. As to such general language of opinion, see § 542, and Comment *d* under that Section, which is applicable here so far as it is pertinent. In addition, the fact misrepresented must be a material one, of importance to the normal purchaser, by which the ultimate buyer may justifiably be expected to be influenced in buying the chattel.

h. "To the public." The rule stated in this Section is limited to misrepresentations which are made by the seller to the public at large, in order to induce purchase of the chattels sold, or are intended by the seller to, and do, reach the public. The form of the representation is not important. It may be made by public advertising in newspapers or television, by literature distributed to the public through dealers, by labels on the product sold, or leaflets accompanying it, or in any other manner, whether it be oral or written.

Illustrations:

2. A manufactures wire rope. He issues a manual containing statements concerning its strength, which he distributes through dealers to buyers, and members of the public who may be expected to buy. In reliance upon the statements made in the manual, B buys a quantity of the wire rope from a dealer, and makes use of it to hoist a weight of 1,000 pounds. The strength of the rope is not as great as is represented in the manual, and as a result the rope breaks and the weight falls on B and injures him. A is subject to strict liability to B.

3. A manufactures a product for use by women at home in giving "permanent waves" to their hair. He places on the bottles labels which state that the product may safely be used in a particular manner, and will not be injurious to the hair. B reads such a label, and in reliance upon it purchases a bottle of the product from a retail dealer. She uses

it as directed, and as a result her hair is destroyed. A is subject to strict liability to B.

i. Consumers. The rule stated in this Section is limited to strict liability for physical harm to consumers of the chattel. The Caveat leaves open the question whether the rule may not also apply to one who is not a consumer, but who suffers physical harm through his justifiable reliance upon the misrepresentation.

"Consumer" is to be understood in the broad sense of one who makes use of the chattel in the manner which a purchaser may be expected to use it. Thus an employee of the ultimate purchaser to whom the chattel is turned over, and who is directed to make use of it in his work, is a consumer, and so is the wife of the purchaser of an automobile who is permitted by him to drive it.

j. Justifiable reliance. The rule here stated applies only where there is justifiable reliance upon the misrepresentation of the seller, and physical harm results because of such reliance, and because of the fact which is misrepresented. It does not apply where the misrepresentation is not known, or there is indifference to it, and it does not influence the purchase or subsequent conduct. At the same time, however, the misrepresentation need not be the sole inducement to purchase, or to use the chattel, and it is sufficient that it has been a substantial factor in that inducement. (Compare § 546 and Comments.) Since the liability here is for misrepresentation, the rules as to what will constitute justifiable reliance stated in §§ 537–545 A are applicable to this Section, so far as they are pertinent.

The reliance need not necessarily be that of the consumer who is injured. It may be that of the ultimate purchaser of the chattel, who because of such reliance passes it on to the consumer who is in fact injured, but is ignorant of the misrepresentation. Thus a husband who buys an automobile in justifiable reliance upon statements concerning its brakes, and permits his wife to drive the car, supplies the element of reliance, even though the wife in fact never learns of the statements.

Illustration:

4. The same facts as in Illustration 2, except that the harm is suffered by C, an employee of B, to whom B turns over the wire rope without informing him of the representations made by A. The same result.

RESTATEMENT (THIRD) OF TORTS: PRODUCTS LIABILITY

Selected Sections*

CHAPTER 1

LIABILITY OF COMMERCIAL PRODUCT SELLERS BASED ON PRODUCT DEFECTS AT TIME OF SALE

TOPIC 1

LIABILITY RULES APPLICABLE TO PRODUCTS GENERALLY

CHAPTER 4

PROVISIONS OF GENERAL APPLICABILITY

TOPIC 1

CAUSATION

TOPIC 2

AFFIRMATIVE DEFENSES

Chapter 1

LIABILITY OF COMMERCIAL PRODUCT SELLERS BASED ON PRODUCT DEFECTS AT TIME OF SALE

TOPIC 1.   LIABILITY RULES APPLICABLE TO PRODUCTS GENERALLY

§ 1. Liability of Commercial Seller or Distributor for Harm Caused by Defective Products

One engaged in the business of selling or otherwise distributing products who sells or distributes a defective product is subject to liability for harm to persons or property caused by the defect.

Comment:

a. History. This Section states a general rule of tort liability applicable to commercial sellers and other distributors of products generally. Rules of liability applicable to special products such as prescription drugs and used products are set forth in separate Sections in Topic 2 of this Chapter.

The liability established in this Section draws on both warranty law and tort law. Historically, the focus of products liability law was on manufacturing defects. A manufacturing defect is a physical departure from a product's intended design. See § 2(a). Typically, manufacturing defects occur in only a small percentage of units in a product line. Courts early began imposing liability without fault on product sellers for harm caused by such defects, holding a seller liable for harm caused by manufacturing defects even though all possible care had been exercised by the seller in the preparation and distribution of the product. In doing so, courts relied on the concept of warranty, in connection with which fault has never been a prerequisite to liability.

The imposition of liability for manufacturing defects has a long history in the common law. As early as 1266, criminal statutes imposed liability upon victualers, vintners, brewers, butchers, cooks, and other persons who supplied contaminated food and drink. In the late 1800s, courts in many states began imposing negligence and strict warranty liability on commercial sellers of defective goods. In the early 1960s, American courts began to recognize that a commercial seller of any product having a manufacturing defect should be liable in tort for harm caused by the defect regardless of the plaintiff's ability to maintain a traditional negligence or warranty action. Liability attached even if the manufacturer's quality control in producing the defective product was reasonable. A plaintiff was not required to be in direct privity with the defendant seller to bring an action. Strict liability in tort for defectively manufactured products merges the concept of implied warranty, in which negligence is not required, with the tort concept of negligence, in which contractual privity is not required. See § 2(a).

Questions of design defects and defects based on inadequate instructions or warnings arise when the specific product unit conforms to the intended design but the intended design itself, or its sale without adequate instructions or warnings, renders the product not reasonably safe. If these forms of defect are found to exist, then every unit in the same product line is potentially defective. See § 2, Comments *d, f,* and *i.* Imposition of liability for design defects and for defects based on inadequate instructions or warnings was relatively infrequent until the late 1960s and early 1970s. A number of restrictive rules made recovery for such defects, especially design defects, difficult to obtain. As these rules eroded, courts sought to impose liability without fault for design defects and defects due to inadequate instructions or warnings under the general principles of § 402A of the Restatement, Second, of Torts. However, it soon became evident that § 402A, created to deal with liability for manufacturing defects, could not appropriately be applied to cases of design defects or defects based on inadequate instructions or warnings. A product unit that fails to meet the manufacturer's design specifications thereby fails to perform its intended function and is, almost by definition, defective. However, when the product unit meets the manufacturer's own design specifications, it is necessary to go outside those specifications to determine whether the product is defective.

Sections 2(b) and 2(c) recognize that the rule developed for manufacturing defects is inappropriate for the resolution of claims of defective design and defects based on inadequate instructions or warnings. These latter categories of cases require determinations that the product could have reasonably been made safer by a better design or instruction or warning. Sections 2(b) and 2(c) rely on a reasonableness test traditionally used in determining whether an actor has been negligent. See Restatement, Second, Torts §§ 291–293. Nevertheless, many courts insist on speaking of liability based on the standards described in §§ 2(b) and 2(c) as being "strict."

Several factors help to explain this rhetorical preference. First, in many design defect cases, if the product causes injury while being put to a reasonably foreseeable use, the seller is held to have known of the risks that foreseeably attend such use. See § 2, Comment *m.* Second, some courts have sought to limit the defense of comparative fault in certain products liability contexts. In furtherance of this objective, they have avoided characterizing the liability test as based in negligence, thereby limiting the effect of comparative or contributory fault. See § 17, Comment *d.* Third, some courts are concerned that a negligence standard might be too forgiving of a small manufacturer who might be excused for its ignorance of risk or for failing to take adequate precautions to avoid risk. Negligence, which focuses on the conduct of the defendant-manufacturer, might allow a finding that a defendant with meager resources was not negligent because it was too burdensome for such a defendant to discover risks or to design or warn against them. The concept of strict liability, which focuses on the product rather than the conduct of the manufacturer, may help make the point that a defendant is held to the expert standard of knowledge available to the relevant manufacturing community at the time the product was manufactured. Finally, the liability of nonmanufacturing sellers in the distributive chain is strict. It is no defense that they acted reasonably and did not discover a defect in the product, be it from manufacturing, design, or failure to warn. See Comment *e*.

Thus, "strict products liability" is a term of art that reflects the judgment that products liability is a discrete area of tort law which borrows from both negligence and warranty. It is not fully congruent with classical tort or contract law. Rather than perpetuating confusion spawned by existing doctrinal categories, §§ 1 and 2 define the liability for each form of defect in terms directly addressing the various kinds of defects. As long as these functional criteria are met, courts may utilize the terminology of negligence, strict liability, or the implied warranty of merchantability, or simply define liability in the terms set forth in the black letter. See § 2, Comment *n*.

b. Sale or other distribution. The rule stated in this Section applies not only to sales transactions but also to other forms of commercial product distribution that are the functional equivalent of product sales. See § 20.

c. One engaged in the business of selling or otherwise distributing. The rule stated in this Section applies only to manufacturers and other commercial sellers and distributors who are engaged in the business of selling or otherwise distributing the type of product that harmed the plaintiff. The rule does not apply to a noncommercial seller or distributor of such products. Thus, it does not apply to one who sells foodstuffs to a neighbor, nor does it apply to the private owner of an automobile who sells it to another.

It is not necessary that a commercial seller or distributor be engaged exclusively or even primarily in selling or otherwise distributing the type of product that injured the plaintiff, so long as the sale of the product is other than occasional or casual. Thus, the rule applies to a motion-picture theater's routine sales of popcorn or ice cream, either for consumption on the premises or in packages to be taken home. Similarly, a service station that does mechanical repair work on cars may also sell tires and automobile equipment as part of its regular business. Such sales are subject to the rule in this Section. However, the rule does not cover occasional sales (frequently referred to as "casual sales") outside the regular course of the seller's business. Thus, an occasional sale of surplus equipment by a business does not fall within the ambit of this rule. Whether a defendant is a commercial seller or distributor within the meaning of this Section is usually a question of law to be determined by the court.

d. Harm to persons or property. The rule stated in this Section applies only to harm to persons or property, commonly referred to as personal injury and property damage. For rules governing economic loss, see § 21.

e. Nonmanufacturing sellers or other distributors of products. The rule stated in this Section provides that all commercial sellers and distributors of products, including nonmanufacturing sellers and distributors such as wholesalers and retailers, are subject to liability for selling products that are defective. Liability attaches even when such nonmanufacturing sellers or distributors do not themselves render the products defective and regardless of whether they are in a position to prevent defects from occurring. See § 2, Comment *o*. Legislation has been enacted in many jurisdictions that, to some extent, immunizes nonmanufacturing sellers or distributors from strict liability. The legislation is premised on the belief that bringing nonmanufacturing sellers or distributors into products liability litigation generates wasteful legal costs. Although liability in most cases is ultimately passed on to the manufacturer who is responsible for creating the product defect, nonmanufacturing sellers or distributors must devote resources to protect their interests. In most situations, therefore, immunizing nonmanufacturers from strict liability saves those resources without jeopardizing the plaintiff's interests. To assure plaintiffs access to a responsible and solvent product seller or distributor, the statutes generally provide that the nonmanufacturing seller or distributor is immunized from strict liability only if: (1) the manufacturer is subject to the jurisdiction of the court of plaintiff's domicile; and (2) the manufacturer is not, nor is likely to become, insolvent.

In connection with these statutes, two problems may need to be resolved to assure fairness to plaintiffs. First, as currently structured, the statutes typically impose upon the plaintiff the risk of insolvency of the manufacturer between the time an action is brought and the time a judgment can be enforced. If a nonmanufacturing seller or distributor is dismissed from an action at the outset when it appears that the manufacturer will be able to pay a judgment, and the manufacturer subsequently becomes insolvent and is unable to pay the judgment, the plaintiff may be left to suffer the loss uncompensated. One possible solution could be to toll the statute of limitations against nonmanufacturers so that they may be brought in if necessary. Second, a nonmanufacturing seller or distributor occasionally will be responsible for the introduction of a defect in a product even though it exercised reasonable care in handling or supervising the product in its control. In such instances, liability for a § 2(a) defect should be imposed on the nonmanufacturing seller or distributor. See § 2, Illustration 2.

---

§ 2. Categories of Product Defect

A product is defective when, at the time of sale or distribution, it contains a manufacturing defect, is defective in design, or is defective because of inadequate instructions or warnings. A product:

(a) contains a manufacturing defect when the product departs from its intended design even though all possible care was exercised in the preparation and marketing of the product;

(b) is defective in design when the foreseeable risks of harm posed by the product could have been reduced or avoided by the adoption of a reasonable alternative design by the seller or other distributor, or a predecessor in the commercial chain of distribution, and the omission of the alternative design renders the product not reasonably safe;

(c) is defective because of inadequate instructions or warnings when the foreseeable risks of harm posed by the product could have been reduced or avoided by the provision of reasonable instructions or warnings by the seller or other distributor, or a predecessor in the commercial chain of distribution, and the omission of the instructions or warnings renders the product not reasonably safe.

Comment:

a. Rationale. The rules set forth in this Section establish separate standards of liability for manufacturing defects, design defects, and defects based on inadequate instructions or warnings. They are generally applicable to most products. Standards of liability applicable to special product categories such as prescription drugs and used products are set forth in separate sections in Topic 2 of this Chapter.

The rule for manufacturing defects stated in Subsection (a) imposes liability whether or not the manufacturer's quality control efforts satisfy standards of reasonableness. Strict liability without fault in this context is generally believed to foster several objectives. On the premise that tort law serves the instrumental function of creating safety incentives, imposing strict liability on manufacturers for harm caused by manufacturing defects encourages greater investment in product safety than does a regime of fault-based liability under which, as a practical matter, sellers may escape their appropriate share of responsibility. Some courts and commentators also have said that strict liability discourages the consumption of defective products by causing the purchase price of products to reflect, more than would a rule of negligence, the costs of defects. And by eliminating the issue of manufacturer fault from plaintiff's case, strict liability reduces the transaction costs involved in litigating that issue.

Several important fairness concerns are also believed to support manufacturers' liability for manufacturing defects even if the plaintiff is unable to show that the manufacturer's quality control fails to meet risk-utility norms. In many cases manufacturing defects are in fact caused by manufacturer negligence but plaintiffs have difficulty proving it. Strict liability therefore performs a function similar to the concept of res ipsa loquitur, allowing deserving plaintiffs to succeed notwithstanding what would otherwise be difficult or insuperable problems of proof. Products that malfunction due to manufacturing defects disappoint reasonable expectations of product performance. Because manufacturers invest in quality control at consciously chosen levels, their knowledge that a predictable number of flawed products will enter the marketplace entails an element of deliberation about the amount of injury that will result from their activity. Finally, many believe that consumers who benefit from products without suffering harm should share, through increases in the prices charged for those products, the burden of unavoidable injury costs that result from manufacturing defects.

An often-cited rationale for holding wholesalers and retailers strictly liable for harm caused by manufacturing defects is that, as between them and innocent victims who suffer harm because of defective products, the product sellers as business entities are in a better position than are individual users and consumers to insure against such losses. In most instances, wholesalers and retailers will be able to pass liability costs up the chain of product distribution to the manufacturer. When joining the manufacturer in the tort action presents the plaintiff with procedural difficulties, local retailers can pay damages to the victims and then seek indemnity from manufacturers. Finally, holding retailers and wholesalers strictly liable creates incentives for them to deal only with reputable, financially responsible manufacturers and distributors, thereby helping to protect the interests of users and consumers. For considerations relevant to reducing nonmanufacturers' liability, see § 1, Comment *e*.

In contrast to manufacturing defects, design defects and defects based on inadequate instructions or warnings are predicated on a different concept of responsibility. In the first place, such defects cannot be determined by reference to the manufacturer's own design or marketing standards because those standards are the very ones that plaintiffs attack as unreasonable. Some sort of independent assessment of advantages and disadvantages, to which some attach the label "risk-utility balancing," is necessary. Products are not generically defective merely because they are dangerous. Many product-related accident costs can be eliminated only by excessively sacrificing product features that make products useful and desirable. Thus, the various trade-offs need to be considered in determining whether accident costs are more fairly and efficiently borne by accident victims, on the one hand, or, on the other hand, by consumers generally through the mechanism of higher product prices attributable to liability costs imposed by courts on product sellers.

Subsections (b) and (c), which impose liability for products that are defectively designed or sold without adequate warnings or instructions and are thus not reasonably safe, achieve the same general objectives as does liability predicated on negligence. The emphasis is on creating incentives for manufacturers to achieve optimal levels of safety in designing and marketing products. Society does not benefit from products that are excessively safe—for example, automobiles designed with maximum speeds of 20 miles per hour—any more than it benefits from products that are too risky. Society benefits most when the right, or optimal, amount of product safety is achieved. From a fairness perspective, requiring individual users and consumers to bear appropriate responsibility for proper product use prevents careless users and consumers from being subsidized by more careful users and consumers, when the former are paid damages out of funds to which the latter are forced to contribute through higher product prices.

In general, the rationale for imposing strict liability on manufacturers for harm caused by manufacturing defects does not apply in the context of imposing liability for defective design and defects based on inadequate instruction or warning. Consumer expectations as to proper product design or warning are typically more difficult to discern than in the case of a manufacturing defect. Moreover, the element of deliberation in setting appropriate levels of design safety is not directly analogous to the setting of levels of quality control by the manufacturer. When a manufacturer sets its quality control at a certain level, it is aware that a given number of products may leave the assembly line in a defective condition and cause injury to innocent victims who can generally do nothing to avoid injury. The implications of deliberately drawing lines with respect to product design safety are different. A reasonably designed product still carries with it elements of risk that must be protected against by the user or consumer since some risks cannot be designed out of the product at reasonable cost.

Most courts agree that, for the liability system to be fair and efficient, the balancing of risks and benefits in judging product design and marketing must be done in light of the knowledge of risks and risk-avoidance techniques reasonably attainable at the time of distribution. To hold a manufacturer liable for a risk that was not foreseeable when the product was marketed might foster increased manufacturer investment in safety. But such investment by definition would be a matter of guesswork. Furthermore, manufacturers may persuasively ask to be judged by a normative behavior standard to which it is reasonably possible for manufacturers to conform. For these reasons, Subsections (b) and (c) speak of products being defective only when risks are reasonably foreseeable.

b. The nonexclusiveness of the definitions of defect in this Section. When a plaintiff seeks recovery under the general rule of liability in § 1, in most instances the plaintiff must establish a prima facie case of product defect by satisfying the requirements of § 2. Section 2 is not, however, the exclusive means by which the plaintiff may establish liability in a products case based on the general rule in § 1. Some courts, for example, while recognizing that in most cases involving defective design the plaintiff must prove the availability of a reasonable alternative design, also observe that such proof is not necessary in every case involving design defects. Sections

3 and 4 and Comment *e* to § 2 provide approaches to the establishment of defective design other than that provided in § 2(b).

Section 3 provides that when circumstantial evidence supports the conclusion that a defect was a contributing cause of the harm and that the defect existed at the time of sale, it is unnecessary to identify the specific nature of the defect and meet the requisites of § 2. Section 3 frees the plaintiff from the strictures of § 2 in circumstances in which common experience teaches that an inference of defect may be warranted under the specific facts, including the failure of the product to perform its manifestly intended function. When the defect established under § 3 may involve product design, some courts recognize consumer expectations as an adequate test for defect, in apparent conflict with the reasonable alternative design requirement in § 2(b). But when the claims involve a product's failure to perform its manifestly intended function and the other requisites of § 3 are met, the apparent conflict disappears.

Section 4, dealing with violations of statutory and regulatory norms, also provides an alternate method of establishing defect. A plaintiff is not required to establish the standard for design or warning under § 2, but merely to identify a government-imposed standard.

Comment *e* provides a further qualification of the rule in § 2(b). This Restatement recognizes the possibility that product sellers may be subject to liability even absent a reasonable alternative design when the product design is manifestly unreasonable. When § 2(b) is read in conjunction with these other provisions that allow for other avenues for determining defective design, it reflects the substantial body of case law suggesting that reasonable alternative design is the predominant, yet not exclusive, method for establishing defective design.

c. Manufacturing defects. As stated in Subsection (a), a manufacturing defect is a departure from a product unit's design specifications. More distinctly than any other type of defect, manufacturing defects disappoint consumer expectations. Common examples of manufacturing defects are products that are physically flawed, damaged, or incorrectly assembled. In actions against the manufacturer, under prevailing rules concerning allocation of burdens of proof the plaintiff ordinarily bears the burden of establishing that such a defect existed in the product when it left the hands of the manufacturer.

Occasionally a defect may arise after manufacture, for example, during shipment or while in storage. Since the product, as sold to the consumer, has a defect that is a departure from the product unit's design specifications, a commercial seller or distributor down the chain of distribution is liable as if the product were defectively manufactured. As long as the plaintiff establishes that the product was defective when it left the hands of a given seller in the distributive chain, liability will attach to that seller. Such defects are referred to in this Restatement as "manufacturing defects" even when they occur after manufacture. When the manufacturer delegates some aspect of manufacture, such as final assembly or inspection, to a subsequent seller, the manufacturer may be subject to liability under rules of vicarious liability for a defect that was introduced into the product after it left the hands of the manufacturer. Although Subsection (a) calls for liability without fault, a plaintiff may seek to recover based upon allegations and proof of negligent manufacture. See Comment *n*. For the rule governing food products that contain impurities or foreign matter, see § 7. For the rule governing commercial used-product sellers' liability for harm caused by manufacturing defects, see § 8.

d. *Design defects: general considerations*. Whereas a manufacturing defect consists of a product unit's failure to meet the manufacturer's design specifications, a product asserted to have a defective design meets the manufacturer's design specifications but raises the question whether the specifications themselves create unreasonable risks. Answering that question requires reference to a standard outside the specifications. Subsection (b) adopts a reasonableness ("risk-utility balancing") test as the standard for judging the defectiveness of product designs. More specifically, the test is whether a reasonable alternative design would, at reasonable cost, have reduced the foreseeable risks of harm posed by the product and, if so, whether the omission of the alternative design by the seller or a predecessor in the distributive chain rendered the product not reasonably safe. (This is the primary, but not the exclusive, test for defective design. See Comment *b*.) Under prevailing rules concerning allocation of burden of proof, the plaintiff must prove that such a reasonable alternative was, or reasonably could have been, available at time of sale or distribution. See Comment *f*.

Assessment of a product design in most instances requires a comparison between an alternative design and the product design that caused the injury, undertaken from the viewpoint of a reasonable person. That approach is also used in administering the traditional reasonableness standard in negligence. See Restatement, Second, Torts § 283, Comment *c*. The policy reasons that support use of a reasonable-person perspective in connection with the general negligence standard also support its use in the products liability context.

How the defendant's design compares with other, competing designs in actual use is relevant to the issue of whether the defendant's design is defective. Defendants often seek to defend their product designs on the ground that the designs conform to the "state of the art." The term "state of the art" has been variously defined to mean that the product design conforms to industry custom, that it reflects the safest and most advanced technology developed and in commercial use, or that it reflects technology at the cutting edge of scientific knowledge. The confusion brought about by these various definitions is unfortunate. This Section states that a design is defective if the product could have been made safer by the adoption of a reasonable alternative design. If such a design could have been practically adopted at time of sale and if the omission of such a design rendered the product not reasonably safe, the plaintiff establishes defect under Subsection (b). When a defendant demonstrates that its product design was the safest in use at the time of sale, it may be difficult for the plaintiff to prove that an alternative design could have been practically adopted. The defendant is thus allowed to introduce evidence with regard to industry practice that bears on whether an alternative design was practicable. Industry practice may also be relevant to whether the omission of an alternative design rendered the product not reasonably safe. While such evidence is admissible, it is not necessarily dispositive. If the plaintiff introduces expert testimony to establish that a reasonable alternative design could practically have been adopted, a trier of fact may conclude that the product was defective notwithstanding that such a design was not adopted by any manufacturer, or even considered for commercial use, at the time of sale.

Early in the development of products liability law, courts held that a claim based on design defect could not be sustained if the dangers presented by the product were open and obvious. Subsection (b) does not recognize the obviousness of a design-related risk as precluding a finding of defectiveness. The fact that a danger is open and obvious is relevant to the issue of defectiveness, but does not necessarily preclude a plaintiff from establishing that a reasonable alternative design should have been adopted that would have reduced or prevented injury to the plaintiff.

The requirement in Subsection (b) that the plaintiff show a reasonable alternative design applies in most instances even though the plaintiff alleges that the category of product sold by the defendant is so dangerous that it should not have been marketed at all. See Comment *e*. Common and widely distributed products such as alcoholic beverages, firearms, and above-ground swimming pools may be found to be defective only upon proof of the requisite conditions in Subsection (a), (b), or (c). If such products are defectively manufactured or sold without reasonable warnings as to their danger when such warnings are appropriate, or if reasonable alternative designs could have been adopted, then liability under §§ 1 and 2 may attach. Absent proof of defect under those Sections, however, courts have not imposed liability for categories of products that are generally available and widely used and consumed, even if they pose substantial risks of harm. Instead, courts generally have concluded that legislatures and administrative agencies can, more appropriately than courts, consider the desirability of commercial distribution of some categories of widely used and consumed, but nevertheless dangerous, products.

e. Design defects: possibility of manifestly unreasonable design. Several courts have suggested that the designs of some products are so manifestly unreasonable, in that they have low social utility and high degree of danger, that liability should attach even absent proof of a reasonable alternative design. In large part the problem is one of how the range of relevant alternative designs is described. For example, a toy gun that shoots hard rubber pellets with sufficient velocity to cause injury to children could be found to be defectively designed within the rule of

Subsection (b). Toy guns unlikely to cause injury would constitute reasonable alternatives to the dangerous toy. Thus, toy guns that project ping-pong balls, soft gelatin pellets, or water might be found to be reasonable alternative designs to a toy gun that shoots hard pellets. However, if the realism of the hard-pellet gun, and thus its capacity to cause injury, is sufficiently important to those who purchase and use such products to justify the court's limiting consideration to toy guns that achieve realism by shooting hard pellets, then no reasonable alternative will, by hypothesis, be available. In that instance, the design feature that defines which alternatives are relevant—the realism of the hard-pellet gun and thus its capacity to injure—is precisely the feature on which the user places value and of which the plaintiff complains. If a court were to adopt this characterization of the product, and deem the capacity to cause injury an egregiously unacceptable quality in a toy for use by children, it could conclude that liability should attach without proof of a reasonable alternative design. The court would declare the product design to be defective and not reasonably safe because the extremely high degree of danger posed by its use or consumption so substantially outweighs its negligible social utility that no rational, reasonable person, fully aware of the relevant facts, would choose to use, or to allow children to use, the product.

f. Design defects: factors relevant in determining whether the omission of a reasonable alternative design renders a product not reasonably safe. Subsection (b) states that a product is defective in design if the omission of a reasonable alternative design renders the product not reasonably safe. A broad range of factors may be considered in determining whether an alternative design is reasonable and whether its omission renders a product not reasonably safe. The factors include, among others, the magnitude and probability of the foreseeable risks of harm, the instructions and warnings accompanying the product, and the nature and strength of consumer expectations regarding the product, including expectations arising from product portrayal and marketing. See Comment *g.* The relative advantages and disadvantages of the product as designed and as it alternatively could have been designed may also be considered. Thus, the likely effects of the alternative design on production costs; the effects of the alternative design on product longevity, maintenance, repair, and esthetics; and the range of consumer choice among products are factors that may be taken into account. A plaintiff is not necessarily required to introduce proof on all of these factors; their relevance, and the relevance of other factors, will vary from case to case. Moreover, the factors interact with one another. For example, evidence of the magnitude and probability of foreseeable harm may be offset by evidence that the proposed alternative design would reduce the efficiency and the utility of the product. On the other hand, evidence that a proposed alternative design would increase production costs may be offset by evidence that product portrayal and marketing created substantial expectations of performance or safety, thus increasing the probability of foreseeable harm. Depending on the mix of these factors, a number of variations in the design of a given product may meet the test in Subsection (b). On the other hand, it is not a factor under Subsection (b) that the imposition of liability would have a negative effect on corporate earnings or would reduce employment in a given industry.

When evaluating the reasonableness of a design alternative, the overall safety of the product must be considered. It is not sufficient that the alternative design would have reduced or prevented the harm suffered by the plaintiff if it would also have introduced into the product other dangers of equal or greater magnitude.

While a plaintiff must prove that a reasonable alternative design would have reduced the foreseeable risks of harm, Subsection (b) does not require the plaintiff to produce expert testimony in every case. Cases arise in which the feasibility of a reasonable alternative design is obvious and understandable to laypersons and therefore expert testimony is unnecessary to support a finding that the product should have been designed differently and more safely. For example, when a manufacturer sells a soft stuffed toy with hard plastic buttons that are easily removable and likely to choke and suffocate a small child who foreseeably attempts to swallow them, the plaintiff should be able to reach the trier of fact with a claim that buttons on such a toy should be an integral part of the toy's fabric itself (or otherwise be unremovable by an infant) without hiring an expert to demonstrate the feasibility of an alternative safer design. Furthermore, other products already available on the market may serve the same or very similar function at lower risk and at comparable cost. Such products may serve as reasonable alternatives to the product in question.

In many cases, the plaintiff must rely on expert testimony. Subsection (b) does not, however, require the plaintiff to produce a prototype in order to make out a prima facie case. Thus, qualified expert testimony on the issue suffices, even though the expert has produced no prototype, if it reasonably supports the conclusion that a reasonable alternative design could have been practically adopted at the time of sale.

The requirements in Subsection (b) relate to what the plaintiff must prove in order to prevail at trial. This Restatement takes no position regarding the requirements of local law concerning the adequacy of pleadings or pretrial demonstrations of genuine issues of fact. It does, however, assume that the plaintiff will have the opportunity to conduct reasonable discovery so as to ascertain whether an alternative design is practical.

A test that considers such a broad range of factors in deciding whether the omission of an alternative design renders a product not reasonably safe requires a fair allocation of proof between the parties. To establish a prima facie case of defect, the plaintiff must prove the availability of a technologically feasible and practical alternative design that would have reduced or prevented the plaintiff's harm. Given inherent limitations on access to relevant data, the plaintiff is not required to establish with particularity the costs and benefits associated with adoption of the suggested alternative design.

In sum, the requirement of Subsection (b) that a product is defective in design if the foreseeable risks of harm could have been reduced by a reasonable alternative design is based on the commonsense notion that liability for harm caused by product designs should attach only when harm is reasonably preventable. For justice to be achieved, Subsection (b) should not be construed to create artificial and unreasonable barriers to recovery.

The necessity of proving a reasonable alternative design as a predicate for establishing design defect is, like any factual element in a case, addressed initially to the courts. Sufficient evidence must be presented so that reasonable persons could conclude that a reasonable alternative could have been practically adopted. Assuming that a court concludes that sufficient evidence on this issue has been presented, the issue is then for the trier of fact. This Restatement takes no position regarding the specifics of how a jury should be instructed. So long as jury instructions are generally consistent with the rule of law set forth in Subsection (b), their specific form and content are matters of local law.

g. Consumer expectations: general considerations. Under Subsection (b), consumer expectations do not constitute an independent standard for judging the defectiveness of product designs. Courts frequently rely, in part, on consumer expectations when discussing liability based on other theories of liability. Some courts, for example, use the term "reasonable consumer expectations" as an equivalent of "proof of a reasonable, safer design alternative," since reasonable consumers have a right to expect product designs that conform to the reasonableness standard in Subsection (b). Other courts, allowing an inference of defect to be drawn when the incident is of a kind that ordinarily would occur as a result of product defect, observe that products that fail when put to their manifestly intended use disappoint reasonable consumer expectations. See § 3. However, consumer expectations do not play a determinative role in determining defectiveness. See Comment *h.* Consumer expectations, standing alone, do not take into account whether the proposed alternative design could be implemented at reasonable cost, or whether an alternative design would provide greater overall safety. Nevertheless, consumer expectations about product performance and the dangers attendant to product use affect how risks are perceived and relate to foreseeability and frequency of the risks of harm, both of which are relevant under Subsection (b). See Comment *f.* Such expectations are often influenced by how products are portrayed and marketed and can have a significant impact on consumer behavior. Thus, although consumer expectations do not constitute an independent standard for judging the defectiveness of product designs, they may substantially influence or even be ultimately determinative on risk-utility balancing in judging whether the omission of a proposed alternative design renders the product not reasonably safe.

Subsection (b) likewise rejects conformance to consumer expectations as a defense. The mere fact that a risk presented by a product design is open and obvious, or generally known, and that the product thus satisfies expectations, does not prevent a finding that the design is defective. But the fact that a product design meets consumer expectations may substantially influence or even be ultimately determinative on risk-utility balancing in judging whether the omission of a proposed alternative design renders the product not reasonably safe. It follows that, while disappointment of consumer expectations may not serve as an independent basis for allowing recovery under Subsection (b), neither may conformance with consumer expectations serve as an independent basis for denying recovery. Such expectations may be relevant in both contexts, but in neither are they controlling.

h. Consumer expectations: food products and used products. With regard to two special product categories consumer expectations play a special role in determining product defect. See § 7 (food products) and § 8 (used products). On occasion it is difficult to determine whether a given food component is an inherent aspect of a product or constitutes an adulteration of the product. Whether, for example, a fish bone in commercially distributed fish chowder constitutes a manufacturing defect within the meaning of § 2(a) is best determined by focusing on reasonable consumer expectations.

Regarding commercially distributed used products, the rules set forth in § 2 are not adequate to the task of determining liability. Variations in the type and condition of used products are such that the stringent rules for imposition of liability for new products are inappropriate. On occasion the seller of a used product may market the product in a manner that would cause a reasonable person in the position of the buyer to expect the used product to present no greater risk of defect than if it were new; or a used product may be remanufactured, justifying heightened seller's responsibility. In these limited settings it is appropriate to treat the sale under rules similar to those applicable to new products. See §§ 8(b) and 8(c).

i. Inadequate instructions or warnings. Commercial product sellers must provide reasonable instructions and warnings about risks of injury posed by products. Instructions inform persons how to use and consume products safely. Warnings alert users and consumers to the existence and nature of product risks so that they can prevent harm either by appropriate conduct during use or consumption or by choosing not to use or consume. In most instances the instructions and warnings will originate with the manufacturer, but sellers down the chain of distribution must warn when doing so is feasible and reasonably necessary. In any event, sellers down the chain are liable if the instructions and warnings provided by predecessors in the chain are inadequate. See Comment *o.* Under prevailing rules concerning allocation of burdens of proof, plaintiff must prove that adequate instructions or warnings were not provided. Subsection (c) adopts a reasonableness test for judging the adequacy of product instructions and warnings. It thus parallels Subsection (b), which adopts a similar standard for judging the safety of product designs. Although the liability standard is formulated in essentially identical terms in Subsections (b) and (c), the defectiveness concept is more difficult to apply in the warnings context. In evaluating the adequacy of product warnings and instructions, courts must be sensitive to many factors. It is impossible to identify anything approaching a perfect level of detail that should be communicated in product disclosures. For example, educated or experienced product users and consumers may benefit from inclusion of more information about the full spectrum of product risks, whereas less-educated or unskilled users may benefit from more concise warnings and instructions stressing only the most crucial risks and safe-handling practices. In some contexts, products intended for special categories of users, such as children, may require more vivid and unambiguous warnings. In some cases, excessive detail may detract from the ability of typical users and consumers to focus on the important aspects of the warnings, whereas in others reasonably full disclosure will be necessary to enable informed, efficient choices by product users. Product warnings and instructions can rarely communicate all potentially relevant information, and the ability of a plaintiff to imagine a hypothetical better warning in the aftermath of an accident does not establish that the warning actually accompanying the product was inadequate. No easy guideline exists for courts to adopt in assessing the adequacy of product warnings and instructions. In making their assessments, courts must focus on various factors, such as content and comprehensibility, intensity of expression, and the characteristics of expected user groups.

Depending on the circumstances, Subsection (c) may require that instructions and warnings be given not only to purchasers, users, and consumers, but also to others who a reasonable seller should know will be in a position to reduce or avoid the risk of harm. There is no general rule as to whether one supplying a product for the use of others through an intermediary has a duty to warn the ultimate product user directly or may rely on the intermediary to relay warnings. The standard is one of reasonableness in the circumstances. Among the factors to be considered are the gravity of the risks posed by the product, the likelihood that the intermediary will convey the information to the ultimate user, and the feasibility and effectiveness of giving a warning directly to the user. Thus, when the purchaser of machinery is the owner of a workplace who provides the machinery to employees for their use, and there is reason to doubt that the employer will pass warnings on to employees, the seller is required to reach the employees directly with necessary instructions and warnings if doing so is reasonably feasible.

In addition to alerting users and consumers to the existence and nature of product risks so that they can, by appropriate conduct during use or consumption, reduce the risk of harm, warnings also may be needed to inform users and consumers of nonobvious and not generally known risks that unavoidably inhere in using or consuming the product. Such warnings allow the user or consumer to avoid the risk warned against by making an informed decision not to purchase or use the product at all and hence not to encounter the risk. In this context, warnings must be provided for inherent risks that reasonably foreseeable product users and consumers would reasonably deem material or significant in deciding whether to use or consume the product. Whether or not many persons would, when warned, nonetheless decide to use or consume the product, warnings are required to protect the interests of those reasonably foreseeable users or consumers who would, based on their own reasonable assessments of the risks and benefits, decline product use or consumption. When such warnings are necessary, their omission renders the product not reasonably safe at time of sale. Notwithstanding the defective condition of the product in the absence of adequate warnings, if a particular user or consumer would have decided to use or consume even if warned, the lack of warnings is not a legal cause of that plaintiff's harm. Judicial decisions supporting the duty to provide warnings for informed decisionmaking have arisen almost exclusively with regard to those toxic agents and pharmaceutical products with respect to which courts have recognized a distinctive need to provide risk information so that recipients of the information can decide whether they wish to purchase or utilize the product. See § 6, Comment *d*.

j. Warnings: obvious and generally known risks. In general, a product seller is not subject to liability for failing to warn or instruct regarding risks and risk-avoidance measures that should be obvious to, or generally known by, foreseeable product users. When a risk is obvious or generally known, the prospective addressee of a warning will or should already know of its existence. Warning of an obvious or generally known risk in most instances will not provide an effective additional measure of safety. Furthermore, warnings that deal with obvious or generally known risks may be ignored by users and consumers and may diminish the significance of warnings about non-obvious, not-generally-known risks. Thus, requiring warnings of obvious or generally known risks could reduce the efficacy of warnings generally. When reasonable minds may differ as to whether the risk was obvious or generally known, the issue is to be decided by the trier of fact. The obviousness of risk may bear on the issue of design defect rather than failure to warn. See Comments *d* and *g*.

k. Warnings: adverse allergic or idiosyncratic reactions. Cases of adverse allergic or idiosyncratic reactions involve a special subset of products that may be defective because of inadequate warnings. Many of these cases involve nonprescription drugs and cosmetics. However, virtually any tangible product can contain an ingredient to which some persons may be allergic. Thus, food, nonprescription drugs, toiletries, paint, solvents, building materials, clothing, and furniture have all been involved in litigation to which this Comment is relevant. Prescription drugs and medical devices are also capable of causing allergic reactions, but they are governed by § 6.

The general rule in cases involving allergic reactions is that a warning is required when the harm-causing ingredient is one to which a substantial number of persons are allergic. The degree of substantiality is not precisely quantifiable. Clearly the plaintiff in most cases must show that the allergic predisposition is not unique to the plaintiff. In determining whether the plaintiff has carried the burden in this regard, however, the court may properly consider the severity of the plaintiff's harm. The more severe the harm, the more justified is a conclusion that the number of persons at risk need not be large to be considered "substantial" so as to require a warning. Essentially, this reflects the same risk-utility balancing undertaken in warnings cases generally. But courts explicitly impose the requirement of substantiality in cases involving adverse allergic reactions.

The ingredient that causes the allergic reaction must be one whose danger or whose presence in the product is not generally known to consumers. When both the presence of an allergenic ingredient in the product and the risks presented by such ingredient are widely known, instructions and warnings about that danger are unnecessary. When the presence of the allergenic ingredient would not be anticipated by a reasonable user or consumer, warnings concerning its presence are required. Similarly, when the presence of the ingredient is generally known to consumers, but its dangers are not, a warning of the dangers must be given.

Finally, as required in Subsection (c), warnings concerning risks of allergic reactions that are not reasonably foreseeable at the time of sale need not be provided. See Comment *m*.

l. Relationship between design and instruction or warning. Reasonable designs and instructions or warnings both play important roles in the production and distribution of reasonably safe products. In general, when a safer design can reasonably be implemented and risks can reasonably be designed out of a product, adoption of the safer design is required over a warning that leaves a significant residuum of such risks. For example, instructions and warnings may be ineffective because users of the product may not be adequately reached, may be likely to be inattentive, or may be insufficiently motivated to follow the instructions or heed the warnings. However, when an alternative design to avoid risks cannot reasonably be implemented, adequate instructions and warnings will normally be sufficient to render the product reasonably safe. Compare Comment *e*. Warnings are not, however, a substitute for the provision of a reasonably safe design.

The fact that a risk is obvious or generally known often serves the same function as a warning. See Comment *j*. However, obviousness of risk does not necessarily obviate a duty to provide a safer design. Just as warnings may be ignored, so may obvious or generally known risks be ignored, leaving a residuum of risk great enough to require adopting a safer design. See Comment *d*.

m. Reasonably foreseeable uses and risks in design and warning claims. Subsections (b) and (c) impose liability only when the product is put to uses that it is reasonable to expect a seller or distributor to foresee. Product sellers and distributors are not required to foresee and take precautions against every conceivable mode of use and abuse to which their products might be put. Increasing the costs of designing and marketing products in order to avoid the consequences of unreasonable modes of use is not required.

In cases involving a claim of design defect in a mechanical product, foreseeability of risk is rarely an issue as a practical matter. Once the plaintiff establishes that the product was put to a reasonably foreseeable use, physical risks of injury are generally known or reasonably knowable by experts in the field. It is not unfair to charge a manufacturer with knowledge of such generally known or knowable risks.

The issue of foreseeability of risk of harm is more complex in the case of products such as prescription drugs, medical devices, and toxic chemicals. Risks attendant to use and consumption of these products may, indeed, be unforeseeable at the time of sale. Unforeseeable risks arising from foreseeable product use or consumption by definition cannot specifically be warned against. Thus, in connection with a claim of inadequate design, instruction, or warning, plaintiff should bear the burden of establishing that the risk in question was known or should have been known to the relevant manufacturing community. The harms that result from unforeseeable risks—for example, in the human body's reaction to a new drug, medical device, or chemical—are not a basis of liability. Of course, a seller bears responsibility to perform reasonable testing prior to marketing a product and to discover risks and risk-avoidance measures that such testing would reveal. A seller is charged with knowledge of what reasonable testing would reveal. If testing is not undertaken, or is performed in an inadequate manner, and this failure results in a defect that causes harm, the seller is subject to liability for harm caused by such defect.

n. Relationship of definitions of defect to traditional doctrinal categories. The rules in this Section and in other provisions of this Chapter define the bases of tort liability for harm caused by product defects existing at time of sale or other distribution. The rules are stated functionally rather than in terms of traditional doctrinal categories. Claims based on product defect at time of sale or other distribution must meet the requisites set forth in Subsection (a), (b), or (c), or the other provisions in this Chapter. As long as these requisites are met, doctrinal tort categories such as negligence or strict liability may be utilized in bringing the claim.

Similarly, a product defect claim satisfying the requisites of Subsection (a), (b), or (c), or other provisions in this Chapter, may be brought under the implied warranty of merchantability provisions of the Uniform Commercial Code. It is recognized that some courts have adopted a consumer expectations definition for design and failure-to-warn defects in implied warranty cases involving harm to persons or property. This Restatement contemplates that a well-coordinated body of law governing liability for harm to persons or property arising out of the sale of defective products requires a consistent definition of defect, and that the definition properly should come from tort law, whether the claim carries a tort label or one of implied warranty of merchantability.

In connection with a claim under §§ 1 and 2 and related provisions of this Restatement, the evidence that the defendant did or did not conduct adequately reasonable research or testing before marketing the product may be admissible (but is not necessarily required) regardless of whether the claim is based on negligence, strict liability, or implied warranty of merchantability. Although a defendant is held objectively responsible for having knowledge that a reasonable seller would have had, the fact that the defendant engaged in substantial research and testing may help to support the contention that a risk was not reasonably foreseeable. Conversely, the fact that the defendant engaged in little or no research or testing may, depending on the circumstances, help to support the contention that, had reasonable research or testing been performed, the risk could have been foreseen. Moreover, as long as the requisites in Subsection (a), (b), or (c), or other provisions in this Chapter, are met, the plaintiff may in appropriate instances—for example, in connection with comparative fault or punitive damage claims—show that the defect resulted from reckless, willfully indifferent, or intentionally wrongful conduct of the defendant.

A separate and more difficult question arises as to whether a case should be submitted to a jury on multiple theories of recovery. Design and failure-to-warn claims may be combined in the same case because they rest on different factual allegations and distinct legal concepts. However, two or more factually identical defective-design claims or two or more factually identical failure-to-warn claims should not be submitted to the trier of fact in the same case under different doctrinal labels. Regardless of the doctrinal label attached to a particular claim, design and warning claims rest on a risk-utility assessment. To allow two or more factually identical risk-utility claims to go to a jury under different labels, whether "strict liability," "negligence," or "implied warranty of merchantability," would generate confusion and may well result in inconsistent verdicts.

In proceedings in which multiple theories are alleged, the Restatement leaves to local law the question of the procedural stage in a tort action at which plaintiff must decide under which theory to pursue the case.

A different approach may be appropriate for claims based on manufacturing defects, since the rule set forth in Subsection (a) does not require risk-utility assessment while a negligence claim does. That is, the two types of manufacturing defect claims are based on different factual predicates. Negligence rests on a showing of fault leading to product defect. Strict liability rests merely on a showing of product defect. When a plaintiff believes a good claim for the negligent creation of (or failure to discover) a manufacturing defect may be established, the plaintiff may assert such a claim in addition to a claim in strict liability under Subsection (a). The plaintiff in such a case should have the opportunity to prove fault and also to assert the right to recover based on strict liability. However, clearly it would be inconsistent for a trier of fact to find no manufacturing defect on a § 2(a) claim and yet return a verdict of liability because the defendant was negligent in having poor quality control. What must be shown under either theory is that the product in question did, in fact, have a manufacturing defect at time of sale that contributed to causing the plaintiff's harm.

In connection with manufacturing defects, a § 2(a) tort claim and an implied warranty of merchantability claim rest on the same factual predicate—the sale by the defendant of a product that departs from the manufacturer's specifications irrespective of anyone's fault. Thus, these two claims are duplicative and may not be pursued together in the same case.

The same analysis applies to claims against a nonmanufacturing supplier. The supplier can be held liable as the seller of a defective product under § 2(a) or can be held liable under a negligence theory for failing reasonably to inspect a product or for negligently introducing a defect into the product. Since these claims are based on different factual predicates, the plaintiff may bring actions in both strict liability and negligence. Again, of course, recovery under either theory requires a finding of defect.

The plaintiff in the nonmanufacturing-supplier case should, once again, not be free to submit a case to a jury based on both the implied warranty of merchantability and strict liability theories since they rest on the same factual base—the sale by the supplier of a defective product regardless of fault. The theories are thus duplicative and do not constitute valid separate claims that may be given to the trier of fact in the same case.

In all instances set forth above in which claims are duplicative, if one or the other theory presents an advantage to the plaintiff—in connection with the statute of limitations, for example—the plaintiff may pursue the more advantageous theory. But the trier of fact may not consider both theories on the same facts.

Plaintiffs may, consistent with the foregoing principles, join claims based on product defect existing at time of sale or other distribution and claims based on theories of recovery that do not rest on a premise of product defect at time of sale. Claims based on misrepresentation, express warranty, and implied warranty of fitness for particular purpose, in particular, are not within the scope of this Chapter and thus are unaffected by it.

Finally, negligence retains its vitality as an independent theory of recovery for a wide range of product-related, harm-causing behavior not involving defects at time of sale. This Restatement includes several such topics in later Chapters, including post-sale failure to warn (see § 10); post-sale failure to recall (see § 11); and a successor's liability for its own failure to warn (see § 13). Other topics are covered in the Restatement, Second, of Torts. Thus, for example, negligent entrustment is treated in § 390.

Liability for negligent service, maintenance, or repair, or negligent overpromotion of a product, is governed by the rules set forth in §§ 291 et seq.

o. Liability of nonmanufacturing sellers for defective design and defects due to inadequate instructions or warnings. Nonmanufacturing sellers such as wholesalers and retailers often are not in a good position feasibly to adopt safer product designs or better instructions or warnings. Nevertheless, once it is determined that a reasonable alternative design or reasonable instructions or warnings could have been provided at or before the time of sale by a predecessor in the chain of distribution and would have reduced plaintiff's harm, it is no defense that a nonmanufacturing seller of such a product exercised due care. Thus, strict liability is imposed on a wholesale or retail seller who neither knew nor should have known of the relevant risks, nor was in a position to have taken action to avoid them, so long as a predecessor in the chain of distribution could have acted reasonably to avoid the risks. See Comment *a*. For exceptions to the general rule regarding the liability of a nonmanufacturer seller, see § 1, Comment *e*.

p. Misuse, modification, and alteration. Product misuse, modification, and alteration are forms of post-sale conduct by product users or others that can be relevant to the determination of the issues of defect, causation, or comparative responsibility. Whether such conduct affects one or more of the issues depends on the nature of the conduct and whether the manufacturer should have adopted a reasonable alternative design or provided a reasonable warning to protect against such conduct.

Under the rule in Subsection (b), liability for defective design attaches only if the risks of harm related to foreseeable product use could have been reduced by the adoption of a reasonable alternative design. Similarly, under the rule in Subsection (c), liability for failure to instruct or warn attaches only if the risks presented by the product could have been reduced by the adoption of reasonable instructions or warnings. Foreseeable product misuse, alteration, and modification must also be considered in deciding whether an alternative design should have been adopted. The post-sale conduct of the user may be so unreasonable, unusual, and costly to avoid that a seller has no duty to design or warn against them. When a court so concludes, the product is not defective within the meaning of Subsection (b) or (c).

A product may, however, be defective as defined in Subsection (b) or (c) due to the omission of a reasonable alternative design or the omission of an adequate warning, yet the risk that eventuates due to misuse, modification, or alteration raises questions whether the extent or scope of liability under the prevailing rules governing legal causation allow for the imposition of liability. See § 15.

Moreover, a product may be found to be defective and causally responsible for plaintiff's harm but the plaintiff may have misused, altered, or modified the product in a manner that calls for the reduction of plaintiff's recovery under the rules of comparative responsibility. Thus, an automobile may be defectively designed so as to provide inadequate protection against harm in the event of a collision, and the plaintiff's negligent modification of the automobile may have caused the collision eventuating in plaintiff's harm. See § 17.

It follows that misuse, modification, and alteration are not discrete legal issues. Rather, when relevant, they are aspects of the concepts of defect, causation, and plaintiff's fault. Jurisdictions differ on the question of who bears the burden of raising and introducing proof regarding conduct that constitutes misuse, modification, and alteration. The allocation of burdens in this regard is not addressed in this Restatement and is left to local law.

q. Causation. Under § 1, the product defect must have caused harm to the plaintiff. See §§ 17 and 18.

r. Warranty. Liability for harm caused by product defects imposed by the rules stated in this Chapter is tort liability, not liability for breach of warranty under the Uniform Commercial Code (U.C.C.). Courts may characterize claims under this Chapter as claims for breaches of the implied warranty of merchantability. But in cases involving defect-caused harm to persons or property, a well-coordinated body of law dealing with liability for such harm arising out of the sale of defective products would adopt the tort definition of product defect. See Comment *n*.

———

§ 3. Circumstantial Evidence Supporting Inference of Product Defect

It may be inferred that the harm sustained by the plaintiff was caused by a product defect existing at the time of sale or distribution, without proof of a specific defect, when the incident that harmed the plaintiff:

(a) was of a kind that ordinarily occurs as a result of product defect; and

(b) was not, in the particular case, solely the result of causes other than product defect existing at the time of sale or distribution.

Comment:

a. History. This Section traces its historical antecedents to the law of negligence, which has long recognized that an inference of negligence may be drawn in cases where the defendant's negligence is the best explanation for the cause of an accident, even if the plaintiff cannot explain the exact nature of the defendant's conduct. See Restatement, Second, Torts § 328D. As products liability law developed, cases arose in which an inference of product defect could be drawn from the incident in which a product caused plaintiff's harm, without proof of the specific nature of the defect. This Section sets forth the formal requisites for drawing such an inference.

b.   Requirement that the harm be of a kind that ordinarily occurs as a result of product defect. The most frequent application of this Section is to cases involving manufacturing defects. When a product unit contains such a defect, and the defect affects product performance so as to cause a harmful incident, in most instances it will cause the product to malfunction in such a way that the inference of product defect is clear. From this perspective, manufacturing defects cause products to fail to perform their manifestly intended functions. Frequently, the plaintiff is able to establish specifically the nature and identity of the defect and may proceed directly under § 2(a). But when the product unit involved in the harm-causing incident is lost or destroyed in the accident, direct evidence of specific defect may not be available. Under that circumstance, this Section may offer the plaintiff the only fair opportunity to recover.

When examination of the product unit is impossible because the unit is lost or destroyed after the harm-causing incident, a somewhat different issue may be presented. Responsibility for spoliation of evidence may be relevant to the fairness of allowing the inference set forth in this Section. In any event, the issues of evidence spoliation and any sanctions that might be imposed for such conduct are beyond the scope of this Restatement Third, Torts: Products Liability.

Although the rules in this Section, for the reasons just stated, most often apply to manufacturing defects, occasionally a product design causes the product to malfunction in a manner identical to that which would ordinarily be caused by a manufacturing defect. Thus, an aircraft may inadvertently be designed in such a way that, in new condition and while flying within its intended performance parameters, the wings suddenly and unexpectedly fall off, causing harm. In theory, of course, the plaintiff in such a case would be able to show how other units in the same production line were designed, leading to a showing of a reasonable alternative design under § 2(b). As a practical matter, however, when the incident involving the aircraft is one that ordinarily occurs as a result of product defect, and evidence in the particular case establishes that the harm was not solely the result of causes other than product defect existing at time of sale, it should not be necessary for the plaintiff to incur the cost of proving whether the failure resulted from a manufacturing defect or from a defect in the design of the product. Section 3 allows the trier of fact to draw the inference that the product was defective whether due to a manufacturing defect or a design defect. Under those circumstances, the plaintiff need not specify the type of defect responsible for the product malfunction.

It is important to emphasize the difference between a general inference of defect under § 3 and claims of defect brought directly under §§ 1 and 2. Section 3 claims are limited to situations in which a product fails to perform its manifestly intended function, thus supporting the conclusion that a defect of some kind is the most probable explanation. If that is not the case, and if no other provision of Chapter 1 allows the plaintiff to establish defect independently of the requirements in § 2 (see § 4 and Comment *e* to § 2), a plaintiff is required to establish a cause of action for defect based on proof satisfying the requirements set forth in § 2. See § 2, Comment *b*.

Illustrations:

1. John purchased a new electric blender. John used the blender approximately 10 times exclusively for making milkshakes. While he was making a milkshake, the blender suddenly shattered. A piece of glass struck John's eye, causing harm. The incident resulting in harm is of a kind that ordinarily occurs as a result of product defect.

2. Same facts as Illustration 1, except that John accidentally dropped the blender, causing the glass to shatter. The product did not fail to function in a manner supporting an inference of defect. Whether liability can be established depends on whether the plaintiff can prove a cause of action under §§ 1 and 2.

3. Mary purchased a new automobile. She drove the car 1,000 miles without incident. One day she stopped the car at a red light and leaned back to rest until the light changed. Suddenly the seat collapsed backward, causing Mary to hit the accelerator and the car to shoot out into oncoming traffic and collide with another car. Mary suffered harm in the ensuing collision. As a result of the collision, Mary's car was set afire, destroying the seat assembly. The incident resulting in the harm is of a kind that ordinarily occurs as a result of product defect. Mary need not establish whether the seat assembly contained a manufacturing defect or a design defect.

4. Same facts as in Illustration 3, except that the seat-back assembly failed when Mary, while stopped at the red light, was rear-ended by another automobile at 40 m.p.h. Mary cannot make out liability under this Section. The product did not fail to function in a manner supporting an inference of defect since the collapse of the seat is not the kind of incident that ordinarily occurs as a result of product defect. Liability must be established under the rules set forth in §§ 1 and 2.

5. While carefully driving a new automobile at legal speed on a well-maintained road, Driver felt something crack below where the steering column connects with the dashboard. The steering wheel spun to the right and the automobile turned sharply. Before Driver could stop, the automobile crashed into a wall and Driver suffered harm. Driver has brought an action against the manufacturer of the automobile. The automobile had been driven on short trips before the accident and had 300 miles on its odometer. Driver's qualified expert witness testifies that in her opinion the accident was caused by a defect in the

steering mechanism. The expert identifies four specific manufacturing and design defects that could have caused the accident, but was unable to say, on a balance of the probabilities, which of the four defects was the cause. Under this Section it is not necessary to identify the specific defect in order to draw the inference that a product defect caused the plaintiff's harm.

c. *No requirement that plaintiff prove what aspect of the product was defective.* The inference of defect may be drawn under this Section without proof of the specific defect. Furthermore, quite apart from the question of what type of defect was involved, the plaintiff need not explain specifically what constituent part of the product failed. For example, if an inference of defect can be appropriately drawn in connection with the catastrophic failure of an airplane, the plaintiff need not establish whether the failure is attributable to fuel-tank explosion or engine malfunction.

d. *Requirement that the incident that harmed the plaintiff was not, in the particular case, solely the result of causes other than product defect existing at the time of sale.* To allow the trier of fact to conclude that a product defect caused the plaintiff's harm under this Section, the plaintiff must establish by a preponderance of the evidence that the incident was not solely the result of causal factors other than defect at time of sale. The defect need not be the only cause of the incident; if the plaintiff can prove that the most likely explanation of the harm involves the causal contribution of a product defect, the fact that there may be other concurrent causes of the harm does not preclude liability under this Section. But when the harmful incident can be attributed solely to causes other than original defect, including the conduct of others, an inference of defect under this Section cannot be drawn.

Evidence may permit the inference that a defect in the product at the time of the harm-causing incident caused the product to malfunction, but not the inference that the defect existed at the time of sale or distribution. Such factors as the age of the product, possible alteration by repairers or others, and misuse by the plaintiff or third parties may have introduced the defect that causes harm.

Illustrations:

6. While driving a new automobile at high speed one night, Driver drove off the highway and crashed into a tree. Driver suffered harm. Driver cannot remember the circumstances surrounding the accident. Driver has brought an action against ABC Company, the manufacturer of the automobile. Driver presents no evidence of a specific defect. However, Driver's qualified expert presents credible testimony that a defect in the automobile must have caused the accident. ABC's qualified expert presents credible testimony that it is equally likely that, independent of any defect, Driver lost control while speeding on the highway. If the trier of fact believes the testimony of

Driver's expert, then an inference of defect may be established under this Section. If, however, ABC's expert is believed, an inference of product defect may not be drawn under this Section because Driver has failed to establish by a preponderance of the evidence that the harm did not result solely from Driver's independent loss of control at high speed.

7. Jack purchased a new ABC Electric Power Screwdriver. He inserted the bit for the appropriate screw size and turned the power button on. The bit shot out of the tool and lodged itself in Jack's arm, causing serious injury. Two weeks after purchasing the electric screwdriver, Jack believed the tool was making too much noise and brought it to the Acme Tool Repair Shop to check it out. Acme removed the mechanism that held the bit, examined it, and then reassembled it. Finding no problem, Acme returned the tool to Jack. The accident occurred the next day. On direct examination Jack's expert testifies that the accident was caused by a defect existing at time of sale. On cross-examination, however, Jack's expert admits it is equally probable that the problem with the tool was introduced by Acme. An inference that the power tool was defective at the time of sale cannot be drawn under this Section.

———

§ 4. Noncompliance and Compliance with Product Safety Statutes or Regulations

In connection with liability for defective design or inadequate instructions or warnings:

(a) a product's noncompliance with an applicable product safety statute or administrative regulation renders the product defective with respect to the risks sought to be reduced by the statute or regulation; and

(b) a product's compliance with an applicable product safety statute or administrative regulation is properly considered in determining whether the product is defective with respect to the risks sought to be reduced by the statute or regulation, but such compliance does not preclude as a matter of law a finding of product defect.

Comment:

a. Product safety statutes or administrative regulations. The safety statutes and administrative regulations referred to in this Section are those, promulgated by federal and state and local legislatures and agencies, intended to promote safety in the design and marketing of products. The phrase "safety statute or administrative regulation" is intended to be inclusive of all final governmental edicts and directives, issued pursuant to such statutes or regulations, that establish binding safety standards for the design and marketing of products. Because liability for manufacturing defects under §§ 1 and 2(a) is liability without fault, the violation of, or compliance with, a safety statute or regulation is not relevant to such a claim. In connection with a claim of manufacturing defect brought under common-law negligence principles, see § 2, Comment n, the relevance of statutory or regulatory compliance and violation should be determined according to general negligence principles.

b. Requirement that the statute or regulation be applicable. For purposes of this Section, the product safety statute or administrative regulation must have been in force and applicable at the time of sale or other distribution.

c. Requirement that the statute or regulation be relevant to the particular claim of product defect. For purposes of this Section, the safety statute or administrative regulation must be such that compliance reduces the risk that caused the plaintiff's harm. Thus, when a plaintiff complains that the design of a product should have been more stable to prevent the product from tipping over, a safety statute or regulation is relevant if it addresses the issue of stability in such a way that compliance with the statute or regulation reduces the risk of the product tipping over in the manner that caused the plaintiff's harm. This Section addresses the issue of product defectiveness. For rules governing causation, see §§ 15 and 16. For rules governing affirmative defenses, see §§ 17 and 18.

d. Noncompliance with product safety statute or administrative regulation. Subsection (a) provides that noncompliance with an applicable product safety statute or administrative regulation renders the product defective in design or defective due to inadequate instructions or warnings with respect to the risks sought to be reduced by the statute or regulation. The general rule does not apply when a regulation merely suggests, but does not require, a safety feature. The general rule also does not apply when, after sale but prior to injury, the statute or regulation is repealed or otherwise rendered invalid so as to cause the product no longer to be in noncompliance. When repeal or invalidation takes place post-injury, but prior to adjudication, the court may take the repeal or invalidation into account in deciding whether noncompliance with the statute or regulation renders the product defective. Moreover, when the statute or regulation is unclear as to its meaning or purpose, or conflicts with other safety statutes or regulations with which the product must also comply, a court may take these circumstances into account in determining whether noncompliance with the statute or regulation renders the product defective. The rule in this Subsection is based on the policy judgment that designs and warnings that fail to comply with applicable safety standards established by statute or regulations are, subject to the foregoing exceptions, by definition defective.

In contrast to Subsection (a), the parallel common-law rule governing noncompliance with safety statutes or regulations in negligence actions not involving products liability claims recognizes that noncompliance with an applicable safety statute or regulation does not constitute failure to use due care when the defendant establishes a justification or excuse for the violation. For example, if noncompliance with an administrative regulation under conditions of emergency or temporary impossibility would not constitute a violation in a direct enforcement proceeding, noncompliance alone does not prove negligence. In connection with the adequacy of product designs and warnings, however, design and marketing decisions are made before distribution to users and consumers. The product seller therefore has the option of deferring sale until statutory or regulatory compliance is achieved. Consequently, justification or excuse of the sort anticipated in connection with negligence claims generally does not apply in connection with failure to comply with statutes or regulations governing product design or warnings.

e. Compliance with product safety statute or administrative regulation. An important distinction must be drawn between the subject addressed in Subsection (b) and the matter of federal preemption of state products liability law. Subsection (b) addresses the question of whether and to what extent, as a matter of state tort law, compliance with product safety statutes or administrative regulations affects liability for product defectiveness. When a court concludes that a defendant is not liable by reason of having complied with a safety design or warnings statute or regulation, it is deciding that the product in question is not defective as a matter of the law of that state. The safety statute or regulation may be a federal provision, but the decision to give it determinative effect is a state-law determination. In contrast, in federal preemption, the court decides as a matter of federal law that the relevant federal statute or regulation reflects, expressly or impliedly, the intent of Congress to displace state law, including state tort law, with the federal statute or regulation. The question of preemption is thus a question of federal law, and a determination that there is preemption nullifies otherwise operational state law. The complex set of rules and standards for resolving questions of federal preemption are beyond the scope of this Restatement. However, when federal preemption is found, the legal effect is clear. Judicial deference to federal product safety statutes or regulations occurs not because the court concludes that compliance with the statute or regulation shows the product to be nondefective; the issue of defectiveness under state law is never reached. Rather, the court defers because, when a federal statute or regulation is preemptive, the Constitution mandates federal supremacy.

Accordingly, Subsection (b) addresses the effects of compliance with a federal statute or regulation found to be nonpreemptive. It addresses the question, under state law, of the effect that compliance with product safety statutes or regulations—federal or state—should have on the issue of product defectiveness. Subsection (b) reflects the traditional view that the standards set by most product safety statutes or regulations generally are only minimum standards. Thus, most product safety statutes or regulations establish a floor of safety below which product sellers fall only at their peril, but they leave open the question of whether a higher standard of product safety should be applied. This is the general rule, applicable in most cases.

Occasionally, after reviewing relevant circumstances, a court may properly conclude that a particular product safety standard set by statute or regulation adequately serves the objectives of tort law and therefore that the product that complies with the standard is not defective as a matter of law. Such a conclusion may be appropriate when the safety statute or regulation was promulgated recently, thus supplying currency to the standard therein established; when the specific standard addresses the very issue of product design or warning presented in the case before the court; and when the court is confident that the deliberative process by which the safety standard was established was full, fair, and thorough and reflected substantial expertise. Conversely, when the deliberative process that led to the safety standard with which the defendant's product complies was tainted by the supplying of false information to, or the withholding of necessary and valid information from, the agency that promulgated the standard or certified or approved the product, compliance with regulation is entitled to little or no weight.

f. Conduct not related to product defect. This Section deals with noncompliance and compliance with product safety statutes or regulations as they relate to the issue of product defect. Conduct involving products but not related to product defect may also be governed by statute or regulation. For example, sale of dangerous instrumentalities may be prohibited by statute or regulation, or statutes or regulations may govern such matters as post-sale warnings or recalls. When and whether liability arises when there has been noncompliance or compliance with such statutes or regulations is governed by Restatement, Second, Torts §§ 286–288C.

––––––––

TOPIC 2.   LIABILITY RULES APPLICABLE TO SPECIAL PRODUCTS OR PRODUCT MARKETS

§ 5. **Liability of Commercial Seller or Distributor of Product Components for Harm Caused by Products Into Which Components Are Integrated**

One engaged in the business of selling or otherwise distributing product components who sells or distributes a component is subject to liability for harm to persons or property caused by a product into which the component is integrated if:

   (a) the component is defective in itself, as defined in this Chapter, and the defect causes the harm; or

   (b)(1) the seller or distributor of the component substantially participates in the integration of the component into the design of the product; and

      (2) the integration of the component causes the product to be defective, as defined in this Chapter; and

   (3) the defect in the product causes the harm.

Comment:

   a. Rationale. Product components include raw materials, bulk products, and other constituent products sold for integration into other products. Some components, such as raw materials, valves, or switches, have no functional capabilities unless integrated into other products. Other components, such as a truck chassis or a multi-functional machine, function on their own but still may be utilized in a variety of ways by assemblers of other products.

   As a general rule, component sellers should not be liable when the component itself is not defective as defined in this Chapter. If the component is not itself defective, it would be unjust and inefficient to impose liability solely on the ground that the manufacturer of the integrated product utilizes the component in a manner that renders the integrated product defective. Imposing liability would require the component seller to scrutinize another's product which the component seller has no role in developing. This would require the component seller to develop sufficient sophistication to review the decisions of the business entity that is already charged with responsibility for the integrated product.

   The refusal to impose liability on sellers of nondefective components is expressed in various ways, such as the "raw material supplier defense" or the "bulk sales/sophisticated purchaser rule." However expressed, these formulations recognize that component sellers who do not participate in the integration of the component into the design of the product should not be liable merely because the integration of the component causes the product to become dangerously defective. This Section subjects component sellers to liability when the components themselves are defective or when component providers substantially participate in the integration of components into the design of the other products.

Illustration:

   1. ABC Chain Co. manufactures chains for a wide range of uses in industrial equipment. XYZ Mach. Co. purchases chains from ABC for use in conveyor-belt systems and informs ABC that the chains will be used for that purpose. In the design of a conveyor system by XYZ, part of the chain is exposed. The conveyor system as designed and manufactured by XYZ is defective in that it should include a safety

guard under the rule stated in § 2(b). XYZ sells a conveyor system to LMN Co. LMN's employee, E, while working near the conveyor, is injured when her shirt sleeve becomes entangled in the unguarded chain in the conveyor. ABC is not subject to liability to E. The chain sold by ABC is not itself defective as defined in § 2, and ABC did not participate in the integration of its chain into the design of the XYZ conveyor. XYZ is subject to liability for harm to E as the seller of a defectively designed conveyor under the rules stated in §§ 1 and 2(b).

    b.   *Liability when a product component is defective in itself.* A commercial seller or other distributor of a product component is subject to liability for harm caused by a defect in the component. See § 19, Comment *b.* For example, if a cut-off switch is sold in defective condition due to loosely connected wiring, the seller of the switch is subject to liability for harm to persons or property caused by the improper wiring after the switch is integrated into another product. Similarly, if aluminum that departs from the aluminum manufacturer's specifications due to the presence of foreign particles is utilized in the manufacture of airplane engines, the seller of the defective aluminum is subject to liability for harm to persons or property caused by the defects in the aluminum. Both the switches in the first instance and the aluminum in the second are defective as defined in § 2(a).

    The same rule applies when a component is defectively designed as defined in § 2(b). For example, if motorcycle headlights intended for rugged off-road use are so designed that they fail when the motorcycle is driven over bumpy roads, they are defective within the meaning of § 2(b). Since reasonable alternative designs are available that prevent such foreseeable failures from occurring, the headlight supplier is subject to liability for harm caused by the defectively designed headlight. Indeed, a defect may be inferable under § 3. However, a component not defective in itself as defined in § 2(b) or § 3 does not become defective merely because a purchaser decides to integrate the component into another product in a way that renders the design of the integrated product defective. See Comment *e.*

    The same principles apply in determining a component seller's duty to supply reasonable instructions and warnings to the component buyer. The component seller is required to provide instructions and warnings regarding risks associated with the use of the component product. See §§ 1 and 2(c). However, when a sophisticated buyer integrates a component into another product, the component seller owes no duty to warn either the immediate buyer or ultimate consumers of dangers arising because the component is unsuited for the special purpose to which the buyer puts it. To impose a duty to warn in such a circumstance would require that component sellers monitor the development of products and systems into which their components are to be integrated. See Comment *a.* Courts have not yet confronted the question of whether, in combination, factors such as the component purchaser's lack of expertise and ignorance of the risks of integrating the component into the purchaser's product, and the component supplier's knowledge of both the relevant risks and the purchaser's ignorance thereof, give rise to a duty on the part of the component supplier to warn of risks attending integration of the component into the purchaser's product. Whether the seller of a component should be subject to liability for selling its product to one who is likely to utilize it dangerously is governed by principles of negligent entrustment. See Restatement, Second, Torts § 390.

Illustrations:

2. The same facts as Illustration 1, except that one of the chains sold by ABC to XYZ contains a manufacturing defect as defined in § 2(a). XYZ installs the defective chain in the conveyor-belt system sold by XYZ to LMN. As a result of the defect, the chain breaks, causing the conveyor belt to stop abruptly. E, LMN's employee, suffers harm when the conveyor's sudden stop causes a heavy object on the conveyor to fall on E. ABC is subject to liability to E for harm caused by the sale of the defective component. XYZ is also subject to liability to E for the sale of a defective conveyor system.

3. ABC Vinyl, Inc., sells vinyl swimming-pool liners for use in above-ground swimming pools. ABC manufactures the liners without depth markers. XYZ Pools, Inc., manufactures and sells above-ground swimming pools. XYZ installs a pool with an ABC liner at the home of Roberta. Jack, while visiting Roberta, dives into the shallow portion of the pool that appears to him to be eight feet deep. In reality the water is only four feet deep. Jack hits his head on the bottom and suffers harm. If a court finds that the absence of the depth markers renders the design of the liner defective within the meaning of § 2(b), ABC is subject to liability to Jack. The fact that the liner is a component of the above-ground swimming pool and has been integrated into a specific swimming pool does not insulate ABC from liability for selling a component product that is defectively designed for all swimming-pool installations. XYZ is also subject to liability to Jack as the seller of a pool with a defectively designed liner.

4. ABC Foam Co. manufactures bulk foam with many different uses. XYZ Co. purchases bulk foam from ABC, then processes the foam and incorporates the processed foam in the manufacture of disposable dishware. ABC becomes aware that XYZ is using processed foam in the dishware. ABC and XYZ are both aware that there is a potential danger that processed foam may cause allergic skin reactions for some users. ABC is aware that XYZ is not warning consumers of this potential problem. ABC has no duty to warn XYZ or ultimate consumers of the dangers attendant to use of the processed foam for disposable dishware. The foam sold by ABC is not defective in itself as defined in this Chapter. A supplier of a component has no duty to warn a knowledgeable buyer of risks attendant to special application of its products when integrated into another's product. ABC did not partici-

pate in the design of the disposable dishware manufactured by XYZ, and is thus not subject to liability under Subsection (b).

c. Raw materials. Product components include raw materials. See Comment *a*. Thus, when raw materials are contaminated or otherwise defective within the meaning of § 2(a), the seller of the raw materials is subject to liability for harm caused by such defects. Regarding the seller's exposure to liability for defective design, a basic raw material such as sand, gravel, or kerosene cannot be defectively designed. Inappropriate decisions regarding the use of such materials are not attributable to the supplier of the raw materials but rather to the fabricator that puts them to improper use. The manufacturer of the integrated product has a significant comparative advantage regarding selection of materials to be used. Accordingly, raw-materials sellers are not subject to liability for harm caused by defective design of the end-product. The same considerations apply to failure-to-warn claims against sellers of raw materials. To impose a duty to warn would require the seller to develop expertise regarding a multitude of different end-products and to investigate the actual use of raw materials by manufacturers over whom the supplier has no control. Courts uniformly refuse to impose such an onerous duty to warn. For a consideration of whether special circumstances may give rise to a duty on the part of raw-material sellers to warn of risks attending integration of raw materials with other components, see Comment *b*.

Illustration:

> 5. LMN Sand Co. sells sand in bulk. ABC Construction Co. purchases sand to use in mixing cement. LMN is aware that the improper mixture of its sand with other ingredients can cause cement to crack. ABC utilizes LMN's sand to form a cement supporting column in a building. As a result of improper mixture the cement column cracks and gives way during a mild earthquake and causes injury to the building's occupants. LMN is not liable to the injured occupants. The sand sold by LMN is not itself defective under §§ 1–4. LMN has no duty to warn ABC about improperly mixing sand for use in cement. LMN did not participate in ABC's design of the cement and is not subject to liability for harm caused by the sand as integrated into the cement.

d. Incomplete products. Product components include products that can be put to different uses depending on how they are integrated into other products. For example, the chassis of a truck can be put to a variety of different uses. A truck chassis may ultimately be used with a cement mixer or a garbage compaction unit or in a flat-bed truck. Similarly, an engine for industrial machines may be adapted to a variety of different industrial uses. A seller ordinarily is not liable for failing to incorporate a safety feature that is peculiar to the specific adaptation for which another utilizes the incomplete product. A safety feature important for one adaptation may be wholly unnecessary or inappropriate for a different adaptation.

The same considerations also militate against imposing a duty on the seller of the incomplete product to warn purchasers of the incomplete product, or end-users of the integrated product, of dangers arising from special adaptations of the incomplete product by others.

e. Substantial participation in the integration of the component into the design of another product. When the component seller is substantially involved in the integration of the component into the design of the integrated product, the component seller is subject to liability when the integration results in a defective product and the defect causes harm to the plaintiff. Substantial participation can take various forms. The manufacturer or assembler of the integrated product may invite the component seller to design a component that will perform specifically as part of the integrated product or to assist in modifying the design of the integrated product to accept the seller's component. Or the component seller may play a substantial role in deciding which component best serves the requirements of the integrated product. When the component seller substantially participates in the design of the integrated product, it is fair and reasonable to hold the component seller responsible for harm caused by the defective, integrated product. A component seller who simply designs a component to its buyer's specifications, and does not substantially participate in the integration of the component into the design of the product, is not liable within the meaning of Subsection (b). Moreover, providing mechanical or technical services or advice concerning a component part does not, by itself, constitute substantial participation that would subject the component supplier to liability. One who provides a design service alone, as distinct from combining the design function with the sale of a component, generally is liable only for negligence and is not treated as a product seller. See § 19(b).

f. Integration of the component as a cause of the harm. The mere fact that the component seller substantially participates in the integration of the component into the design of a product does not subject the seller to liability unless the integration causes the product to be defective and the resulting defect causes the plaintiff's harm. The component seller is not liable for harm caused by defects in the integrated product that are unrelated to the component. For example, a manufacturer of a component valve may substantially participate in redesigning the valve so that it can be integrated into a particular kind of tank. If the tank fails due to defective steel in the body of the tank and the failure has nothing to do with the installation of the valve, the seller of the valve is not subject to liability under Subsection (b). The valve manufacturer is not liable under Subsection (b) even if it is sufficiently involved in the design of the tank so that it would be liable for harm caused by a failure of the valve as integrated into the tank. Similarly, if a raw-material supplier offers advice about processing the material and there is no evidence that the processing advice was a cause of the allegedly defective condition, the raw-material supplier should not be subject to liability.

Illustration:

6. ABC Chemical Co. sells plastic resins in bulk. XYZ Hot Water Heater Manufacturing Co. informs ABC that XYZ wishes to purchase resin for use in making its hot-water heaters and specifies resin that can withstand heat up to 212° Fahrenheit. ABC recommends that XYZ use a certain type of resin which, in ABC's testing under specified laboratory conditions, including thickness of one-quarter inch or more, was shown to be capable of withstanding temperatures in excess of 212° Fahrenheit. ABC explains these conditions to XYZ. ABC also provides XYZ with technical support and general processing advice. XYZ purchases the recommended resin from ABC and decides upon design and processing parameters, molds the resin into a plastic part, and combines the part with other materials and parts to produce hot-water heaters. XYZ tests its hot-water heaters for safety and durability and formulates instructions and warnings to accompany them. An XYZ hot-water heater subsequently fails because the plastic walls specified by its design, one-eighth inch thick, are too thin to withstand the stress imposed by its normal operating temperatures, resulting in injury to a homeowner. ABC is not liable to the homeowner. The resin sold by ABC was not in itself defective. ABC did not substantially participate in the design, manufacture or assembly of the hot-water heater.

---

§ 6. Liability of Commercial Seller or Distributor for Harm Caused by Defective Prescription Drugs and Medical Devices

(a) A manufacturer of a prescription drug or medical device who sells or otherwise distributes a defective drug or medical device is subject to liability for harm to persons caused by the defect. A prescription drug or medical device is one that may be legally sold or otherwise distributed only pursuant to a health-care provider's prescription.

(b) For purposes of liability under Subsection (a), a prescription drug or medical device is defective if at the time of sale or other distribution the drug or medical device:

    (1) contains a manufacturing defect as defined in § 2(a); or

    (2) is not reasonably safe due to defective design as defined in Subsection (c); or

    (3) is not reasonably safe due to inadequate instructions or warnings as defined in Subsection (d).

(c) A prescription drug or medical device is not reasonably safe due to defective design if the foreseeable risks of harm posed by the drug or medical device are sufficiently great in relation to its foreseeable therapeutic benefits that reasonable health-care providers, knowing of such foreseeable risks and therapeutic benefits, would not prescribe the drug or medical device for any class of patients.

(d) A prescription drug or medical device is not reasonably safe due to inadequate instructions or warnings if reasonable instructions or warnings regarding foreseeable risks of harm are not provided to:

(1) prescribing and other health-care providers who are in a position to reduce the risks of harm in accordance with the instructions or warnings; or

(2) the patient when the manufacturer knows or has reason to know that health-care providers will not be in a position to reduce the risks of harm in accordance with the instructions or warnings.

(e) A retail seller or other distributor of a prescription drug or medical device is subject to liability for harm caused by the drug or device if:

(1) at the time of sale or other distribution the drug or medical device contains a manufacturing defect as defined in § 2(a); or

(2) at or before the time of sale or other distribution of the drug or medical device the retail seller or other distributor fails to exercise reasonable care and such failure causes harm to persons.

Comment:

a. History. Subsections (b)(1) and (d)(1) state the traditional rules that drug and medical-device manufacturers are liable only when their products contain manufacturing defects or are sold without adequate instructions and warnings to prescribing and other health-care providers. Until recently, courts refused to impose liability based on defective designs of drugs and medical devices sold only by prescription. However, consistent with recent trends in the case law, two limited exceptions from these traditional rules are generally recognized. Subsection (d)(2) sets forth situations when a prescription-drug or medical-device manufacturer is required to warn the patient directly of risks associated with consumption or use of its product. And Subsection (c) imposes liability for a drug or medical device whose risks of harm so far outweigh its therapeutic benefits that reasonable, properly informed health-care providers would not prescribe it.

b. Rationale. The obligation of a manufacturer to warn about risks attendant to the use of drugs and medical devices that may be sold only pursuant to a health-care provider's prescription traditionally has required warnings directed to health-care providers and not to patients. The rationale supporting this "learned intermediary" rule is that only health-care professionals are in a position to understand the significance of the risks involved and to assess the relative advantages and disadvantages of a given form of prescription-based therapy. The duty then devolves on the health-care provider to supply to the patient such information as is deemed appropriate under the circumstances so that the patient can make an informed choice as to therapy. Subsection (d)(1) retains the "learned intermediary" rule. However, in certain limited therapeutic relationships the physician or other health-care provider has a much-diminished role as an evaluator or decisionmaker. In these instances it may be appropriate to impose on the manufacturer the duty to warn the patient directly. See Subsection (d)(2).

The traditional refusal by courts to impose tort liability for defective designs of prescription drugs and medical devices is based on the fact that a prescription drug or medical device entails a unique set of risks and benefits. What may be harmful to one patient may be beneficial to another. Under Subsection (c) a drug is defectively designed only when it provides no net benefit to any class of patients. Courts have concluded that as long as a drug or medical device provides net benefits to some persons under some circumstances, the drug or device manufacturer should be required to instruct and warn health-care providers of the foreseeable risks and benefits. Courts have also recognized that the regulatory system governing prescription drugs is a legitimate mechanism for setting the standards for drug design. In part, this deference reflects concerns over the possible negative effects of judicially imposed liability on the cost and availability of valuable medical technology. This deference also rests on two further assumptions: first, that prescribing health-care providers, when adequately informed by drug manufacturers, are able to assure that the right drugs and medical devices reach the right patients; and second, that governmental regulatory agencies adequately review new prescription drugs and devices, keeping unreasonably dangerous designs off the market.

Nevertheless, unqualified deference to these regulatory mechanisms is considered by a growing number of courts to be unjustified. An approved prescription drug or medical device can present significant risks without corresponding advantages. At the same time, manufacturers must have ample discretion to develop useful drugs and devices without subjecting their design decisions to the ordinary test applicable to products generally under § 2(b). Accordingly, Subsection (c) imposes a more rigorous test for defect than does § 2(b), which does not apply to prescription drugs and medical devices. The requirement for establishing defective design of a prescription drug or medical device under Subsection (c) is that the drug or device have so little merit compared with its risks that reasonable health-care providers, possessing knowledge of risks that were known or reasonably should have been known, would not have prescribed the drug or device for any class of patients. Thus, a prescription drug or medical device that has usefulness to any class of patients is not defective in design even if it is harmful to other patients. Because of the special nature of prescription drugs and medical devices, the determination of whether such products are not reasonably safe is to be made under Subsections (c) and (d) rather than under §§ 2(b) and 2(c).

The rules imposing liability on a manufacturer for inadequate warning or defective design of prescription drugs and medical devices assume that the federal regulatory standard has not preempted the imposition of tort liability under state law. When such preemption is found, liability cannot attach if the manufacturer has complied with the applicable federal standard. See § 4, Comment *e*.

The doctrine of preemption based on supremacy of federal law should be distinguished from the proposition that compliance with statutory and regulatory standards satisfies the state's requirement for product safety. Subsections (c) and (d) recognize common-law causes of action for defective drug design and for failure to provide reasonable instructions or warnings, even though the manufacturer complied with governmental standards. For the rules governing compliance with governmental standards generally, see § 4(b).

c. Manufacturers' liability for manufacturing defects. Limitations on the liability for prescription drug and medical-device designs do not support treating drug and medical-device manufacturers differently from commercial sellers of other products with respect to manufacturing defects. Courts have traditionally subjected manufacturers of prescription products to liability for harm caused by manufacturing defects.

d. Manufacturers' liability for failure adequately to instruct or warn prescribing and other health-care providers. Failure to instruct or warn is the major basis of liability for manufacturers of prescription drugs and medical devices. When prescribing health-care providers are adequately informed of the relevant benefits and risks associated with various prescription drugs and medical devices, they can reach appropriate decisions regarding which drug or device is best for specific patients. Sometimes a warning serves to inform health-care providers of unavoidable risks that inhere in the drug or medical device. By definition, such a warning would not aid the health-care provider in reducing the risk of injury to the patient by taking precautions in how the drug is administered or the medical device is used. However, warnings of unavoidable risks allow the health-care provider, and thereby the patient, to make an informed choice whether to utilize the drug or medical device. Beyond informing prescribing health-care providers, a drug or device manufacturer may have a duty under the law of negligence to use reasonable measures to supply instructions or warnings to nonprescribing health-care providers who are in positions to act on such information so as to reduce or prevent injury to patients.

e. Direct warnings to patients. Warnings and instructions with regard to drugs or medical devices that can be sold legally only pursuant to a prescription are, under the "learned intermediary" rule, directed to health-care providers. Subsection (d)(2) recognizes that direct warnings and instructions to patients are warranted for drugs that are dispensed or administered to patients without the personal intervention or evaluation of a health-care provider. An example is the administration of a vaccine in clinics where mass inoculations are performed. In many such programs, health-care providers are not in a position to evaluate the risks attendant upon use of the drug or device or to relate them to patients. When a manufacturer supplies prescription drugs for distribution to patients in this type of unsupervised environment, if a direct warning to patients is feasible and can be effective, the law requires measures to that effect.

Although the learned intermediary rule is generally accepted and a drug manufacturer fulfills its legal obligation to warn by providing adequate warnings to the health-care provider, arguments have been advanced that in two other areas courts should consider imposing tort liability on drug manufacturers that fail to provide direct warnings to consumers. In the first, governmental regulatory agencies have mandated that patients be informed of risks attendant to the use of a drug. A noted example is the FDA requirement that birth control pills be sold to patients accompanied by a patient package insert. In the second, manufacturers have advertised a prescription drug and its indicated use in the mass media. Governmental regulations require that, when drugs are so advertised, they must be accompanied by appropriate information concerning risk so as to provide balanced advertising. The question in both instances is whether adequate warnings to the appropriate health-care provider should insulate the manufacturer from tort liability.

Those who assert the need for adequate warnings directly to consumers contend that manufacturers that communicate directly with consumers should not escape liability simply because the decision to prescribe the drug was made by the health-care provider. Proponents of the learned intermediary rule argue that, notwithstanding direct communications to the consumer, drugs cannot be dispensed unless a health-care provider makes an individualized decision that a drug is appropriate for a particular patient, and that it is for the health-care provider to decide which risks are relevant to the particular patient. The Institute leaves to developing case law whether exceptions to the learned intermediary rule in these or other situations should be recognized.

When the content of the warnings is mandated or approved by a governmental agency regulation and a court finds that compliance with such regulation federally preempts tort liability, then no liability under this

Section can attach. For the rules governing compliance with governmental standards generally, see § 4(b).

f. Manufacturers' liability for defectively designed prescription drugs and medical devices. Subsection (c) reflects the judgment that, as long as a given drug or device provides net benefits for a class of patients, it should be available to them, accompanied by appropriate warnings and instructions. Learned intermediaries must generally be relied upon to see that the right drugs and devices reach the right patients. However, when a drug or device provides net benefits to no class of patients—when reasonable, informed health-care providers would not prescribe it to any class of patients—then the design of the product is defective and the manufacturer should be subject to liability for the harm caused.

A prescription drug or device manufacturer defeats a plaintiff's design claim by establishing one or more contexts in which its product would be prescribed by reasonable, informed health-care providers. That some individual providers do, in fact, prescribe defendant's product does not in itself suffice to defeat the plaintiff's claim. Evidence regarding the actual conduct of health-care providers, while relevant and admissible, is not necessarily controlling. The issue is whether, objectively viewed, reasonable providers, knowing of the foreseeable risks and benefits of the drug or medical device, would prescribe it for any class of patients. Given this very demanding objective standard, liability is likely to be imposed only under unusual circumstances. The court has the responsibility to determine when the plaintiff has introduced sufficient evidence so that reasonable persons could conclude that plaintiff has met this demanding standard.

g. Foreseeability of risks of harm in prescription drug and medical device cases. Duties concerning the design and marketing of prescription drugs and medical devices arise only with respect to risks of harm that are reasonably foreseeable at the time of sale. Imposing liability for unforeseeable risks can create inappropriate disincentives for the development of new drugs and therapeutic devices. Moreover, because actuaries cannot accurately assess unknown and unknowable risks, insuring against losses due to unknowable risks would be problematic. Drug and medical device manufacturers have the responsibility to perform reasonable testing prior to marketing a product and to discover risks and risk-avoidance measures that such testing would reveal. See § 2, Comments *a* and *m*.

h. Liability of retail seller of prescription drugs and medical devices for defective designs and defects due to inadequate instructions or warnings. The rule governing most products imposes liability on wholesalers and retailers for selling a defectively designed product, or one without adequate instructions or warnings, even though they have exercised reasonable care in marketing the product. See § 1, Comment *e*, and § 2, Comment *o*. Courts have refused to apply this general rule to nonmanufacturing retail sellers of prescription drugs and medical devices and, instead, have adopted the rule stated in Subsection (e). That rule subjects retailers to liability only if the product contains a manufacturing defect or if the retailer fails to exercise reasonable care in connection with distribution of the drug or medical device. In so limiting the liability of intermediary parties, courts have held that they should be permitted to rely on the special expertise of manufacturers, prescribing and treating health-care providers, and governmental regulatory agencies. They have also emphasized the needs of medical patients to have ready access to prescription drugs at reasonable prices.

———

§ 7. Liability of Commercial Seller or Distributor for Harm Caused by Defective Food Products

One engaged in the business of selling or otherwise distributing food products who sells or distributes a food product that is defective under § 2, § 3, or § 4 is subject to liability for harm to persons or property caused by the defect. Under § 2(a), a harm-causing ingredient of the food product constitutes a defect if a reasonable consumer would not expect the food product to contain that ingredient.

Comment:

a. General applicability of §§ 2, 3, and 4 to food products. Except for the special problems identified in Comment *b*, liability for harm caused by defects in commercially distributed food products are determined under the same rules generally applicable to non-food products. A food product may contain a manufacturing defect under § 2(a), as when a can of peas contains a pebble; may be defectively designed under § 2(b), as when the recipe for potato chips contains a dangerous chemical preservative; or may be sold without adequate warnings under § 2(c), as when the seller fails to inform consumers that the dye applied to the skins of oranges contains a well-known allergen. Section 3 may allow a plaintiff to reach the trier of fact when, unable to identify the specific defect, the plaintiff becomes violently ill immediately after consuming the defendant's food product and other causes are sufficiently eliminated. And § 4 may apply when a commercially distributed food product fails to conform to applicable safety statutes or administrative regulations.

b. The special problem under § 2(a). When a plaintiff suffers harm due to the presence in food of foreign matter clearly not intended by the product seller, such as a pebble in a can of peas or the pre-sale spoilage of a jar of mayonnaise, the claim is readily treated under § 2(a), which deals with harm caused by manufacturing defects. Food product cases, however, sometimes present unique difficulties when it is unclear whether the ingredient that caused the plaintiff's harm is an unanticipated adulteration or is an inherent aspect of the product. For example, is a one-inch chicken bone in a chicken enchilada, or a fish bone in fish chowder, a manufacturing defect or, instead, an inherent aspect of the product? The analytical problem stems from the circumstance that food products in many instances do not have specific product designs that may be used as a basis for determining whether the offending product ingredient constitutes a departure from design, and is thus a manufacturing defect. Food recipes vary over time, within the same restaurant or other commercial food-preparation facility, from facility to facility, and from locale to locale.

Faced with this indeterminacy, some courts have attempted to rely on a distinction between "foreign" and "natural" characteristics of food products to determine liability. Under that distinction, liability attaches only if the alleged adulteration is foreign rather than natural to the product. Most courts have found this approach inadequate, however. Although a one-inch chicken bone may in some sense be "natural" to a chicken enchilada, depending on the context in which consumption takes place, the bone may still be unexpected by the reasonable consumer, who will not be able to avoid injury, thus rendering the product not reasonably safe. The majority view is that, in this circumstance of uncertainty, the issue of whether a food product containing a dangerous but arguably natural component is defective under § 2(a) is to be determined by reference to reasonable consumer expectations within the relevant context of consumption. A consumer expectations test in this context relies upon culturally defined, widely shared standards that food products ought to meet. Although consumer expectations are not adequate to supply a standard for defect in other contexts, assessments of what consumers have a right to expect in various commercial food preparations are sufficiently well-formed that judges and triers of fact can sensibly resolve whether liability should be imposed using this standard.

———

§ 8. Liability of Commercial Seller or Distributor of Defective Used Products

One engaged in the business of selling or otherwise distributing used products who sells or distributes a defective used product is subject to liability for harm to persons or property caused by the defect if the defect:

(a) arises from the seller's failure to exercise reasonable care; or

(b) is a manufacturing defect under § 2(a) or a defect that may be inferred under § 3 and the seller's marketing of the product would cause a reasonable person in the position of the buyer to expect the used product to present no greater risk of defect than if the product were new; or

(c) is a defect under § 2 or § 3 in a used product remanufactured by the seller or a predecessor in the commercial chain of distribution of the used product; or

(d) arises from a used product's noncompliance under § 4 with a product safety statute or regulation applicable to the used product.

A used product is a product that, prior to the time of sale or other distribution referred to in this Section, is commercially sold or otherwise distributed to a buyer not in the commercial chain of distribution and used for some period of time.

Chapter 2

LIABILITY OF COMMERCIAL PRODUCT SELLERS NOT BASED ON PRODUCT DEFECTS AT TIME OF SALE

§ 9. Liability of Commercial Product Seller or Distributor for Harm Caused by Misrepresentation

One engaged in the business of selling or otherwise distributing products who, in connection with the sale of a product, makes a fraudulent, negligent, or innocent misrepresentation of material fact concerning the product is subject to liability for harm to persons or property caused by the misrepresentation.

Comment:

[Section 9 incorporates the causes of action for fraud, negligent misrepresentation, and innocent misrepresentation available under Restatement (Second) of Torts §§ 310, 311, and 402B as applicable to commercial product sellers and distributors.]

---

§ 10. Liability of Commercial Product Seller or Distributor for Harm Caused by Post–Sale Failure to Warn

(a) One engaged in the business of selling or otherwise distributing products is subject to liability for harm to persons or property caused by the seller's failure to provide a warning after the time of sale or distribution of a product if a reasonable person in the seller's position would provide such a warning.

(b) A reasonable person in the seller's position would provide a warning after the time of sale if:

(1) the seller knows or reasonably should know that the product poses a substantial risk of harm to persons or property; and

(2) those to whom a warning might be provided can be identified and can reasonably be assumed to be unaware of the risk of harm; and

(3) a warning can be effectively communicated to and acted on by those to whom a warning might be provided; and

(4) the risk of harm is sufficiently great to justify the burden of providing a warning.

Comment:

a. Rationale. Judicial recognition of the seller's duty to warn of a product-related risk after the time of sale, whether or not the product is defective at the time of original sale within the meaning of other Sections of this Restatement, is relatively new. Nonetheless, a growing body of decisional and statutory law imposes such a duty. Courts recognize that warnings about risks discovered after sale are sometimes necessary to prevent significant harm to persons and property. Nevertheless, an unbounded post-sale duty to warn would impose unacceptable burdens on product sellers. The costs of identifying and communicating with product users years after sale are often daunting. Furthermore, as product designs are developed and improved over time, many risks are reduced or avoided by subsequent design changes. If every post-sale improvement in a product design were to give rise to a duty to warn users of the risks of continuing to use the existing design, the burden on product sellers would be unacceptably great.

As with all rules that raise the question whether a duty exists, courts must make the threshold decisions that, in particular cases, triers of fact could reasonably find that product sellers can practically and effectively discharge such an obligation and that the risks of harm are sufficiently great to justify what is typically a substantial post-sale undertaking. In deciding whether a claim based on breach of a post-sale duty to warn should reach the trier of fact, the court must determine whether the requirements in Subsection (b)(1) through (4) are supported by proof. The legal standard is whether a reasonable person would provide a post-sale warning. In light of the serious potential for overburdening sellers in this regard, the court should carefully examine the circumstances for and against imposing a duty to provide a post-sale warning in a particular case.

b. When a reasonable person in the seller's position would provide a warning. The standard governing the liability of the seller is objective: whether a reasonable person in the seller's position would provide a warning. This is the standard traditionally applied in determining negligence. See Restatement, Second, Torts § 283, Comment *c*. In applying the reasonableness standard to members of the chain of distribution it is possible that one party's conduct may be reasonable and another's unreasonable. For example, a manufacturer may discover information under circumstances satisfying Subsection (b)(1) through (4) and thus be required to provide a post-sale warning. In contrast, a retailer is generally not in a position to know about the risk discovered by the manufacturer after sale and thus is not subject to liability because it neither knows nor should know of the risk. Once the retailer is made aware of the risk, however, whether the retailer is subject to liability for failing to issue a post-sale warning depends on whether a reasonable person in the retailer's position would warn under the criteria set forth in Subsection (b)(1) through (4).

c. Requirement that seller or other distributor knows or should know of the product-related risk. A duty to warn after the time of sale cannot arise unless the product seller or other distributor knows or in the exercise of reasonable care should know of the product-related risk that causes plaintiff's harm. The seller may have known or should have known of the risk at the time of sale, in which case failure to warn will cause the product to be defective under § 2(c). But even if the product is not defective at the time of sale because no reasonable seller would have known of the risk under § 2(c), knowledge of the risk may come after sale and may give rise to a duty to warn at that time.

As a practical matter, most post-sale duties to warn arise when new information is brought to the attention of the seller, after the time of sale, concerning risks accompanying the product's use or consumption. When risks are not actually brought to the attention of sellers, the burden of constantly monitoring product performance in the field is usually too burdensome to support a post-sale duty to warn. However, when reasonable grounds exist for the seller to suspect that a hitherto unknown risk exists, especially when the risk involved is great, the duty of reasonable care may require investigation. With regard to one class of products, prescription drugs and devices, courts traditionally impose a continuing duty of reasonable care to test and monitor after sale to discover product-related risks.

Illustration:

    1. ABC manufactures and sells Model 1220 power drills used exclusively in heavy industry. Three years after the Model 1220 is first put on the market, ABC learns that when the drill is used continuously for more than four hours it overheats, causing it to fracture. ABC

learns of the overheating problem when the Model 1220 is first used on a new metal alloy that was not previously available, and thus not in use, at the time of first distribution. The new alloy causes the drill to heat well beyond temperatures caused by any other metal for which the Model 1220 has ever been used. No reasonable person could have foreseen the development of the new alloy when any of the drills were sold. Because the risk of overheating was not foreseeable at the time of sale of many of the Model 1220s, those units are not defective within the meaning of § 2. Whether ABC is subject to liability for failing to issue a post-sale warning regarding the risks of overheating is determined based on the factors set forth in Subsection (b)(1) through (4).

d. *Requirement that the risk of harm be substantial.* For a post-sale duty to arise under this Section, the risk of harm must be at least as great as the level of risk that would require a warning under § 2(c). Because post-sale warnings are invariably costly to provide, and post-sale increases in knowledge of risks are to some extent inevitable, no duty arises after the time of sale to issue warnings regarding product-related accidents that occur infrequently and are not likely to cause substantial harm. If post-sale acquisition of knowledge of adverse outcomes that are both infrequent and insubstantial were to trigger a post-sale duty to warn, sellers would face costly and potentially crushing burdens.

e. *Requirement that those to whom a warning might be provided be identifiable.* The problem of identifying those to whom product warnings might be provided is especially relevant in the post-sale context. When products are originally sold or distributed, most often the seller accompanies the product, together with its packaging, with whatever warnings are appropriate. When knowledge of product-related risk is available to the seller only after sale, it may be difficult for the seller to determine who, in the general population of product users and consumers, is in a position to respond to warnings effectively. In some instances, customer records may identify the population to whom warnings should be provided. Individual names and addresses are not necessarily required. Records may indicate classes of product users, or geographically limited markets. But when no such records are available, the seller's inability to identify those for whom warnings would be useful may properly prevent a post-sale duty to warn from arising. See Comment g.

Illustration:

2. ABC has manufactured and distributed vacuum cleaners commercially to millions of consumers over the course of many years. Only scanty and incomplete sales records have been kept by retailers, and it is practically impossible for ABC to identify who among the consuming public owns and operates its vacuums. Five years after the first commercial distribution of Model 14, ABC discovers a risk when the Model 14 is used to vacuum dust from a chemical carpet cleaner newly introduced to the market. No reasonable person in ABC's position

would have foreseen the risk previously, and thus the Model 14 was not defective at time of original sale. The difficulty of ABC's identifying users of its Model 14 vacuum, together with the frequency and severity of the risk, must be weighed by the court in determining whether ABC owes a post-sale duty to warn of the newly discovered risk.

f. The reasonableness of assuming that those to whom a warning might be provided are unaware of the risk. To justify the cost of providing a post-sale warning, it must reasonably appear that those to whom a warning might be provided are unaware of the risk. See § 2, Comment *j*. Similarly, even if knowledge of the risk reasonably becomes available to the seller only after the original sale, if users and consumers are at that time generally aware of the risk a post-sale warning is not required.

g. The seller's ability to communicate the warning effectively to those who are in a position to act to prevent harm. For a post-sale duty to warn to arise, the seller must reasonably be able to communicate the warning to those identified as appropriate recipients. When original customer sales records indicate which individuals are probably using and consuming the product in question, direct communication of a warning may be feasible. When direct communication is not feasible, it may be necessary to utilize the public media to disseminate information regarding risks of substantial harm. As the group to whom warnings might be provided increases in size, costs of communicating warnings may increase and their effectiveness may decrease.

h. Requirement that those to whom a post-sale warning might be provided be able to act effectively to reduce the risk. To justify the potentially high cost of providing a post-sale warning, those to whom such warnings are provided must be in a position to reduce or prevent product-caused harm. Such recipients of warnings need not be original purchasers of the product, so long as they are able to reduce risk effectively.

i. Requirement that the risk of harm be sufficiently great to justify providing a post-sale warning. Compared with the costs of providing warnings attendant upon the original sale of a product, the costs of providing post-sale warnings are typically greater. In the post-sale context, identifying those who should receive a warning and communicating the warning to them can require large expenditures. Courts recognize these burdens and hold that a post-sale warning is required only when the risk of harm is sufficiently great to justify undertaking a post-sale warning program. Subsection (b)(4) requires that, even for a substantial risk, a seller owes a duty to warn after the time of sale only if the risk of harm is sufficiently great to justify the cost of providing a post-sale warning. The test defining unreasonable conduct is that which governs negligence generally. See Restatement, Second, Torts § 291.

j. Distinguishing post-sale failures to warn from defects existing at the time of sale. When a product is defective at the time of sale liability can be established without reference to a post-sale duty to warn. A seller who discovers after sale that its product was defective at the time of sale within the meaning of this Restatement cannot generally absolve itself of liability by issuing a post-sale warning. As long as the original defect is causally related to the harm suffered by the plaintiff, a prima facie case under this Restatement can be established notwithstanding reasonable post-sale efforts to warn. Of course, even when a product is defective at the time of sale a seller may have an independent obligation to issue a post-sale warning based on the rule stated in this Section. Thus, a plaintiff may seek recovery based on both a time-of-sale defect and a post-sale failure to warn.

Illustrations:

3. ABC manufactures and sells Model 1220 power drills used exclusively in heavy industry. ABC sells a Model 1220 drill to XYZ Industries. Six months after the sale to XYZ, ABC learns that when the Model 1220 drill is used continuously for more than four hours it overheats, causing the drill to fracture. ABC should have discovered this problem through reasonable testing before the drill was put on the market. Had ABC done so, it could have adopted a reasonable alternative design that would have avoided the problem. Model 1220 is thus defective within the meaning of § 2(b). After ABC discovers the overheating problem, it sends warning letters to all owners of the Model 1220, including XYZ, that the machine should not be used for more than four hours continuously and that after prolonged use the machine should be turned off for 30 minutes to cool. The post-sale warning states that failure to do so could cause harm. XYZ posts the warning in its plant. Several months thereafter, XYZ's employee, E, is working on the machine during a rush job and the Model 1220 is allowed to run continuously for more than four hours. The machine overheats and the drill shatters, causing harm to E. Notwithstanding ABC's post-sale efforts to warn, ABC is subject to liability for the harm to E caused by the defectively designed Model 1220 under §§ 1 and 2. Whether E's recovery should be reduced because of contributory negligence or comparative fault is governed by § 17. Whether E should be denied recovery due to the absence of proximate causation is governed by § 15.

4. Same facts as Illustration 3 except that ABC fails to issue a post-sale warning after it discovers the overheating problem. E may bring an action based on a § 2 defect and may also assert the failure of ABC to provide a post-sale warning of the overheating problem. Whether it is reasonable also to subject ABC to liability for failure to issue a post-sale warning is determined by applying the factors set forth in Subsection (b)(1) through (4).

———

§ 11. Liability of Commercial Product Seller or Distributor for Harm Caused by Post–Sale Failure to Recall Product

One engaged in the business of selling or otherwise distributing products is subject to liability for harm to persons or property caused by the seller's failure to recall a product after the time of sale or distribution if:

(a)(1) a governmental directive issued pursuant to a statute or administrative regulation specifically requires the seller or distributor to recall the product; or

(2) the seller or distributor, in the absence of a recall requirement under Subsection (a)(1), undertakes to recall the product; and

(b) the seller or distributor fails to act as a reasonable person in recalling the product.

Comment:

a. Rationale. Duties to recall products impose significant burdens on manufacturers. Many product lines are periodically redesigned so that they become safer over time. If every improvement in product safety were to trigger a common-law duty to recall, manufacturers would face incalculable costs every time they sought to make their product lines better and safer. Moreover, even when a product is defective within the meaning of § 2, § 3, or § 4, an involuntary duty to recall should be imposed on the seller only by a governmental directive issued pursuant to statute or regulation. Issues relating to product recalls are best evaluated by governmental agencies capable of gathering adequate data regarding the ramifications of such undertakings. The duty to recall or repair should be distinguished from a post-sale duty to warn about product hazards discovered after sale. See §§ 10 and 13.

Illustration:

1. MNO Corp. has manufactured and distributed washing machines for five years. MNO develops an improved model that includes a safety device that reduces the risk of harm to users. The washing machines sold previously conformed to the best technology available at time of sale and were not defective when sold. MNO is under no common-law obligation to recall previously-distributed machines in order to retrofit them with the new safety device.

b. Failure to recall when recall is specifically required by a governmental directive issued pursuant to statute or other governmental regulation. When a product recall is specifically required by a governmental directive issued pursuant to a statute or regulation, failure reasonably to comply with the relevant directive subjects the seller or other distributor to liability for harm caused by such failure. For the product seller or other distributor to be subject to liability under Subsection (a)(1), the directive must specifically require recall. It is not sufficient that an agency has the power to direct product recalls with regard to the product in question if the agency has failed to issue a specific recall directive, nor will it suffice that a general duty to recall is imposed by statute or regulation and the plaintiff alleges that the defendant breached that duty by failing to recall in the absence of a specific directive to do so. When a directive issued pursuant to a statute or regulation specifically requires product recall, the violation by the seller of that requirement constitutes actionable negligence. See § 4, Comment *f*.

To give rise to the duty to recall under this Section, the governmental directive must require the defendant to recall the product during the time period in which the plaintiff claims the defendant breached the duty to recall. For example, if the regulatory scheme calls for a stay of the recall directive pending appeal, no duty to recall arises under this Section until the appeal is decided in a way that makes the recall directive binding on the defendant.

Illustrations:

    2. The same facts as Illustration 1, except that a federal agency directs MNO to recall the machines distributed by MNO. Thereafter, MNO unreasonably fails to notify machine owners, whom it can reasonably identify, about the recall. MNO is subject to liability for harm caused by its noncompliance with the governmental directive to recall the machines.

    3. The same facts as Illustration 1, except that the agency issues no directive to MNO regarding the washing machines. A plaintiff argues that MNO owed a general tort duty under the statute to recall the washing machine, which the plaintiff claims was defectively designed as defined in § 2(b) and caused the claimant's harm. MNO is not subject to liability under Subsection (a)(1).

    c. When seller or other distributor voluntarily undertakes to recall. Some courts have held that, when a seller, under no statutory or regulatory obligation to undertake a recall, volunteers to do so, the seller is subject to liability for failing to act reasonably to recall the product. The rationale for this rule lies partly in the general rule that one who undertakes a rescue, and thus induces other would-be rescuers to forbear, must act reasonably in following through. In the context of products liability, courts appear to assume that voluntary recalls are typically undertaken in the anticipation that, if the seller does not recall voluntarily, it will be directed to do so by a governmental regulator. Having presumably forestalled the regulatory recall directive, the seller should be under a common-law duty to follow through on its commitment to recall. In some instances voluntary recalls are subject to regulation by governmental agencies. Whether product sellers are subject to, or protected from, liability for harm caused by noncompliance or compliance with the terms of such regulations is governed by Restatement, Second, of Torts §§ 286–288C. See § 4, Comment *f*.

Illustration:

4. The same facts as Illustration 1, except that MNO voluntarily announces that it will recall and retrofit the washing machines it distributed earlier, and it thereafter unreasonably fails to notify owners whom it can reasonably identify about the recall. MNO is subject to liability under Subsection (a)(2) for harm caused by its failure to act reasonably in undertaking to recall the machines.

d. Distinguishing liability for post-sale failure to recall from liability for the sale or other distribution of defective products. When a product is defective at the time of sale and the defect causes harm to persons or property, the seller is subject to liability whether or not the seller attempts to eliminate the defect by post-sale recall. The fact that one who owns or possesses a product that was defective at time of sale does not respond to a recall notice does not necessarily eliminate the causal connection between the original defect and the plaintiff's harm. See § 15. It may be foreseeable that product owners will fail to respond to recall notices. In a case involving harm caused by an original defect at the time of sale, the plaintiff's failure to act on a recall notice may be taken into account under the rules stated in § 17 governing comparative responsibility. In appropriate cases a plaintiff may seek recovery based on both a claim of original defect and a claim of post-sale failure to recall.

Illustrations:

5. XYZ Motor Co. manufactures and sells the Buster Sedan. XYZ learned that the Buster tends to oversteer dangerously. XYZ should have discovered the problem before the Buster Sedan was put on the market, when it could have adopted a reasonable alternative design. The Buster Sedan was thus defectively designed within the meaning of § 2(b). The National Highway Traffic Safety Administration directed XYZ to recall the Buster to correct the oversteering problem. Sonia Rand, who had purchased a Buster Sedan, received a recall notice. Sonia did not respond to the notice. Six months later, while driving on the highway, Sonia lost control of her car. A trier of fact could find that the oversteering in Sonia's Buster contributed to her loss of control. XYZ is subject to liability under §§ 1 and 2(b) for the injury caused by the defectively designed Buster Sedan. In her action based on the design defect, Sonia's failure to bring her car in for repair is relevant to the issue of legal causation under § 15 and the issue of comparative responsibility under § 17.

6. Same facts as Illustration 5, except that XYZ failed to undertake the recall directed by the National Highway Traffic Safety Administration. Sonia suffers injury after the time a recall notice should have been issued. XYZ is subject to liability under this Section for failure to

recall. XYZ is also subject to liability under § 2(b) based on defective design. Whether XYZ is subject to liability for post-sale failure to warn is governed by the rules stated in § 10.

7. Same facts as Illustration 5, except that the National Highway Traffic Safety Administration refused, after considering the problem, to direct a recall. XYZ is subject to liability to Sonia based on a § 2(b) design defect. XYZ is not subject to liability under this Section for failure to recall. Whether XYZ is subject to liability for post-sale failure to warn is governed by the rules stated in § 10.

e. Causal relationship between failure to recall and plaintiff's harm. For a seller to be subject to liability for post-sale failure to recall, the plaintiff must establish not only that the seller unreasonably failed to recall the product under this Section, but also that the defect that was the subject of recall was a legal cause of the plaintiff's harm. See § 15.

Chapter 3

LIABILITY OF SUCCESSORS AND APPARENT MANUFACTURERS

§ 12. Liability of Successor for Harm Caused by Defective Products Sold Commercially by Predecessor

A successor corporation or other business entity that acquires assets of a predecessor corporation or other business entity is subject to liability for harm to persons or property caused by a defective product sold or otherwise distributed commercially by the predecessor if the acquisition:

(a) is accompanied by an agreement for the successor to assume such liability; or

(b) results from a fraudulent conveyance to escape liability for the debts or liabilities of the predecessor; or

(c) constitutes a consolidation or merger with the predecessor; or

(d) results in the successor becoming a continuation of the predecessor.

Comment:

a. History. The rule that a corporation or other business entity is not, in the absence of the circumstances described in Subsections (a) through (d), subject to liability for harm caused by defective products sold by a corporation from which it purchases productive assets derives from both products liability and corporate law principles. When the alleged successor purchases the assets piecemeal with little or no further continuity of operations between the two corporations or other business entities, the nonliability of the alleged successor derives primarily from the fact that the successor is not within the basic liability rule in § 1 of this Restatement: "one ... *who sells or distributes* a defective product is subject to liability for harm ... caused by the defective product." (Emphasis added.) Thus, when one corporation commercially sells products, some of which are defective, and later transfers its productive assets to another corporation that uses those assets to manufacture products of its own, the purchaser of the assets is not liable for harm caused by a defective product sold earlier by the transferor because the transferee did not "sell or distribute" the defective product that caused the harm. When the alleged successor receives value in the form of the transferor's goodwill and continues to manufacture products of the same sort as manufactured earlier by the predecessor, and thus to some extent constitutes a continuation of the predecessor, the general rule of nonliability derives primarily from the law governing corporations, which favors the free alienability of corporate assets and limits shareholders' exposures to liability in order to facilitate the formation and investment of capital.

When the transferor goes out of business upon, or shortly after, a transfer of productive assets, the rights of plaintiffs injured by defective products sold earlier by the transferor may be adversely affected. For tort plaintiffs who have existing judgments outstanding against the predecessor at the time of transfer and dissolution, the law governing corporations and other business entities provides, within limits, legal protection. Creditors, including tort creditors, who hold existing judgments against a corporation that is in the process of transferring its assets and going out of business may satisfy those claims out of the proceeds from the transfer of assets. Moreover, if the proceeds from the transfer of assets are distributed to shareholders of the transferor corporation in violation of applicable state corporation law or fraudulent transfer law, existing creditors of the corporation may pursue the proceeds in the hands of the transferor's shareholders. These rules, in some states expressed in statutes, are designed to protect, within the limits of practicality, creditors who are identifiable at the time of the transfer of the predecessor's assets to the successor corporation and the transferor's dissolution. The same principles have been applied to the transfer of assets of proprietorships, partnerships, and other business entities.

Tort claimants who, as a result of defective products sold by a predecessor corporation, seek recovery only after transfer of assets to a successor corporation often face difficulties in attempting to bring their claims within the foregoing legal rules. Their claims typically accrue after the predecessor corporation has lawfully distributed to its shareholders the proceeds from the transfer of assets and has ceased to exist. Under these circumstances, tort claimants who were not existing creditors at the time of the transfer of assets ordinarily have no recourse against the predecessor's shareholders. Unless they can pursue their claims against the successor corporation, or can reach other funds provided by existing insurance or by a statute, their only practical remedy lies with retailers and wholesalers in the predecessor's distributive chain, who may not be available as a practical matter. Statutes and judicial precedents governing the rights of creditors after a corporate assets transfer and dissolution generally do not address this problem of post-transfer claims accrual.

Few precedents recognize tort claims against the successor corporation for harm caused by defective products sold by the predecessor unless the transaction by which productive assets are acquired meets criteria established by one of several traditional exceptions. These exceptions apply generally to creditors whose claims accrue after dissolution of the predecessor, and are not limited to products liability claimants. They fall into two basic categories: those in which some conduct of the successor, in addition to acquiring the predecessor's assets, justifies holding the successor responsible (the successor either contractually agrees to be liable or knowingly participates in a fraudulent asset transfer); and those in which the successor itself can be said to have sold or distributed the defective products because the successor constitutes the same juridical entity as the predecessor, perhaps in somewhat different form (the successor merges with, or constitutes a "mere continuation" of, the predecessor). Under this Section, a products liability claimant has a recognized claim against a successor for harm caused by defective products distributed by the predecessor in these circumstances.

A minority of jurisdictions impose liability on a successor corporation based on a broader concept of continuation of the business enterprise, even when there is no continuity of shareholders, officers, or directors. Some courts hold that the continuation of a predecessor's product line by the successor is sufficient to support imposition of successor liability for harm caused by defects in products sold before the assets transfer.

b. *Rationale.* Limiting the liability of successor corporations to the circumstances described in this Section is supported by fairness and efficiency considerations. An alleged successor that purchases the predecessor's productive assets piecemeal, other than as part of a going concern, cannot, by that fact alone, be said to have either manufactured or sold defective products distributed by the predecessor before the transfer of assets. In the absence of circumstances in which the successor could be said to constitute a continuation of the predecessor, or somehow to have prejudiced subsequent tort plaintiffs by its own pre-acquisition conduct, imposing liability on a business entity that did not make or distribute the defective products that caused harm could be justified only because it increases the amount of money available post-acquisition out of which to satisfy plaintiffs' claims. But that alone cannot be justification for successor liability. Thus, imposing liability on the piecemeal purchase of productive assets would, for no compelling reason, impede the free alienability of corporate assets, thereby discouraging shareholder investment of capital and increasing social costs.

Imposing liability on successor corporations constitutes acceptable public policy when the successor either agrees to be liable or is implicated in the transfer of assets in a way that, without such liability, would unfairly deprive future products liability plaintiffs of the remedies that would otherwise have been available against the predecessor. Subsections (a) through (d) describe the types of corporate asset transfers that have been determined to justify imposing liability on the successor. Subsection (a) recognizes that contractual promises by the successor to pay subsequent tort claims, for which promises the successor has presumably been compensated, should be honored. Subsection (b) provides that when a business entity makes a fraudulent transfer in which the transferee is implicated, successor liability is appropriate for the same reason that liability would be imposed in favor of other creditors. Thus, a predecessor may arrange an asset transfer at an artificially deflated price, accompanied by an agreement by the successor to compensate either the predecessor, its owners, or its managers in ways that escape easy detection; or a successor may knowingly participate in an asset transfer coupled with a liquidating dividend by the predecessor to its shareholders for the purpose of leaving tort plaintiffs without remedy. If those transfers are fraudulent under applicable state law, imposing tort liability on the transferee for having knowingly participated in such transfers is justified.

Subsections (c) and (d) deal with successors that, in a real sense, did produce and distribute the product that caused the harm, though in a somewhat different organizational form. Subsection (c) deals with the transferor corporation that merges by law or in fact into the transferee, typically with no substantial change in corporate management or ownership. Subsection (d) concerns the transfer of corporate assets in the context of a transaction involving only a change in organizational form. In both these situations, liability for harm caused by defective products distributed previously should be imposed on the business entity that emerges from the transaction. In substance, if not in form, the post-transfer entity distributed the defective products and should be held responsible for them. If mere changes in form were allowed to control substance, corporations intending to continue operations could periodically wash themselves clean of potential liability at practically zero cost, in sham transactions, and thereby unreasonably undermine incentives for producers and distributors to invest in product safety and unfairly deny tort plaintiffs adequate remedies when defective products later cause harm.

A small minority of courts have fashioned successor liability rules more advantageous to products liability claimants than the rules stated in this Section. Those minority rules, in effect, extend the "change in form only" exception just described to include circumstances in which the successor continues a product line previously distributed by the predecessor. The minority position is based on the belief that a successor who purchases productive assets should not be allowed to benefit from receiving the goodwill and reputation of the predecessor's business without the burden of responding in tort to claims for harm caused by products sold by the predecessor prior to transfer. An argument advanced to support this minority view is that holding successors liable reduces the price that predecessors receive for transferring assets, thereby helping to strengthen incentives for the managers to invest in care before the transfer of the business.

This reasoning has proven unpersuasive to a substantial majority of courts that have considered the issue. Extending successor liability beyond the exceptions set forth in Subsections (a) through (d) would, in the judgment of most courts, be unfair and socially wasteful. Post-transfer plaintiffs harmed by pre-transfer defects have a right to expect that a transfer of assets will not be allowed to prejudice financially their chances of satisfying a judgment; they have no legitimate claim that the transfer should increase those chances over what they would have been if no transfer had occurred. In the likely event that the successor is financially stronger than the predecessor, imposing a broader liability for pre-transfer product defects would unjustifiably increase the funds available to those injured by such defects compared with what would have been available to them if no transfer had taken place.

As courts have recognized, it would be difficult, and often impossible, to implement and administer a liability rule that attempted to limit post-transfer plaintiffs' rights to an aggregate amount equal to the net value of the predecessor before transfer. Tort judgments are imposed independently of one another, in various jurisdictions; no central authority exists to assure that, in the aggregate, tort judgments do not exceed a predetermined total amount. Thus, the expanded successor liability rules in a minority of states, not limited to time-of-transfer net value, replace one risk of injustice—that the assets transfer may unfairly reduce plaintiffs' recoveries in cases that do not satisfy the traditional exceptions (reflected in Subsections (a) through (d))—with another, possibly greater, injustice: that the transfer may give tort plaintiffs a windfall at the expense of companies who engage in asset transfers and, in turn, at the expense of the consuming public.

Moreover, a majority of courts have concluded that the substantial social costs of a more expansive liability rule would be incurred without actually benefiting very many tort plaintiffs. In most instances, the magnitude of future liability for products distributed pre-transfer is difficult, if not impossible, to assess. As a majority of courts have recognized, the result of imposing successor liability as a general rule would be to depress the prices for transferred assets to the point that piecemeal disposition of assets, which clearly would not subject the buyers to liability, would be a preferable alternative to sale of the assets as part of a going concern. In that event, the products liability claimant harmed by a pre-transfer product defect would still run the risk of ending up with an uncollectible judgment.

The benefits to society of preserving the predecessor's assets as a going concern would be sacrificed, with no commensurate benefits to tort claimants.

And even if a more expansive successor liability rule did not invariably lead to piecemeal asset transfers, such a liability rule would depress the prices received for going-concern transfers to an extent that would threaten to undermine the objectives of the law governing corporations. One of the purposes served by the corporate structure is to provide limitation and certainty of risk to shareholders in order to encourage capital formation. Thus, the shareholders' initial risk is limited to the value of their shares of stock and they are able to withdraw from an investment by sale of the stock without incurring future potential liability. A more expansive successor liability rule might threaten shareholders' investments by significantly restraining corporate assets transfers, thereby tending to frustrate corporation law's objective of encouraging shareholder investment.

Some critics of the majority rule argue that, when the successor continues to manufacture the same products as the predecessor, often under the same trademark, consumers have legitimate expectations that the successor will stand behind the predecessor's products. Disappointing these expectations is unfair, according to the critics, quite apart from the effects of successor liability upon the formation of capital. But this argument overlooks the reality that the predecessor's products that cause harm in these cases were distributed prior to the assets transfer, when there could be no reliance by consumers on the financial viability of the successor. One cannot logically rely on post-transfer expectations regarding the successor to justify the imposition of liability on the successor for pre-transfer distributions by the predecessor.

c. Nonliability in the absence of special circumstances. In the absence of the circumstances described in Subsections (a) through (d), a successor company that buys productive assets from another company is not liable for harm caused by a defective product sold or otherwise distributed by the predecessor prior to the successor's acquisition of assets. When the assets are purchased piecemeal, the alleged successor did not "sell or distribute" the product under the liability rule stated in § 1; and attempts to establish continuation of the corporate entity are recognized only under the terms set forth in this Section. The successor is liable under §§ 1–4 for harm caused by defective products it sells after acquisition. In the absence of the circumstances described in this Section, however, the successor is not liable for defective products sold by another prior to that time.

d. Agreement for successor to assume liability. When the successor agrees to assume liabilities for defective products sold by its predecessor, liability is imposed under Subsection (a) in accordance with the terms of the agreement. As a general matter, contract law governs the application of this exception. Courts have interpreted general statements that the successor agrees to assume the liabilities of the predecessor to include products liability claims even though the agreement makes no specific mention of products liability. However, assumption of products liability is not implied by the successor's assumption of specific duties with regard to product service or replacement.

e. Fraudulent transfer in order to avoid debts or liabilities. Subsection (b) incorporates by reference the relevant state law governing fraudulent conveyances and transfers. In contexts other than successor products liability, fraudulent transfers can be set aside on behalf of existing creditors of the transferor. In this context, fraudulent transfers provide a basis for holding successors liable to post-transfer tort plaintiffs. The fact that general creditors are pursuing remedies against the transferee does not prevent tort plaintiffs from pursuing remedies under Subsection (b). What constitutes a fraudulent conveyance or transfer is determined by reference to applicable state law.

f. Consolidation or merger. When statutory consolidation or merger of two corporations takes place, products liability devolves on the successor corporation under Subsection (c). A more difficult question is whether, absent statutory merger, a de facto merger has taken place. Local law governing de facto mergers is determinative. Whether a de facto merger under Subsection (c) has occurred generally depends on whether: (1) there is a continuity of management, employees, location, and assets; (2) the successor corporation acquires the assets of the predecessor with shares of its own stock so that shareholders of the transferor corporation become shareholders of the transferee corporation; (3) the predecessor corporation ceases its ordinary business operations immediately or shortly after the transfer of assets; and (4) the successor assumes those liabilities and obligations of the predecessor necessary for the uninterrupted continuation of the normal operations of the predecessor.

g. Continuation of the predecessor. The exception recognized in Subsection (d), referred to by many courts as the "mere continuation" exception, applies when there has been a formal redesignation of the predecessor corporate entity but little or no change in underlying substance. The most important indicia of continuation, in addition to the continuation of the predecessor's business activities, are common identities of officers, directors, and shareholders in the predecessor and successor corporations. A minority of jurisdictions recognize a broader exception, referred to as the "continuity of enterprise" exception, that imposes liability on the successor for continuing the business activities of the predecessor even when the corporate form of the successor is different from the predecessor. This Section does not follow that minority position.

h. Necessity for the predecessor to transfer all of its assets and go out of business. Almost all of the reported decisions applying the bases of successor liability stated in this Section involve predecessors that transfer all of their assets to successors and then dissolve or otherwise cease operations. Indeed, the predecessor's termination is the circumstance that, as a practical matter, most often gives rise to the need for a post-transfer tort plaintiff to look to the successor for recovery. The exceptions set forth in Subsections (c) and (d), merger and continuation, most frequently have significance when the predecessor has transferred all of its assets to the successor and, at least formally, has ceased to exist. But there is no reason that the exceptions set forth in Subsections (c) and (d) might not arise in connection with the transfer of a division of a large company, leaving the company in existence after the transfer. And the exceptions in Subsections (a) and (b) could arise in connection with transfers involving less than all of the predecessor's assets where the predecessor continues in existence after the transfer.

i. Relationship between the rule in this Section and the successor's independent duty to warn. This Section deals with a successor's liability for harm caused by the predecessor's defective products and is not premised on post-transfer wrongdoing by the successor itself. For the rules governing the liability of a successor for its own post-transfer failure to warn its predecessor's customers, see § 13.

————

§ 13. Liability of Successor for Harm Caused by Successor's Own Post–Sale Failure to Warn

(a) A successor corporation or other business entity that acquires assets of a predecessor corporation or other business entity, whether or not liable under the rule stated in § 12, is subject to liability for harm to persons or property caused by the successor's failure to warn of a risk created by a product sold or distributed by the predecessor if:

(1) the successor undertakes or agrees to provide services for maintenance or repair of the product or enters into a similar relationship with purchasers of the predecessor's products giving rise to actual or potential economic advantage to the successor, and

(2) a reasonable person in the position of the successor would provide a warning.

(b) A reasonable person in the position of the successor would provide a warning if:

(1) the successor knows or reasonably should know that the product poses a substantial risk of harm to persons or property; and

(2) those to whom a warning might be provided can be identified and can reasonably be assumed to be unaware of the risk of harm; and

**(3) a warning can be effectively communicated to
and acted on by those to whom a warning might be
provided; and**

**(4) the risk of harm is sufficiently great to justify
the burden of providing a warning.**

Comment:

a. Rationale. Corporations that acquire assets from other corporations are liable for harm caused by defective products sold by predecessors only in limited circumstances. See § 12. This Section subjects a successor to liability for its own failure to warn after acquiring the predecessor's assets when certain conditions are satisfied and when a reasonable person in the successor's position would provide a warning. Liability under this Section is similar to liability under § 10, in which a seller is liable for harm caused by breach of a post-sale duty to warn even if the product was not defective at the time of original sale. Unlike product sellers in § 10, the successor governed by this Section did not manufacture or sell the defective product. However, by virtue of succeeding to the predecessor's interests, the successor is often in a good position to learn of problems arising from use of the predecessor's product and to prevent harm to persons or property. When the relationship between the successor and pre-transfer purchasers of the predecessor's products gives rise to actual or potential economic benefit to the successor, it is both fair and efficient to require the successor to act reasonably to prevent such harm.

b. Relationship between the successor and the predecessor's customers. Absent some additional circumstance besides having become a successor, the successor remains a pure volunteer upon whom the law usually imposes no duty to act or to warn. Many courts have recognized four elements as being significant in determining the existence of a duty to warn: (1) succession to a predecessor's service contracts; (2) coverage of the defective product under a service contract made directly with the successor; (3) actual service of the defective product by the successor; and (4) the successor's knowledge of the existence of defects and the identities of the predecessor's customers who own the defective product. However, these factors are not exhaustive and the inquiry should be whether the successor's relationships with the predecessor's customers give rise to actual or potential economic advantage.

In most instances, in the absence of service contracts governing the predecessor's products or actual service of the defective product by the successor, it will be difficult to establish that the successor's relationships with the predecessor's customers give rise to actual or potential economic benefit to the successor. Furthermore, in the absence of service contracts, it may be difficult to establish under Subsection (b)(1) through (4) that a reasonable person in the position of the successor would provide a warning. Thus, when the successor has established no systematic relationships with the predecessor's customers through service contracts, usually the successor has no practical method of identifying those customers and communicating effectively with them. The successor who has no continuing contacts with a predecessor's customers may also be unable to discover risks that should be addressed through warnings. Similarly, when a successor has discontinued both the sale of a predecessor's product line and the provision of services to the predecessor's customers, it may not be in a position reasonably to discover risks about the discontinued line or to determine the persons to whom a warning should be addressed.

Notwithstanding the importance of service contracts in the application of this Section, a contract is not the only method of establishing a relationship with a predecessor's customers. For example, a successor may sell or offer to sell spare parts to the predecessor's customers for machinery sold by the predecessor when the successor knows or should know the machinery is defective. Such conduct should be considered by courts in deciding whether sufficient actual or potential economic advantage has accrued to the successor to warrant the imposition of a duty to warn the predecessor's customers.

c. *Factors in determining whether a reasonable successor would provide a warning.* Whether a reasonable person in the successor's position would provide a warning is governed by the same requirements that determine whether a reasonable seller should provide a post-sale warning under § 10. Subsection (b)(1) through (4) are identical to the requirements set forth in Subsection (b)(1) through (4) of § 10 and are explained in the Comments to § 10.

———

§ 14. Selling or Distributing as One's Own a Product Manufactured by Another

One engaged in the business of selling or otherwise distributing products who sells or distributes as its own a product manufactured by another is subject to the same liability as though the seller or distributor were the product's manufacturer.

Comment:

a. *History.* The rule stated in this Section derives from § 400 of the Restatement, Second, of Torts, promulgated in 1965. Section 400 incorporates by reference §§ 394–398, setting forth the rules governing the liability of manufacturers of chattels. These rules establish a regime of fault-based manufacturers' liability and treat product manufacturers differently than other actors, including nonmanufacturer product sellers. After inclusion of § 402A in the Restatement, Second, imposing strict liability on all commercial sellers of defective products for harm caused by product defects, it was questionable whether § 400 remained relevant in the context of products liability. Once § 402A imposed strict liability on all product sellers it made little, if any, difference whether the seller of a defective product was a retailer or a manufacturer. Compare Comment *b*.

b. Relevance of this Section when all commercial product sellers are held to the same standards of liability under §§ 1–4. To the extent that nonmanufacturers in the chain of distribution are held to the same standards as manufacturers, the rule stated in this Section is of little practical significance. However, many jurisdictions by statute treat nonmanufacturers more leniently. See § 1, Comment *e*. To the extent that a statute specifies responsibilities, the statutory terms control. But to the extent that a statute does not, the rule in this Section states the common-law rule.

c. Representing oneself as the manufacturer or one for whom the product has been specially manufactured. When a commercial seller sells a product manufactured by another under its own trademark or logo, the seller is liable as though it were the manufacturer of the product. This rule applies even if the seller discloses that the product was produced by an identified manufacturer specifically for the seller. In this circumstance, the seller is presumed to cause the product to be used or consumed, in part at least, in reliance on the seller. The seller's reputation is an implied assurance of the quality of the product, and the seller should be estopped from denying that it stands behind that assurance.

d. Liability of trademark licensors. The rule stated in this Section does not, by its terms, apply to the owner of a trademark who licenses a manufacturer to place the licensor's trademark or logo on the manufacturer's product and distribute it as though manufactured by the licensor. In such a case, even if purchasers of the product might assume that the trademark owner was the manufacturer, the licensor does not "sell or distribute as its own a product manufactured by another." Thus, the manufacturer may be liable under §§ 1–4, but the licensor, who does not sell or otherwise distribute products, is not liable under this Section of this Restatement.

Trademark licensors are liable for harm caused by defective products distributed under the licensor's trademark or logo when they participate substantially in the design, manufacture, or distribution of the licensee's products. In these circumstances they are treated as sellers of the products bearing their trademarks.

———

Chapter 4

PROVISIONS OF GENERAL APPLICABILITY

TOPIC 1. CAUSATION

§ 15. General Rule Governing Causal Connection Between Product Defect and Harm

> **Whether a product defect caused harm to persons or property is determined by the prevailing rules and principles governing causation in tort.**

Comment:

a. Requirement of causal connection between defect and harm. Sections 1, 5, 6, 7, and 8 require that the defect of which the plaintiff complains cause harm to person or property. The rules that govern causation in tort law generally are, subject to § 16, also applicable in products liability cases.

b. Misuse, alteration, and modification. When the plaintiff establishes product defect under the rules stated in Chapter 1, a question can arise whether the misuse, alteration, or modification of the product by the user or a third party contributed to the plaintiff's harm in such a way as to absolve the defendant from liability, in whole or in part. Such a question is to be resolved under the prevailing rules and principles governing causation or the prevailing rules and principles governing comparative responsibility, as the case may be. See § 17.

Illustrations:

1. XYZ Co. manufactures and sells automobiles. Sam purchased a new XYZ Model 300 and drove it around town for several days. Unknown to Sam, the lug nuts that hold the right front wheel to the axle were too large, allowing them to loosen and present a serious risk of eventual failure. On Sam's fifth day of ownership, a large truck rear-ended the XYZ automobile while Sam was driving it. Both Sam and the automobile suffer harm. XYZ Co. is not liable to Sam. Although the automobile was defective when Sam purchased it, and although the automobile was a cause of Sam's injuries, the defect was not a substantial factor in causing the injuries, which would have occurred even if the defect had not been present.

2. XYZ Co. manufactures and sells automobiles. Sam purchased a new XYZ Model 300 and drove it around town for several days. On one trip Sam felt the right front wheel wobbling. Upon examination Sam discovered that the five lug nuts holding the wheel to the axle were too large, causing them to loosen. Had Sam not stopped when he did, the

wheel would have fallen off. Sam removed the five over-sized lug nuts, borrowed two correct-sized nuts from the right rear wheel, and reattached the right front wheel with them. Sam did nothing more about the wheels for more than a month, whereupon he loaned the automobile to a friend, saying nothing about the wheels. The friend inadvertently drove into a large pothole, causing the two nuts on the right front wheel to break. The wheel came off and both the automobile and Sam's friend suffered harm. Had five proper-sized lug nuts been on the wheel instead of just two, they would not have broken and the accident would not have occurred. XYZ Co. is not liable to Sam or Sam's friend. Although the XYZ automobile was defective when sold, and although the defect was a necessary condition to the occurrence of the accident, Sam's modification and subsequent failure to effect adequate repair were sufficiently unforeseeable that the defect was not a substantial factor in causing the friend's injury.

c. Causation and proportional liability. In certain cases involving generic toxic substances, the plaintiffs may be unable to identify which among a number of manufacturers produced the particular product that caused a particular plaintiff's harm. In this context, especially with respect to the drug diethylstilbestrol (DES), some courts have relieved the plaintiff of responsibility to identify the causal producer, and allow recovery instead against each producer named by the plaintiff in proportion to each defendant's market share. Other courts have refused to effect such a basic change in traditional rules of causation.

In deciding whether to adopt a rule of proportional liability, courts have considered the following factors: (1) the generic nature of the product; (2) the long latency period of the harm; (3) the inability of plaintiffs to discover which defendant's product caused plaintiff's harm, even after exhaustive discovery; (4) the clarity of the causal connection between the defective product and the harm suffered by plaintiffs; (5) the absence of other medical or environmental factors that could have caused or materially contributed to the harm; and (6) the availability of sufficient "market share" data to support a reasonable apportionment of liability. The Institute leaves to developing law the question of whether, given the appropriate factors, a rule of proportional liability should be adopted.

However, if a court does adopt some form of proportional liability, the liability of each defendant is properly limited to the individual defendant's share of the market. The rules of joint and several liability are incompatible with a market-share approach to causation. Unlike the case of concurrent tortfeasors, in which several parties contribute to a single plaintiff's entire harm, it is not established in the market-share context that all the defendants contributed to the plaintiff's injury. Instead, each defendant should pay for harm in proportion to the risk that it caused in the market at large. Joint and several liability would impose liability on each defendant for the entirety of the harm based on its presence in the market with other defendants. In the absence of some concerted conduct among the defendants, such liability is inappropriate.

———

§ 16. Increased Harm Due to Product Defect

(a) **When a product is defective at the time of commercial sale or other distribution and the defect is a substantial factor in increasing the plaintiff's harm beyond that which would have resulted from other causes, the product seller is subject to liability for the increased harm.**

(b) **If proof supports a determination of the harm that would have resulted from other causes in the absence of the product defect, the product seller's liability is limited to the increased harm attributable solely to the product defect.**

(c) **If proof does not support a determination under Subsection (b) of the harm that would have resulted in the absence of the product defect, the product seller is liable for all of the plaintiff's harm attributable to the defect and other causes.**

(d) **A seller of a defective product that is held liable for part of the harm suffered by the plaintiff under Subsection (b), or all of the harm suffered by the plaintiff under Subsection (c), is jointly and severally liable or severally liable with other parties who bear legal responsibility for causing the harm, determined by applicable rules of joint and several liability.**

Comment:

a. Liability for increased harm. This Section deals with the problem of increased harm, often referred to as the issue of "enhancement" of harm. Liability for increased harm arises most frequently in automobile crashworthiness cases, but can also arise in connection with other products. Typically, the plaintiff is involved in an automobile accident caused by conduct or circumstances other than a product defect. The plaintiff would have suffered some injury as a result of the accident even in the absence of the claimed product defect. However, the plaintiff contends that the injuries were aggravated by the vehicle's failure reasonably to protect occupants in the event of an accident.

In the early era of product design litigation, controversy arose over whether a manufacturer owed any obligation to design its product so that injuries would be reasonably minimized in the event of an accident. That controversy is now settled. Although accidents are not intended uses of products, they are generally foreseeable. A manufacturer has a duty to design and manufacture its product so as reasonably to reduce the foreseeable harm that may occur in an accident brought about by causes other than a product defect. See Comment *b*. Since the product seller is responsible only for the increased harm, and not for the harm that would have occurred even in the absence of the product defect, basic principles of causation limit the damages to those resulting from the increased harm caused by the defect. The plaintiff must establish that the defect was a substantial factor in increasing the harm beyond that which would have resulted from other causes. Once the plaintiff establishes such increased harm, Subsection (b) or (c) applies. If proof supports a determination of what harm would have occurred without a defect, then liability is limited to the increased harm. If proof does not support such a determination, then the product seller is liable for all of the plaintiff's harm from both the defect and other causes.

Illustrations:

1. Bob negligently lost control of his car and collided with Ann's car, causing Ann to suffer harm from being thrown against her car's steering wheel. Ann was driving a car manufactured by XYZ Motor Co. In addition to suing Bob for his negligence, Ann sues XYZ. Expert testimony establishes that a reasonable alternative design of the steering mechanism was available that would have cushioned the impact between Ann and the steering column and that its omission rendered the car not reasonably safe. Further expert testimony describes the extent to which the omission of the alternative design increased the harm. Defendant XYZ is liable for harm that the trier of fact concludes the plaintiff suffered beyond the harm that would have been suffered had the car been equipped with the reasonable alternative design.

2. While Arthur was driving a snowmobile manufactured by ABC Co., the snowmobile hit a snow-covered rock. On impact, Arthur fell off the snowmobile and his face struck a brake bracket on the side of the snowmobile. Two sharp metal protrusions on the bracket caused serious facial injury. Competent testimony establishes that the brake bracket could have been covered by a safety guard that would have prevented such serious injury and that omission of the guard rendered the product not reasonably safe. Competent testimony also indicates the extent to which absence of the guard increased Arthur's harm. ABC is subject to liability for the harm that the trier of fact finds would have been prevented by a safety guard.

b. Establishing defect in increased-harm cases. To establish liability for increased harm, the plaintiff must prove that a product defect caused the harm under the rules stated in §§ 1–4. When the plaintiff alleges that a manufacturing defect caused increased harm, the plaintiff must establish a defect as set forth in § 2(a). When the plaintiff alleges that a design defect or a defect due to inadequate instructions or warnings caused increased harm, the plaintiff must establish that a reasonable alternative design could have been adopted, or that reasonable instructions or warnings could have been provided, as set forth in §§ 2(b) and 2(c).

In connection with a design defect claim in the context of increased harm, the plaintiff must establish that a reasonable alternative design would have reduced the plaintiff's harm. The factors enumerated in § 2, Comment *f*, for determining the reasonableness of an alternative design and the reasonable safety of the product are fully applicable to establishing defect in an increased-harm case. Furthermore, the alternative to the product design must increase the overall safety of the product. It is not sufficient that the alternative design would have reduced or prevented the harm the plaintiff suffered if the alternative would introduce into the product other dangers of equal or greater magnitude.

Proof of defect does not, of itself, establish a case of increased harm. The plaintiff must also establish that the defect was a substantial factor in increasing the plaintiff's harm beyond the harm that would have occurred from other causes. Subsection (c) provides that, when proof does not support a determination of increased harm, the product seller is liable for all harm suffered by the victim. However, the rule stated in Subsection (c) does not take effect until the plaintiff establishes under Subsection (a), by competent testimony, that the plaintiff's harm was increased as a result of the product defect.

Illustrations:

3. George was a passenger in a van manufactured by the XYZ Motor Co. The van was driven by a co-worker, Alice, who was proceeding non-negligently along a highway at 50 mph. To avoid a dog that unexpectedly ran across the highway, Alice swerved and lost control of the van, which struck an abutment. The force and angle of the collision caused the van to fly in the air and travel 75 feet before coming to rest upside down. During or after the initial collision, the roof panel separated from the van. George was thrown through the roof area and landed 50 feet from the van. Competent testimony by George's expert establishes that the welds meant to hold the roof to the body of the van were defective and did not meet the XYZ design standards. George's expert evidence also supports a determination that, had the roof been properly welded, it would not have come off as a result of the collision, that George would have remained in the van, and that the harm he suffered as a result of being thrown from the van was more serious than it would have been if the roof had kept George inside the van. Expert testimony also supports a determination of the extent to which George would have been harmed if he had stayed in the van, and thus the extent to which George's harm was increased by the failure of the roof to remain attached to the van. XYZ is liable for George's harm above that which the trier of fact determines George would have suffered in the absence of the defective welds.

4. Alice was operating a tractor manufactured by XYZ Farm Equipment. The tractor was designed for use on hills and sharp inclines. The tractor struck a large rock protruding from the ground, causing the tractor to roll over down a slope. Alice was thrown from the tractor and pinned beneath it. Alice's expert testifies that, had the tractor been designed with a rollover protection system, Alice would not have been thrown from the tractor and that the omission of the rollover protection system rendered the product not reasonably safe. This testimony supports a finding of defective design. Expert testimony also describes the extent to which Alice's harm was increased by the omission of the rollover protection system. Defendant XYZ is subject to liability for Alice's harm beyond that which the trier of fact finds she would have suffered had the tractor been equipped with the rollover protection system.

5. Richard suffered harm as a result of an automobile accident that occurred when he lost control of his car on a rain-soaked highway. The car slid off the highway and collided sideways with a steel pole. As a result of the force of the collision, the pole ripped through the body of the car and crushed Richard between the front seat and the area of the roof just above the windshield. Richard brings suit against the XYZ Motor Co., the manufacturer of the car, alleging that the car was defective in design in that it did not have a continuous steel frame extending through the door panels. Richard's experts assert that, had the vehicle been so designed, it would have bounced off the pole, preventing penetration by the pole into the passenger space. XYZ's experts assert that a continuous steel frame would also reduce front-to-back deformation of the body of the vehicle in a head-on crash. Deformation is desirable in head-on crashes because it absorbs the impact of the crash and decreases risk of harm to the occupants of the vehicle. Richard's experts admit on cross-examination that, for head-on automobile accidents, the alternative design offered by Richard would decrease safety. Even if the design alternative offered by Richard would have reduced his harm, if the trier of fact finds that Richard's proposed alternative would have decreased the overall safety of the vehicle, it should return a verdict for XYZ.

c. *Determination of what harm would have resulted in the absence of the product defect.* The task of determining what harm would have resulted had the product not been defective under Subsection (b) is often difficult. Outright guesswork is not permitted, but neither should anything approaching certainty be required. When an expert offers a rational explanation derived from a causal analysis, the testimony should, subject to the normal discretion of the trial court, be admitted for consideration by the trier of fact.

d. *Extent of liability for increased harm when proof does not support determination of what harm would have resulted in the absence of the product defect.* Subsection (c) provides that when the plaintiff has proved

103

defect-caused increased harm, the product seller is subject to liability for all harm suffered by the plaintiff if proof does not support a determination of what harm would have resulted if the product had not been defective. The defendant, a wrongdoer who in fact has caused harm to the plaintiff, should not escape liability because the nature of the harm makes such a determination impossible. Compare § 433B(2) of the Restatement, Second, of Torts.

Illustration:

6. The same facts as Illustration 3, in that George proves that the defect was a substantial factor in increasing the harm beyond that which he would have suffered if the roof had kept him inside the van, but George is unable to quantify the extent of the increased harm. Neither party introduces proof that supports the apportionment of liability. XYZ is liable for all of George's harm.

e. Joint and several liability for increased harm. When the plaintiff proves defect-caused increased harm, and the seller of the defective product is held liable for part of the harm suffered by the plaintiff under Subsection (b) or all of the harm suffered by the plaintiff under Subsection (c), liability of the seller and other tortfeasors is joint and several. In a case under Subsection (b), the manufacturer is jointly and severally liable only for the increased harm; in a case under Subsection (c), for the entire harm. Joint and several liability is imposed because there is no practical method of apportioning responsibility that would reflect the separate causal contributions of those tortfeasors who caused the increased harm. The general rules governing joint and several liability determine the liability of the parties to the injured plaintiff. In those jurisdictions that retain the common-law rule, all parties bear full responsibility for the entirety of the harm. In many jurisdictions, the common-law rules of joint and several liability have undergone significant legislative modification limiting liability to the percentage of fault allocated to each party.

Illustrations:

7. Same facts as Illustration 6, except that Alice's negligent driving caused her to lose control of her van. The XYZ Motor Co. is liable under Subsection (c) for all of George's harm. The case is governed by the law of State A, which follows the common-law rule of joint and several liability. George may recover all of his damages from either Alice or XYZ.

8. Same facts as Illustration 7. The XYZ Motor Co. is liable under Subsection (c) for all of George's harm. The case is governed by the law of State B, whose statute limits the liability of joint tortfeasors to the percentage of responsibility allocated to each party. The trier of fact allocates 40 percent of the responsibility to Alice and 60 percent of the responsibility to XYZ. XYZ's liability is limited to 60 percent of the total damages.

9. Same facts as Illustration 7. The XYZ Motor Co. is liable under Subsection (c) for all of George's harm. The case is governed by the law of State C, whose statute retains the common-law rule of joint and several liability for economic loss but limits the liability of joint tortfeasors for noneconomic loss to the percentage of responsibility allocated to each party. The trier of fact has allocated 40 percent of the responsibility to Alice and 60 percent to XYZ. George may recover all of his economic loss damages from either Alice or XYZ. His recovery from XYZ for noneconomic damages is limited to 60 percent.

f. Plaintiff's fault in cases of increased harm. Section 17 sets forth the general rules governing plaintiff's fault in products liability litigation. It provides that plaintiff's fault is relevant in apportioning liability between the plaintiff and the product seller. The seriousness of the plaintiff's fault and the nature of the product defect are relevant in apportioning the appropriate percentages of responsibility between the plaintiff and the product seller. See § 17, Comment *d*. Accordingly, the contributory fault of the plaintiff in causing an accident that results in defect-related increased harm is relevant in apportioning responsibility between or among the parties, according to applicable apportionment law. In apportioning responsibility in such cases, it may be important that requiring a product to be designed reasonably to prevent increased harm aims to protect persons in circumstances in which they are unable to protect themselves.

TOPIC 2. AFFIRMATIVE DEFENSES

§ 17. Apportionment of Responsibility Between or Among Plaintiff, Sellers and Distributors of Defective Products, and Others

(a) A plaintiff's recovery of damages for harm caused by a product defect may be reduced if the conduct of the plaintiff combines with the product defect to cause the harm and the plaintiff's conduct fails to conform to generally applicable rules establishing appropriate standards of care.

(b) The manner and extent of the reduction under Subsection (a) and the apportionment of plaintiff's recovery among multiple defendants are governed by generally applicable rules apportioning responsibility.

Comment:

a. History. The rule stated in this Section recognizes that the fault of the plaintiff is relevant in assessing liability for product-caused harm. Section 402A of the Restatement, Second, of Torts, recognizing strict liability for harm caused by defective products, was adopted in 1964 when the overwhelming majority rule treated contributory negligence as a total bar to recovery. Understandably, the Institute was reluctant to bar a plaintiff's products liability claim in tort based on conduct that was not egregious. Thus, § 402A, Comment *n*, altered the general tort defenses by narrowing the applicability of contributory negligence and emphasizing assumption of risk as the primary defense. Since then, comparative fault has swept the country. Only a tiny minority of states retain contributory fault as a total bar.

A strong majority of jurisdictions apply the comparative responsibility doctrine to products liability actions. Courts today do not limit the relevance of plaintiff's fault as did the Restatement, Second, of Torts to conduct characterized as voluntary assumption of the risk. See Comment *d*.

Certain forms of consumer behavior—product misuse and product alteration or modification—have been the subject of much confusion and misunderstanding. Early decisions treated product misuse, alteration, and modification, whether by the plaintiff or a third party, as a total bar to recovery against a product seller. Today misuse, alteration, and modification relate to one of three issues in a products liability action. In some cases, misuse, alteration, and modification are important in determining whether the product is defective. In others, they are relevant to the issue of legal cause. Finally, when the plaintiff misuses, alters, or modifies the product, such conduct may constitute contributory fault and reduce the plaintiff's recovery under the rules of comparative responsibility. See Comment *c*.

b. Conduct of the plaintiff. The applicable rules of apportionment of responsibility vary among jurisdictions. Some states have adopted "pure" comparative fault, which allocates responsibility to each actor purely in proportion to the actor's percentage of total fault. Others follow some variant of "modified" comparative fault, in which actors' responsibilities are adjusted according to predetermined thresholds of responsibility. For example, in many modified jurisdictions the plaintiff is totally barred if found more than 50 percent at fault. The apportionment of responsibility principles as they have developed in each jurisdiction should be applied to products liability cases. With respect to whether special exceptions should be made in products liability cases for certain categories of plaintiff conduct, see Comment *d*.

c. Misuse, alteration, and modification. Product misuse, alteration, and modification, whether by a third party or the plaintiff, are not discrete doctrines within products liability law. Instead such conduct is relevant to the determination of the issues of defect, causation, and comparative responsibility. See § 2, Comment *p*.

Jurisdictions differ on the question of who bears the burden of proof regarding conduct that constitutes misuse, modification, and alteration. The allocation of burdens in this regard is not addressed in this Restatement and is left to local law.

d. *Particular forms or categories of plaintiff's conduct.* Some courts accord different treatment to special categories of plaintiff conduct. For example, some decisions hold that when the plaintiff's negligence is the failure to discover a product defect, reduction of damages on the basis of apportionment of responsibility is improper, reasoning that a consumer has a right to expect a defect-free product and should not be burdened with a duty to inspect for defects. Other decisions hold that apportionment of responsibility is improper when the product lacked a safety feature that would protect against the risk that resulted in the injury in question, reasoning that the defendant's responsibility should not be diminished when the plaintiff engages in the very conduct that the product design should have prevented. On the other hand, some decisions hold that a plaintiff's assumption of the risk is a complete defense to a products liability action, not merely a basis for apportionment of responsibility. Product misuse, alteration, and modification have been treated by some courts as an absolute bar to recovery and by others as a form of plaintiff fault that should be compared with that of other parties to reduce recovery. The majority position is that all forms of plaintiff's failure to conform to applicable standards of care are to be considered for the purpose of apportioning responsibility between the plaintiff and the product seller or distributor.

Before the court will allow any apportionment of responsibility, the defendant must introduce sufficient evidence to support a finding of fault on the part of the plaintiff. Thus, for example, when the defendant claims that the plaintiff failed to discover a defect, there must be evidence that the plaintiff's conduct in failing to discover a defect did, in fact, fail to meet a standard of reasonable care. In general, a plaintiff has no reason to expect that a new product contains a defect and would have little reason to be on guard to discover it. Or when a plaintiff is injured due to inattention to a danger that should have been eliminated by a safety feature, there must be evidence supporting the conclusion that the plaintiff's momentary inattention or inadvertence in a workplace setting constitutes failure to exercise reasonable care. In the absence of such evidence courts refuse to submit the plaintiff's conduct to the trier of fact for apportionment based on the principles of comparative responsibility. When evidence of plaintiff fault is established, how much responsibility to attribute to a plaintiff will vary with the circumstances. The seriousness of the plaintiff's fault and the nature of the product defect are relevant in apportioning the appropriate percentages of responsibility between the plaintiff and the product seller.

———

§ 18. Disclaimers, Limitations, Waivers, and Other Contractual Exculpations as Defenses to Products Liability Claims for Harm to Persons

Disclaimers and limitations of remedies by product sellers or other distributors, waivers by product purchas-

ers, and other similar contractual exculpations, oral or written, do not bar or reduce otherwise valid products liability claims against sellers or other distributors of new products for harm to persons.

Comment:

a. Effects of contract defenses on products liability tort claims for harm to persons. A commercial seller or other distributor of a new product is not permitted to avoid liability for harm to persons through limiting terms in a contract governing the sale of a product. It is presumed that the ordinary product user or consumer lacks sufficient information and bargaining power to execute a fair contractual limitation of rights to recover. For a limited exception to this general rule, see Comment *d.* The rule in this Section applies only to "sellers or other distributors of new products." For rules governing commercial sellers of used products, including whether they may rely on disclaimers, waivers, and other contractual defenses, see § 8. Nothing in this Section is intended to constrain parties within the commercial chain of distribution from contracting inter se for indemnity agreements or save-harmless clauses.

b. Distinguishing disclaimers from warnings. This Section invalidates disclaimers and contractual exculpations of liability by sellers of new products when they are interjected to bar or limit claims by plaintiffs for harm to persons. Disclaimers should be distinguished from warnings. Warnings convey information to the buyer about avoiding risk in using the product. In some cases warnings inform the consumer of risks that cannot be avoided. Both types of warnings provide consumers with valuable information concerning the risks attendant to using the product. A product sold with reasonable instructions or warnings may be nondefective. See § 2, Comments *i, j, k,* and *l.* Disclaimers attempt contractually to avoid liability for defective products. For the reasons set forth in Comment *a,* courts refuse to enforce disclaimers that purport to deny recovery for harm to persons caused by new products that were defective at the time of sale.

c. Effects of disclaimers on claims for harm to property or for economic loss. For the effect of disclaimers on tort claims for defect-caused harm to property or for economic loss, see § 21, Comment *f.*

d. Waiver of rights in contractual settings in which product purchasers possess both adequate knowledge and sufficient economic power. The rule in this Section applies to cases in which commercial product sellers attempt unfairly to disclaim or otherwise limit their liability to the majority of users and consumers who are presumed to lack information and bargaining power adequate to protect their interests. This Section does not address whether consumers, especially when represented by informed and economically powerful consumer groups or intermediaries, with full information and sufficient bargaining power, may contract with product sellers to accept curtailment of liability in exchange for concomitant benefits, or whether such consumers might be allowed to agree to substitute alternative dispute resolution mechanisms in place of traditional adjudication. When such contracts are accompanied by alternative nontort remedies that serve as an adequate quid pro quo for reducing or eliminating rights to recover in tort, arguments may support giving effect to such agreements. Such contractual arrangements raise policy questions different from those raised by this Section and require careful consideration by the courts.

————

TOPIC 3. DEFINITIONS

§ 19. Definition of "Product"

For purposes of this Restatement:

(a) A product is tangible personal property distributed commercially for use or consumption. Other items, such as real property and electricity, are products when the context of their distribution and use is sufficiently analogous to the distribution and use of tangible personal property that it is appropriate to apply the rules stated in this Restatement.

(b) Services, even when provided commercially, are not products.

(c) Human blood and human tissue, even when provided commercially, are not subject to the rules of this Restatement.

Comment:

a. History. The question of whether something distributed in commerce is a product for purposes of tort liability is important in this Restatement, but relatively less so than it was in the period from the early 1960s to the early 1980s. Before 1960, American courts had not yet recognized strict liability in tort for harm caused by defective products, particularly if there was no privity of contract between plaintiff and defendant. Thus, prior to that time, plaintiffs claiming in tort against product sellers were required to prove causal negligence; if they could prove negligence they could usually recover in tort whether or not a product was involved. Once the era of strict products liability in tort arrived in the early 1960s, liability turned primarily on whether what the defendant distributed was, or was not, a product. Most of the focus during this period was on liability for harm caused by manufacturing defects, in connection with which strict liability had a distinctive character. See § 2(a).

By the early 1980s, the emphasis of products liability litigation had shifted from manufacturing defects to defective designs and defects due to inadequate instructions and warnings. Thereafter, design and warning cases came to dominate. Given that design and warning cases turn on essentially risk-utility evaluations, see § 2, Comment *d*, the practical importance of whether something is, or is not, a product has diminished somewhat. Nevertheless, that issue remains important in the modern era to the extent that the concept of strict liability retains functional meaning. See § 1, Comment *a*. Statutes enacted to reform products liability law, many of which impose nontraditional conditions and limitations on product-related liability, tend to enhance the importance of classifying something as a product.

Apart from statutes that define "product" for purposes of determining products liability, in every instance it is for the court to determine as a matter of law whether something is, or is not, a product.

b.   Tangible personal property: in general. For purposes of this Restatement, most but not necessarily all products are tangible personal property. In certain situations, however, intangible personal property (see Comment *d*) and real property (see Comment *e*) may be products. Component parts are products, whether sold or distributed separately or assembled with other component parts. An assemblage of component parts is also, itself, a product. Raw materials are products, whether manufactured, such as sheet metal; processed, such as lumber; or gathered and sold or distributed in raw condition, such as unwashed gravel and farm produce. For treatment of the special problems presented when plaintiffs join sellers of component parts and raw materials in actions against those who subsequently combined those materials to create defective products, see § 10.

Courts are divided regarding whether living animals, such as pets or livestock, should be considered to be products for the purpose of determining a commercial seller's liability in tort. Frequently, as when diseased livestock are sold and subsequently must be destroyed, the claim to recover for their value involves a claim for harm to the product itself and thus represents a claim for pure economic loss not permitted by this Restatement. See § 21. But when a living animal is sold commercially in a diseased condition and causes harm to other property or to persons, the animal constitutes a product for purposes of this Restatement.

c.   Tangible personal property: human blood and human tissue. Although human blood and human tissue meet the formal requisites of Subsection (a), they are specifically excluded from the coverage of this Restatement. Almost all the litigation regarding such products has dealt with contamination of human blood and blood-related products by the hepatitis virus or the HIV virus. Absent a special rule dealing with human blood and tissue, such contamination presumably would be subject to the rules of §§ 1 and 2(a). Those Sections impose strict liability when a product departs from its intended design even though all possible care was exercised in the preparation and marketing of the product. However, legislation in almost all jurisdictions limits the liability of sellers of human blood and human tissue to the failure to exercise reasonable care, often by providing that human blood and human tissue are not "products" or that their provision is a "service." Where legislation has not addressed the problem, courts have concluded that strict liability is inappropriate for harm caused by such product contamination.

What constitutes reasonable care for those engaged in providing professional services is defined in § 299A of the Restatement, Second, of Torts.

d. Intangible personal property. Two basic types of intangible personal property are involved. The first consists of information in media such as books, maps, and navigational charts. Plaintiffs allege that the information delivered was false and misleading, causing harm when actors relied on it. They seek to recover against publishers in strict liability in tort based on product defect, rather than on negligence or some form of misrepresentation. Although a tangible medium such as a book, itself clearly a product, delivers the information, the plaintiff's grievance in such cases is with the information, not with the tangible medium. Most courts, expressing concern that imposing strict liability for the dissemination of false and defective information would significantly impinge on free speech have, appropriately, refused to impose strict products liability in these cases. One area in which some courts have imposed strict products liability involves false information contained in maps and navigational charts. In that context the falsity of the factual information is unambiguous and more akin to a classic product defect. However, the better view is that false information in such documents constitutes a misrepresentation that the user may properly rely upon.

The second major category of intangible, harm-causing products involves the transmission of intangible forces such as electricity and X rays. With respect to transmission of electricity, a majority of courts have held that electricity becomes a product only when it passes through the customer's meter and enters the customer's premises. Until then, the system of high-voltage transmission provides, not a product, but a service; before passing the meter and entering the plaintiff's premises, so it is said, the electricity has not entered the stream of commerce. Some courts employ this analysis to conclude that, while electricity is a "product" prior to delivery, it has not yet been "sold or otherwise distributed." Whether or not these rationales are cogent, the distinction drawn between pre-and post-delivery is reasonable. Plaintiffs in the post-delivery cases typically complain of unexpected drops or surges in voltage, resulting in personal injury or property damage. Those claims seem better governed by principles of strict liability for physical deviations from intended design. Plaintiffs in the pre-delivery, high-voltage cases complain of the inherent dangers that unavoidably accompany the transmission of high-voltage electricity. Courts have refused to impose strict liability on electric utilities for high voltage-related accidents either on a strict products liability basis or under the abnormally dangerous activities doctrine set out in § 520 of the Restatement, Second, of Torts. This Restatement does not alter that approach.

The cases involving harm caused by X-rays and radiation treatments rest not on assertions that the X-rays themselves were defective, but rather on assertions that they were improperly administered by medical technicians. Courts have refused to impose liability in the absence of a showing by plaintiff either that the X-rays or other forms of radiation treatment were defective or that the medical technicians acted negligently. These cases may also reflect courts' traditional refusal to impose strict liability on providers of medical care.

e.   Real property. Traditionally, courts have been reluctant to impose products liability on sellers of improved real property in that such property does not constitute goods or personalty. A housing contractor, building and selling one house at a time, does not fit the pattern of a mass producer of manufactured products, nor is such a builder perceived to be more capable than are purchasers of controlling or insuring against risks presented by weather conditions or earth movements. More recently, courts have treated sellers of improved real property as product sellers in a number of contexts. When a building contractor sells a building that contains a variety of appliances or other manufactured equipment, the builder, together with the equipment manufacturer and other distributors, are held as product sellers with respect to such equipment notwithstanding the fact that the built-in equipment may have become, for other legal purposes, attachments to and thus part of the underlying real property. Moreover, the builder may be treated as a product seller even with respect to the building itself when the building has been prefabricated—and thus manufactured—and later assembled on-or off-site. Finally, courts impose strict liability for defects in construction when dwellings are built, even if on-site, on a major scale, as in a large housing project.

f.   The distinction between services and products. Services, even when provided commercially, are not products for purposes of this Restatement. Thus, apart from the sale of a product incidental to the service, one who agrees for a monetary fee to mow the lawn of another is the provider of a service even if the provider is a large firm engaged commercially in lawn care. Moreover, it is irrelevant that the service provided relates directly to products commercially distributed. For example, one who contracts to inspect, repair, and maintain machinery owned and operated by another is the provider of a product-related service rather than the provider of a product. If a product repairer replaces a worn-out component part with a new part, the replacement constitutes a sale of the part; but the repair itself constitutes a service. For consideration of commercial transactions combining elements of both sale and service, see § 20(c).

————

§ 20.   Definition of "One Who Sells or Otherwise Distributes"

For purposes of this Restatement:

(a) One sells a product when, in a commercial context, one transfers ownership thereto either for use or consump-

tion or for resale leading to ultimate use or consumption. Commercial product sellers include, but are not limited to, manufacturers, wholesalers, and retailers.

(b) One otherwise distributes a product when, in a commercial transaction other than a sale, one provides the product to another either for use or consumption or as a preliminary step leading to ultimate use or consumption. Commercial nonsale product distributors include, but are not limited to, lessors, bailors, and those who provide products to others as a means of promoting either the use or consumption of such products or some other commercial activity.

(c) One also sells or otherwise distributes a product when, in a commercial transaction, one provides a combination of products and services and either the transaction taken as a whole, or the product component thereof, satisfies the criteria in Subsection (a) or (b).

Comment:

a. History. Until the mid–1960s, the only transactions that gave rise to what today is known as "products liability" were commercial product sales, as defined in Subsection (a). In large part this limitation reflects the origins of liability without fault in the law of warranty, which has traditionally focused on sales transactions. During the formative years in the development of strict products liability, courts extended liability to some nonsale transactions, but always by assimilating such transactions to sales. Section 402A of the Restatement, Second, of Torts, approved in 1964, limited itself to "one who *sells* a product in a defective condition...." (Emphasis added). After the promulgation of § 402A, courts began to extend strict liability for harm caused by product defects to some nonsale commercial transactions involving the distribution of products. Rather than stretching to call these transactions "sales," courts simply declared that the same policy objectives that supported strict liability in the sales context supported strict liability in other contexts. The first significant extension involved commercial product lessors. Although title does not pass in lease transactions, courts have reasoned that the same policy objectives that are served by holding commercial product sellers strictly liable also apply to commercial product lessors. Over time, courts have extended strict products liability to a wide range of nonsale, nonlease transactions.

b. Product sales and giveaways. Sales occur at all levels in the distributive chain including manufacturer sellers, wholesale sellers, and retail sellers. Food served in a restaurant is sold to the customer, as are products given away free of separate charge in the context of a commercial sales promotion. Thus, businesses are liable for defects in free samples or defects in products given away for other promotional purposes. Even if the final transaction through which a defective product reaches the plaintiff is not a commercial sales transaction, with the result that products liability is not imposed on the final transferor—as when one buys a soft drink at a store and then gives it to a friend—a plaintiff may recover in tort for resulting harm against all commercial sellers who sold the product in a defective condition.

c. Commercial product leases. A commercial lessor of new and like-new products is generally subject to the rules governing new product sellers. When an individual rents a new or an almost-new used product on a short-term basis, with the lessee having no opportunity to inspect the product or adequately to assess its condition, and the product unit is drawn from a pool of rental units that includes new and almost-new used units with no attempt by the leasing agent to distinguish among units on the basis of age and condition, the lessor is subject to liability as if it were the retail seller of a new product. When the rental units are in obviously used condition, liability of the lessor depends on the rules stated in § 8.

d. Sales-service combinations. When the same person provides both products and services in a commercial transaction, whether a product has been sold may be difficult to determine. When the product and service components are kept separate by the parties to the transaction, as when a lawn-care firm bills separately for fertilizer applied to a customer's lawn or when a machinery repairer replaces a component part and bills separately for it, the firm will be held to be the seller of the product. This is especially true when the parties to the transaction explicitly characterize the property aspect as a sale.

When the parties do not clearly separate the product and service components, courts differ in their treatment of these so-called "sale-service hybrid transactions." These transactions tend to fall into two categories. In the first, the product component is consumed in the course of providing the service, as when a hair dye is used in treating a customer's hair in a salon. Even when the service provider does not charge the customer separately for the dye, the transaction ordinarily is treated as a sale of the material that is consumed in providing the service. When the product component in the sale-service transaction is not consumed or permanently transferred to the customer—as when defective scissors are used in the hair salon—the transaction ordinarily is treated as one not involving a sale of the product to the customer. But while the salon is not a seller, all commercial sellers in the chain of distribution of the scissors, from the manufacturer through the retailer who sold them to the salon, are clearly sellers of the scissors and are subject to liability to the salon customer under the rules of this Restatement. It should be noted that, in a strong majority of jurisdictions, hospitals are held not to be sellers of products they supply in connection with the provision of medical care, regardless of the circumstances.

e. Other means of commercial distribution: finance leases. A finance lessor, as distinct from a commercial lessor under Comment *c*, is not subject to the rule of this Section in the absence of active participation in the underlying commercial product distribution.

f. Other means of commercial distribution: product bailments. Bailments typically involve short-term transfers of possession. Several categories of cases are fairly clear. When the defendant is in the business of selling the same type of product as is the subject of the bailment, the seller/bailor is subject to strict liability for harm caused by defects. Thus, an automobile dealer who allows a prospective customer to test-drive a demonstrator will be treated the same as a seller of the demonstrator car. Even when sale of a product is not contemplated, the commercial bailor is subject to strict liability if a charge is imposed as a condition of the bailment. Thus, a laundromat is subject to strict liability for a defective clothes dryer, and a roller rink that rents skates is treated similarly. When products are made available as a convenience to customers who are on the defendant's premises primarily for different, although related purposes, and no separate charge is made, strict liability is not imposed. Thus, bowling alleys that supply bowling balls for customer use and markets that supply shopping carts are not subject to strict products liability for harm caused by defects in those items. Similarly, doctors who use medical devices while treating patients are not considered distributors of those products.

g. Other means of commercial distribution: product distribution facilitators. Persons assisting or providing services to product distributors, while indirectly facilitating the commercial distribution of products, are not subject to liability under the rules of this Restatement. Thus, commercial firms engaged in advertising products are outside the rules of this Restatement, as are firms engaged exclusively in the financing of product sale or lease transactions. Sales personnel and commercial auctioneers are also outside the rules of this Restatement.

---

§ 21. Definition of "Harm to Persons or Property": Recovery for Economic Loss

For purposes of this Restatement, harm to persons or property includes economic loss if caused by harm to:

(a) the plaintiff's person; or

(b) the person of another when harm to the other interferes with an interest of the plaintiff protected by tort law; or

(c) the plaintiff's property other than the defective product itself.

Comment:

a.   Rationale. This Section limits the kinds of harm for which recovery is available under this Restatement. Two major constraints on tort recovery give content to this Section. First, products liability law lies at the boundary between tort and contract. Some categories of loss, including those often referred to as "pure economic loss," are more appropriately assigned to contract law and the remedies set forth in Articles 2 and 2A of the Uniform Commercial Code. When the Code governs a claim, its provisions regarding such issues as statutes of limitation, privity, notice of claim, and disclaimer ordinarily govern the litigation. Second, some forms of economic loss have traditionally been excluded from the realm of tort law even when the plaintiff has no contractual remedy for a claim.

b.   Economic loss resulting from harm to plaintiff's person. Loss of earnings and reductions in earning capacity are common forms of economic loss resulting from harm to the plaintiff's person and are included in Subsection (a). Other forms of economic loss resulting from harm to the plaintiff's person are recoverable if they are within the general principles of legal cause. See Restatement, Second, Torts §§ 430–461.

c.   When harm to another interferes with an interest of the plaintiff protected by tort law. When tort law recognizes the right of a plaintiff to recover for economic loss arising from harm to another's person, that right is included within the rules of this Restatement Third, Torts: Products Liability. Thus, for example, actions under local common law and statutes for loss of consortium or wrongful death on behalf of next of kin, although not direct harms to the plaintiff's person, are included in Subsection (b). Other examples of such rights may be recognized under local law, but the categories included in Subsection (b) have traditionally been limited in number.

d.   Harm to the defective product itself. When a product defect results in harm to the product itself, the law governing commercial transactions sets forth a comprehensive scheme governing the rights of the buyer and seller. Harm to the product itself takes two forms. A product defect may render the product ineffective so that repair or replacement is necessary. Such a defect may also result in consequential loss to the buyer. For example, a machine that becomes inoperative may cause the assembly line in which it is being used to break down and may lead to a wide range of consequential economic losses to the business that owns the machine. These losses are not recoverable in tort under the rules of this Restatement. A somewhat more difficult question is presented when the defect in the product renders it unreasonably dangerous, but the product does not cause harm to persons or property. In these situations the danger either (1) never eventuates in harm because the product defect is discovered before it causes harm, or (2) eventuates in harm to the product itself but not in harm to persons or other property. A plausible argument can be made that products that are dangerous, rather than merely ineffectual, should be governed by the rules governing products liability law. However, a majority of courts have concluded that the remedies provided under the Uniform Commercial Code—repair and replacement costs and, in appropriate circumstances, consequential economic loss—are sufficient. Thus, the rules of this Restatement do not apply in such situations.

A second category of economic loss excluded from the coverage of this Restatement includes losses suffered by a plaintiff but not as a direct result of harm to the plaintiff's person or property. For example, a defective product may destroy a commercial business establishment, whose employees patronize a particular restaurant, resulting in economic loss to the restaurant. The loss suffered by the restaurant generally is not recoverable in tort and in any event is not cognizable under products liability law.

e. Harm to the plaintiff's property other than the defective product itself. A defective product that causes harm to property other than the defective product itself is governed by the rules of this Restatement. What constitutes harm to other property rather than harm to the product itself may be difficult to determine. A product that nondangerously fails to function due to a product defect has clearly caused harm only to itself. A product that fails to function and causes harm to surrounding property has clearly caused harm to other property. However, when a component part of a machine or a system destroys the rest of the machine or system, the characterization process becomes more difficult. When the product or system is deemed to be an integrated whole, courts treat such damage as harm to the product itself. When so characterized, the damage is excluded from the coverage of this Restatement. A contrary holding would require a finding of property damage in virtually every case in which a product harms itself and would prevent contractual rules from serving their legitimate function in governing commercial transactions.

The characterization of a claim as harm to other property may trigger liability not only for the harm to physical property but also for incidental economic loss. The extent to which incidental economic loss is recoverable in tort is governed by general principles of legal cause. See Restatement, Second, Torts §§ 430–461.

One category of claims stands apart. In the case of asbestos contamination in buildings, most courts have taken the position that the contamination constitutes harm to the building as other property. The serious health threat caused by asbestos contamination has led the courts to this conclusion. Thus, actions seeking recovery for the costs of asbestos removal have been held to be within the purview of products liability law rather than commercial law.

f. Harm to other property: disclaimers and limitations of remedies. Although recovery for harm to property other than the defective product itself is governed by this Restatement, the Institute leaves to developing case law the questions of whether and under what circumstances contracting parties may disclaim or limit remedies for harm to other property. Of course, such contractual limitations would be effective only between the parties themselves. When a defective product causes harm to property owned by third persons, the contractual arrangements between the contracting parties should not shield the seller from liability to the third party. However, contractual limitations on tort liability for harm to property, when fairly bargained for, may provide an effective way for the contracting parties efficiently to allocate risks of such harm between themselves.

UNIFORM COMMERCIAL CODE

Selected Sections*

Table of Jurisdictions Adopting Code.

* Copyright © 1987 by The American Law Institute and the National Conference of Commissioners on Uniform State Laws. Reprinted with permission of the Permanent Editorial Board for the Uniform Commercial Code.

119

UNIFORM COMMERCIAL CODE
*Table of Jurisdictions Wherein Code Has Been Adopted**

Jurisdiction	Laws	Effective Date	Statutory Citation
Alabama	1965, Act No. 549	1–1–1967	Code 1975, §§ 7–1–101 to 7–11–108
Alaska	1962, c. 114	1–1–1963	AS §§ 45.01 to 45.09, 45.12, 45.14
Arizona	1967, c. 3	1–1–1968	A.R.S. §§ 47–1101 to 47–11107
Arkansas	1961, Act No. 185	1–1–1962	Code 1987, §§ 4–1–101 to 4–10–104
California	Stats.1963, c. 819	1–1–1965	West's Ann.Cal.Com.Code, §§ 1101 to 15104
Colorado	1965, c. 330	7–1–1966	C.R.S. §§ 4–1–101 to 4–11–102
Connecticut	1959, No. 133	10–1–1961	C.G.S.A. §§ 42a–1–101 to 42a–10–109
Delaware	1966, c. 349	7–1–1967	6 Del.C. §§ 1–101 to 11–109
Dist. of Columbia	P.L. 88–243	1–1–1965	D.C.Code 1981, §§ 28:1–101 to 28:11–108
Florida	1965, c. 65–254	1–1–1967	West's F.S.A. §§ 670.101 to 670.507; 671.101 to 680.532
Georgia	1962, Act 713	1–1–1964	O.C.G.A. §§ 11–1–101 to 11–11–104
Hawaii	1965, No. 208	1–1–1967	HRS §§ 490:1–101 to 490:11–108
Idaho	1967, c. 161	1–1–1968	I.C. §§ 28–1–101 to 28–10–104; 28–12–101 to 28–12–532
Illinois	1961, p. 2101	7–2–1962	S.H.A. 810 ILCS 5/1–101 to 5/12–102
Indiana	1963, c. 317	7–1–1964	West's A.I.C. 26–1–1–101 to 26–1–10–104
Iowa	1965, (61 G.A.) c. 413	7–4–1966	I.C.A. §§ 554.1101 to 554.13532
Kansas	1965, c. 564	1–1–1966	K.S.A. 84–1–101 to 84–10–102
Kentucky	1958, c. 77	7–1–1960	KRS 355.1–101 to 355.11–108
Louisiana	1974, No. 92	1–1–1975	LSA–R.S. 10:1–101 to 10:5–117
Maine	1963, c. 362	12–31–1964	11 M.R.S.A. §§ 1–101 to 10–108
Maryland	1963, c. 538	2–1–1964	Code, Commercial Law, §§ 1–101 to 10–112
Massachusetts	1957, c. 765	10–1–1958	M.G.L.A. c. 106, §§ 1–101 to 9–507
Michigan	1962, P.A. 174	1–1–1964	M.C.L.A. §§ 440.1101 to 440.11102
Minnesota	1965, c. 811	7–1–1966	M.S.A. §§ 336.1–101 to 336.11–108
Mississippi	1966, c. 316	3–31–1968	Code 1972, §§ 75–1–101 to 75–11–108
Missouri	1963, p. 503	7–1–1965	V.A.M.S. §§ 400.1–101 to 400.11–107
Montana	1963, c. 264	1–2–1965	MCA 30–1–101 to 30–9–511
Nebraska	1963, c. 544	9–2–1965	Neb.U.C.C. §§ 1–101 to 10–104
Nevada	1965, c. 353	3–1–1967	N.R.S. 104.1101 to 104.9507; 104A.010 to 104A.2531

* For the versions of the UCC adopted in each state, see Uniform Commercial Code (U.L.A.) at 1–2 (1989 and Supp.2004). Eds.

Jurisdiction	Laws	Effective Date	Statutory Citation
New Hampshire	1959, c. 247	7–1–1961	RSA 382–A:1–101 to 382–A:9–507
New Jersey	1961, c. 120	1–1–1963	N.J.S.A. 12A:1–101 to 12A:11–108
New Mexico	1961, c. 96	1–1–1962	NMSA 1978, §§ 55–1–101 to 55–12–108
New York	1962, c. 553	9–27–1964	McKinney's Uniform Commercial Code, §§ 1–101 to 13–105
North Carolina	1965, c. 700	7–1–1967	G.S. §§ 25–1–101 to 25–11–108
North Dakota	1965, c. 296	7–1–1966	NDCC 41–01–02 to 41–09–53
Ohio.................	1961, p. 13	7–1–1962	R.C. §§ 1301.01 to 1310.78
Oklahoma	1961, p. 70	1–1–1963	12A Okl.St.Ann. §§ 1–101 to 11–107
Oregon................	1961, c. 726	9–1–1963	ORS 71.1010 to 79.6010
Pennsylvania	1953, P.L. 3	7–1–1954	13 Pa.C.S.A. §§ 1101 to 9507
Rhode Island..........	1960, c. 147	1–2–1962	Gen.Laws 1956, §§ 6A–1–101 to 6A–9–507
South Carolina	1966, c. 1065	1–1–1968	Code 1976, §§ 36–1–101 to 36–11–108
South Dakota	1966, c. 150	7–1–1967	SDCL 57A–1–101 to 57A–11–108
Tennessee	1963, c. 81	7–1–1964	West's Tenn.Code §§ 47–1–101 to 47–9–607
Texas.................	1965, c. 721	7–1–1966	V.T.C.A., Bus. & C. §§ 1.101 to 11.108
Utah	1965, c. 154	1–1–1966	U.C.A.1953, 70A–1–101 to 70A–11–108
Vermont	1966, No. 29	1–1–1967	9A V.S.A. §§ 1–101 to 9–607
Virgin Islands	1965, No. 1299	7–1–1965	11A V.I.C. §§ 1–101 to 9–507
Virginia...............	1964, c. 219	1–1–1966	Code 1950, §§ 8.1–101 to 8.11–108
Washington............	1965, Ex.Sess., c. 157	7–1–1967	West's RCWA 62A.1–101 to 62A.11–109
West Virginia	1963, c. 193	7–1–1964	Code, 46–1–101 to 46–11–108
Wisconsin	1963, c. 158	7–1–1965	W.S.A. 401.101 to 411.901
Wyoming..............	1961, c. 219	1–2–1962	W.S.1977, §§ 34.1–1–101 to 34.1–10–104

ARTICLE 1

GENERAL PROVISIONS

PART 1
SHORT TITLE, CONSTRUCTION, APPLICATION AND SUBJECT MATTER OF THE ACT

§ 1–101. Short Title

This Act shall be known and may be cited as Uniform Commercial Code.

* * *

§ 1–102. Purposes; Rules of Construction; Variation by Agreement

(1) This Act shall be liberally construed and applied to promote its underlying purposes and policies.

(2) Underlying purposes and policies of this Act are

(a) to simplify, clarify and modernize the law governing commercial transactions;

(b) to permit the continued expansion of commercial practices through custom, usage and agreement of the parties;

(c) to make uniform the law among the various jurisdictions.

(3) The effect of provisions of this Act may be varied by agreement, except as otherwise provided in this Act and except that the obligations of good faith, diligence, reasonableness and care prescribed by this Act may not be disclaimed by agreement but the parties may by agreement determine the standards by which the performance of such obligations is to be measured if such standards are not manifestly unreasonable.

(4) The presence in certain provisions of this Act of the words "unless otherwise agreed" or words of similar import does not imply that the effect of other provisions may not be varied by agreement under subsection (3).

(5) In this Act unless the context otherwise requires

(a) words in the singular number include the plural, and in the plural include the singular;

(b) words of the masculine gender include the feminine and the neuter, and when the sense so indicates words of the neuter gender may refer to any gender.

* * *

§ 1–103. Supplementary General Principles of Law Applicable

Unless displaced by the particular provisions of this Act, the principles of law and equity, including the law merchant and the law relative to capacity to contract, principal and agent, estoppel, fraud, misrepresentation, duress, coercion, mistake, bankruptcy, or other validating or invalidating cause shall supplement its provisions.

* * *

§ 1–104. Construction Against Implicit Repeal

This Act being a general act intended as a unified coverage of its subject matter, no part of it shall be deemed to be impliedly repealed by subsequent legislation if such construction can reasonably be avoided.

* * *

§ 1–105. Territorial Application of the Act; Parties' Power to Choose Applicable Law

(1) Except as provided hereafter in this section, when a transaction bears a reasonable relation to this state and also to another state or nation

the parties may agree that the law either of this state or of such other state or nation shall govern their rights and duties. Failing such agreement this Act applies to transactions bearing an appropriate relation to this state.

* * *

Official Comment

Prior Uniform Statutory Provision: None.

Purposes:

1. Subsection (1) states affirmatively the right of the parties to a multi-state transaction or a transaction involving foreign trade to choose their own law. That right is subject to the firm rules stated in the five sections listed in subsection (2), and is limited to jurisdictions to which the transaction bears a "reasonable relation." In general, the test of "reasonable relation" is similar to that laid down by the Supreme Court in Seeman v. Philadelphia Warehouse Co., 274 U.S. 403, 47 S.Ct. 626, 71 L.Ed. 1123 (1927). Ordinarily the law chosen must be that of a jurisdiction where a significant enough portion of the making or performance of the contract is to occur or occurs. But an agreement as to choice of law may sometimes take effect as a shorthand expression of the intent of the parties as to matters governed by their agreement, even though the transaction has no significant contact with the jurisdiction chosen.

2. Where there is no agreement as to the governing law, the Act is applicable to any transaction having an "appropriate" relation to any state which enacts it. Of course, the Act applies to any transaction which takes place in its entirety in a state which has enacted the Act. But the mere fact that suit is brought in a state does not make it appropriate to apply the substantive law of that state. Cases where a relation to the enacting state is not "appropriate" include, for example, those where the parties have clearly contracted on the basis of some other law, as where the law of the place of contracting and the law of the place of contemplated performance are the same and are contrary to the law under the Code.

3. Where a transaction has significant contacts with a state which has enacted the Act and also with other jurisdictions, the question what relation is "appropriate" is left to judicial decision. In deciding that question, the court is not strictly bound by precedents established in other contexts. Thus a conflict-of-laws decision refusing to apply a purely local statute or rule of law to a particular multi-state transaction may not be valid precedent for refusal to apply the Code in an analogous situation. Application of the Code in such circumstances may be justified by its comprehensiveness, by the policy of uniformity, and by the fact that it is in large part a reformulation and restatement of the law merchant and of the understanding of a business community which transcends state and even national boundaries. Compare Global Commerce Corp. v. Clark–Babbitt Industries, Inc., 239 F.2d 716, 719 (2d Cir.1956). In particular, where a transaction is governed in large part by the Code, application of another law to some detail of performance because of an accident of geography may violate the commercial understanding of the parties.

4. The Act does not attempt to prescribe choice-of-law rules for states which do not enact it, but this section does not prevent application of the Act in a court of such a state. Common-law choice of law often rests on policies of giving effect to agreements and of uniformity of result regardless of where suit is brought. To the extent that such

policies prevail, the relevant considerations are similar in such a court to those outlined above.

* * *

§ 1–106. Remedies to Be Liberally Administered

(1) The remedies provided by this Act shall be liberally administered to the end that the aggrieved party may be put in as good a position as if the other party had fully performed but neither consequential or special nor penal damages may be had except as specifically provided in this Act or by other rule of law.

(2) Any right or obligation declared by this Act is enforceable by action unless the provision declaring it specifies a different and limited effect.

Official Comment

Prior Uniform Statutory Provision: Subsection (1)—none; Subsection (2)—Section 72, Uniform Sales Act.

Changes: Reworded.

Purposes of Changes and New Matter: Subsection (1) is intended to effect three things:

1. First, to negate the unduly narrow or technical interpretation of some remedial provisions of prior legislation by providing that the remedies in this Act are to be liberally administered to the end stated in the section. Second, to make it clear that compensatory damages are limited to compensation. They do not include consequential or special damages, or penal damages; and the Act elsewhere makes it clear that damages must be minimized. Cf. Sections 1–203, 2–706(1), and 2–712(2). The third purpose of subsection (1) is to reject any doctrine that damages must be calcula-ble with mathematical accuracy. Compensatory damages are often at best approximate: they have to be proved with whatever definiteness and accuracy the facts permit, but no more. Cf. Section 2–204(3).

2. Under subsection (2) any right or obligation described in this Act is enforceable by court action, even though no remedy may be expressly provided, unless a particular provision specifies a different and limited effect. Whether specific performance or other equitable relief is available is determined not by this section but by specific provisions and by supplementary principles. Cf. Sections 1–103, 2–716.

3. "Consequential" or "special" damages and "penal" damages are not defined in terms in the Code, but are used in the sense given them by the leading cases on the subject.

§ 1–107. Waiver or Renunciation of Claim or Right After Breach

Any claim or right arising out of an alleged breach can be discharged in whole or in part without consideration by a written waiver or renunciation signed and delivered by the aggrieved party.

Official Comment

Prior Uniform Statutory Provision:
Compare Section 1, Uniform Written Obligations Act; Sections 119(3), 120(2) and 122, Uniform Negotiable Instruments Law.

Purposes:

This section makes consideration unnecessary to the effective renunciation or waiver of rights or claims arising out of an alleged breach of a commercial contract where such renunciation is in writing and signed and delivered by the aggrieved party. Its provisions, however, must be read in conjunction with the section imposing an obligation of good faith. (Section 1–203). There may, of course, also be an oral renunciation or waiver sustained by consideration but subject to Statute of Frauds provisions and to the section of Article 2 on Sales dealing with the modification of signed writings (Section 2–209). As is made express in the latter section this Act fully recognizes the effectiveness of waiver and estoppel.

* * *

PART 2
GENERAL DEFINITIONS AND PRINCIPLES OF INTERPRETATION

§ 1–201. General Definitions

Subject to additional definitions contained in the subsequent Articles of this Act which are applicable to specific Articles or Parts thereof, and unless the context otherwise requires, in this Act:

(1) "Action" in the sense of a judicial proceeding includes recoupment, counterclaim, set-off, suit in equity and any other proceedings in which rights are determined.

(2) "Aggrieved party" means a party entitled to resort to a remedy.

(3) "Agreement" means the bargain of the parties in fact as found in their language or by implication from other circumstances including course of dealing or usage of trade or course of performance as provided in this Act (Sections 1–205 and 2–208). Whether an agreement has legal consequences is determined by the provisions of this Act, if applicable; otherwise by the law of contracts (Section 1–103). (Compare "Contract".)

* * *

(10) "Conspicuous": A term or clause is conspicuous when it is so written that a reasonable person against whom it is to operate ought to have noticed it. A printed heading in capitals (as: NON-NEGOTIABLE BILL OF LADING) is conspicuous. Language in the body of a form is "conspicuous" if it is in larger or other contrasting type or color. But in a telegram any stated term is "conspicuous". Whether a term or clause is "conspicuous" or not is for decision by the court.

(11) "Contract" means the total legal obligation which results from the parties' agreement as affected by this Act and any other applicable rules of law. (Compare "Agreement".)

* * *

(13) "Defendant" includes a person in the position of defendant in a cross-action or counterclaim.

* * *

(16) "Fault" means wrongful act, omission or breach.

* * *

(19) "Good faith" means honesty in fact in the conduct or transaction concerned.

* * *

(25) A person has "notice" of a fact when

(a) he has actual knowledge of it; or

(b) he has received a notice or notification of it; or

(c) from all the facts and circumstances known to him at the time in question he has reason to know that it exists.

A person "knows" or has "knowledge" of a fact when he has actual knowledge of it. "Discover" or "learn" or a word or phrase of similar import refers to knowledge rather than to reason to know. The time and circumstances under which a notice or notification may cease to be effective are not determined by this Act.

(26) A person "notifies" or "gives" a notice or notification to another by taking such steps as may be reasonably required to inform the other in ordinary course whether or not such other actually comes to know of it. A person "receives" a notice or notification when

(a) it comes to his attention; or

(b) it is duly delivered at the place of business through which the contract was made or at any other place held out by him as the place for receipt of such communications.

(27) Notice, knowledge or a notice or notification received by an organization is effective for a particular transaction from the time when it is brought to the attention of the individual conducting that transaction, and in any event from the time when it would have been brought to his attention if the organization had exercised due diligence. An organization exercises due diligence if it maintains reasonable routines for communicating significant information to the person conducting the transaction and there is reasonable compliance with the routines. Due diligence does not require an individual acting for the organization to communicate information unless such communication is part of his regular duties or unless he has reason to know of the transaction and that the transaction would be materially affected by the information.

(28) "Organization" includes a corporation, government or governmental subdivision or agency, business trust, estate, trust, partnership or

association, two or more persons having a joint or common interest, or any other legal or commercial entity.

(29) "Party", as distinct from "third party", means a person who has engaged in a transaction or made an agreement within this Act.

(30) "Person" includes an individual or an organization (See Section 1–102).

(31) "Presumption" or "presumed" means that the trier of fact must find the existence of the fact presumed unless and until evidence is introduced which would support a finding of its non-existence.

(32) "Purchase" includes taking by sale, discount, negotiation, mortgage, pledge, lien, issue or re-issue, gift or any other voluntary transaction creating an interest in property.

(33) "Purchaser" means a person who takes by purchase.

(34) "Remedy" means any remedial right to which an aggrieved party is entitled with or without resort to a tribunal.

(35) "Representative" includes an agent, an officer of a corporation or association, and a trustee, executor or administrator of an estate, or any other person empowered to act for another.

(36) "Rights" includes remedies.

* * *

Official Comment

* * *

10. "Conspicuous". New. This is intended to indicate some of the methods of making a term attention-calling. But the test is whether attention can reasonably be expected to be called to it.

* * *

19. "Good faith". See Section 76(2), Uniform Sales Act; Section 58(2), Uniform Warehouse Receipts Act; Section 53(2), Uniform Bills of Lading Act; Section 22(2), Uniform Stock Transfer Act. "Good faith", whenever it is used in the Code, means at least what is here stated. In certain Articles, by specific provision, additional requirements are made applicable. See, e.g., Secs. 2–103(1)(b), 7–404. To illustrate, in the Article on Sales, Section 2–103, good faith is expressly defined as including in the case of a merchant observance of reasonable commercial standards of fair dealing in the trade, so that throughout that Article wherever a merchant appears in the case an inquiry into his observance of such standards is necessary to determine his good faith.

* * *

25. "Notice". New. Compare N.I.L. Sec. 56. Under the definition a person has notice when he has received a notification of the fact in question. But by the last sentence the act leaves open the time and circumstances under which notice or notification may cease to be effective. Therefore such cases as Graham v. White–Phillips Co., 296 U.S. 27, 56 S.Ct. 21, 80 L.Ed. 20 (1935), are not overruled.

26. "Notifies". New. This is the word used when the essential fact is the proper dispatch of the notice, not its receipt. Compare "Send". When the essential fact is the other party's receipt of

the notice, that is stated. The second sentence states when a notification is received.

27. New. This makes clear that reason to know, knowledge, or a notification, although "received" for instance by a clerk in Department A of an organization, is effective for a transaction conducted in Department B only from the time when it was or should have been communicated to the individual conducting that transaction.

28. "Organization". This is the definition of every type of entity or association, excluding an individual, acting as such. Definitions of "person" were included in Section 191, Uniform Negotiable Instruments Law; Section 76, Uniform Sales Act; Section 58, Uniform Warehouse Receipts Act; Section 53, Uniform Bills of Lading Act; Section 22, Uniform Stock Transfer Act; Section 1, Uniform Trust Receipts Act. The definition of "organization" given here includes a number of entities or associations not specifically mentioned in prior definition of "person", namely, government, governmental subdivision or agency, business trust, trust and estate.

* * *

§ 1–203. Obligation of Good Faith

Every contract or duty within this Act imposes an obligation of good faith in its performance or enforcement.

Official Comment

Prior Uniform Statutory Provision:
None.

Purposes:

This section sets forth a basic principle running throughout this Act. The principle involved is that in commercial transactions good faith is required in the performance and enforcement of all agreements or duties. * * *

It is to be noted that under the Sales Article definition of good faith (Section 2–103), contracts made by a merchant have incorporated in them the explicit standard not only of honesty in fact (Section 1–201), but also of observance by the merchant of reasonable commercial standards of fair dealing in the trade.

* * *

§ 1–204. Time; Reasonable Time; "Seasonably"

(1) Whenever this Act requires any action to be taken within a reasonable time, any time which is not manifestly unreasonable may be fixed by agreement.

(2) What is a reasonable time for taking any action depends on the nature, purpose and circumstances of such action.

(3) An action is taken "seasonably" when it is taken at or within the time agreed or if no time is agreed at or within a reasonable time.

Official Comment

Prior Uniform Statutory Provision:
None.

Purposes:

1. Subsection (1) recognizes that nothing is stronger evidence of a reasonable time than the fixing of such time by a fair agreement between the parties.

However, provision is made for disregarding a clause which whether by inadvertence or overreaching fixes a time so unreasonable that it amounts to eliminating all remedy under the contract. The parties are not required to fix the most reasonable time but may fix any time which is not obviously unfair as judged by the time of contracting.

2. Under the section, the agreement which fixes the time need not be part of the main agreement, but may occur separately. Notice also that under the definition of "agreement" (Section 1–201) the circumstances of the transaction, including course of dealing or usages of trade or course of performance may be material. On the question what is a reasonable time these matters will often be important.

* * *

§ 1–205. Course of Dealing and Usage of Trade

(1) A course of dealing is a sequence of previous conduct between the parties to a particular transaction which is fairly to be regarded as establishing a common basis of understanding for interpreting their expressions and other conduct.

(2) A usage of trade is any practice or method of dealing having such regularity of observance in a place, vocation or trade as to justify an expectation that it will be observed with respect to the transaction in question. The existence and scope of such a usage are to be proved as facts. If it is established that such a usage is embodied in a written trade code or similar writing the interpretation of the writing is for the court.

(3) A course of dealing between parties and any usage of trade in the vocation or trade in which they are engaged or of which they are or should be aware give particular meaning to and supplement or qualify terms of an agreement.

(4) The express terms of an agreement and an applicable course of dealing or usage of trade shall be construed wherever reasonable as consistent with each other; but when such construction is unreasonable express terms control both course of dealing and usage of trade and course of dealing controls usage of trade.

(5) An applicable usage of trade in the place where any part of performance is to occur shall be used in interpreting the agreement as to that part of the performance.

(6) Evidence of a relevant usage of trade offered by one party is not admissible unless and until he has given the other party such notice as the court finds sufficient to prevent unfair surprise to the latter.

Official Comment

Prior Uniform Statutory Provision: No such general provision but see Sections 9(1), 15(5), 18(2), and 71, Uniform Sales Act.

Purposes: This section makes it clear that:

1. This Act rejects both the "lay-dictionary" and the "conveyancer's" reading of a commercial agreement. Instead the meaning of the agreement of

the parties is to be determined by the language used by them and by their action, read and interpreted in the light of commercial practices and other surrounding circumstances. The measure and background for interpretation are set by the commercial context, which may explain and supplement even the language of a formal or final writing.

2. Course of dealing under subsection (1) is restricted, literally, to a sequence of conduct between the parties previous to the agreement. However, the provisions of the Act on course of performance make it clear that a sequence of conduct after or under the agreement may have equivalent meaning. (Section 2–208.)

3. "Course of dealing" may enter the agreement either by explicit provisions of the agreement or by tacit recognition.

4. This Act deals with "usage of trade" as a factor in reaching the commercial meaning of the agreement which the parties have made. The language used is to be interpreted as meaning what it may fairly be expected to mean to parties involved in the particular commercial transaction in a given locality or in a given vocation or trade. By adopting in this context the term "usage of trade" this Act expresses its intent to reject those cases which see evidence of "custom" as representing an effort to displace or negate "established rules of law." A distinction is to be drawn between mandatory rules of law such as the Statute of Frauds provisions of Article 2 on Sales whose very office is to control and restrict the actions of the parties, and which cannot be abrogated by agreement, or by a usage of trade, and those rules of law (such as those in Part 3 of Article 2 on Sales) which fill in points which the parties have not considered and in fact agreed upon. The latter rules hold "unless otherwise agreed" but yield to the contrary agreement of the parties. Part of the agreement of the parties to which such rules yield is to be sought for in the usages of trade which furnish the background and give particular meaning to the language used, and are the framework of common understanding controlling any general rules of law which hold only when there is no such understanding.

5. A usage of trade under subsection (2) must have the "regularity of observance" specified. The ancient English tests for "custom" are abandoned in this connection. Therefore, it is not required that a usage of trade be "ancient or immemorial," "universal" or the like. Under the requirement of subsection (2) full recognition is thus available for new usages and for usages currently observed by the great majority of decent dealers, even though dissidents ready to cut corners do not agree. There is room also for proper recognition of usage agreed upon by merchants in trade codes.

6. The policy of this Act controlling explicit unconscionable contracts and clauses (Sections 1–203, 2–302) applies to implicit clauses which rest on usage of trade and carries forward the policy underlying the ancient requirement that a custom or usage must be "reasonable." However, the emphasis is shifted. The very fact of commercial acceptance makes out a prima facie case that the usage is reasonable, and the burden is no longer on the usage to establish itself as being reasonable. But the anciently established policing of usage by the courts is continued to the extent necessary to cope with the situation arising if an unconscionable or dishonest practice should become standard.

7. Subsection (3), giving the prescribed effect to usages of which the parties "are or should be aware", reinforces the provision of subsection (2) requiring not universality but only the described "regularity of observance" of the practice or method. This subsection

also reinforces the point of subsection (2) that such usages may be either general to trade or particular to a special branch of trade.

8. Although the terms in which this Act defines "agreement" include the elements of course of dealing and usage of trade, the fact that express reference is made in some sections to those elements is not to be construed as carrying a contrary intent or implication elsewhere. Compare Section 1–102(4).

9. In cases of a well established line of usage varying from the general rules of this Act where the precise amount of the variation has not been worked out into a single standard, the party relying on the usage is entitled, in any event, to the minimum variation demonstrated. The whole is not to be disregarded because no particular line of detail has been established. In case a dominant pattern has been fairly evidenced, the party relying on the usage is entitled under this section to go to the trier of fact on the question of whether such dominant pattern has been incorporated into the agreement.

10. Subsection (6) is intended to insure that this Act's liberal recognition of the needs of commerce in regard to usage of trade shall not be made into an instrument of abuse.

* * *

ARTICLE 2

SALES

PART 1
SHORT TITLE, GENERAL CONSTRUCTION AND SUBJECT MATTER

§ 2–101. Short Title

This Article shall be known and may be cited as Uniform Commercial Code—Sales.

Official Comment

This Article is a complete revision and modernization of the Uniform Sales Act which was promulgated by the National Conference of Commissioners on Uniform State Laws in 1906 and has been adopted in 34 states and Alaska, the District of Columbia and Hawaii.

The coverage of the present Article is much more extensive than that of the old Sales Act and extends to the various bodies of case law which have been developed both outside of and under the latter.

The arrangement of the present Article is in terms of contract for sale and the various steps of its performance. The legal consequences are stated as following directly from the contract and action taken under it without resorting to the idea of when property or title passed or was to pass as being the determining factor. The purpose is to avoid making practical issues between practical men turn upon the location of an intangible something, the passing of which no man can prove by evidence and to substitute for such abstractions proof of words and actions of a tangible character.

* * *

§ 2–103. Definitions and Index of Definitions

(1) In this Article unless the context otherwise requires

(a) "Buyer" means a person who buys or contracts to buy goods.

(b) "Good faith" in the case of a merchant means honesty in fact and the observance of reasonable commercial standards of fair dealing in the trade.

(c) "Receipt" of goods means taking physical possession of them.

(d) "Seller" means a person who sells or contracts to sell goods.

* * *

§ 2–104. Definitions: "Merchant"; "Between Merchants"; "Financing Agency"

(1) "Merchant" means a person who deals in goods of the kind or otherwise by his occupation holds himself out as having knowledge or skill peculiar to the practices or goods involved in the transaction or to whom such knowledge or skill may be attributed by his employment of an agent or broker or other intermediary who by his occupation holds himself out as having such knowledge or skill.

* * *

(3) "Between merchants" means in any transaction with respect to which both parties are chargeable with the knowledge or skill of merchants.

Official Comment

Prior Uniform Statutory Provision: None. But see Sections 15(2), (5), 16(c), 45(2) and 71, Uniform Sales Act, and Sections 35 and 37, Uniform Bills of Lading Act for examples of the policy expressly provided for in this Article.

Purposes:

1. This Article assumes that transactions between professionals in a given field require special and clear rules which may not apply to a casual or inexperienced seller or buyer. It thus adopts a policy of expressly stating rules applicable "between merchants" and "as against a merchant", wherever they are needed instead of making them depend upon the circumstances of each case as in the statutes cited above. This section lays the foundation of this policy by defining those who are to be regarded as professionals or "merchants" and by stating when a transaction is deemed to be "between merchants".

2. The term "merchant" as defined here roots in the "law merchant" concept of a professional in business. The professional status under the definition may be based upon specialized knowledge as to the goods, specialized knowledge as to business practices, or specialized knowledge as to both and which kind of specialized knowledge may be sufficient to establish the merchant status is indicated by the nature of the provisions.

The special provisions as to merchants appear only in this Article and they are of three kinds. Sections 2–201(2), 2–205, 2–207 and 2–209 dealing with the statute of frauds, firm offers, confirmatory memoranda and modification rest on normal business practices which are or ought to be typical of and familiar to any person in business. For purposes of these sections almost every person in business would, therefore, be deemed to be a "merchant" under the language "who ... by his occupation holds himself out as having knowledge or skill peculiar to the practices ... involved in the transaction ..." since the practices involved in the transaction are non-specialized business practices such as answering mail. In this type of provision, banks or even universities, for example, well may be "merchants." But even these sections only apply to a merchant in his mercantile capacity; a lawyer or bank president buying fishing tackle for his own use is not a merchant.

On the other hand, in Section 2–314 on the warranty of merchantability, such warranty is implied only "if the seller is a merchant with respect to goods of that kind." Obviously this qualification restricts the implied warranty to a much smaller group than everyone who is engaged in business and requires a professional status as to particular kinds of goods. The exception in Section 2–402(2) for retention of possession by a merchant-seller falls in the same class;

as does Section 2–403(2) on entrusting of possession to a merchant "who deals in goods of that kind".

A third group of sections includes 2–103(1)(b), which provides that in the case of a merchant "good faith" includes observance of reasonable commercial standards of fair dealing in the trade; 2–327(1)(c), 2–603 and 2–605, dealing with responsibilities of merchant buyers to follow seller's instructions, etc.; 2–509 on risk of loss, and 2–609 on adequate assurance of performance. This group of sections applies to persons who are merchants under either the "practices" or the "goods" aspect of the definition of merchant.

3. The "or to whom such knowledge or skill may be attributed by his employment of an agent or broker ..." clause of the definition of merchant means that even persons such as universities, for example, can come within the definition of merchant if they have regular purchasing departments or business personnel who are familiar with business practices and who are equipped to take any action required.

* * *

§ 2–105. Definitions: Transferability; "Goods"; "Future" Goods; "Lot"; "Commercial Unit"

(1) "Goods" means all things (including specially manufactured goods) which are movable at the time of identification to the contract for sale other than the money in which the price is to be paid, investment securities (Article 8) and things in action. "Goods" also includes the unborn young of animals and growing crops and other identified things attached to realty as described in the section on goods to be severed from realty (Section 2–107).

distinguishes goods from real estate.

* * *

Official Comment

Prior Uniform Statutory Provision: Subsections (1), (2), (3) and (4)—Sections 5, 6 and 76, Uniform Sales Act; Subsections (5) and (6)—none.

Changes: Rewritten.

Purposes of Changes and New Matter:

1. Subsection (1) on "goods": The phraseology of the prior uniform statutory provision has been changed so that:

The definition of goods is based on the concept of movability and the term "chattels personal" is not used. It is not intended to deal with things which are not fairly identifiable as movables before the contract is performed.

Growing crops are included within the definition of goods since they are frequently intended for sale. The concept of "industrial" growing crops has been abandoned, for under modern practices fruit, perennial hay, nursery stock and the like must be brought within the scope of this Article. The young of animals are also included expressly in this definition since they, too, are frequently intended for sale and may be contracted for before birth. The period of gestation of domestic animals is such that the provisions of the section on identification can apply as in the case of crops to be planted. The reason of this definition also leads to the inclusion of a wool crop or the like as "goods" subject to identification under this Article.

The exclusion of "money in which the price is to be paid" from the definition of goods does not mean that foreign currency which is included in the definition of money may not be the subject matter of a sales transaction. Goods is intended to cover the sale of money when money is being treated as a commodity but not to include it when money is the medium of payment.

As to contracts to sell timber, minerals, or structures to be removed from the land Section 2–107(1)(Goods to be severed from Realty: recording) controls.

The use of the word "fixtures" is avoided in view of the diversity of definitions of that term. This Article in including within its scope "things attached to realty" adds the further test that they must be capable of severance without material harm thereto. As between the parties any identified things which fall within that definition become "goods" upon the making of the contract for sale.

* * *

§ 2–106. Definitions: "Contract"; "Agreement"; "Contract for Sale"; "Sale"; "Present Sale"; "Conforming" to Contract; "Termination"; "Cancellation"

(1) In this Article unless the context otherwise requires "contract" and "agreement" are limited to those relating to the present or future sale of goods. "Contract for sale" includes both a present sale of goods and a contract to sell goods at a future time. A "sale" consists in the passing of title from the seller to the buyer for a price (Section 2–401). A "present sale" means a sale which is accomplished by the making of the contract.

(2) Goods or conduct including any part of a performance are "conforming" or conform to the contract when they are in accordance with the obligations under the contract.

(3) "Termination" occurs when either party pursuant to a power created by agreement or law puts an end to the contract otherwise than for its breach. On "termination" all obligations which are still executory on both sides are discharged but any right based on prior breach or performance survives.

(4) "Cancellation" occurs when either party puts an end to the contract for breach by the other and its effect is the same as that of

"termination" except that the cancelling party also retains any remedy for breach of the whole contract or any unperformed balance.

Official Comment

Prior Uniform Statutory Provision: Subsection (1)—Section 1(1) and (2), Uniform Sales Act; Subsection (2)—none, but subsection generally continues policy of Sections 11, 44 and 69, Uniform Sales Act; Subsections (3) and (4)—none.

Changes: Completely rewritten.

Purposes of Changes and New Matter:

1. Subsection (1): "Contract for sale" is used as a general concept throughout this Article, but the rights of the parties do not vary according to whether the transaction is a present sale or a contract to sell unless the Article expressly so provides.

2. Subsection (2): It is in general intended to continue the policy of requiring exact performance by the seller of his obligations as a condition to his right to require acceptance. However, the seller is in part safeguarded against surprise as a result of sudden technicality on the buyer's part by the provisions of Section 2–508 on seller's cure of improper tender or delivery. Moreover usage of trade frequently permits commercial leeways in performance and the language of the agreement itself must be read in the light of such custom or usage and also, prior course of dealing, and in a long term contract, the course of performance.

3. Subsections (3) and (4): These subsections are intended to make clear the distinction carried forward throughout this Article between termination and cancellation.

* * *

PART 2
FORM, FORMATION AND READJUSTMENT OF CONTRACT

§ 2–201.   Formal Requirements; Statute of Frauds

(1) Except as otherwise provided in this section a contract for the sale of goods for the price of $500 or more is not enforceable by way of action or defense unless there is some writing sufficient to indicate that a contract for sale has been made between the parties and signed by the party against whom enforcement is sought or by his authorized agent or broker. A writing is not insufficient because it omits or incorrectly states a term agreed upon but the contract is not enforceable under this paragraph beyond the quantity of goods shown in such writing.

(2) Between merchants if within a reasonable time a writing in confirmation of the contract and sufficient against the sender is received and the party receiving it has reason to know its contents, it satisfies the requirements of subsection (1) against such party unless written notice of objection to its contents is given within 10 days after it is received.

(3) A contract which does not satisfy the requirements of subsection (1) but which is valid in other respects is enforceable

(a) if the goods are to be specially manufactured for the buyer and are not suitable for sale to others in the ordinary course of the seller's business and the seller, before notice of repudiation is received and under circumstances which reasonably indicate that the goods are for the buyer, has made either a substantial beginning of their manufacture or commitments for their procurement; or

(b) if the party against whom enforcement is sought admits in his pleading, testimony or otherwise in court that a contract for sale was made, but the contract is not enforceable under this provision beyond the quantity of goods admitted; or

(c) with respect to goods for which payment has been made and accepted or which have been received and accepted (Sec. 2–606).

Official Comment

Prior Uniform Statutory Provision: Section 4, Uniform Sales Act (which was based on Section 17 of the Statute of 29 Charles II).

Changes: Completely rephrased; restricted to sale of goods. See also Sections 1–206, 8–319 and 9–203.

Purposes of Changes: The changed phraseology of this section is intended to make it clear that:

1. The required writing need not contain all the material terms of the contract and such material terms as are stated need not be precisely stated. All that is required is that the writing afford a basis for believing that the offered oral evidence rests on a real transaction. It may be written in lead pencil on a scratch pad. It need not indicate which party is the buyer and which the seller. The only term which must appear is the quantity term which need not be accurately stated but recovery is limited to the amount stated. The price, time and place of payment or delivery, the general quality of the goods, or any particular warranties may all be omitted.

Special emphasis must be placed on the permissibility of omitting the price term in view of the insistence of some courts on the express inclusion of this term even where the parties have contracted on the basis of a published price list. In many valid contracts for sale the parties do not mention the price in express terms, the buyer being bound to pay and the seller to accept a reasonable price which the trier of the fact may well be trusted to determine. Again, frequently the price is not mentioned since the parties have based their agreement on a price list or catalogue known to both of them and this list serves as an efficient safeguard against perjury. Finally, "market" prices and valuations that are current in the vicinity constitute a similar check. Thus if the price is not stated in the memorandum it can normally be supplied without danger of fraud. Of course if the "price" consists of goods rather than money the quantity of goods must be stated.

Only three definite and invariable requirements as to the memorandum are made by this subsection. First, it must evidence a contract for the sale of goods; second, it must be "signed", a word which includes any authentication which identifies the party to be charged; and third, it must specify a quantity.

2. "Partial performance" as a substitute for the required memorandum can validate the contract only for the goods which have been accepted or for which payment has been made and accepted.

Receipt and acceptance either of goods or of the price constitutes an unambiguous overt admission by both parties that a contract actually exists. If the court can make a just apportionment, therefore, the agreed price of any goods actually delivered can be recovered without a writing or, if the price has been paid, the seller can be forced to deliver an apportionable part of the goods. The overt actions of the parties make admissible evidence of the other terms of the contract necessary to a just apportionment. This is true even though the actions of the parties are not in themselves inconsistent with a different transaction such as a consignment for resale or a mere loan of money.

Part performance by the buyer requires the delivery of something by him that is accepted by the seller as such performance. Thus, part payment may be made by money or check, accepted by the seller. If the agreed price consists of goods or services, then they must also have been delivered and accepted.

3. Between merchants, failure to answer a written confirmation of a contract within ten days of receipt is tantamount to a writing under subsection (2) and is sufficient against both parties under subsection (1). The only effect, however, is to take away from the party who fails to answer the defense of the Statute of Frauds; the burden of persuading the trier of fact that a contract was in fact made orally prior to the written confirmation is unaffected. Compare the effect of a failure to reply under Section 2–207.

4. Failure to satisfy the requirements of this section does not render the contract void for all purposes, but merely prevents it from being judicially enforced in favor of a party to the contract. For example, a buyer who takes possession of goods as provided in an oral contract which the seller has not meanwhile repudiated, is not a trespasser. Nor would the Statute of Frauds provisions of this section be a defense to a third person who wrongfully induces a party to refuse to perform an oral contract, even though the injured party cannot maintain an action for damages against the party so refusing to perform.

5. The requirement of "signing" is discussed in the comment to Section 1–201.

6. It is not necessary that the writing be delivered to anybody. It need not be signed or authenticated by both parties but it is, of course, not sufficient against one who has not signed it. Prior to a dispute no one can determine which party's signing of the memorandum may be necessary but from the time of contracting each party should be aware that to him it is signing by the other which is important.

7. If the making of a contract is admitted in court, either in a written pleading, by stipulation or by oral statement before the court, no additional writing is necessary for protection against fraud. Under this section it is no longer possible to admit the contract in court and still treat the Statute as a defense. However, the contract is not thus conclusively established. The admission so made by a party is itself evidential against him of the truth of the facts so admitted and of nothing more; as against the other party, it is not evidential at all.

* * *

§ 2–202. Final Written Expression: Parol or Extrinsic Evidence

Terms with respect to which the confirmatory memoranda of the parties agree or which are otherwise set forth in a writing intended by the parties as a final expression of their agreement with respect to such terms as are included therein may not be contradicted by evidence of any prior agreement or of a contemporaneous oral agreement but may be explained or supplemented:

(a) by course of dealing or usage of trade (Section 1–205) or by course of performance (Section 2–208); and

(b) by evidence of consistent additional terms unless the court finds the writing to have been intended also as a complete and exclusive statement of the terms of the agreement.

Official Comment

Prior Uniform Statutory Provision: None.

Purposes:

1. This section definitely rejects:

(a) Any assumption that because a writing has been worked out which is final on some matters, it is to be taken as including all the matters agreed upon;

(b) The premise that the language used has the meaning attributable to such language by rules of construction existing in the law rather than the meaning which arises out of the commercial context in which it was used; and

(c) The requirement that a condition precedent to the admissibility of the type of evidence specified in paragraph (a) is an original determination by the court that the language used is ambiguous.

2. Paragraph (a) makes admissible evidence of course of dealing, usage of trade and course of performance to explain or supplement the terms of any writing stating the agreement of the parties in order that the true understanding of the parties as to the agreement may be reached. Such writings are to be read on the assumption that the course of prior dealings between the parties and the usages of trade were taken for granted when the document was phrased. Unless carefully negated they have become an element of the meaning of the words used. Similarly, the course of actual performance by the parties is considered the best indication of what they intended the writing to mean.

3. Under paragraph (b) consistent additional terms, not reduced to writing, may be proved unless the court finds that the writing was intended by both parties as a complete and exclusive statement of all the terms. If the additional terms are such that, if agreed upon, they would certainly have been included in the document in the view of the court, then evidence of their alleged making must be kept from the trier of fact.

* * *

§ 2–204. Formation in General

(1) A contract for sale of goods may be made in any manner sufficient to show agreement, including conduct by both parties which recognizes the existence of such a contract.

(2) An agreement sufficient to constitute a contract for sale may be found even though the moment of its making is undetermined.

(3) Even though one or more terms are left open a contract for sale does not fail for indefiniteness if the parties have intended to make a contract and there is a reasonably certain basis for giving an appropriate remedy.

* * *

§ 2–206. Offer and Acceptance in Formation of Contract

(1) Unless otherwise unambiguously indicated by the language or circumstances

　(a) an offer to make a contract shall be construed as inviting acceptance in any manner and by any medium reasonable in the circumstances;

　(b) an order or other offer to buy goods for prompt or current shipment shall be construed as inviting acceptance either by a prompt promise to ship or by the prompt or current shipment of conforming or non-conforming goods, but such a shipment of non-conforming goods does not constitute an acceptance if the seller seasonably notifies the buyer that the shipment is offered only as an accommodation to the buyer.

(2) Where the beginning of a requested performance is a reasonable mode of acceptance an offeror who is not notified of acceptance within a reasonable time may treat the offer as having lapsed before acceptance.

* * *

§ 2–207. Additional Terms in Acceptance or Confirmation

(1) A definite and seasonable expression of acceptance or a written confirmation which is sent within a reasonable time operates as an acceptance even though it states terms additional to or different from those offered or agreed upon, unless acceptance is expressly made conditional on assent to the additional or different terms.

(2) The additional terms are to be construed as proposals for addition to the contract. Between merchants such terms become part of the contract unless:

　(a) the offer expressly limits acceptance to the terms of the offer;

　(b) they materially alter it; or

　(c) notification of objection to them has already been given or is given within a reasonable time after notice of them is received.

(3) Conduct by both parties which recognizes the existence of a contract is sufficient to establish a contract for sale although the writings of the parties do not otherwise establish a contract. In such case the terms of the particular contract consist of those terms on which the writings of the parties agree, together with any supplementary terms incorporated under any other provisions of this Act.

* * *

§ 2–208. Course of Performance or Practical Construction

(1) Where the contract for sale involves repeated occasions for performance by either party with knowledge of the nature of the performance

and opportunity for objection to it by the other, any course of performance accepted or acquiesced in without objection shall be relevant to determine the meaning of the agreement.

(2) The express terms of the agreement and any such course of performance, as well as any course of dealing and usage of trade, shall be construed whenever reasonable as consistent with each other; but when such construction is unreasonable, express terms shall control course of performance and course of performance shall control both course of dealing and usage of trade (Section 1–205).

(3) Subject to the provisions of the next section on modification and waiver, such course of performance shall be relevant to show a waiver or modification of any term inconsistent with such course of performance.

Official Comment

Prior Uniform Statutory Provision: No such general provision but concept of this section recognized by terms such as "course of dealing", "the circumstances of the case," "the conduct of the parties," etc., in Uniform Sales Act.

Purposes:

1. The parties themselves know best what they have meant by their words of agreement and their action under that agreement is the best indication of what that meaning was. This section thus rounds out the set of factors which determines the meaning of the "agreement" and therefore also of the "unless otherwise agreed" qualification to various provisions of this Article.

2. Under this section a course of performance is always relevant to determine the meaning of the agreement. Express mention of course of performance elsewhere in this Article carries no contrary implication when there is a failure to refer to it in other sections.

3. Where it is difficult to determine whether a particular act merely sheds light on the meaning of the agreement or represents a waiver of a term of the agreement, the preference is in favor of "waiver" whenever such construction, plus the application of the provisions on the reinstatement of rights waived (see Section 2–209), is needed to preserve the flexible character of commercial contracts and to prevent surprise or other hardship.

4. A single occasion of conduct does not fall within the language of this section but other sections such as the ones on silence after acceptance and failure to specify particular defects can affect the parties' rights on a single occasion (see Sections 2–605 and 2–607).

* * *

§ 2–209. Modification, Rescission and Waiver

(1) An agreement modifying a contract within this Article needs no consideration to be binding.

(2) A signed agreement which excludes modification or rescission except by a signed writing cannot be otherwise modified or rescinded, but except as between merchants such a requirement on a form supplied by the merchant must be separately signed by the other party.

(3) The requirements of the statute of frauds section of this Article (Section 2–201) must be satisfied if the contract as modified is within its provisions.

(4) Although an attempt at modification or rescission does not satisfy the requirements of subsection (2) or (3) it can operate as a waiver.

(5) A party who has made a waiver affecting an executory portion of the contract may retract the waiver by reasonable notification received by the other party that strict performance will be required of any term waived, unless the retraction would be unjust in view of a material change of position in reliance on the waiver.

Official Comment

Prior Uniform Statutory Provision: Subsection (1)—Compare Section 1, Uniform Written Obligations Act; Subsections (2) to (5)—none.

Purposes of Changes and New Matter:

1. This section seeks to protect and make effective all necessary and desirable modifications of sales contracts without regard to the technicalities which at present hamper such adjustments.

2. Subsection (1) provides that an agreement modifying a sales contract needs no consideration to be binding.

However, modifications made thereunder must meet the test of good faith imposed by this Act. The effective use of bad faith to escape performance on the original contract terms is barred, and the extortion of a "modification" without legitimate commercial reason is ineffective as a violation of the duty of good faith. Nor can a mere technical consideration support a modification made in bad faith.

The test of "good faith" between merchants or as against merchants includes "observance of reasonable commercial standards of fair dealing in the trade" (Section 2–103), and may in some situations require an objectively demonstrable reason for seeking a modification. But such matters as a market shift which makes performance come to involve a loss may provide such a reason even though there is no such unforeseen difficulty as would make out a legal excuse from performance under Sections 2–615 and 2–616.

3. Subsections (2) and (3) are intended to protect against false allegations of oral modifications. "Modification or rescission" includes abandonment or other change by mutual consent, contrary to the decision in Green v. Doniger, 300 N.Y. 238, 90 N.E.2d 56 (1949); it does not include unilateral "termination" or "cancellation" as defined in Section 2–106.

The Statute of Frauds provisions of this Article are expressly applied to modifications by subsection (3). Under those provisions the "delivery and acceptance" test is limited to the goods which have been accepted, that is, to the past. "Modification" for the future cannot therefore be conjured up by oral testimony if the price involved is $500.00 or more since such modification must be shown at least by an authenticated memo. And since a memo is limited in its effect to the quantity of goods set forth in it there is safeguard against oral evidence.

Subsection (2) permits the parties in effect to make their own Statute of Frauds as regards any future modification of the contract by giving effect to a clause in a signed agreement which expressly requires any modification to be by signed writing. But note that if a consumer is to be held to such a clause on a form supplied by a merchant it must be separately signed.

4. Subsection (4) is intended, despite the provisions of subsections (2) and (3), to prevent contractual provi-

sions excluding modification except by a signed writing from limiting in other respects the legal effect of the parties' actual later conduct. The effect of such conduct as a waiver is further regulated in subsection (5).

* * *

PART 3
GENERAL OBLIGATION AND CONSTRUCTION OF CONTRACT

§ 2–301. General Obligations of Parties

The obligation of the seller is to transfer and deliver and that of the buyer is to accept and pay in accordance with the contract.

Official Comment

Prior Uniform Statutory Provision: Sections 11 and 41, Uniform Sales Act.

Changes: Rewritten.

Purposes of Changes: This section uses the term "obligation" in contrast to the term "duty" in order to provide for the "condition" aspects of delivery and payment insofar as they are not modified by other sections of this Article such as those on cure of tender. It thus replaces not only the general provisions of the Uniform Sales Act on the parties' duties, but also the general provisions of that Act on the effect of conditions. In order to determine what is "in accordance with the contract" under this Article usage of trade, course of dealing and performance, and the general background of circumstances must be given due consideration in conjunction with the lay meaning of the words used to define the scope of the conditions and duties.

* * *

§ 2–302. Unconscionable Contract or Clause

(1) If the court as a matter of law finds the contract or any clause of the contract to have been unconscionable at the time it was made the court may refuse to enforce the contract, or it may enforce the remainder of the contract without the unconscionable clause, or it may so limit the application of any unconscionable clause as to avoid any unconscionable result.

(2) When it is claimed or appears to the court that the contract or any clause thereof may be unconscionable the parties shall be afforded a reasonable opportunity to present evidence as to its commercial setting, purpose and effect to aid the court in making the determination.

Official Comment

Prior Uniform Statutory Provision: None.

Purposes:

1. This section is intended to make it possible for the courts to police explicitly against the contracts or clauses which they find to be unconscionable. In the past such policing has been accomplished by adverse construction of language, by manipulation of the rules of offer and acceptance or by determinations that the clause is contrary to public policy or to the dominant purpose of the contract. This section is intended to allow the court to pass directly on the unconscionability of the contract or particular clause therein and to make a

conclusion of law as to its unconscionability. The basic test is whether, in the light of the general commercial background and the commercial needs of the particular trade or case, the clauses involved are so one-sided as to be unconscionable under the circumstances existing at the time of the making of the contract. Subsection (2) makes it clear that it is proper for the court to hear evidence upon these questions. The principle is one of the prevention of oppression and unfair surprise (Cf. Campbell Soup Co. v. Wentz, 172 F.2d 80 (3d Cir.1948)) and not of disturbance of allocation of risks because of superior bargaining power. The underlying basis of this section is illustrated by the results in cases such as the following:

Kansas City Wholesale Grocery Co. v. Weber Packing Corporation, 93 Utah 414, 73 P.2d 1272 (1937), where a clause limiting time for complaints was held inapplicable to latent defects in a shipment of catsup which could be discovered only by microscopic analysis; Hardy v. General Motors Acceptance Corporation, 38 Ga.App. 463, 144 S.E. 327 (1928), holding that a disclaimer of warranty clause applied only to express warranties, thus letting in a fair implied warranty; Andrews Bros. v. Singer & Co. (1934 CA) 1 K.B. 17, holding that where a car with substantial mileage was delivered instead of a "new" car, a disclaimer of warranties, including those "implied," left unaffected an "express obligation" on the description, even though the Sale of Goods Act called such an implied warranty; New Prague Flouring Mill Co. v. Spears, 194 Iowa 417, 189 N.W. 815 (1922), holding that a clause permitting the seller, upon the buyer's failure to supply shipping instructions, to cancel, ship, or allow delivery date to be indefinitely postponed 30 days at a time by the inaction, does not indefinitely postpone the date of measuring damages for the buyer's breach, to the seller's advantage; and Kansas Flour

Mills Co. v. Dirks, 100 Kan. 376, 164 P. 273 (1917), where under a similar clause in a rising market the court permitted the buyer to measure his damages for non-delivery at the end of only one 30 day postponement; Green v. Arcos, Ltd. (1931 CA) 47 T.L.R. 336, where a blanket clause prohibiting rejection of shipments by the buyer was restricted to apply to shipments where discrepancies represented merely mercantile variations; Meyer v. Packard Cleveland Motor Co., 106 Ohio St. 328, 140 N.E. 118 (1922), in which the court held that a "waiver" of all agreements not specified did not preclude implied warranty of fitness of a rebuilt dump truck for ordinary use as a dump truck; F.C. Austin Co. v. J.H. Tillman Co., 104 Or. 541, 209 P. 131 (1922), where a clause limiting the buyer's remedy to return was held to be applicable only if the seller had delivered a machine needed for a construction job which reasonably met the contract description; Bekkevold v. Potts, 173 Minn. 87, 216 N.W. 790, 59 A.L.R. 1164 (1927), refusing to allow warranty of fitness for purpose imposed by law to be negated by clause excluding all warranties "made" by the seller; Robert A. Munroe & Co. v. Meyer (1930) 2 K.B. 312, holding that the warranty of description overrides a clause reading "with all faults and defects" where adulterated meat not up to the contract description was delivered.

2. Under this section the court, in its discretion, may refuse to enforce the contract as a whole if it is permeated by the unconscionability, or it may strike any single clause or group of clauses which are so tainted or which are contrary to the essential purpose of the agreement, or it may simply limit unconscionable clauses so as to avoid unconscionable results.

3. The present section is addressed to the court, and the decision is to be made by it. The commercial evidence referred to in subsection (2) is for the

court's consideration, not the jury's. Only the agreement which results from the court's action on these matters is to be submitted to the general triers of the facts.

* * *

§ 2–303. Allocation or Division of Risks

Where this Article allocates a risk or a burden as between the parties "unless otherwise agreed", the agreement may not only shift the allocation but may also divide the risk or burden.

Official Comment

Prior Uniform Statutory Provision: None.

Purposes:

1. This section is intended to make it clear that the parties may modify or allocate "unless otherwise agreed" risks or burdens imposed by this Article as they desire, always subject, of course, to the provisions on unconscionability.

Compare Section 1–102(4).

2. The risk or burden may be divided by the express terms of the agreement or by the attending circumstances, since under the definition of "agreement" in this Act the circumstances surrounding the transaction as well as the express language used by the parties enter into the meaning and substance of the agreement.

* * *

§ 2–313. Express Warranties by Affirmation, Promise, Description, Sample

(1) Express warranties by the seller are created as follows:

(a) Any affirmation of fact or promise made by the seller to the buyer which relates to the goods and becomes part of the basis of the bargain creates an express warranty that the goods shall conform to the affirmation or promise.

(b) Any description of the goods which is made part of the basis of the bargain creates an express warranty that the goods shall conform to the description.

(c) Any sample or model which is made part of the basis of the bargain creates an express warranty that the whole of the goods shall conform to the sample or model.

(2) It is not necessary to the creation of an express warranty that the seller use formal words such as "warrant" or "guarantee" or that he have a specific intention to make a warranty, but an affirmation merely of the value of the goods or a statement purporting to be merely the seller's opinion or commendation of the goods does not create a warranty.

Official Comment

Prior Uniform Statutory Provision: Sections 12, 14 and 16, Uniform Sales Act.

Changes: Rewritten.

Purposes of Changes: To consolidate and systematize basic principles with the result that:

1. "Express" warranties rest on "dickered" aspects of the individual bargain, and go so clearly to the essence of that bargain that words of disclaimer in a form are repugnant to the basic dickered terms. "Implied" warranties rest so clearly on a common factual situation or set of conditions that no particular language or action is necessary to evidence them and they will arise in such a situation unless unmistakably negated.

This section reverts to the older case law insofar as the warranties of description and sample are designated "express" rather than "implied".

2. Although this section is limited in its scope and direct purpose to warranties made by the seller to the buyer as part of a contract for sale, the warranty sections of this Article are not designed in any way to disturb those lines of case law growth which have recognized that warranties need not be confined either to sales contracts or to the direct parties to such a contract. They may arise in other appropriate circumstances such as in the case of bailments for hire, whether such bailment is itself the main contract or is merely a supplying of containers under a contract for the sale of their contents. The provisions of Section 2–318 on third party beneficiaries expressly recognize this case law development within one particular area. Beyond that, the matter is left to the case law with the intention that the policies of this Act may offer useful guidance in dealing with further cases as they arise.

3. The present section deals with affirmations of fact by the seller, descriptions of the goods or exhibitions of samples, exactly as any other part of a negotiation which ends in a contract is dealt with. No specific intention to make a warranty is necessary if any of these factors is made part of the basis of the bargain. In actual practice affirmations of fact made by the seller about the goods during a bargain are regarded as part of the description of those goods; hence no particular reliance on such statements need be shown in order to weave them into the fabric of the agreement. Rather, any fact which is to take such affirmations, once made, out of the agreement requires clear affirmative proof. The issue normally is one of fact.

4. In view of the principle that the whole purpose of the law of warranty is to determine what it is that the seller has in essence agreed to sell, the policy is adopted of those cases which refuse except in unusual circumstances to recognize a material deletion of the seller's obligation. Thus, a contract is normally a contract for a sale of something describable and described. A clause generally disclaiming "all warranties, express or implied" cannot reduce the seller's obligation with respect to such description and therefore cannot be given literal effect under Section 2–316.

This is not intended to mean that the parties, if they consciously desire, cannot make their own bargain as they wish. But in determining what they have agreed upon good faith is a factor and consideration should be given to the fact that the probability is small that a real price is intended to be exchanged for a pseudo-obligation.

5. Paragraph (1)(b) makes specific some of the principles set forth above when a description of the goods is given by the seller.

A description need not be by words. Technical specifications, blueprints and the like can afford more exact description than mere language and if made part of the basis of the bargain goods must conform with them. Past deliveries may set the description of quality, either expressly or impliedly by course of dealing. Of course, all descriptions by merchants must be read against the applicable trade usages with the general rules as to merchantability resolving any doubts.

6. The basic situation as to statements affecting the true essence of the bargain is no different when a sample or model is involved in the transaction. This section includes both a "sample" actually drawn from the bulk of goods which is the subject matter of the sale, and a "model" which is offered for inspection when the subject matter is not at hand and which has not been drawn from the bulk of the goods.

Although the underlying principles are unchanged, the facts are often ambiguous when something is shown as illustrative, rather than as a straight sample. In general, the presumption is that any sample or model just as any affirmation of fact is intended to become a basis of the bargain. But there is no escape from the question of fact. When the seller exhibits a sample purporting to be drawn from an existing bulk, good faith of course requires that the sample be fairly drawn. But in mercantile experience the mere exhibition of a "sample" does not of itself show whether it is merely intended to "suggest" or to "be" the character of the subject-matter of the contract. The question is whether the seller has so acted with reference to the sample as to make him responsible that the whole shall have at least the values shown by it. The circumstances aid in answering this question. If the

sample has been drawn from an existing bulk, it must be regarded as describing values of the goods contracted for unless it is accompanied by an unmistakable denial of such responsibility. If, on the other hand, a model of merchandise not on hand is offered, the mercantile presumption that it has become a literal description of the subject matter is not so strong, and particularly so if modification on the buyer's initiative impairs any feature of the model.

7. The precise time when words of description or affirmation are made or samples are shown is not material. The sole question is whether the language or samples or models are fairly to be regarded as part of the contract. If language is used after the closing of the deal (as when the buyer when taking delivery asks and receives an additional assurance), the warranty becomes a modification, and need not be supported by consideration if it is otherwise reasonable and in order (Section 2-209).

8. Concerning affirmations of value or a seller's opinion or commendation under subsection (2), the basic question remains the same: What statements of the seller have in the circumstances and in objective judgment become part of the basis of the bargain? As indicated above, all of the statements of the seller do so unless good reason is shown to the contrary. The provisions of subsection (2) are included, however, since common experience discloses that some statements or predictions cannot fairly be viewed as entering into the bargain. Even as to false statements of value, however, the possibility is left open that a remedy may be provided by the law relating to fraud or misrepresentation.

* * *

§ 2-314. Implied Warranty: Merchantability; Usage of Trade

(1) Unless excluded or modified (Section 2-316), a warranty that the goods shall be merchantable is implied in a contract for their sale if the

seller is a merchant with respect to goods of that kind. Under this section the serving for value of food or drink to be consumed either on the premises or elsewhere is a sale.

(2) Goods to be merchantable must be at least such as

(a) pass without objection in the trade under the contract description; and

(b) in the case of fungible goods, are of fair average quality within the description; and

(c) are fit for the ordinary purposes for which such goods are used; and

(d) run, within the variations permitted by the agreement, of even kind, quality and quantity within each unit and among all units involved; and

(e) are adequately contained, packaged, and labeled as the agreement may require; and

(f) conform to the promises or affirmations of fact made on the container or label if any.

(3) Unless excluded or modified (Section 2–316) other implied warranties may arise from course of dealing or usage of trade.

Official Comment

Prior Uniform Statutory Provision: Section 15(2), Uniform Sales Act.

Changes: Completely rewritten.

Purposes of Changes: This section, drawn in view of the steadily developing case law on the subject, is intended to make it clear that:

1. The seller's obligation applies to present sales as well as to contracts to sell subject to the effects of any examination of specific goods. (Subsection (2) of Section 2–316). Also, the warranty of merchantability applies to sales for use as well as to sales for resale.

2. The question when the warranty is imposed turns basically on the meaning of the terms of the agreement as recognized in the trade. Goods delivered under an agreement made by a merchant in a given line of trade must be of a quality comparable to that generally acceptable in that line of trade under the description or other designation of the goods used in the agreement. The responsibility imposed rests on any mer-

chant-seller, and the absence of the words "grower or manufacturer or not" which appeared in Section 15(2) of the Uniform Sales Act does not restrict the applicability of this section.

3. A specific designation of goods by the buyer does not exclude the seller's obligation that they be fit for the general purposes appropriate to such goods. A contract for the sale of second-hand goods, however, involves only such obligation as is appropriate to such goods for that is their contract description. A person making an isolated sale of goods is not a "merchant" within the meaning of the full scope of this section and, thus, no warranty of merchantability would apply. His knowledge of any defects not apparent on inspection would, however, without need for express agreement and in keeping with the underlying reason of the present section and the provisions on good faith, impose an obligation that known material but hidden defects be fully disclosed.

4. Although a seller may not be a "merchant" as to the goods in question,

if he states generally that they are "guaranteed" the provisions of this section may furnish a guide to the content of the resulting express warranty. This has particular significance in the case of second-hand sales, and has further significance in limiting the effect of fine-print disclaimer clauses where their effect would be inconsistent with large-print assertions of "guarantee".

5. The second sentence of subsection (1) covers the warranty with respect to food and drink. Serving food or drink for value is a sale, whether to be consumed on the premises or elsewhere. Cases to the contrary are rejected. The principal warranty is that stated in subsections (1) and (2)(c) of this section.

6. Subsection (2) does not purport to exhaust the meaning of "merchantable" nor to negate any of its attributes not specifically mentioned in the text of the statute, but arising by usage of trade or through case law. The language used is "must be at least such as ...," and the intention is to leave open other possible attributes of merchantability.

7. Paragraphs (a) and (b) of subsection (2) are to be read together. Both refer, as indicated above, to the standards of that line of the trade which fits the transaction and the seller's business. "Fair average" is a term directly appropriate to agricultural bulk products and means goods centering around the middle belt of quality, not the least or the worst that can be understood in the particular trade by the designation, but such as can pass "without objection." Of course a fair percentage of the least is permissible but the goods are not "fair average" if they are all of the least or worst quality possible under the description. In cases of doubt as to what quality is intended, the price at which a merchant closes a contract is an excellent index of the nature and scope of his obligation under the present section.

8. Fitness for the ordinary purposes for which goods of the type are used is a fundamental concept of the present section and is covered in paragraph (c). As stated above, merchantability is also a part of the obligation owing to the purchaser for use. Correspondingly, protection, under this aspect of the warranty, of the person buying for resale to the ultimate consumer is equally necessary, and merchantable goods must therefore be "honestly" resalable in the normal course of business because they are what they purport to be.

9. Paragraph (d) on evenness of kind, quality and quantity follows case law. But precautionary language has been added as a reminder of the frequent usages of trade which permit substantial variations both with and without an allowance or an obligation to replace the varying units.

10. Paragraph (e) applies only where the nature of the goods and of the transaction require a certain type of container, package or label. Paragraph (f) applies, on the other hand, wherever there is a label or container on which representations are made, even though the original contract, either by express terms or usage of trade, may not have required either the labelling or the representation. This follows from the general obligation of good faith which requires that a buyer should not be placed in the position of reselling or using goods delivered under false representations appearing on the package or container. No problem of extra consideration arises in this connection since, under this Article, an obligation is imposed by the original contract not to deliver mislabeled articles, and the obligation is imposed where mercantile good faith so requires and without reference to the doctrine of consideration.

11. Exclusion or modification of the warranty of merchantability, or of any part of it, is dealt with in the sec-

tion to which the text of the present section makes explicit precautionary references. That section must be read with particular reference to its subsection (4) on limitation of remedies. The warranty of merchantability, wherever it is normal, is so commonly taken for granted that its exclusion from the contract is a matter threatening surprise and therefore requiring special precaution.

12. Subsection (3) is to make explicit that usage of trade and course of dealing can create warranties and that they are implied rather than express warranties and thus subject to exclusion or modification under Section 2–316. A typical instance would be the obligation to provide pedigree papers to evidence conformity of the animal to the contract in the case of a pedigreed dog or blooded bull.

13. In an action based on breach of warranty, it is of course necessary to show not only the existence of the warranty but the fact that the warranty was broken and that the breach of the warranty was the proximate cause of the loss sustained. In such an action an affirmative showing by the seller that the loss resulted from some action or event following his own delivery of the goods can operate as a defense. Equally, evidence indicating that the seller exercised care in the manufacture, processing or selection of the goods is relevant to the issue of whether the warranty was in fact broken. Action by the buyer following an examination of the goods which ought to have indicated the defect complained of can be shown as matter bearing on whether the breach itself was the cause of the injury.

* * *

§ 2–315. Implied Warranty: Fitness for Particular Purpose

Where the seller at the time of contracting has reason to know any particular purpose for which the goods are required and that the buyer is relying on the seller's skill or judgment to select or furnish suitable goods, there is unless excluded or modified under the next section an implied warranty that the goods shall be fit for such purpose.

Official Comment

Prior Uniform Statutory Provision: Section 15(1), (4), (5), Uniform Sales Act.

Changes: Rewritten.

Purposes of Changes:

1. Whether or not this warranty arises in any individual case is basically a question of fact to be determined by the circumstances of the contracting. Under this section the buyer need not bring home to the seller actual knowledge of the particular purpose for which the goods are intended or of his reliance on the seller's skill and judgment, if the circumstances are such that the seller has reason to realize the purpose intended or that the reliance exists. The buyer, of course, must actually be relying on the seller.

2. A "particular purpose" differs from the ordinary purpose for which the goods are used in that it envisages a specific use by the buyer which is peculiar to the nature of his business whereas the ordinary purposes for which goods are used are those envisaged in the concept of merchantability and go to uses which are customarily made of the goods in question. For example, shoes are generally used for the purpose of walking upon ordinary ground, but a seller may know that a particular pair was selected to be used for climbing mountains.

A contract may of course include both a warranty of merchantability and one of fitness for a particular purpose.

The provisions of this Article on the cumulation and conflict of express and implied warranties must be considered on the question of inconsistency between or among warranties. In such a case any question of fact as to which warranty was intended by the parties to apply must be resolved in favor of the warranty of fitness for particular purpose as against all other warranties except where the buyer has taken upon himself the responsibility of furnishing the technical specifications.

3. In connection with the warranty of fitness for a particular purpose the provisions of this Article on the allocation or division of risks are particularly applicable in any transaction in which the purpose for which the goods are to be used combines requirements both as to the quality of the goods themselves and compliance with certain laws or regulations. How the risks are divided is a question of fact to be determined, where not expressly contained in the agreement, from the circumstances of contracting, usage of trade, course of performance and the like, matters which may constitute the "otherwise agreement" of the parties by which they may divide the risk or burden.

4. The absence from this section of the language used in the Uniform Sales Act in referring to the seller, "whether he be the grower or manufacturer or not," is not intended to impose any requirement that the seller be a grower or manufacturer. Although normally the warranty will arise only where the seller is a merchant with the appropriate "skill or judgment," it can arise as to non-merchants where this is justified by the particular circumstances.

5. The elimination of the "patent or other trade name" exception constitutes the major extension of the warranty of fitness which has been made by the cases and continued in this Article. Under the present section the existence of a patent or other trade name and the designation of the article by that name, or indeed in any other definite manner, is only one of the facts to be considered on the question of whether the buyer actually relied on the seller, but it is not of itself decisive of the issue. If the buyer himself is insisting on a particular brand he is not relying on the seller's skill and judgment and so no warranty results. But the mere fact that the article purchased has a particular patent or trade name is not sufficient to indicate nonreliance if the article has been recommended by the seller as adequate for the buyer's purposes.

6. The specific reference forward in the present section to the following section on exclusion or modification of warranties is to call attention to the possibility of eliminating the warranty in any given case. However it must be noted that under the following section the warranty of fitness for a particular purpose must be excluded or modified by a conspicuous writing.

* * *

§ 2-316. Exclusion or Modification of Warranties

(1) Words or conduct relevant to the creation of an express warranty and words or conduct tending to negate or limit warranty shall be construed wherever reasonable as consistent with each other; but subject to the provisions of this Article on parol or extrinsic evidence (Section 2-202) negation or limitation is inoperative to the extent that such construction is unreasonable.

(2) Subject to subsection (3), to exclude or modify the implied warranty of merchantability or any part of it the language must mention merchantability and in case of a writing must be conspicuous, and to exclude or modify any implied warranty of fitness the exclusion must be by a writing and conspicuous. Language to exclude all implied warranties of fitness is sufficient if it states, for example, that "There are no warranties which extend beyond the description on the face hereof."

(3) Notwithstanding subsection (2)

(a) unless the circumstances indicate otherwise, all implied warranties are excluded by expressions like "as is," "with all faults" or other language which in common understanding calls the buyer's attention to the exclusion of warranties and makes plain that there is no implied warranty; and

(b) when the buyer before entering into the contract has examined the goods or the sample or model as fully as he desired or has refused to examine the goods there is no implied warranty with regard to defects which an examination ought in the circumstances to have revealed to him; and

(c) an implied warranty can also be excluded or modified by course of dealing or course of performance or usage of trade.

(4) Remedies for breach of warranty can be limited in accordance with the provisions of this Article on liquidation or limitation of damages and on contractual modification of remedy (Sections 2–718 and 2–719).

Official Comment

Prior Uniform Statutory Provision: None. See sections 15 and 71, Uniform Sales Act.

Purposes:

1. This section is designed principally to deal with those frequent clauses in sales contracts which seek to exclude "all warranties, express or implied." It seeks to protect a buyer from unexpected and unbargained language of disclaimer by denying effect to such language when inconsistent with language of express warranty and permitting the exclusion of implied warranties only by conspicuous language or other circumstances which protect the buyer from surprise.

2. The seller is protected under this Article against false allegations of oral warranties by its provisions on parol and extrinsic evidence and against unauthorized representations by the customary "lack of authority" clauses. This Article treats the limitation or avoidance of consequential damages as a matter of limiting remedies for breach, separate from the matter of creation of liability under a warranty. If no warranty exists, there is of course no problem of limiting remedies for breach of warranty. Under subsection (4) the question of limitation of remedy is governed by the sections referred to rather than by this section.

3. Disclaimer of the implied warranty of merchantability is permitted under subsection (2), but with the safeguard that such disclaimers must mention merchantability and in case of a writing must be conspicuous.

4. Unlike the implied warranty of merchantability, implied warranties of

fitness for a particular purpose may be excluded by general language, but only if it is in writing and conspicuous.

5. Subsection (2) presupposes that the implied warranty in question exists unless excluded or modified. Whether or not language of disclaimer satisfies the requirements of this section, such language may be relevant under other sections to the question whether the warranty was ever in fact created. Thus, unless the provisions of this Article on parol and extrinsic evidence prevent, oral language of disclaimer may raise issues of fact as to whether reliance by the buyer occurred and whether the seller had "reason to know" under the section on implied warranty of fitness for a particular purpose.

6. The exceptions to the general rule set forth in paragraphs (a), (b) and (c) of subsection (3) are common factual situations in which the circumstances surrounding the transaction are in themselves sufficient to call the buyer's attention to the fact that no implied warranties are made or that a certain implied warranty is being excluded.

7. Paragraph (a) of subsection (3) deals with general terms such as "as is," "as they stand," "with all faults," and the like. Such terms in ordinary commercial usage are understood to mean that the buyer takes the entire risk as to the quality of the goods involved. The terms covered by paragraph (a) are in fact merely a particularization of paragraph (c) which provides for exclusion or modification of implied warranties by usage of trade.

8. Under paragraph (b) of subsection (3) warranties may be excluded or modified by the circumstances where the buyer examines the goods or a sample or model of them before entering into the contract. "Examination" as used in this paragraph is not synonymous with inspection before acceptance or at any other time after the contract

has been made. It goes rather to the nature of the responsibility assumed by the seller at the time of the making of the contract. Of course if the buyer discovers the defect and uses the goods anyway, or if he unreasonably fails to examine the goods before he uses them, resulting injuries may be found to result from his own action rather than proximately from a breach of warranty. See Sections 2-314 and 2-715 and comments thereto.

In order to bring the transaction within the scope of "refused to examine" in paragraph (b), it is not sufficient that the goods are available for inspection. There must in addition be a demand by the seller that the buyer examine the goods fully. The seller by the demand puts the buyer on notice that he is assuming the risk of defects which the examination ought to reveal. The language "refused to examine" in this paragraph is intended to make clear the necessity for such demand.

Application of the doctrine of "caveat emptor" in all cases where the buyer examines the goods regardless of statements made by the seller is, however, rejected by this Article. Thus, if the offer of examination is accompanied by words as to their merchantability or specific attributes and the buyer indicates clearly that he is relying on those words rather than on his examination, they give rise to an "express" warranty. In such cases the question is one of fact as to whether a warranty of merchantability has been expressly incorporated in the agreement. Disclaimer of such an express warranty is governed by subsection (1) of the present section.

The particular buyer's skill and the normal method of examining goods in the circumstances determine what defects are excluded by the examination. A failure to notice defects which are obvious cannot excuse the buyer. However, an examination under circumstances which do not permit chemical or other testing of the goods would not exclude defects which could be ascertained only by such testing. Nor can latent defects be excluded by a simple examination. A professional buyer examining a product in his field will be held to have assumed the risk as to all defects which a professional in the field ought to observe, while a nonprofessional buyer will be held to have assumed the risk only for such defects as a layman might be expected to observe.

9. The situation in which the buyer gives precise and complete specifications to the seller is not explicitly covered in this section, but this is a frequent circumstance by which the implied warranties may be excluded. The warranty of fitness for a particular pur-

pose would not normally arise since in such a situation there is usually no reliance on the seller by the buyer. The warranty of merchantability in such a transaction, however, must be considered in connection with the next section on the cumulation and conflict of warranties. Under paragraph (c) of that section in case of such an inconsistency the implied warranty of merchantability is displaced by the express warranty that the goods will comply with the specifications. Thus, where the buyer gives detailed specifications as to the goods, neither of the implied warranties as to quality will normally apply to the transaction unless consistent with the specifications.

* * *

§ 2–317. Cumulation and Conflict of Warranties Express or Implied

Warranties whether express or implied shall be construed as consistent with each other and as cumulative, but if such construction is unreasonable the intention of the parties shall determine which warranty is dominant. In ascertaining that intention the following rules apply:

(a) Exact or technical specifications displace an inconsistent sample or model or general language of description.

(b) A sample from an existing bulk displaces inconsistent general language of description.

(c) Express warranties displace inconsistent implied warranties other than an implied warranty of fitness for a particular purpose.

Official Comment

Prior Uniform Statutory Provision: On cumulation of warranties see Sections 14, 15, and 16, Uniform Sales Act.

Changes: Completely rewritten into one section.

Purposes of Changes:

1. The present section rests on the basic policy of this Article that no warranty is created except by some conduct (either affirmative action or failure to disclose) on the part of the seller. Therefore, all warranties are made cumulative

unless this construction of the contract is impossible or unreasonable.

This Article thus follows the general policy of the Uniform Sales Act except that in case of the sale of an article by its patent or trade name the elimination of the warranty of fitness depends solely on whether the buyer has relied on the seller's skill and judgment; the use of the patent or trade name is but one factor in making this determination.

2. The rules of this section are designed to aid in determining the inten-

tion of the parties as to which of inconsistent warranties which have arisen from the circumstances of their transaction shall prevail. These rules of intention are to be applied only where factors making for an equitable estoppel of the seller do not exist and where he has in perfect good faith made warranties which later turn out to be inconsistent. To the extent that the seller has led the buyer to believe that all of the warranties can be performed, he is estopped from setting up any essential inconsistency as a defense.

3. The rules in subsections (a), (b) and (c) are designed to ascertain the intention of the parties by reference to the factor which probably claimed the attention of the parties in the first instance. These rules are not absolute but may be changed by evidence showing that the conditions which existed at the time of contracting make the construction called for by the section inconsistent or unreasonable.

* * *

§ 2–318. Third Party Beneficiaries of Warranties Express or Implied

Note: *If this Act is introduced in the Congress of the United States this section should be omitted. (States to select one alternative.)*

Alternative A

A seller's warranty whether express or implied extends to any natural person who is in the family or household of his buyer or who is a guest in his home if it is reasonable to expect that such person may use, consume or be affected by the goods and who is injured in person by breach of the warranty. A seller may not exclude or limit the operation of this section.

Alternative B

A seller's warranty whether express or implied extends to any natural person who may reasonably be expected to use, consume or be affected by the goods and who is injured in person by breach of the warranty. A seller may not exclude or limit the operation of this section.

Alternative C

A seller's warranty whether express or implied extends to any person who may reasonably be expected to use, consume or be affected by the goods and who is injured by breach of the warranty. A seller may not exclude or limit the operation of this section with respect to injury to the person of an individual to whom the warranty extends. As amended 1966.

Official Comment

Purposes:

1. The last sentence of this section does not mean that a seller is precluded from excluding or disclaiming a warranty which might otherwise arise in connection with the sale provided such exclusion or modification is permitted by Section 2–316. Nor does that sentence preclude the seller from limiting the remedies of his own buyer and of any beneficiaries, in any manner provided in Sections 2–718 or 2–719. To the extent that the contract of sale contains provisions under which warranties are ex-

cluded or modified, or remedies for breach are limited, such provisions are equally operative against beneficiaries of warranties under this section. What this last sentence forbids is exclusion of liability by the seller to the persons to whom the warranties which he has made to his buyer would extend under this section.

2. The purpose of this section is to give certain beneficiaries the benefit of the same warranty which the buyer received in the contract of sale, thereby freeing any such beneficiaries from any technical rules as to "privity." It seeks to accomplish this purpose without any derogation of any right or remedy resting on negligence. It rests primarily upon the merchant-seller's warranty under this Article that the goods sold are merchantable and fit for the ordinary purposes for which such goods are used rather than the warranty of fitness for a particular purpose. Implicit in the section is that any beneficiary of a warranty may bring a direct action for breach of warranty against the seller whose warranty extends to him [As amended in 1966].

3. The first alternative expressly includes as beneficiaries within its provisions the family, household and guests of the purchaser. Beyond this, the section in this form is neutral and is not intended to enlarge or restrict the developing case law on whether the seller's warranties, given to his buyer who resells, extend to other persons in the distributive chain. The second alternative is designed for states where the case law has already developed further and for those that desire to expand the class of beneficiaries. The third alternative goes further, following the trend of modern decisions as indicated by Restatement of Torts 2d § 402 A (Tentative Draft No. 10, 1965) in extending the rule beyond injuries to the person [As amended in 1966].

* * *

PART 5
PERFORMANCE

* * *

§ 2-503. Manner of Seller's Tender of Delivery

(1) Tender of delivery requires that the seller put and hold conforming goods at the buyer's disposition and give the buyer any notification reasonably necessary to enable him to take delivery. The manner, time and place for tender are determined by the agreement and this Article, and in particular

    (a) tender must be at a reasonable hour, and if it is of goods they must be kept available for the period reasonably necessary to enable the buyer to take possession; but

    (b) unless otherwise agreed the buyer must furnish facilities reasonably suited to the receipt of the goods.

(2) Where the case is within the next section respecting shipment tender requires that the seller comply with its provisions.

(3) Where the seller is required to deliver at a particular destination tender requires that he comply with subsection (1) and also in any

appropriate case tender documents as described in subsections (4) and (5) of this section.

(4) Where goods are in the possession of a bailee and are to be delivered without being moved

(a) tender requires that the seller either tender a negotiable document of title covering such goods or procure acknowledgment by the bailee of the buyer's right to possession of the goods; but

(b) tender to the buyer of a non-negotiable document of title or of a written direction to the bailee to deliver is sufficient tender unless the buyer seasonably objects, and receipt by the bailee of notification of the buyer's rights fixes those rights as against the bailee and all third persons; but risk of loss of the goods and of any failure by the bailee to honor the non-negotiable document of title or to obey the direction remains on the seller until the buyer has had a reasonable time to present the document or direction, and a refusal by the bailee to honor the document or to obey the direction defeats the tender.

(5) Where the contract requires the seller to deliver documents

(a) he must tender all such documents in correct form, except as provided in this Article with respect to bills of lading in a set (subsection (2) of Section 2–323); and

(b) tender through customary banking channels is sufficient and dishonor of a draft accompanying the documents constitutes non-acceptance or rejection.

* * *

§ 2–507. Effect of Seller's Tender; Delivery on Condition

(1) Tender of delivery is a condition to the buyer's duty to accept the goods and, unless otherwise agreed, to his duty to pay for them. Tender entitles the seller to acceptance of the goods and to payment according to the contract.

(2) Where payment is due and demanded on the delivery to the buyer of goods or documents of title, his right as against the seller to retain or dispose of them is conditional upon his making the payment due.

* * *

§ 2–508. Cure by Seller of Improper Tender or Delivery; Replacement

(1) Where any tender or delivery by the seller is rejected because nonconforming and the time for performance has not yet expired, the seller may seasonably notify the buyer of his intention to cure and may then within the contract time make a conforming delivery.

(2) Where the buyer rejects a non-conforming tender which the seller had reasonable grounds to believe would be acceptable with or without money allowance the seller may if he seasonably notifies the buyer have a further reasonable time to substitute a conforming tender.

Official Comment

Prior Uniform Statutory Provision: None.

Purposes:

1. Subsection (1) permits a seller who has made a non-conforming tender in any case to make a conforming delivery within the contract time upon seasonable notification to the buyer. It applies even where the seller has taken back the non-conforming goods and refunded the purchase price. He may still make a good tender within the contract period. The closer, however, it is to the contract date, the greater is the necessity for extreme promptness on the seller's part in notifying of his intention to cure, if such notification is to be "seasonable" under this subsection.

The rule of this subsection, moreover, is qualified by its underlying reasons. Thus if, after contracting for June delivery, a buyer later makes known to the seller his need for shipment early in the month and the seller ships accordingly, the "contract time" has been cut down by the supervening modification and the time for cure of tender must be referred to this modified time term.

2. Subsection (2) seeks to avoid injustice to the seller by reason of a surprise rejection by the buyer. However, the seller is not protected unless he had "reasonable grounds to believe" that the tender would be acceptable. Such reasonable grounds can lie in prior course of dealing, course of performance or usage of trade as well as in the particular circumstances surrounding the making of the contract. The seller is charged with commercial knowledge of any factors in a particular sales situation which require him to comply strictly with his obligations under the contract as, for example, strict conformity of documents in an overseas shipment or the sale of precision parts or chemicals for use in manufacture. Further, if the buyer gives notice either implicitly, as by a prior course of dealing involving rigorous inspections, or expressly, as by the deliberate inclusion of a "no replacement" clause in the contract, the seller is to be held to rigid compliance. If the clause appears in a "form" contract evidence that it is out of line with trade usage or the prior course of dealing and was not called to the seller's attention may be sufficient to show that the seller had reasonable grounds to believe that the tender would be acceptable.

3. The words "a further reasonable time to substitute a conforming tender" are intended as words of limitation to protect the buyer. What is a "reasonable time" depends upon the attending circumstances. Compare Section 2–511 on the comparable case of a seller's surprise demand for legal tender.

4. Existing trade usages permitting variations without rejection but with price allowance enter into the agreement itself as contractual limitations of remedy and are not covered by this section.

* * *

§ 2–515. Preserving Evidence of Goods in Dispute

In furtherance of the adjustment of any claim or dispute

   (a) either party on reasonable notification to the other and for the purpose of ascertaining the facts and preserving evidence has the right to inspect, test and sample the goods including such of them as may be in the possession or control of the other; and

(b) the parties may agree to a third party inspection or survey to determine the conformity or condition of the goods and may agree that the findings shall be binding upon them in any subsequent litigation or adjustment.

Official Comment

Prior Uniform Statutory Provision: None.

Purposes:

1. To meet certain serious problems which arise when there is a dispute as to the quality of the goods and thereby perhaps to aid the parties in reaching a settlement, and to further the use of devices which will promote certainty as to the condition of the goods, or at least aid in preserving evidence of their condition.

2. Under paragraph (a), to afford either party an opportunity for preserving evidence, whether or not agreement has been reached, and thereby to reduce uncertainty in any litigation and, in turn perhaps, to promote agreement.

Paragraph (a) does not conflict with the provisions on the seller's right to resell rejected goods or the buyer's similar right. Apparent conflict between these provisions which will be suggested in certain circumstances is to be resolved by requiring prompt action by the parties. Nor does paragraph (a) impair the effect of a term for payment before inspection. Short of such defects as amount to fraud or substantial failure of consideration, non-conformity is neither an excuse nor a defense to an action for non-acceptance of documents. Normally, therefore, until the buyer has made payment, inspected and rejected the goods, there is no occasion or use for the rights under paragraph (a).

3. Under paragraph (b), to provide for third party inspection upon the agreement of the parties, thereby opening the door to amicable adjustments based upon the findings of such third parties.

The use of the phrase "conformity or condition" makes it clear that the parties' agreement may range from a complete settlement of all aspects of the dispute by a third party to the use of a third party merely to determine and record the condition of the goods so that they can be resold or used to reduce the stake in controversy. "Conformity", at one end of the scale of possible issues, includes the whole question of interpretation of the agreement and its legal effect, the state of the goods in regard to quality and condition, whether any defects are due to factors which operate at the risk of the buyer, and the degree of non-conformity where that may be material. "Condition", at the other end of the scale, includes nothing but the degree of damage or deterioration which the goods show. Paragraph (b) is intended to reach any point in the gamut which the parties may agree upon.

The principle of the section on reservation of rights reinforces this paragraph in simplifying such adjustments as the parties wish to make in partial settlement while reserving their rights as to any further points. Paragraph (b) also suggests the use of arbitration, where desired, of any points left open, but nothing in this section is intended to repeal or amend any statute governing arbitration. Where any question arises as to the extent of the parties' agreement under the paragraph, the presumption should be that it was meant to extend only to the relation between the contract description and the goods as delivered, since that is what a craftsman in the trade would normally be expected to report upon. Finally, a written and authenticated report of inspection or tests by a third party, whether or not sampling has been practicable, is entitled to be admitted as evidence under this Act, for it is a third party document.

* * *

PART 6

BREACH, REPUDIATION AND EXCUSE

§ 2–601. Buyer's Rights on Improper Delivery

Subject to the provisions of this Article on breach in installment contracts (Section 2–612) and unless otherwise agreed under the sections on contractual limitations of remedy (Sections 2–718 and 2–719), if the goods or the tender of delivery fail in any respect to conform to the contract, the buyer may

(a) reject the whole; or

(b) accept the whole; or

(c) accept any commercial unit or units and reject the rest.

Official Comment

Prior Uniform Statutory Provision: No one general equivalent provision but numerous provisions, dealing with situations of non-conformity where buyer may accept or reject, including Sections 11, 44 and 69(1), Uniform Sales Act.

Changes: Partial acceptance in good faith is recognized and the buyer's remedies on the contract for breach of warranty and the like, where the buyer has returned the goods after transfer of title, are no longer barred.

Purposes of Changes: To make it clear that:

1. A buyer accepting a nonconforming tender is not penalized by the loss of any remedy otherwise open to him. This policy extends to cover and regulate the acceptance of a part of any lot improperly tendered in any case where the price can reasonably be apportioned. Partial acceptance is permitted whether the part of the goods accepted conforms or not. The only limitation on partial acceptance is that good faith and commercial reasonableness must be used to avoid undue impairment of the value of the remaining portion of the goods. This is the reason for the insistence on the "commercial unit" in paragraph (c). In this respect, the test is not only what unit has been the basis of contract, but whether the partial acceptance produces so materially adverse an effect on the remainder as to constitute bad faith.

2. Acceptance made with the knowledge of the other party is final. An original refusal to accept may be withdrawn by a later acceptance if the seller has indicated that he is holding the tender open. However, if the buyer attempts to accept, either in whole or in part, after his original rejection has caused the seller to arrange for other disposition of the goods, the buyer must answer for any ensuing damage since the next section provides that any exercise of ownership after rejection is wrongful as against the seller. Further, he is liable even though the seller may choose to treat his action as acceptance rather than conversion, since the damage flows from the misleading notice. Such arrangements for resale or other

disposition of the goods by the seller must be viewed as within the normal contemplation of a buyer who has given notice of rejection. However, the buyer's attempts in good faith to dispose of defective goods where the seller has failed to give instructions within a reasonable time are not to be regarded as an acceptance.

* * *

§ 2–602. Manner and Effect of Rightful Rejection

(1) Rejection of goods must be within a reasonable time after their delivery or tender. It is ineffective unless the buyer seasonably notifies the seller.

(2) Subject to the provisions of the two following sections on rejected goods (Sections 2–603 and 2–604),

(a) after rejection any exercise of ownership by the buyer with respect to any commercial unit is wrongful as against the seller; and

(b) if the buyer has before rejection taken physical possession of goods in which he does not have a security interest under the provisions of this Article (subsection (3) of Section 2–711), he is under a duty after rejection to hold them with reasonable care at the seller's disposition for a time sufficient to permit the seller to remove them; but

(c) the buyer has no further obligations with regard to goods rightfully rejected.

(3) The seller's rights with respect to goods wrongfully rejected are governed by the provisions of this Article on Seller's remedies in general (Section 2–703).

Official Comment

Prior Uniform Statutory Provision: Section 50, Uniform Sales Act.

Changes: Rewritten.

Purposes of Changes: To make it clear that:

1. A tender or delivery of goods made pursuant to a contract of sale, even though wholly non-conforming, requires affirmative action by the buyer to avoid acceptance. Under subsection (1), therefore, the buyer is given a reasonable time to notify the seller of his rejection, but without such seasonable notification his rejection is ineffective. The sections of this Article dealing with inspection of goods must be read in connection with the buyer's reasonable time for action under this subsection. Contract provisions limiting the time for rejection fall within the rule of the section on "Time" and are effective if the time set gives the buyer a reasonable time for discovery of defects. What constitutes a due "notifying" of rejection by the buyer to the seller is defined in Section 1–201.

2. Subsection (2) lays down the normal duties of the buyer upon rejection, which flow from the relationship of the parties. Beyond his duty to hold the goods with reasonable care for the buyer's [seller's] disposition, this section continues the policy of prior uniform legislation in generally relieving the buyer from any duties with respect to them, except when the circumstances impose the limited obligation of salvage upon him under the next section.

3. The present section applies only to rightful rejection by the buyer. If the seller has made a tender which in all respects conforms to the contract, the buyer has a positive duty to accept and his failure to do so constitutes a "wrongful rejection" which gives the seller immediate remedies for breach. Subsection (3) is included here to em-phasize the sharp distinction between the rejection of an improper tender and the non-acceptance which is a breach by the buyer.

4. The provisions of this section are to be appropriately limited or modified when a negotiation is in process.

* * *

§ 2–605. Waiver of Buyer's Objections by Failure to Particularize

(1) The buyer's failure to state in connection with rejection a particular defect which is ascertainable by reasonable inspection precludes him from relying on the unstated defect to justify rejection or to establish breach

(a) where the seller could have cured it if stated seasonably; or

(b) between merchants when the seller has after rejection made a request in writing for a full and final written statement of all defects on which the buyer proposes to rely.

(2) Payment against documents made without reservation of rights precludes recovery of the payment for defects apparent on the face of the documents.

* * *

§ 2–606. What Constitutes Acceptance of Goods

(1) Acceptance of goods occurs when the buyer

(a) after a reasonable opportunity to inspect the goods signifies to the seller that the goods are conforming or that he will take or retain them in spite of their nonconformity; or

(b) fails to make an effective rejection (subsection (1) of Section 2–602), but such acceptance does not occur until the buyer has had a reasonable opportunity to inspect them; or

(c) does any act inconsistent with the seller's ownership; but if such act is wrongful as against the seller it is an acceptance only if ratified by him.

(2) Acceptance of a part of any commercial unit is acceptance of that entire unit.

Official Comment

Prior Uniform Statutory Provision: Section 48, Uniform Sales Act.

Changes: Rewritten, the qualification in paragraph (c) and subsection (2) being new; otherwise the general policy of the prior legislation is continued.

Purposes of Changes and New Matter: To make it clear that:

1. Under this Article "acceptance" as applied to goods means that the buyer, pursuant to the contract, takes particular goods which have been appropriated to the contract as his own, whether or not he is obligated to do so, and whether he does so by words, action, or silence when it is time to speak. If the goods conform to the contract, acceptance amounts only to the performance by the buyer of one part of his legal obligations.

2. Under this Article acceptance of goods is always acceptance of identified goods which have been appropriated to the contract or are appropriated by the contract. There is no provision for "acceptance of title" apart from acceptance in general, since acceptance of title is not material under this Article to the detailed rights and duties of the parties. (See Section 2–401). The refinements of the older law between acceptance of goods and of title become unnecessary in view of the provisions of the sections on effect and revocation of acceptance, on effects of identification and on risk of loss, and those sections which free the seller's and buyer's remedies from the complications and confusions caused by the question of whether title has or has not passed to the buyer before breach.

3. Under paragraph (a), payment made after tender is always one circumstance tending to signify acceptance of the goods but in itself it can never be more than one circumstance and is not conclusive. Also, a conditional communication of acceptance always remains subject to its expressed conditions.

4. Under paragraph (c), any action taken by the buyer, which is inconsistent with his claim that he has rejected the goods, constitutes an acceptance. However, the provisions of paragraph (c) are subject to the sections dealing with rejection by the buyer which permit the buyer to take certain actions with respect to the goods pursuant to his options and duties imposed by those sections, without effecting an acceptance of the goods. The second clause of paragraph (c) modifies some of the prior case law and makes it clear that "acceptance" in law based on the wrongful act of the acceptor is acceptance only as against the wrongdoer and then only at the option of the party wronged.

In the same manner in which a buyer can bind himself, despite his insistence that he is rejecting or has rejected the goods, by an act inconsistent with the seller's ownership under paragraph (c), he can obligate himself by a communication of acceptance despite a prior rejection under paragraph (a). However, the sections on buyer's rights on improper delivery and on the effect of rightful rejection, make it clear that after he once rejects a tender, paragraph (a) does not operate in favor of the buyer unless the seller has re-tendered the goods or has taken affirmative action indicating that he is holding the tender open. See also Comment 2 to Section 2–601.

5. Subsection (2) supplements the policy of the section on buyer's rights on improper delivery, recognizing the validity of a partial acceptance but insisting that the buyer exercise this right only as to whole commercial units.

* * *

§ 2–607. Effect of Acceptance; Notice of Breach; Burden of Establishing Breach After Acceptance; Notice of Claim or Litigation to Person Answerable Over

(1) The buyer must pay at the contract rate for any goods accepted.

(2) Acceptance of goods by the buyer precludes rejection of the goods accepted and if made with knowledge of a non-conformity cannot be revoked because of it unless the acceptance was on the reasonable assumption that the non-conformity would be seasonably cured but acceptance does not of itself impair any other remedy provided by this Article for non-conformity.

(3) Where a tender has been accepted

   (a) the buyer must within a reasonable time after he discovers or should have discovered any breach notify the seller of breach or be barred from any remedy; and

   (b) if the claim is one for infringement or the like (subsection (3) of Section 2–312) and the buyer is sued as a result of such a breach he must so notify the seller within a reasonable time after he receives notice of the litigation or be barred from any remedy over for liability established by the litigation.

(4) The burden is on the buyer to establish any breach with respect to the goods accepted.

(5) Where the buyer is sued for breach of a warranty or other obligation for which his seller is answerable over

   (a) he may give his seller written notice of the litigation. If the notice states that the seller may come in and defend and that if the seller does not do so he will be bound in any action against him by his buyer by any determination of fact common to the two litigations, then unless the seller after seasonable receipt of the notice does come in and defend he is so bound.

   (b) if the claim is one for infringement or the like (subsection (3) of Section 2–312) the original seller may demand in writing that his buyer turn over to him control of the litigation including settlement or else be barred from any remedy over and if he also agrees to bear all expense and to satisfy any adverse judgment, then unless the buyer after seasonable receipt of the demand does turn over control the buyer is so barred.

(6) The provisions of subsections (3), (4) and (5) apply to any obligation of a buyer to hold the seller harmless against infringement or the like (subsection (3) of Section 2–312).

Official Comment

Prior Uniform Statutory Provision: Subsection (1)—Section 41, Uniform Sales Act; Subsections (2) and (3)—Sections 49 and 69, Uniform Sales Act.

Changes: Rewritten.

Purposes of Changes: To continue the prior basic policies with respect to acceptance of goods while making a number of minor though material changes in the interest of simplicity and commercial convenience so that:

1. Under subsection (1), once the buyer accepts a tender the seller acquires a right to its price on the contract terms. In cases of partial acceptance, the

price of any part accepted is, if possible, to be reasonably apportioned, using the type of apportionment familiar to the courts in quantum valebat cases, to be determined in terms of "the contract rate," which is the rate determined from the bargain in fact (the agreement) after the rules and policies of this Article have been brought to bear.

2. Under subsection (2) acceptance of goods precludes their subsequent rejection. Any return of the goods thereafter must be by way of revocation of acceptance under the next section. Revocation is unavailable for a non-conformity known to the buyer at the time of acceptance, except where the buyer has accepted on the reasonable assumption that the non-conformity would be seasonably cured.

3. All other remedies of the buyer remain unimpaired under subsection (2). This is intended to include the buyer's full rights with respect to future installments despite his acceptance of any earlier non-conforming installment.

4. The time of notification is to be determined by applying commercial standards to a merchant buyer. "A reasonable time" for notification from a retail consumer is to be judged by different standards so that in his case it will be extended, for the rule of requiring notification is designed to defeat commercial bad faith, not to deprive a good faith consumer of his remedy.

The content of the notification need merely be sufficient to let the seller know that the transaction is still troublesome and must be watched. There is no reason to require that the notification which saves the buyer's rights under this section must include a clear statement of all the objections that will be relied on by the buyer, as under the section covering statements of defects upon rejection (Section 2–605). Nor is there reason for requiring the notification to be a claim for damages or of any

threatened litigation or other resort to a remedy. The notification which saves the buyer's rights under this Article need only be such as informs the seller that the transaction is claimed to involve a breach, and thus opens the way for normal settlement through negotiation.

5. Under this Article various beneficiaries are given rights for injuries sustained by them because of the seller's breach of warranty. Such a beneficiary does not fall within the reason of the present section in regard to discovery of defects and the giving of notice within a reasonable time after acceptance, since he has nothing to do with acceptance. However, the reason of this section does extend to requiring the beneficiary to notify the seller that an injury has occurred. What is said above, with regard to the extended time for reasonable notification from the lay consumer after the injury is also applicable here; but even a beneficiary can be properly held to the use of good faith in notifying, once he has had time to become aware of the legal situation.

6. Subsection (4) unambiguously places the burden of proof to establish breach on the buyer after acceptance. However, this rule becomes one purely of procedure when the tender accepted was non-conforming and the buyer has given the seller notice of breach under subsection (3). For subsection (2) makes it clear that acceptance leaves unimpaired the buyer's right to be made whole, and that right can be exercised by the buyer not only by way of cross-claim for damages, but also by way of recoupment in diminution or extinction of the price.

7. Subsections (3)(b) and (5)(b) give a warrantor against infringement an opportunity to defend or compromise third-party claims or be relieved of his liability. Subsection (5)(a) codifies for all warranties the practice of voucher to

defend. Compare Section 3–803. Subsection (6) makes these provisions applicable to the buyer's liability for infringement under Section 2–312.

8. All of the provisions of the present section are subject to any explicit reservation of rights.

* * *

§ 2–608.   Revocation of Acceptance in Whole or in Part

(1) The buyer may revoke his acceptance of a lot or commercial unit whose non-conformity substantially impairs its value to him if he has accepted it

    (a) on the reasonable assumption that its non-conformity would be cured and it has not been seasonably cured; or

    (b) without discovery of such non-conformity if his acceptance was reasonably induced either by the difficulty of discovery before acceptance or by the seller's assurances.

(2) Revocation of acceptance must occur within a reasonable time after the buyer discovers or should have discovered the ground for it and before any substantial change in condition of the goods which is not caused by their own defects. It is not effective until the buyer notifies the seller of it.

(3) A buyer who so revokes has the same rights and duties with regard to the goods involved as if he had rejected them.

Official Comment

Prior Uniform Statutory Provision: Section 69(1)(d), (3), (4) and (5), Uniform Sales Act.

Changes: Rewritten.

Purposes of Changes: To make it clear that:

1. Although the prior basic policy is continued, the buyer is no longer required to elect between revocation of acceptance and recovery of damages for breach. Both are now available to him. The non-alternative character of the two remedies is stressed by the terms used in the present section. The section no longer speaks of "rescission," a term capable of ambiguous application either to transfer of title to the goods or to the contract of sale and susceptible also of confusion with cancellation for cause of an executed or executory portion of the contract. The remedy under this section is instead referred to simply as "revocation of acceptance" of goods tendered

under a contract for sale and involves no suggestion of "election" of any sort.

2. Revocation of acceptance is possible only where the non-conformity substantially impairs the value of the goods to the buyer. For this purpose the test is not what the seller had reason to know at the time of contracting; the question is whether the non-conformity is such as will in fact cause a substantial impairment of value to the buyer though the seller had no advance knowledge as to the buyer's particular circumstances.

3. "Assurances" by the seller under paragraph (b) of subsection (1) can rest as well in the circumstances or in the contract as in explicit language used at the time of delivery. The reason for recognizing such assurances is that they induce the buyer to delay discovery. These are the only assurances involved in paragraph (b). Explicit assurances may be made either in good faith or bad faith. In either case any remedy accord-

ed by this Article is available to the buyer under the section on remedies for fraud.

4. Subsection (2) requires notification of revocation of acceptance within a reasonable time after discovery of the grounds for such revocation. Since this remedy will be generally resorted to only after attempts at adjustment have failed, the reasonable time period should extend in most cases beyond the time in which notification of breach must be given, beyond the time for discovery of non-conformity after acceptance and beyond the time for rejection after tender. The parties may by their agreement limit the time for notification under this section, but the same sanctions and considerations apply to such agreements as are discussed in the comment on manner and effect of rightful rejection.

5. The content of the notice under subsection (2) is to be determined in this case as in others by considerations of good faith, prevention of surprise, and reasonable adjustment. More will generally be necessary than the mere notification of breach required under the preceding section. On the other hand the requirements of the section on waiver of buyer's objections do not apply here. The fact that quick notification of trouble is desirable affords good ground for being slow to bind a buyer by his first statement. Following the general policy of this Article, the requirements of the content of notification are less stringent in the case of a non-merchant buyer.

6. Under subsection (2) the prior policy is continued of seeking substantial justice in regard to the condition of goods restored to the seller. Thus the buyer may not revoke his acceptance if the goods have materially deteriorated except by reason of their own defects. Worthless goods, however, need not be offered back and minor defects in the articles reoffered are to be disregarded.

7. The policy of the section allowing partial acceptance is carried over into the present section and the buyer may revoke his acceptance, in appropriate cases, as to the entire lot or any commercial unit thereof.

* * *

PART 7
REMEDIES

* * *

§ 2–711. Buyer's Remedies in General; Buyer's Security Interest in Rejected Goods

(1) Where the seller fails to make delivery or repudiates or the buyer rightfully rejects or justifiably revokes acceptance then with respect to any goods involved, and with respect to the whole if the breach goes to the whole contract (Section 2–612), the buyer may cancel and whether or not he has done so may in addition to recovering so much of the price as has been paid

(a) "cover" and have damages under the next section as to all the goods affected whether or not they have been identified to the contract; or

(b) recover damages for non-delivery as provided in this Article (Section 2–713).

(2) Where the seller fails to deliver or repudiates the buyer may also

(a) if the goods have been identified recover them as provided in this Article (Section 2–502); or

(b) in a proper case obtain specific performance or replevy the goods as provided in this Article (Section 2–716).

(3) On rightful rejection or justifiable revocation of acceptance a buyer has a security interest in goods in his possession or control for any payments made on their price and any expenses reasonably incurred in their inspection, receipt, transportation, care and custody and may hold such goods and resell them in like manner as an aggrieved seller (Section 2–706).

Official Comment

Prior Uniform Statutory Provision: No comparable index section; Subsection (3)—Section 69(5), Uniform Sales Act.

Changes: The prior uniform statutory provision is generally continued and expanded in Subsection (3).

Purposes of Changes and New Matter:

1. To index in this section the buyer's remedies, subsection (1) covering those remedies permitting the recovery of money damages, and subsection (2) covering those which permit reaching the goods themselves. The remedies listed here are those available to a buyer who has not accepted the goods or who has justifiably revoked his acceptance. The remedies available to a buyer with regard to goods finally accepted appear in the section dealing with breach in regard to accepted goods. The buyer's right to proceed as to all goods when the breach is as to only some of the goods is determined by the section on breach in installment contracts and by the section on partial acceptance.

Despite the seller's breach, proper retender of delivery under the section on cure of improper tender or replacement can effectively preclude the buyer's remedies under this section, except for any delay involved.

2. To make it clear in subsection (3) that the buyer may hold and resell rejected goods if he has paid a part of the price or incurred expenses of the type specified. "Paid" as used here includes acceptance of a draft or other time negotiable instrument or the signing of a negotiable note. His freedom of resale is coextensive with that of a seller under this Article except that the buyer may not keep any profit resulting from the resale and is limited to retaining only the amount of the price paid and the costs involved in the inspection and handling of the goods. The buyer's security interest in the goods is intended to be limited to the items listed in subsection (3), and the buyer is not permitted to retain such funds as he might believe adequate for his damages. The buyer's right to cover, or to have damages for non-delivery, is not impaired by his exercise of his right of resale.

3. It should also be noted that this Act requires its remedies to be liberally administered and provides that any right or obligation which it declares is enforceable by action unless a different effect is specifically prescribed (Section 1–106).

* * *

§ 2–714. Buyer's Damages for Breach in Regard to Accepted Goods

(1) Where the buyer has accepted goods and given notification (subsection (3) of Section 2–607) he may recover as damages for any non-

conformity of tender the loss resulting in the ordinary course of events from the seller's breach as determined in any manner which is reasonable.

(2) The measure of damages for breach of warranty is the difference at the time and place of acceptance between the value of the goods accepted and the value they would have had if they had been as warranted, unless special circumstances show proximate damages of a different amount.

(3) In a proper case any incidental and consequential damages under the next section may also be recovered.

Official Comment

Prior Uniform Statutory Provision: Section 69(6) and (7), Uniform Sales Act.

Changes: Rewritten.

Purposes of Changes:

1. This section deals with the remedies available to the buyer after the goods have been accepted and the time for revocation of acceptance has gone by. In general this section adopts the rule of the prior uniform statutory provision for measuring damages where there has been a breach of warranty as to goods accepted, but goes further to lay down an explicit provision as to the time and place for determining the loss.

The section on deduction of damages from price provides an additional remedy for a buyer who still owes part of the purchase price, and frequently the two remedies will be available concurrently. The buyer's failure to notify of his claim under the section on effects of acceptance, however, operates to bar his remedies under either that section or the present section.

2. The "non-conformity" referred to in subsection (1) includes not only breaches of warranties but also any failure of the seller to perform according to his obligations under the contract. In the case of such non-conformity, the buyer is permitted to recover for his loss "in any manner which is reasonable."

3. Subsection (2) describes the usual, standard and reasonable method of ascertaining damages in the case of breach of warranty but it is not intended as an exclusive measure. It departs from the measure of damages for non-delivery in utilizing the place of acceptance rather than the place of tender. In some cases the two may coincide, as where the buyer signifies his acceptance upon the tender. If, however, the non-conformity is such as would justify revocation of acceptance, the time and place of acceptance under this section is determined as of the buyer's decision not to revoke.

4. The incidental and consequential damages referred to in subsection (3), which will usually accompany an action brought under this section, are discussed in detail in the comment on the next section.

* * *

§ 2–715. Buyer's Incidental and Consequential Damages

(1) Incidental damages resulting from the seller's breach include expenses reasonably incurred in inspection, receipt, transportation and care and custody of goods rightfully rejected, any commercially reasonable charges, expenses or commissions in connection with effecting cover and any other reasonable expense incident to the delay or other breach.

(2) Consequential damages resulting from the seller's breach include

(a) any loss resulting from general or particular requirements and needs of which the seller at the time of contracting had reason to know and which could not reasonably be prevented by cover or otherwise; and

(b) injury to person or property proximately resulting from any breach of warranty.

Official Comment

Prior Uniform Statutory Provisions: Subsection (2)(b)—Sections 69(7) and 70, Uniform Sales Act.

Changes: Rewritten.

Purposes of Changes and New Matter:

1. Subsection (1) is intended to provide reimbursement for the buyer who incurs reasonable expenses in connection with the handling of rightfully rejected goods or goods whose acceptance may be justifiably revoked, or in connection with effecting cover where the breach of the contract lies in nonconformity or non-delivery of the goods. The incidental damages listed are not intended to be exhaustive but are merely illustrative of the typical kinds of incidental damage.

2. Subsection (2) operates to allow the buyer, in an appropriate case, any consequential damages which are the result of the seller's breach. The "tacit agreement" test for the recovery of consequential damages is rejected. Although the older rule at common law which made the seller liable for all consequential damages of which he had "reason to know" in advance is followed, the liberality of that rule is modified by refusing to permit recovery unless the buyer could not reasonably have prevented the loss by cover or otherwise. Subparagraph (2) carries forward the provisions of the prior uniform statutory provision as to consequential damages resulting from breach of warranty, but modifies the rule by requiring first that the buyer attempt to minimize his damages in good faith, either by cover or otherwise.

3. In the absence of excuse under the section on merchant's excuse by failure of presupposed conditions, the seller is liable for consequential damages in all cases where he had reason to know of the buyer's general or particular requirements at the time of contracting. It is not necessary that there be a conscious acceptance of an insurer's liability on the seller's part, nor is his obligation for consequential damages limited to cases in which he fails to use due effort in good faith.

Particular needs of the buyer must generally be made known to the seller while general needs must rarely be made known to charge the seller with knowledge.

Any seller who does not wish to take the risk of consequential damages has available the section on contractual limitation of remedy.

4. The burden of proving the extent of loss incurred by way of consequential damage is on the buyer, but the section on liberal administration of remedies rejects any doctrine of certainty which requires almost mathematical precision in the proof of loss. Loss may be determined in any manner which is reasonable under the circumstances.

5. Subsection (2)(b) states the usual rule as to breach of warranty, allowing recovery for injuries "proximately" resulting from the breach. Where the injury involved follows the use of goods without discovery of the defect causing the damage, the question of "proximate" cause turns on whether it was reasonable for the buyer to use the goods without such inspection as would have revealed the defects. If it was not

reasonable for him to do so, or if he did in fact discover the defect prior to his use, the injury would not proximately result from the breach of warranty.

6. In the case of sale of wares to one in the business of reselling them, resale is one of the requirements of which the seller has reason to know within the meaning of subsection (2)(a).

* * *

§ 2–716. Buyer's Right to Specific Performance or Replevin

(1) Specific performance may be decreed where the goods are unique or in other proper circumstances.

(2) The decree for specific performance may include such terms and conditions as to payment of the price, damages, or other relief as the court may deem just.

(3) The buyer has a right of replevin for goods identified to the contract if after reasonable effort he is unable to effect cover for such goods or the circumstances reasonably indicate that such effort will be unavailing or if the goods have been shipped under reservation and satisfaction of the security interest in them has been made or tendered.

Official Comment

Prior Uniform Statutory Provision: Section 68, Uniform Sales Act.

Changes: Rephrased.

Purposes of Changes: To make it clear that:

1. The present section continues in general prior policy as to specific performance and injunction against breach. However, without intending to impair in any way the exercise of the court's sound discretion in the matter, this Article seeks to further a more liberal attitude than some courts have shown in connection with the specific performance of contracts of sale.

2. In view of this Article's emphasis on the commercial feasibility of replacement, a new concept of what are "unique" goods is introduced under this section. Specific performance is no longer limited to goods which are already specific or ascertained at the time of contracting. The test of uniqueness under this section must be made in terms of the total situation which characterizes the contract. Output and requirements contracts involving a particular or peculiarly available source or market present today the typical commercial specific performance situation, as contrasted with contracts for the sale of heirlooms or priceless works of art which were usually involved in the older cases. However, uniqueness is not the sole basis of the remedy under this section for the relief may also be granted "in other proper circumstances" and inability to cover is strong evidence of "other proper circumstances".

3. The legal remedy of replevin is given the buyer in cases in which cover is reasonably unavailable and goods have been identified to the contract. This is in addition to the buyer's right to recover identified goods on the seller's insolvency (Section 2–502).

4. This section is intended to give the buyer rights to the goods comparable to the seller's rights to the price.

5. If a negotiable document of title is outstanding, the buyer's right of replevin relates of course to the document not directly to the goods. See Article 7, especially Section 7–602.

* * *

§ 2–717. Deduction of Damages From the Price

The buyer on notifying the seller of his intention to do so may deduct all or any part of the damages resulting from any breach of the contract from any part of the price still due under the same contract.

Official Comment

Prior Uniform Statutory Provision:
See Section 69(1)(a), Uniform Sales Act.

Purposes:

1. This section permits the buyer to deduct from the price damages resulting from any breach by the seller and does not limit the relief to cases of breach of warranty as did the prior uniform statutory provision. To bring this provision into application the breach involved must be of the same contract under which the price in question is claimed to have been earned.

2. The buyer, however, must give notice of his intention to withhold all or part of the price if he wishes to avoid a default within the meaning of the section on insecurity and right to assurances. In conformity with the general policies of this Article, no formality of notice is required and any language which reasonably indicates the buyer's reason for holding up his payment is sufficient.

* * *

§ 2–718. Liquidation or Limitation of Damages; Deposits

(1) Damages for breach by either party may be liquidated in the agreement but only at an amount which is reasonable in the light of the anticipated or actual harm caused by the breach, the difficulties of proof of loss, and the inconvenience or nonfeasibility of otherwise obtaining an adequate remedy. A term fixing unreasonably large liquidated damages is void as a penalty.

(2) Where the seller justifiably withholds delivery of goods because of the buyer's breach, the buyer is entitled to restitution of any amount by which the sum of his payments exceeds

(a) the amount to which the seller is entitled by virtue of terms liquidating the seller's damages in accordance with subsection (1), or

(b) in the absence of such terms, twenty per cent of the value of the total performance for which the buyer is obligated under the contract or $500, whichever is smaller.

(3) The buyer's right to restitution under subsection (2) is subject to offset to the extent that the seller establishes

(a) a right to recover damages under the provisions of this Article other than subsection (1), and

(b) the amount or value of any benefits received by the buyer directly or indirectly by reason of the contract.

(4) Where a seller has received payment in goods their reasonable value or the proceeds of their resale shall be treated as payments for the

purposes of subsection (2); but if the seller has notice of the buyer's breach before reselling goods received in part performance, his resale is subject to the conditions laid down in this Article on resale by an aggrieved seller (Section 2–706).

Official Comment

Prior Uniform Statutory Provision: None.

Purposes:

1. Under subsection (1) liquidated damage clauses are allowed where the amount involved is reasonable in the light of the circumstances of the case. The subsection sets forth explicitly the elements to be considered in determining the reasonableness of a liquidated damage clause. A term fixing unreasonably large liquidated damages is expressly made void as a penalty. An unreasonably small amount would be subject to similar criticism and might be stricken under the section on unconscionable contracts or clauses.

2. Subsection (2) refuses to recognize a forfeiture unless the amount of the payment so forfeited represents a reasonable liquidation of damages as de-termined under subsection (1). A special exception is made in the case of small amounts (20% of the price or $500, whichever is smaller) deposited as security. No distinction is made between cases in which the payment is to be applied on the price and those in which it is intended as security for performance. Subsection (2) is applicable to any deposit or down or part payment. In the case of a deposit or turn in of goods resold before the breach, the amount actually received on the resale is to be viewed as the deposit rather than the amount allowed the buyer for the trade in. However, if the seller knows of the breach prior to the resale of the goods turned in, he must make reasonable efforts to realize their true value, and this is assured by requiring him to comply with the conditions laid down in the section on resale by an aggrieved seller.

* * *

§ 2–719. Contractual Modification or Limitation of Remedy

(1) Subject to the provisions of subsections (2) and (3) of this section and of the preceding section on liquidation and limitation of damages,

(a) the agreement may provide for remedies in addition to or in substitution for those provided in this Article and may limit or alter the measure of damages recoverable under this Article, as by limiting the buyer's remedies to return of the goods and repayment of the price or to repair and replacement of non-conforming goods or parts; and

(b) resort to a remedy as provided is optional unless the remedy is expressly agreed to be exclusive, in which case it is the sole remedy.

(2) Where circumstances cause an exclusive or limited remedy to fail of its essential purpose, remedy may be had as provided in this Act.

(3) Consequential damages may be limited or excluded unless the limitation or exclusion is unconscionable. Limitation of consequential damages for injury to the person in the case of consumer goods is prima facie

unconscionable but limitation of damages where the loss is commercial is not.

Official Comment
Prior Uniform Statutory Provision: None.

Purposes:

1. Under this section parties are left free to shape their remedies to their particular requirements and reasonable agreements limiting or modifying remedies are to be given effect.

However, it is of the very essence of a sales contract that at least minimum adequate remedies be available. If the parties intend to conclude a contract for sale within this Article they must accept the legal consequence that there be at least a fair quantum of remedy for breach of the obligations or duties outlined in the contract. Thus any clause purporting to modify or limit the remedial provisions of this Article in an unconscionable manner is subject to deletion and in that event the remedies made available by this Article are applicable as if the stricken clause had never existed. Similarly, under subsection (2), where an apparently fair and reasonable clause because of circumstances fails in its purpose or operates to deprive either party of the substantial value of the bargain, it must give way to the general remedy provisions of this Article.

2. Subsection (1)(b) creates a presumption that clauses prescribing remedies are cumulative rather than exclusive. If the parties intend the term to describe the sole remedy under the contract, this must be clearly expressed.

3. Subsection (3) recognizes the validity of clauses limiting or excluding consequential damages but makes it clear that they may not operate in an unconscionable manner. Actually such terms are merely an allocation of unknown or undeterminable risks. The seller in all cases is free to disclaim warranties in the manner provided in Section 2-316.

* * *

§ 2-720. Effect of "Cancellation" or "Rescission" on Claims for Antecedent Breach

Unless the contrary intention clearly appears, expressions of "cancellation" or "rescission" of the contract or the like shall not be construed as a renunciation or discharge of any claim in damages for an antecedent breach.

Official Comment
Prior Uniform Statutory Provision: None.

Purpose: This section is designed to safeguard a person holding a right of action from any unintentional loss of rights by the ill-advised use of such terms as "cancellation", "rescission", or the like. Once a party's rights have accrued they are not to be lightly impaired by concessions made in business decency and without intention to forego them. Therefore, unless the cancellation of a contract expressly declares that it is "without reservation of rights", or the like, it cannot be considered to be a renunciation under this section.

* * *

§ 2-721. Remedies for Fraud

Remedies for material misrepresentation or fraud include all remedies available under this Article for non-fraudulent breach. Neither rescission or a claim for rescission of the contract for sale nor rejection or return of the goods shall bar or be deemed inconsistent with a claim for damages or other remedy.

Official Comment

Prior Uniform Statutory Provision: None.

Purposes: To correct the situation by which remedies for fraud have been more circumscribed than the more modern and mercantile remedies for breach of warranty. Thus the remedies for fraud are extended by this section to coincide in scope with those for non-fraudulent breach. This section thus makes it clear that neither rescission of the contract for fraud nor rejection of the goods bars other remedies unless the circumstances of the case make the remedies incompatible.

* * *

§ 2-725. Statute of Limitations in Contracts for Sale

(1) An action for breach of any contract for sale must be commenced within four years after the cause of action has accrued. By the original agreement the parties may reduce the period of limitation to not less than one year but may not extend it.

(2) A cause of action accrues when the breach occurs, regardless of the aggrieved party's lack of knowledge of the breach. A breach of warranty occurs when tender of delivery is made, except that where a warranty explicitly extends to future performance of the goods and discovery of the breach must await the time of such performance the cause of action accrues when the breach is or should have been discovered.

(3) Where an action commenced within the time limited by subsection (1) is so terminated as to leave available a remedy by another action for the same breach such other action may be commenced after the expiration of the time limited and within six months after the termination of the first action unless the termination resulted from voluntary discontinuance or from dismissal for failure or neglect to prosecute.

(4) This section does not alter the law on tolling of the statute of limitations nor does it apply to causes of action which have accrued before this Act becomes effective.

Official Comment

Prior Uniform Statutory Provision: None.

Purposes: To introduce a uniform statute of limitations for sales contracts, thus eliminating the jurisdictional variations and providing needed relief for concerns doing business on a nationwide scale whose contracts have heretofore been governed by several different periods of limitation depending upon the state in which the transaction occurred. This Article takes sales contracts out of the general laws limiting the time for commencing contractual actions and selects a four year period as the most appropriate to modern business practice. This is within the normal commercial record keeping period.

Subsection (1) permits the parties to reduce the period of limitation. The minimum period is set at one year. The parties may not, however, extend the statutory period.

Subsection (2), providing that the cause of action accrues when the breach occurs, states an exception where the warranty extends to future performance.

Subsection (3) states the saving provision included in many state statutes and permits an additional short period for bringing new actions, where suits begun within the four year period have been terminated so as to leave a remedy still available for the same breach.

Subsection (4) makes it clear that this Article does not purport to alter or modify in any respect the law on tolling of the statute of limitations as it now prevails in the various jurisdictions.

* * *

STATE REFORM STATUTES

ALABAMA CODE

(1979)

§ 6–5–500. Intent of Legislature; legislative findings. It is the intent of the Legislature that a comprehensive system consisting of the time for commencement of actions, for discoverability of actions based upon insidious disease and the repose of actions shall be instituted in this state. The Legislature finds that in order to assure the rights of all persons, and to provide for the fair, orderly and efficient administration of product liability actions in the courts of this state, a complete and unified approach to the time in which product liability actions may be brought and maintained is required. The Legislature finds that product liability actions and litigation have increased substantially, and the cost of such litigation has risen in recent years. The Legislature further finds that these increases are having an impact upon consumer prices, and upon the availability, cost and use of product liability insurance, thus, affecting the availability of compensation for injured consumers. Therefore, it is the intent of the Legislature to provide a comprehensive time framework for the commencement and maintenance of all product liability actions brought in this state.

§ 6–5–501. Definitions. The following definitions are applicable in this division:

(1) ORIGINAL SELLER. Any person, firm, corporation, association, partnership, or other legal or business entity, which in the course of business or as an incident to business, sells or otherwise distributes a manufactured product (a) prior to or (b) at the time the manufactured product is first put to use by any person or business entity who did not acquire the manufactured product for either resale or other distribution in its unused condition or for incorporation as a component part in a manufactured product which is to be sold or otherwise distributed in its unused condition.

(2) PRODUCT LIABILITY ACTION. Any action brought by a natural person for personal injury, death, or property damage caused by the manufacture, construction, design, formula, preparation, assembly, installation, testing, warnings, instructions, marketing, packaging, or labeling of a manufactured product when such action is based upon (a) negligence, (b) innocent or negligent misrepresentation, (c) the manufacturer's liability doctrine, (d) the Alabama extended manufacturer's liability doctrine, as it exists or is hereafter construed or modified, (e) breach of any implied warranty, or (f) breach of any oral express warranty and no other. A

product liability action does not include an action for contribution or indemnity.

(3) The definitions used herein are to be used for purposes of this division and are not to be construed to expand or limit the status of the common or statutory law except as expressly modified by the provisions of this division.

§ 6–5–502. Limitation periods for product liability actions.

(a) All product liability actions against an original seller must be commenced within the following time limits and not otherwise:

(1) Except as specifically provided in subsections (b), (c), and (e) of this section, within one year of the time the personal injury, death, or property damage occurs; and

(2) Except as specifically provided in subsections (b), (c), and (e) of this section, each element of a product liability action shall be deemed to accrue at the time the personal injury, death, or property damage occurs;

(b) Where the personal injury, including personal injury resulting in death, or property damage (i) either is latent or by its nature is not discoverable in the exercise of reasonable diligence at the time of its occurrence, and (ii) is the result of ingestion of or exposure to some toxic or harmful or injury-producing substance, element or particle, including radiation, over a period of time as opposed to resulting from a sudden and fortuitous trauma, then, in that event, the product liability action claiming damages for such personal injury, or property damage must be commenced within one year from the date such personal injury or property damage is or in the exercise of reasonable diligence should have been discovered by the plaintiff or the plaintiff's decedent, and in such cases each of the elements of the product liability action shall be deemed to accrue at the time the personal injury is or in the exercise of reasonable diligence should have been discovered by the plaintiff or the plaintiff's decedent; and

(c) Notwithstanding the provisions of subsections (a) and (b) of this section, a product liability action against an original seller must be brought within 10 years after the manufactured product is first put to use by any person or business entity who did not acquire the manufactured product for either resale or other distribution in its unused condition or for incorporation as a component part in a manufactured product which is to be sold or otherwise distributed in its unused condition.

(d) The original seller may by express written agreement only waive or extend the period of time provided for in subsection (c) of this section; and

(e)(1) Notwithstanding the provisions of subsection (c) of this section, if a plaintiff or plaintiff's decedent is entitled to maintain a product liability action because of the failure of an original seller to alter, repair, recall, inspect, or issue warnings or instructions about the manufactured product, or otherwise to take any action or precautions with regard to the safety of the manufactured product for the benefit of users or consumers after the manufactured product was sold or otherwise distributed by an original seller, and, if any federal or state governmental agency shall impose a requirement so to alter, repair, recall, inspect, or issue warnings or instructions about the manufactured product or otherwise to take any actions or precautions with regard to the safety of the manufactured product for the benefit of users or consumers after the manufactured product was sold or otherwise distributed by an original seller, then, if these two events have occurred, a product liability action for damages on account of such failure for personal injury, death, or property damage must be commenced within one year of the time the personal injury, death, or property damage resulting from such failure occurs;

(2) In product liability actions predicated upon the failure to act and the governmental action, set forth in subdivision (1) of this subsection, where the personal injury, including personal injury resulting in death, or property damage (I) either is latent or by its nature is not discoverable in the exercise of reasonable diligence at the time of its occurrence, and (ii) is the result of the ingestion of or exposure to some toxic or harmful or injury-producing substance, element, or particle, including radiation, over a period of time as opposed to resulting from a sudden and fortuitous trauma, then in that event, the product liability action claiming damages for such personal injury or property damage must be commenced within one year from the date such personal injury or property damage is or in the exercise of reasonable diligence should have been discovered by the plaintiff or the plaintiff's decedent and in such cases each of the elements of the product liability action shall be deemed to accrue at the time the personal injury or property damage is or in the exercise of reasonable diligence should have been discovered by the plaintiff or plaintiff's decedent; and

(3) Notwithstanding the provisions of subdivisions (1) and (2) of this subsection, a product liability action against an original seller must be brought within 10 years after the date of the imposition of such requirement by such governmental agency.

§ 6–5–503. Applicability of division; not retroactive. This division and each section thereof shall apply only to product liability actions, wherein each element accrues after the effective date of this division, and no provision of this division shall have retroactive application.

§ 6–5–520. Intent of Legislature; legislative findings; collateral source rule modified. The Legislature finds that product liability litigation has increased substantially and the cost of such litigation has risen in recent years. The Legislature further finds that these increases have an impact upon the price and availability of products. It is the belief of the Legislature that there are special reasons for modifying the collateral source rule in this state as it applies to product liability actions. The Legislature finds that the recovery by plaintiffs of medical and hospital expenses as damages where plaintiffs are reimbursed for the same medical and hospital expenses from other sources contributes to the increase in the cost of product liability litigation. It is the intent of the Legislature that plaintiffs be compensated fully for any medical or hospital expenses incurred as a result of injuries sustained from a breach of product liability laws, but that plaintiffs not receive compensation more than once for the same medical and hospital expenses.

§ 6–5–521. "Product liability action" defined. (a) A "product liability action" means any action brought by a natural person for personal injury, death, or property damage caused by the manufacture, construction, design, formula, preparation, assembly, installation, testing, warnings, instructions, marketing, packaging, or labeling of a manufactured product when such action is based upon (1) negligence, (2) innocent or negligent misrepresentation, (3) the manufacturer's liability doctrine, (4) the Alabama extended manufacturer's liability doctrine as it exists or is hereafter construed or modified, (5) breach of any implied warranty, or (6) breach of any oral express warranty and no other. A product liability action does not include an action for contribution or indemnity.

(b) The definition used herein is to be used for purposes of this division and is not to be construed to expand or limit the status of the common or statutory law except as expressly modified by the provisions of this division.

§ 6–5–522. Evidence of medical expense reimbursement mitigates damages; cost of obtaining reimbursement recoverable. In all product liability actions where damages for any medical or hospital expenses are claimed and are legally recoverable for personal injury or death, evidence that the plaintiff's medical or hospital expenses have been or will be paid or reimbursed (1) by medical or hospital insurance, or (2) pursuant to the medical and hospital payment provisions of law governing workmen's compensation, shall be admissible as competent evidence in mitigation of such medical or hospital expense damages. In such actions upon admission of evidence respecting reimbursement or payment of medical or hospital expenses, the plaintiff shall be entitled to introduce evidence of the cost of obtaining reimbursement or payment of medical or hospital expenses. Such portion of the costs of obtaining reimbursement or payment of medical or hospital expenses as the trier of fact finds is reasonably related to the reimbursement or payment received or to be received by the plaintiff shall be a recoverable item of such damages for medical or hospital expenses.

§ 6–5–523. Reimbursement for medical expenses discoverable. In all product liability actions information respecting reimbursement or payment obtained or which may be obtained by the plaintiff for medical or hospital expenses shall be subject to discovery.

§ 6–5–524. Evidence of reimbursement inadmissible if recipient must repay. Upon proof by the plaintiff to the court that the plaintiff is obligated to repay the medical or hospital expenses which have been or will be paid or reimbursed, no evidence relating to such reimbursement or payment not otherwise admissible shall be admissible as a result of this division.

§ 6–5–525. Prior rights not affected. This division shall not affect any rights which have accrued prior to July 30, 1979.

ARIZONA REVISED STATUTES ANNOTATED

(1978, 1989 (§ 12–701), 1995, and 2004 (§ 12–688))

§ **12–551. Product liability.** A product liability action as defined in § 12–681 shall be commenced and prosecuted within the period prescribed in § 12–542, except that no product liability action may be commenced and prosecuted if the cause of action accrues more than twelve years after the product was first sold for use or consumption, unless the cause of action is based upon the negligence of the manufacturer or seller or a breach of an express warranty provided by the manufacturer or seller.

§ **12–681. Definitions.** In this article, unless the context otherwise requires:

1. "Defective and unreasonably dangerous" does not include a food product that is otherwise fit for human consumption and nourishment.

2. "Food product" means any product that is grown, prepared, provided, served or sold and that is primarily intended for human consumption and nourishment.

3. "Manufacturer" means a person or entity that designs, assembles, fabricates, produces, constructs or otherwise prepares a product or component part of a product before its sale to a user or consumer, including a seller owned in whole or significant part by the manufacturer or a seller owning the manufacturer in whole or significant part.

4. "Product" means the individual product or any component part of the product that is the subject of a product liability action.

5. "Product liability action" means any action brought against a manufacturer or seller of a product for damages for bodily injury, death or property damage caused by or resulting from the manufacture, construction, design, formula, installation, preparation, assembly, testing, packaging, labeling, sale, use or consumption of any product, the failure to warn or protect against a danger or hazard in the use or misuse of the product or the failure to provide proper instructions for the use or consumption of any product.

6. "Product safety analysis or review" means any investigation, inquiry, review, evaluation or other means by which a person or entity seeks to determine, calculate, predict, estimate, evaluate or report the safety or health effects of the use of any of its products, systems, services or processes. Product safety analysis or review includes an analysis or review by a component manufacturer of the safety and health effects of component parts in end products. A product safety analysis or review may be conducted by employees of the person or entity or by consultants engaged specifically to perform the analysis or review.

7. "Reasonable remedial measures" means actions taken as a result of a product safety analysis or review and intended to improve the safety of

products, systems, services or processes or to lessen the likelihood of a safety-related accident. These actions include:

(a) Modifications to the product, system, service or process.

(b) Changes in quality assurance procedures or policies.

(c) Modifications made to the design or method of manufacturing, to manufacturing equipment or to the testing of the product, system, service or process.

(d) Changes or additions to training programs or safety education programs.

(e) Personnel or human resources measures related to the product, system, service or process.

(f) The use or modification of warnings, notices or changes to owner manuals and related materials.

(g) The recall of products.

8. "Reasonably foreseeable alteration, modification, use or consumption" means an alteration, modification, use or consumption of the product that would be expected of an ordinary and prudent purchaser, user or consumer and that an ordinary and prudent manufacturer should have anticipated.

9. "Seller" means a person or entity, including a wholesaler, distributor, retailer or lessor, that is engaged in the business of leasing any product or selling any product for resale, use or consumption.

10. "State of the art" means the technical, mechanical and scientific knowledge of manufacturing, designing, testing or labeling the same or similar products that was in existence and reasonably feasible for use at the time of manufacture.

§ 12–682. Limitation. The previously existing common law of products liability is modified only to the extent specifically stated in this article and § 12–551.

§ 12–683. Affirmative defenses. In any product liability action, a defendant shall not be liable if the defendant proves that any of the following apply:

1. The defect in the product is alleged to result from inadequate design or fabrication, and if the plans or designs for the product or the methods and techniques of manufacturing, inspecting, testing and labeling the product conformed with the state of the art at the time the product was first sold by the defendant.

2. The proximate cause of the incident giving rise to the action was an alteration or modification of the product that was not reasonably foreseeable, made by a person other than the defendant and subsequent to the time the product was first sold by the defendant.

3. The proximate cause of the incident giving rise to the action was a use or consumption of the product that was for a purpose, in a manner or in an activity other than that which was reasonably foreseeable or was contrary to any express and adequate instructions or warnings appearing on or attached to the product or on its original container or wrapping, if the injured person knew or with the exercise of reasonable and diligent care should have known of such instructions or warnings.

4. The proximate cause of the incident or incidents giving rise to the action was the repeated consumption of a food product that is not defective and unreasonably dangerous if consumed in reasonable quantities.

§ 12–684. Indemnification—Tender of defense—Execution. A. In any product liability action where the manufacturer refuses to accept a tender of defense from the seller, the manufacturer shall indemnify the seller for any judgment rendered against the seller and shall also reimburse the seller for reasonable attorneys' fees and costs incurred by the seller in defending such action, unless either paragraph 1 or 2 applies:

1. The seller had knowledge of the defect in the product.

2. The seller altered, modified or installed the product, and such alteration, modification or installation was a substantial cause of the incident giving rise to the action, was not authorized or requested by the manufacturer and was not performed in compliance with the directions or specifications of the manufacturer.

B. If a judgment is rendered in favor of the plaintiff and a seller is granted indemnity against a manufacturer, the plaintiff shall first attempt to satisfy the judgment by levying execution upon the manufacturer in this state or in the state where the manufacturer's principal place of business is located and by making demand upon any liability insurance carrier of the manufacturer whose identity is known to plaintiff before attempting to collect the judgment from the seller or the seller's liability insurance carrier. The return of a writ of execution partially or wholly unsatisfied or the failure of the manufacturer's insurance carrier to pay the judgment upon demand shall be deemed full compliance with the plaintiff's obligation to attempt to collect from the manufacturer.

C. In any product liability action the manufacturer of the product shall be indemnified by the seller of the product for any judgment rendered against the manufacturer and shall also reimburse the manufacturer for reasonable attorneys' fees and costs incurred in defending such action, if the seller provided the plans or specifications for the manufacturer or preparation of the product and such plans or specifications were a substantial cause of the product's alleged defect and if the product was manufactured in compliance with and according to the plans or specifications of the seller. If a judgment is rendered in favor of the plaintiff and a manufacturer is granted indemnity against a seller, the plaintiff shall first attempt to satisfy the judgment by levying execution upon the seller in this state or in the state where the seller's principal place of business is located and by making demand upon any liability insurance carrier of the seller whose identity is known to plaintiff before attempting to collect the judgment from the manufacturer or manufacturer's liability insurance carrier. The return of a writ of execution partially or wholly unsatisfied or the failure of the seller's insurance carrier to pay the judgment upon demand shall be deemed full compliance with the plaintiff's obligation to attempt to collect from the seller. The provisions of this subsection shall not apply if the manufacturer had knowledge or with the exercise of reasonable and diligent care should have had knowledge of the defect in the product.

§ 12–685. Contents of complaint—Amount of recovery. In any product liability action no dollar amount or figure shall be included in the complaint. The complaint shall pray for such damages as are reasonable in the premises. The complaint shall include a statement reciting that the jurisdictional amount established for filing the action is satisfied.

§ 12–686. Inadmissible evidence—State of the art—Modification. In any product liability action, the following shall not be admissible as direct evidence of a defect:

1.   Evidence of advancements or changes in the state of the art subsequent to the time the product was first sold by the defendant.

2.   Evidence of any change made in the design or methods of manufacturing or testing the product or any similar product subsequent to the time the product was first sold by the defendant.

§ 12–687. Reasonable remedial measures; cause of action; punitive damages. If a person or entity conducts a product safety analysis or review and, as a result, takes reasonable remedial measures, the following shall apply to a product liability action brought against the person or entity:

1.   The plaintiff may not use the product safety analysis or review or the reasonable remedial measures to prove negligence, that the product was defective or unreasonably dangerous, or other culpable conduct in a product liability action. However, the plaintiff may use the product safety analysis or review or reasonable remedial measures for other purposes, such as proving feasibility of precautionary measures, impeachment or to controvert any position taken by a defendant in litigation which is inconsistent with the contents of the product safety analysis or review or reasonable remedial measures.

2.   This subsection does not prevent a plaintiff in a product liability action from proving negligence, that the product was defective or unreasonably dangerous, or other culpable conduct by other independent evidence or sources, even if such evidence or sources are mentioned or included in the product safety analysis or review or reasonable remedial measures.

3.   The plaintiff may not use the product safety analysis or review or the reasonable remedial measures to prove conduct that would subject the person or entity that caused the product safety analysis or review to be

performed to punitive or exemplary damages, unless the plaintiff establishes that the analysis or review, or the reasonable remedial measures, were undertaken in bad faith or solely for the purpose of affecting the litigation instituted by the plaintiff.

4. The existence and contents of a product safety analysis or review and any resulting reasonable remedial measures are discoverable and subject to disclosure in a product liability action unless otherwise privileged. However, a portion of a product safety analysis or review may be designated and maintained as confidential and protected from public disclosure pursuant to applicable rules of civil procedures if the portion involves trade secrets as defined in section 44–401, proprietary material or competitively sensitive information. Any dispute as to confidentiality shall be determined by a court following an in camera review of the portion of the analysis or review in question.

§ 12–688. **Duty to warn; food products.** There is no duty to warn a purchaser, user or consumer or any other person, regardless of age, that the consumption of a food product that is not defective and unreasonably dangerous may cause health problems if consumed excessively.

§ 12–701. **Drugs—Exemplary or punitive damages—Definition.** A. The manufacturer or seller of a drug is not liable for exemplary or punitive damages if the drug alleged to cause the harm either:

1. was manufactured and labeled in relevant and material respects in accordance with the terms of an approval or license issued by the federal Food and Drug Administration under the Food, Drug and Cosmetic Act (21 United States Code Section 301, et seq.) or the Public Health Service Act (42 United States Code Section 201, et seq.) or

2. is generally recognized as safe and effective pursuant to conditions established by the federal food and drug administration and applicable regulations, including packaging and labeling regulations.

B. Subsection A does not apply if the plaintiff proves, by clear and convincing evidence, that the defendant, either before or after making the drug available for public use, knowingly, in violation of applicable federal food and drug administration regulations, withheld from or misrepresented to the administration information known to be material and relevant to the harm which the plaintiff allegedly suffered.

C. In this section, "drug" means the same as provided in Section 201(g)(1) of the federal food, drug and cosmetic act (21 United States Code Section 321(g)(1)).

ARKANSAS CODE ANNOTATED

(1973, 1987)

§ 4–86–102. Suppliers liability. (a) A supplier of a product is subject to liability in damages for harm to a person or to property if:

(1) The supplier is engaged in the business of manufacturing, assembling, selling, leasing, or otherwise distributing the product;

(2) The product was supplied by him or her in a defective condition which rendered it unreasonably dangerous; and

(3) The defective condition was a proximate cause of the harm to person or to property.

(b) The provisions of subsection (a) of this section apply although the claiming party has not obtained the product from or entered into any contractual relation with the supplier.

§ 16–116–102. Definitions. As used in this subchapter:

(1) "Anticipated life" means the period over which the product may reasonably be expected to be useful to the user as determined by the trier of facts;

(2) "Defective condition" means a condition of a product that renders it unsafe for reasonably foreseeable use and consumption;

(3) "Manufacturer" means the designer, fabricator, producer, compounder, processor, or assembler of any product or its component parts;

(4) "Product" means any tangible object or goods produced;

(5) "Product liability action" includes all actions brought for or on account of personal injury, death, or property damage caused by, or resulting from, the manufacture, construction, design, formula, preparation, assembly, testing, service, warning, instruction, marketing, packaging, or labeling of any product;

(6)(A) "Supplier" means any individual or entity engaged in the business of selling a product, whether the sale is for resale, or for use or consumption.

(B) "Supplier" includes a retailer, wholesaler, or distributor and also includes a lessor or bailor engaged in the business of leasing or bailment of a product; and

(7)(A) "Unreasonably dangerous" means that a product is dangerous to an extent beyond that which would be contemplated by the ordinary and reasonable buyer, consumer, or user who acquires or uses the product, assuming the ordinary knowledge of the community or of similar buyers, users, or consumers as to its characteristics, propensities, risks, dangers, and proper and improper uses, as well as any special knowledge, training, or experience possessed by the particular buyer, user, or consumer or which he or she was required to possess.

(B) However, as to a minor, "unreasonably dangerous" means that a product is dangerous to an extent beyond that which would be contemplated by an ordinary and reasonably careful minor considering his or her age and intelligence.

§ 16–116–103. Three year commencement requirement. All product liability actions shall be commenced within three (3) years after the date on which the death, injury, or damage complained of occurs.

§ 16–116–104. Certain knowledge considered evidence. (a)(1) In determining the liability of the manufacturer, the state of scientific and technological knowledge available to the manufacturer or supplier at the time the product was placed on the market, rather than at the time of the injury, may be considered as evidence.

(2) Consideration may also be given to the customary designs, methods, standards, and techniques of manufacturing, inspecting, and testing by other manufacturers or sellers of similar products.

(b) The provisions of this section shall not apply to an action based on express warranty or misrepresentation regarding the product.

§ 16–116–105. Regulation compliance of evidence. (a) Compliance by a manufacturer or supplier with any federal or state statute or administrative regulation existing at the time a product was manufactured and prescribing standards of design, inspection, testing, manufacture, labeling, warning, or instructions for use of a product shall be considered as evidence that the product is not in an unreasonably dangerous condition in regard to matters covered by these standards.

(b) Supplying of a product after its anticipated life may be considered as a defense by the manufacturer as between the manufacturer and supplier if the product is supplied after the expiration date placed on the product by the manufacturer as required by law.

(c) Use of a product beyond its anticipated life by a consumer where the consumer knew or should have known the anticipated life of the product may be considered as evidence of fault on the part of the consumer.

§ 16–116–106. Unreasonably dangerous by alteration. If a product is not unreasonably dangerous at the time it leaves the control of the manufacturer or supplier but was made unreasonably dangerous by subsequent unforeseeable alteration, change, improper maintenance, or abnormal use, such conduct may be considered as evidence of fault on the part of the user.

§ 16–116–107. Supplier's action for indemnity. A supplier of a defective product who was not the manufacturer shall have a cause of action for indemnity from the manufacturer of a defective product arising from the supplying of the defective product.

CALIFORNIA CIVIL CODE

(1987, 1997, 1998 concerning certain inherent dangers)

§ 1714.45.   (a) In a products liability action, a manufacturer or seller shall not be liable if both of the following apply:

(1) The product is inherently unsafe and the product is known to be unsafe by the ordinary consumer who consumes the product with the ordinary knowledge common to the community.

(2) The product is a common consumer product intended for personal consumption, such as sugar, castor oil, alcohol, and butter, as identified in Comment *i* to Section 402A of the *Restatement (Second) of Torts*.

(b) This section does not exempt the manufacture or sale of tobacco products by tobacco manufacturers and their successors in interest from product liability actions, but does exempt the sale or distribution of tobacco products by any other person, including, but not limited to, retailers or distributors.

(c) For purposes of this section, the term "product liability action" means any action for injury or death caused by a product, except that the term does not include an action based on a manufacturing defect or breach of an express warranty.

(d) This section is intended to be declarative of and does not alter or amend existing California law, including *Cronin v. J.B.E. Olson Corp.*, (1972) 8 Cal.3d 121, and shall apply to all product liability actions pending on, or commenced after, January 1, 1988.

(e) This section does not apply to, and never applied to, an action brought by a public entity to recover the value of benefits provided to individuals injured by a tobacco-related illness caused by the tortious conduct of a tobacco company or its successor in interest, including, but not limited to, an action brought pursuant to Section 14124.71 of the Welfare and Institutions Code. In the action brought by a public entity, the fact that the injured individual's claim against the defendant may be barred by a prior version of this section shall not be a defense. This subdivision does not constitute a change in, but is declaratory of, existing law relating to tobacco products.

(f) It is the intention of the Legislature in enacting the amendments to subdivisions (a) and (b) of this section adopted at the 1997–98 Regular Session to declare that there exists no statutory bar to tobacco-related personal injury, wrongful death, or other tort claims against tobacco manufacturers and their successors in interest by California smokers or others who have suffered or incurred injuries, damages, or costs arising from the promotion, marketing, sale, or consumption of tobacco products. It is also the intention of the Legislature to clarify that such claims which were or are brought shall be determined on their merits, without the imposition of any claim of statutory bar or categorical defense.

(g) This section shall not be construed to grant immunity to a tobacco industry research organization.

COLORADO REVISED STATUTES

(1977, 1981, 1986–87, 2003)

§ 13–21–102.5. Limitations on damages for noneconomic loss or injury. (1) The general assembly finds, determines, and declares that awards in civil actions for noneconomic losses or injuries often unduly burden the economic, commercial, and personal welfare of persons in this state; therefore, for the protection of the public peace, health, and welfare, the general assembly enacts this section placing monetary limitations on such damages for noneconomic losses or injuries.

(2) As used in this section:

(a) "Derivative noneconomic loss or injury" means nonpecuniary harm or emotional stress to persons other than the person suffering the direct or primary loss or injury.

(b) "Noneconomic loss or injury" means nonpecuniary harm for which damages are recoverable by the person suffering the direct or primary loss or injury, including pain and suffering, inconvenience, emotional stress, and impairment of the quality of life. "Noneconomic loss or injury" includes a damage recovery for nonpecuniary harm for actions brought under section 13–21–201 or 13–21–202.

(3)(a) In any civil action other than medical malpractice actions in which damages for noneconomic loss or injury may be awarded, the total of such damages shall not exceed the sum of two hundred fifty thousand dollars, unless the court finds justification by clear and convincing evidence therefor. In no case shall the amount of noneconomic loss or injury damages exceed five hundred thousand dollars. The damages for noneconomic loss or injury in a medical malpractice action shall not exceed the limitations on noneconomic loss or injury specified in section 13–64–302.

(b) In any civil action, no damages for derivative noneconomic loss or injury may be awarded unless the court finds justification by clear and convincing evidence therefor. In no case shall the amount of such damages exceed two hundred fifty thousand dollars.

(c)(I) The limitations on damages set forth in paragraphs (a) and (b) of this subsection (3) shall be adjusted for inflation as of January 1, 1998. The adjustment made on January 1, 1998, shall be based on the cumulative annual adjustment for inflation for each year since the effective date of the damages limitations in paragraphs (a) and (b) of this subsection (3). The adjustment made pursuant to this subparagraph (I) shall be rounded upward or downward to the nearest ten-dollar increment.

(II) As used in this paragraph (c), "inflation" means the annual percentage change in the United States department of labor, bureau of labor statistics, consumer price index for Denver–Boulder, all items, all urban consumers, or its successor index.

(III) The secretary of state shall certify the adjusted limitation on damages within fourteen days after the appropriate information is available, and such adjusted limitation on damages shall be the limitation applicable to all claims for relief that accrue on or after January 1, 1998.

(IV) Nothing in this subsection (3) shall change the limitations on damages set forth in section 13–64–302, or the limitation on damages set forth in section 33–44–113, C.R.S.

(4) The limitations specified in subsection (3) of this section shall not be disclosed to a jury in any such action, but shall be imposed by the court before judgment.

(5) Nothing in this section shall be construed to limit the recovery of compensatory damages for physical impairment or disfigurement.

(6)(a)(I) In any claim for breach of contract, damages for noneconomic loss or injury or for derivative noneconomic loss or injury are recoverable only if:

(A) The recovery for such damages is specifically authorized in the contract that is the subject of the claim; or

(B) In any first-party claim brought against an insurer for breach of an insurance contract, the plaintiff demonstrates by clear and convincing evidence that the defendant committed willful and wanton breach of contract.

(II) For purposes of this paragraph (a), "willful and wanton breach of contract" means that:

(A) The defendant intended to breach the contract;

(B) The defendant breached the contract without any reasonable justification; and

(C) The contract clearly indicated that damages for noneconomic loss or injury or for derivative noneconomic damages or loss were within the contemplation or expectation of the parties.

(b) Except for the breach of contract damages that are permitted pursuant to sub-subparagraph (B) of subparagraph (I) of paragraph (a) of this subsection (6), nothing in this subsection (6) shall be construed to prohibit one or more parties from waiving the recovery of damages for noneconomic loss or injury or for derivative noneconomic loss or injury on a breach of contract claim so long as the waiver is explicit and in writing.

(c) The limitations on damages set forth in subsection (3) of this section shall apply in any civil action to the aggregate sum of any noneconomic damages awarded under this section for breach of contract including but not limited to bad faith breach of contract.

(d) In any civil action in which an award of damages for noneconomic loss or injury or for derivative noneconomic loss or injury is made on a breach of contract claim, the court shall state such award in the judgment separately from any other damages award.

(e) Except as otherwise provided in paragraph (c) of this subsection (6), nothing in this subsection (6) shall be construed to govern the recovery of noneconomic damages on a tort claim for bad faith breach of contract.

§ 13–21–401. Definitions. As used in this part 4, unless the context otherwise requires:

(1) "Manufacturer" means a person or entity who designs, assembles, fabricates, produces, constructs, or otherwise prepares a product or a component part of a product prior to the sale of the product to a user or consumer. The term includes any seller who has actual knowledge of a defect in a product or a seller of a product who creates and furnishes a manufacturer with specifications relevant to the alleged defect for producing the product or who otherwise exercises some significant control over all or a portion of the manufacturing process or who alters or modifies a product in any significant manner after the product comes into his possession and before it is sold to the ultimate user or consumer. The term also includes any seller of a product who is owned in whole or significant part by the manufacturer or who owns, in whole or significant part, the manufacturer. A seller not otherwise a manufacturer shall not be deemed to be a manufacturer merely because he places or has placed a private label on a product if he did not otherwise specify how the product shall be produced or control, in some significant manner, the manufacturing process of the product and the seller discloses who the actual manufacturer is.

(2) "Product liability action" means any action brought against a manufacturer or seller of a product, regardless of the substantive legal theory or theories upon which the action is brought, for or on account of personal injury, death, or property damage caused by or resulting from the manufacture, construction, design, formula, installation, preparation, assembly, testing, packaging, labeling, or sale of any product, or the failure to warn or protect against a danger or hazard in the use, misuse, or unintended use of any product, or the failure to provide proper instructions for the use of any product.

(3) "Seller" means any individual or entity, including a manufacturer, wholesaler, distributor, or retailer, who is engaged in the business of selling or leasing any product for resale, use, or consumption.

§ 13–21–402. Innocent seller. (1) No product liability action shall be commenced or maintained against any seller of a product unless said seller is also the manufacturer of said product or the manufacturer of the part thereof giving rise to the product liability action. Nothing in this part 4 shall be construed to limit any other action from being brought against any seller of a product.

(2) If jurisdiction cannot be obtained over a particular manufacturer of a product or a part of a product alleged to be defective, then that

manufacturer's principal distributor or seller over whom jurisdiction can be obtained shall be deemed, for the purposes of this section, the manufacturer of the product.

§ 13–21–402.5. Product misuse. A product liability action may not be commenced or maintained against a manufacturer or seller of a product that caused injury, death, or property damage if, at the time the injury, death, or property damage occurred, the product was used in a manner or for a purpose other than that which was intended and which could not reasonably have been expected, and such misuse of the product was a cause of the injury, death, or property damage.

§ 13–21–403. Presumptions. (1) In any product liability action, it shall be rebuttably presumed that the product which caused the injury, death, or property damage was not defective and that the manufacturer or seller thereof was not negligent if the product:

(a) Prior to sale by the manufacturer, conformed to the state of the art, as distinguished from industry standards, applicable to such product in existence at the time of sale; or

(b) Complied with, at the time of sale by the manufacturer, any applicable code, standard, or regulation adopted or promulgated by the United States or by this state, or by any agency of the United States or of this state.

(2) In like manner, noncompliance with a government code, standard, or regulation existing and in effect at the time of sale of the product by the manufacturer which contributed to the claim or injury shall create a rebuttable presumption that the product was defective or negligently manufactured.

(3) Ten years after a product is first sold for use or consumption, it shall be rebuttably presumed that the product was not defective and that the manufacturer or seller thereof was not negligent and that all warnings and instructions were proper and adequate.

(4) In a product liability action in which the court determines by a preponderance of the evidence that the necessary facts giving rise to a presumption have been established, the court shall instruct the jury concerning the presumption.

§ 13–21–404. Inadmissible evidence. In any product liability action, evidence of any scientific advancements in technical or other knowledge or techniques, or in design theory or philosophy, or in manufacturing or testing knowledge, techniques, or processes, or in labeling, warnings of risks or hazards, or instructions for the use of such product, where such advancements were discovered subsequent to the time the product in issue was sold by the manufacturer, shall not be admissible for any purpose other than to show a duty to warn.

§ 13–80–106. Limitation of actions against manufacturers or sellers of products. (1) Notwithstanding any other statutory provisions to the contrary, all actions except those governed by section 4–2–725, C.R.S., brought against a manufacturer or seller of a product, regardless of the substantive legal theory or theories upon which the action is brought, for or on account of personal injury, death, or property damage caused by or resulting from the manufacture, construction, design, formula, installation, preparation, assembly, testing, packaging, labeling, or sale of any product, or the failure to warn or protect against a danger or hazard in the use, misuse, or unintended use of any product, or the failure to provide proper instructions for the use of any product shall be brought within two years after the claim for relief arises and not thereafter.

(2) If any person entitled to bring any action mentioned in this section is under the age of eighteen years, mentally incompetent, imprisoned, or absent from the United States at the time the cause of action accrues and is without spouse or natural or legal guardian, such person may bring said action within the time limit specified in this section after the disability is removed. If such person has a legal representative, such person's representative shall bring the action within the period of limitation imposed by this section.

§ 13–80–107. Limitation of actions against manufacturers, sellers, or lessors of new manufacturing equipment. (1)(a) Notwithstanding any statutory provision to the contrary, all actions for or on account of personal injury, death, or property damage brought against a person or entity on account of the design, assembly, fabrication, production, or construction of new manufacturing equipment, or any component part thereof, or involving the sale or lease of such equipment shall be brought within the time provided in section 13–80–102 and not thereafter.

(b) Except as provided in paragraph (c) of this subsection (1), no such action shall be brought on a claim arising more than seven years after such equipment was first used for its intended purpose by someone not engaged in the business of manufacturing, selling, or leasing such equipment, except when the claim arises from injury due to hidden defects or prolonged exposure to hazardous material.

(c) The time limitation specified in paragraph (b) of this subsection (1) shall not apply if the manufacturer, seller, or lessor intentionally misrepresented or fraudulently concealed any material fact concerning said equipment which is a proximate cause of the injury, death, or property damage.

(2) As used in this section, "manufacturing equipment" means equipment used in the operation or process of producing a new product, article, substance, or commodity for the purposes of commercial sale and different from and having a distinctive name, character, or use from the raw or prepared materials used in the operation or process.

(3) The provisions of subsection (1) of this section shall not apply to a claim against a manufacturer, seller, or lessor, who, in an express written warranty, warranted manufacturing equipment to be free of defects in design, manufacture, or materials for a period of time greater than that set

forth in paragraph (b) of subsection (1) of this section, if the injury complained of occurred and the claim for relief arose during the period of the express written warranty.

(4) The provisions of subsection (1) of this section shall not be applicable to indemnity actions brought by a manufacturer, seller, or lessor of manufacturing equipment or any other product against any other person who is or may be liable to said manufacturer, seller, or lessor for all or a portion of any judgment rendered against said manufacturer, seller, or lessor.

CONNECTICUT GENERAL STATUTES

(1982–99)

§ 52–572l. Strict tort liability, contributory negligence and comparative negligence not bar to recovery. In causes of action based on strict tort liability, contributory negligence or comparative negligence shall not be a bar to recovery. The provisions of this section shall apply to all actions pending on or brought after June 7, 1977, claiming strict tort liability notwithstanding the date on which the cause of action accrued. Nothing in this section shall be construed as barring the defense of misuse of the product or the defense of knowingly using the product in a defective condition in an action based on strict tort liability.

§ 52–572m. Product liability actions—Definitions. As used in this section and sections 52–240a, 52–572n to 52–572r, inclusive, and 52–577a, as amended by sections 243 to 245, inclusive, and 247 of this act:

(a) "Product seller" means any person or entity, including a manufacturer, wholesaler, distributor or retailer who is engaged in the business of selling such products whether the sale is for resale or for use or consumption. The term "product seller" also includes lessors or bailors of products who are engaged in the business of leasing or bailment of products.

(b) "Product liability claim" includes all claims or actions brought for personal injury, death or property damage caused by the manufacture, construction, design, formula, preparation, assembly, installation, testing, warnings, instructions, marketing, packaging or labeling of any product. "Product liability claim" shall include, but is not limited to, all actions based on the following theories: strict liability in tort; negligence; breach of or failure to discharge a duty to warn or instruct, whether negligent or innocent; misrepresentation or nondisclosure, whether negligent or innocent.

(c) "Claimant" means a person asserting a product liability claim for damages incurred by the claimant or one for whom the claimant is acting in a representative capacity.

(d) "Harm" includes damage to property, including the product itself, and personal injuries including wrongful death. As between commercial parties, "harm" does not include commercial loss.

(e) "Manufacturer" includes product sellers who design, assemble, fabricate, construct, process, package or otherwise prepare a product or component part of a product prior to its sale to a user or consumer. It includes a product seller or entity not otherwise a manufacturer that holds itself out as a manufacturer.

§ 52–572n. Product liability claims. (a) A product liability claim as provided in sections 52–240a, 52–240b, 52–572m to 52–572r, inclusive, and 52–577a may be asserted and shall be in lieu of all other claims against product sellers, including actions of negligence, strict liability and warranty, for harm caused by a product.

(b) A claim may be asserted successfully under said sections notwithstanding the claimant did not buy the product from or enter into any contractual relationship with the product seller.

(c) As between commercial parties, commercial loss caused by a product is not harm and may not be recovered by a commercial claimant in a product liability claim. An action for commercial loss caused by a product may be brought only under, and shall be governed by, title 42a, the Uniform Commercial Code.

§ 52–572o. Comparative responsibility—Award of damages—Action for contribution. (a) In any claim under sections 52–240a, 52–240b, 52–572m to 52–572r, inclusive, or 52–577a, the comparative responsibility of, or attributed to, the claimant, shall not bar recovery but shall diminish the award of compensatory damages proportionately, according to the measure of responsibility attributed to the claimant.

(b) In any claim involving comparative responsibility, the court may instruct the jury to give answers to special interrogatories, or if there is no jury, the court may make its own findings, indicating (1) the amount of damages each claimant would receive if comparative responsibility were disregarded, and (2) the percentage of responsibility allocated to each party, including the claimant, as compared with the combined responsibility of all parties to the action. For this purpose, the court may decide that it is appropriate to treat two or more persons as a single party.

(c) In determining the percentage of responsibility, the trier of fact shall consider, on a comparative basis, both the nature and quality of the conduct of the party.

(d) The court shall determine the award for each claimant according to these findings and shall enter judgment against parties liable on the basis of the common law joint and several liability of joint tortfeasors. The judgment shall also specify the proportionate amount of damages allocated against each party liable, according to the percentage of responsibility established for such party.

(e) If a judgment has been rendered, any action for contribution must be brought within one year after the judgment becomes final. If no judgment has been rendered, the person bringing the action for contribution either must have (1) discharged by payment the common liability within the period of the statute of limitations applicable to the right of action of the claimant against him and commenced the action for contribution within one year after payment, or (2) agreed while action was pending to discharge the common liability and, within one year after the agreement, have paid the liability and brought an action for contribution.

§ 52–572p. Limitation of liability of product seller. (a) A product seller shall not be liable for harm that would not have occurred but for the fact that his product was altered or modified by a third party unless: (1) The alteration or modification was in accordance with the instructions or specifications of the product seller; (2) the alteration or modification was made with the consent of the product seller; or (3) the alteration or modification was the result of conduct that reasonably should have been anticipated by the product seller.

(b) For the purposes of this section, alteration or modification includes changes in the design, formula, function or use of the product from that originally designed, tested or intended by the product seller.

§ 52–572q. Liability of product seller due to lack of adequate warnings or instructions. (a) A product seller may be subject to liability for harm caused to a claimant who proves by a fair preponderance of the evidence that the product was defective in that adequate warnings or instructions were not provided.

(b) In determining whether instructions or warnings were required and, if required, whether they were adequate the trier of fact may consider: (1) The likelihood that the product would cause the harm suffered by the claimant; (2) the ability of the product seller to anticipate at the time of manufacture that the expected product user would be aware of the product risk, and the nature of the potential harm; and (3) the technological feasibility and cost of warnings and instructions.

(c) In claims based on this section, the claimant shall prove by a fair preponderance of the evidence that if adequate warnings or instructions had been provided, the claimant would not have suffered the harm.

(d) A product seller may not be considered to have provided adequate warnings or instructions unless they were devised to communicate with the person best able to take or recommend precautions against the potential harm.

§ 52–577a. Limitation of action based on product liability claim. (a) No product liability claim, as defined in section 52–572m, shall be brought but within three years from the date when the injury, death or property damage is first sustained or discovered or in the exercise of reasonable care should have been discovered, except that, subject to the provisions of subsections (c), (d) and (e) of this section, no such action may be brought against any party nor may any party be impleaded pursuant to subsection (b) of this section later than ten years from the date that the party last parted with possession or control of the product.

(b) In any such action, a product seller may implead any third party who is or may be liable for all or part of the claimant's claim, if such third party defendant is served with the third party complaint within one year from the date the cause of action brought under subsection (a) of this section is returned to court.

(c) The ten-year limitation provided for in subsection (a) of this section shall not apply to any product liability claim brought by a claimant who is not entitled to compensation under chapter 568, provided the claimant can prove that the harm occurred during the useful safe life of the product. In determining whether a product's useful safe life has expired, the trier of fact may consider among other factors: (1) The effect on the product of wear and tear or deterioration from natural causes; (2) the effect of climatic and other local conditions in which the product was used; (3) the policy of the user and similar users as to repairs, renewals and replacements; (4) representations, instructions and warnings made by the product seller about the useful safe life of the product; and (5) any modification or alteration of the product by a user or third party.

(d) The ten-year limitation provided for in subsection (a) of this section shall be extended pursuant to the terms of any express written warranty that the product can be used for a period longer than ten years, and shall not preclude any action against a product seller who intentionally misrepresents a product or fraudulently conceals information about it, provided the misrepresentation or fraudulent concealment was the proximate cause of harm of the claimant.

(e) The ten-year limitation provided for in subsection (a) of this section shall not apply to any product liability claim, whenever brought, involving injury, death or property damage caused by contact with or exposure to asbestos, except that (1) no such action for personal injury or death may be brought by the claimant later than sixty years from the date that the claimant last had contact with or exposure to asbestos, and (2) no such action for damage to property may be brought by the claimant later than thirty years from the date of last contact with or exposure to asbestos.

(f) The definitions contained in section 52–572m shall apply to this section.

(g) The provisions of this section shall apply to all product liability claims brought on or after October 1, 1979.

(1979)

§ 52–240a. Award of attorney's fees in product liability action. If the court determines that the claim or defense is frivolous, the court may award reasonable attorney's fees to the prevailing party in a products liability action.

§ 52–240b. Punitive damages in product liability actions. Punitive damages may be awarded if the claimant proves that the harm suffered was the result of the product seller's reckless disregard for the safety of product users, consumers or others who were injured by the product. If the trier of fact determines that punitive damages should be awarded, the court shall determine that amount of damages not to exceed an amount equal to twice the damages awarded to the plaintiff.

(1991, concerning AIDS vaccine)

§ 19a–591. Definitions. As used in sections 19a–591 to 19a–591c, inclusive:

(1) "AIDS vaccine" means a vaccine which has been developed by a manufacturer, is being tested and administered at a research institution for purposes of determining whether it provides immunity to acquired immune deficiency syndrome or is of therapeutic benefit to persons or fetuses infected with the acquired immune deficiency syndrome virus, and for which an investigational new drug application is on file with the federal Food and Drug Administration and is in effect.

(2) "Manufacturer" means any person who is domiciled or has his principal place of business in this state and has developed an AIDS vaccine.

(3) "Research institution" means a hospital which is accredited by the Joint Commission on the Accreditation of Healthcare Organizations, or a recognized medical school which operates, or is affiliated with, or is operated by an accredited hospital.

(4) "Research subject" means a person who is administered an AIDS vaccine, or a fetus of a person administered an AIDS vaccine, or a child born to a person administered an AIDS vaccine.

(5) "Researcher" means a person employed by or affiliated with a manufacturer or a research institution, who participates in the development or testing or administration of an AIDS vaccine, or who is involved in the diagnosis and treatment of a research subject.

§ 19a–591a. Administration of AIDS vaccine. A manufacturer, research institution or researcher shall, prior to the administration of an AIDS vaccine to a person, provide a written explanation of the immunity provisions of section 19a–591b to such person and obtain such person's informed consent. A parent or legal guardian of a child may give informed consent for such child. A copy of the informed consent shall be maintained with such person's medical records.

§ 19a–591b. Immunity from liability for civil damages for personal injury to research subject. Exceptions. A manufacturer, research institution or researcher shall not be liable to a research subject for civil damages for personal injury resulting from the administration of any AIDS vaccine to such research subject, unless such injury was caused by the gross negligence or reckless, wilful or wanton misconduct of such manufacturer, research institution or researcher or such manufacturer, research institution or researcher has failed to comply with the provisions of section 19a–591a. The immunity provided by this section shall not apply to a manufacturer, research institution or researcher who intentionally provided false information in connection with an investigational new drug application.

§ 19a–591c. Research subjects. No person shall be denied the opportunity to be a research subject because of the inability to pay for medical treatment.

DELAWARE CODE ANNOTATED

(1987)

§ 7001. Sealed container defense in product liability. (a) In this section, the following words have the meanings indicated:

(1) a. "Manufacturer" means a designer, assembler, fabricator, constructor, compounder, producer or processor of any product or its component parts.

b. "Manufacturer" includes an entity not otherwise a manufacturer that imports a product or otherwise holds itself out as a manufacturer.

(2) "Product" means any tangible article, including attachments, accessories and component parts and accompanying labels, warnings, instructions and packaging.

(3) "Sealed container" means a box, container, package, wrapping, encasement or housing of any nature that covers a product so that it would be unreasonable to expect a seller to detect or discover the existence of a dangerous or defective condition in the product. A product shall be deemed to be in a sealed container if the product, by its nature and design, is encased or sold in any other manner making it unreasonable to expect a seller to detect or discover the existence of a dangerous or defective condition.

(4) a. "Seller" means a wholesaler, distributor, retailer or other individual or entity other than a manufacturer that is regularly engaged in the selling of a product whether the sale is for resale by the purchaser or is for use or consumption by the ultimate consumer.

b. "Seller" includes a lessor or bailor regularly engaged in the business of the lease or bailment of the product.

(5) "Similar product" means another article of the same design produced by the same manufacturer.

(b) It shall be a defense to an action against a seller of a product for property damage or personal injury allegedly caused by the defective design or manufacture of a product if the seller establishes that:

(1) The product was acquired and then sold or leased by the seller in a sealed container and in unaltered form;

(2) The seller had no knowledge of the defect;

(3) In the performance of the duties the seller performed or while the product was in the seller's possession could not have discovered the defect while exercising reasonable care;

(4) The seller did not manufacturer, produce, design or designate the specifications for the product, which conduct was the proximate and substantial cause of the claimant's injury;

(5) The seller did not alter, modify, assemble or mishandle the product while in the seller's possession in a manner which was the proximate and substantial cause of the claimant's injury; and

(6) The seller had not received notice of the defect from purchasers of similar products.

(c) The defense provided in subsection (b) of this section is not available if:

(1) The claimant is unable to identify the manufacturer through reasonable effort;

(2) The manufacturer is insolvent, immune from suit or not subject to suit in Delaware; or

(3) The seller made any express warranties, the breach of which were the proximate and substantial cause of the claimant's injury.

(d)(1) Except in an action based on an expressed indemnity agreement, if the seller shows by unrebutted facts that he/she had satisfied subsection (b) of this section and that subsection (c) of this section does not apply, summary judgment shall be entered in his/her favor as to the original or third party actions.

(2) Notwithstanding the granting of a motion for summary judgment pursuant to paragraph (1) of this subsection, the seller will thereafter continue to be treated as though he/she were still a party for all purposes of discovery including the uses thereof.

(3) On a subsequent showing of the occurrence of any condition described in subsection (c) of this section, or that 1 or more of the conditions of subsection (b) of this section did not exist, during the pending litigation, the actions dismissed by summary judgment pursuant to subsection (d)(1) of this section shall be reinstated and are not barred by the passage of time.

FLORIDA STATUTES ANNOTATED

(1999)

§ 768.1256. **Government rules defense.** (1) In a product liability action brought against a manufacturer or seller for harm allegedly caused by a product, there is a rebuttable presumption that the product is not defective or unreasonably dangerous and the manufacturer or seller is not liable if, at the time the specific unit of the product was sold or delivered to the initial purchaser or user, the aspect of the product that allegedly caused the harm:

(a) Complied with federal or state codes, statutes, rules, regulations, or standards relevant to the event causing the death or injury;

(b) The codes, statutes, rules, regulations, or standards are designed to prevent the type of harm that allegedly occurred; and

(c) Compliance with the codes, statutes, rules, regulations, or standards is required as a condition for selling or distributing the product.

(2) In a product liability action as described in subsection (1), there is a rebuttable presumption that the product is defective or unreasonably dangerous and the manufacturer or seller is liable if the manufacturer or seller did not comply with the federal or state codes, statutes, rules, regulations, or standards which:

(a) Were relevant to the event causing the death or injury;

(b) Are designed to prevent the type of harm that allegedly occurred; and

(c) Require compliance as a condition for selling or distributing the product.

(3) This section does not apply to an action brought for harm allegedly caused by a drug that is ordered off the market or seized by the Federal Food and Drug Administration.

§ 768.1257. **State-of-the-art defense for products liability.** In an action based upon defective design, brought against the manufacturer of a product, the finder of fact shall consider the state of the art of scientific and technical knowledge and other circumstances that existed at the time of manufacture, not at the time of loss or injury.

§ 90.407. **Subsequent remedial measures.** Evidence of measures taken after an injury or harm caused by an event, which measures if taken before the event would have made injury or harm less likely to occur, is not admissible to prove negligence, the existence of a product defect, or culpable conduct in connection with the event. This rule does not require the exclusion of evidence of subsequent remedial measures when offered for another purpose, such as proving ownership, control, or the feasibility of precautionary measures, if controverted, or impeachment.

GEORGIA CODE ANNOTATED

(1968, 1978, 1987)

§ 51–1–11. Privity to support action. (a) Except as otherwise provided in this Code section, no privity is necessary to support a tort action; but, if the tort results from the violation of a duty which is itself the consequence of a contract, the right of action is confined to the parties and those in privity to that contract, except in cases where the party would have a right of action for the injury done independently of the contract and except as provided in Code Section 11–2–318.

(b)(1) The manufacturer of any personal property sold as new property directly or through a dealer or any other person shall be liable in tort, irrespective of privity, to any natural person who may use, consume, or reasonably be affected by the property and who suffers injury to his person or property because the property when sold by the manufacturer was not merchantable and reasonably suited to the use intended, and its condition when sold is the proximate cause of the injury sustained.

(2) No action shall be commenced pursuant to this subsection with respect to an injury after ten years from the date of the first sale for use or consumption of the personal property causing or otherwise bringing about the injury.

(3) A manufacturer may not exclude or limit the operation of this subsection.

(c) The limitation of paragraph (2) of subsection (b) of this Code section regarding bringing an action within ten years from the date of the first sale for use or consumption of personal property shall also apply to the commencement of an action claiming negligence of a manufacturer as the basis of liability, except an action seeking to recover from a manufacturer for injuries or damages arising out of the negligence of such manufacturer in manufacturing products which cause a disease or birth defect, or arising out of conduct which manifests a willful, reckless, or wanton disregard for life or property. Nothing contained in this subsection shall relieve a manufacturer from the duty to warn of a danger arising from use of a product once that danger becomes known to the manufacturer.

§ 51–1–11.1. Liability of product seller as manufacturer in product liability action based on doctrine of strict liability in tort. (a) As used in this Code section, the term "product seller" means a person who, in the course of a business conducted for the purpose leases or sells and distributes; installs; prepares; blends; packages; labels; markets; or assembles pursuant to a manufacturer's plan, intention, design, specifications, or formulation; or repairs; maintains; or otherwise is involved in placing a product in the stream of commerce. This definition does not include a manufacturer which, because of certain activities, may additionally be included within all or a portion of the definition of a product seller.

(b) For purposes of a product liability action based in whole or in part on the doctrine of strict liability in tort, a product seller is not a manufacturer as provided in Code Section 51–1–11 and is not liable as such.

(c) Nothing contained in this Code section shall be construed to grant a cause of action in strict liability in tort or any other legal theory or to affect the right of any person to seek and obtain indemnity or contribution.

(d) This Code section shall apply to all causes of action accruing on or after July 1, 1987.

IDAHO CODE

(1980 and (§ 6–1410) 1986)

§ 6–1401. Scope. The previous existing applicable law of this state on product liability is modified only to the extent set forth in this act.

§ 6–1402. Definitions. (1) "Product seller" means any person or entity that is engaged in the business of selling products, whether the sale is for resale, or for use or consumption. The term includes a manufacturer, wholesaler, distributor, or retailer of the relevant product. The term also includes a party who is in the business of leasing or bailing such products. The term "product seller" does not include:

(a) A provider of professional services who utilizes or sells products within the legally authorized scope of its professional practice. A nonprofessional provider of services is not included unless the sale or use of a product is the principal part of the transaction, and the essence of the relationship between the seller and purchaser is not the furnishing of judgment, skill, or services;

(b) A commercial seller of used products who resells a product after use by a consumer or other product user, provided the used product is in essentially the same condition as when it was acquired for resale; and

(c) A finance lessor who is not otherwise a product seller. A "finance lessor" is one who acts in a financial capacity, who is not a manufacturer, wholesaler, distributor, or retailer, and who leases a product without having a reasonable opportunity to inspect and discover defects in the product, under a lease arrangement in which the selection, possession, maintenance, and operation of the product are controlled by a person other than the lessor.

(2) "Manufacturer" includes a product seller who designs, produces, makes, fabricates, constructs, or remanufactures the relevant product or component part of a product before its sale to a user or consumer. It includes a product seller or entity not otherwise a manufacturer that holds itself out as a manufacturer. A product seller acting primarily as a wholesaler, distributor, or retailer of a product may be a "manufacturer" but only to the extent that it designs, produces, makes, fabricates, constructs, or remanufactures the product before its sale.

(3) "Product" means any object possessing intrinsic value, capable of delivery either as an assembled whole or as a component part or parts, and produced for introduction into trade or commerce. Human tissue and organs, including human blood and its components, are excluded from this term. The "relevant product" under this chapter is that product, or its component part or parts, which gave rise to the product liability claim.

(4) "Claimant" means a person or entity asserting a product liability claim, including a wrongful death action, and, if the claim is asserted

through or on behalf of an estate, the term includes claimant's decedent. "Claimant" includes any person or entity that suffers harm.

(5) "Reasonably anticipated conduct" means the conduct which would be expected of an ordinary reasonably prudent person who is likely to use the product in the same or similar circumstances.

§ 6–1403. Length of time product sellers are subject to liability.

(1) Useful safe life.

(a) Except as provided in subsection (1)(b) hereof, a product seller shall not be subject to liability to a claimant for harm under this chapter if the product seller proves by a preponderance of the evidence that the harm was caused after the product's "useful safe life" had expired.

"Useful safe life" begins at the time of delivery of the product and extends for the time during which the product would normally be likely to perform or be stored in a safe manner. For the purposes of this chapter, "time of delivery" means the time of delivery of a product to its first purchaser or lessee who was not engaged in the business of either selling such products or using them as component parts of another product to be sold.

(b) A product seller may be subject to liability for harm caused by a product used beyond its useful safe life to the extent that the product seller has expressly warranted the product for a longer period.

(2) Statute of repose.

(a) Generally. In claims that involve harm caused more than ten (10) years after time of delivery, a presumption arises that the harm was caused after the useful safe life had expired. This presumption may only be rebutted by clear and convincing evidence.

(b) Limitations on statute of repose.

1. If a product seller expressly warrants that its product can be utilized safely for a period longer than ten (10) years, the period of repose, after which the presumption created in subsection (2)(a) hereof arises, shall be extended according to that warranty or promise.

2. The ten (10) year period of repose established in subsection (2)(a) hereof does not apply if the product seller intentionally misrepresents facts about its product, or fraudulently conceals information about it, and that conduct was a substantial cause of the claimant's harm.

3. Nothing contained in subsection (2) of this section shall affect the right of any person found liable under this chapter to seek and obtain contribution or indemnity from any other person who is responsible for harm under this chapter.

4. The ten (10) year period of repose established in subsection (2)(a) hereof shall not apply if the harm was caused by prolonged exposure to a defective product, or if the injury-causing aspect of the product that existed at the time of delivery was not discoverable by an ordinary reasonably

prudent person until more than ten (10) years after the time of delivery, or if the harm, caused within ten (10) years after the time of delivery, did not manifest itself until after that time.

(3) Statute of limitation. No claim under this chapter may be brought more than two (2) years from the time the cause of action accrued as defined in section 5–219, Idaho Code.

§ 6–1404. Comparative responsibility. Comparative responsibility shall not bar recovery in an action by any person or his legal representative to recover damages for product liability resulting in death or injury to person or property, if such responsibility was not as great as the responsibility of the person against whom recovery is sought, but any damages allowed shall be diminished in the proportion to the amount of responsibility attributable to the person recovering.

§ 6–1405. Conduct affecting comparative responsibility. (1) Failure to discover a defective condition.

(a) Claimant's failure to inspect. A claimant is not required to have inspected the product for a defective condition. Failure to have done so does not render the claimant responsible for the harm caused or reduce the claimant's damages.

(b) Claimant's failure to observe an obvious defective condition. When the product seller proves by a preponderance of the evidence that the claimant, while using the product, was injured by a defective condition that would have been obvious to an ordinary reasonably prudent person, the claimant's damages shall be subject to reduction.

(c) A nonclaimant's failure to inspect for defects or to observe an obvious defective condition. A nonclaimant's failure to inspect for a defective condition or to observe a defective condition that would have been obvious to an ordinary reasonably prudent person, shall not reduce claimant's damages.

(2) Use of a product with a known defective condition.

(a) By a claimant. When the product seller proves, by a preponderance of the evidence, that the claimant knew about the product's defective condition, and voluntarily used the product or voluntarily assumed the risk of harm from the product, the claimant's damages shall be subject to reduction to the extent that the claimant did not act as an ordinary reasonably prudent person under the circumstances.

(b) By a nonclaimant product user. If the product seller proves by a preponderance of the evidence that a product user, other than the claimant, knew about a product's defective condition, but voluntarily and unreasonably used or stored the product and thereby proximately caused claimant's harm, the claimant's damages shall be subject to apportionment.

(3) Misuse of a product.

(a) "Misuse" occurs when the product user does not act in a manner that would be expected of an ordinary reasonably prudent person who is likely to use the product in the same or similar circumstances.

(b) When the product seller proves, by a preponderance of the evidence, that product misuse by a claimant, or by a party other than the claimant or the product seller has proximately caused the claimant's harm, the claimant's damages shall be subject to reduction or apportionment to the extent that the misuse was a proximate cause of the harm.

(4) Alteration or modification of a product.

(a) "Alteration or modification" occurs when a person or entity other than the product seller changes the design, construction, or formula of the product, or changes or removes warnings or instructions that accompanied or were displayed on the product. "Alteration or modification" of a product includes the failure to observe routine care and maintenance, but does not include ordinary wear and tear.

(b) When the product seller proves, by a preponderance of the evidence, that an alteration or modification of the product by the claimant, or by a party other than the claimant or the product seller has proximately caused the claimant's harm, the claimant's damages shall be subject to reduction or apportionment to the extent that the alteration or modification was a proximate cause of the harm.

This subsection shall not be applicable if:

1.   The alteration or modification was in accord with the product seller's instructions or specifications;

2.   The alteration or modification was made with the express or implied consent of the product seller; or

3.   The alteration or modification was reasonably anticipated conduct, and the product was defective because of the product seller's failure to provide adequate warnings or instructions with respect to the alteration or modification.

§ 6–1406. Relevance of industry custom, safety or performance standards, and technological feasibility. (1) Evidence of changes in (a) a product's design, (b) warnings or instructions concerning the product, (c) technological feasibility, (d) "state of the art," or (e) the custom of the product seller's industry or business, occurring after the product was manufactured and delivered to its first purchaser or lessee who was not engaged in the business of either selling such products or using them as component parts of another product to be sold, is not admissible for the purpose of proving that the product was defective in design or that a warning or instruction should have accompanied the product at the time of manufacture. The provisions of this section shall not relieve the product seller of any duty to warn of known defects discovered after the product was designed and manufactured.

(2) If the court finds outside the presence of a jury that the probative value of such evidence substantially outweighs its prejudicial effect and that there is no other proof available, this evidence may be admitted for other relevant purposes, including but not limited to proving ownership or control, or impeachment.

(3) For purposes of this section, "custom" refers to the practices followed by an ordinary product seller in the product seller's industry or business.

(4) For purposes of this section, "technological feasibility" means the technological, mechanical and scientific knowledge relating to product safety that was reasonably feasible for use, in light of economic practicality, at the time of manufacture.

§ 6–1407. Individual rights and responsibilities of product sellers other than manufacturers. (1) In the absence of express warranties to the contrary, product sellers other than manufacturers shall not be subject to liability in circumstances where they do not have a reasonable opportunity to inspect the product in a manner which would or should, in the exercise of reasonable care, reveal the existence of the defective condition which is in issue; or where the product seller acquires the product in a sealed package or container and sells the product in the same sealed package or container. The liability limitation of this subsection shall not apply if:

(a) The product seller had knowledge or reason to know of the defect in the product;

(b) The product seller altered, modified, or installed the product, and such alteration, modification or installation was a substantial proximate cause of the incident giving rise to the action, was not authorized or requested by the manufacturer and was not performed in compliance with the directions or specifications of the manufacturer;

(c) The product seller provided the plans or specifications for the manufacturer or preparation of the product and such plans or specifications were a substantial cause of the product's alleged defect;

(d) The product seller is a wholly-owned subsidiary of the manufacturer, the manufacturer is a wholly-owned subsidiary of the product seller;

(e) The product seller sold the product after the expiration date placed on the product or its package by the manufacturer.

(2) In an action where the liability limitation of subsection (1) applies, any manufacturer who refuses to accept a tender of defense from the product seller, shall indemnify the product seller for reasonable attorney's fees and costs incurred by the product seller in defending such action.

(3) In any product liability action, the manufacturer of the product shall be indemnified by the product seller of the product for any judgment

rendered against the manufacturer and shall also be reimbursed for reasonable attorney's fees and costs incurred in defending such action:

(a) If the product seller provided the plans or specifications for the manufacture or preparation of the product;

(b) If such plans or specifications were a substantial cause of the product's alleged defect; and

(c) If the product was manufactured in compliance with and according to the plans or specifications of the seller.

The provisions of this subsection shall not apply if the manufacturer had knowledge or with the exercise of reasonable and diligent care should have had knowledge of the defect in the product.

(4) A product seller, other than a manufacturer, is also subject to the liability of manufacturer if:

(a) The manufacturer is not subject to service of process under the laws of the claimant's domicile; or

(b) The manufacturer has been judicially declared insolvent in that the manufacturer is unable to pay its debts as they become due in the ordinary course of business; or

(c) The court outside the presence of a jury determines that it is highly probable that the claimant would be unable to enforce a judgment against the product manufacturer.

§ 6–1408. Contents of complaint—Amount of recovery. In any product liability action no dollar amount or figure shall be included in the complaint. The complaint shall pray for such damages as are reasonable in the premises. The complaint shall include a statement reciting that the jurisdictional amount established for filing the action is satisfied.

§ 6–1409. Short title. This act shall be known and may be cited as the "Idaho Product Liability Reform Act."

§ 6–1410. Products liability—Defectiveness of firearms or ammunition. (1) In a products liability action, no firearm or ammunition shall be deemed defective in design on the basis that the benefits of the product do not outweigh the risk of injury posed by its potential to cause serious injury, damage, or death when discharged.

(2) For purposes of this section:

(a) The potential of a firearm or ammunition to cause serious injury, damage, or death when discharged does not make the product defective in design;

(b) Injuries or damages resulting from the discharge of a firearm or ammunition are not proximately caused by its potential to cause serious injury, damage, or death, but are proximately caused by the actual discharge of the product;

(3) The provisions of this section shall not affect a products liability cause of action based upon the improper selection of design alternatives.

INDIANA CODE ANNOTATED

(1998, 1999 (34–20–8–1))

§ 34–6–2–115. "Product Liability Action." "Product liability action," for purposes of IC 34–20, means an action that is brought:

(1) against a manufacturer or seller of a product; and

(2) for or on account of physical harm; regardless of the substantive legal theory or theories upon which the action is brought.

§ 34–20–1–1. Application of Article. This article governs all actions that are:

(1) brought by a user or consumer;

(2) against a manufacturer or seller; and

(3) for physical harm caused by a product;

regardless of the substantive legal theory or theories upon which the action is brought.

§ 34–20–1–2. Remedies cumulative. This article shall not be construed to limit any other action from being brought against a seller of a product.

§ 34–20–1–3. Severability. If a provision of this article or its application to a person or circumstance is held invalid, the invalidity does not affect other provisions or applications, and to this end the provisions of this article are severable.

§ 34–20–1–4. Effective date. This article does not apply to a cause of action that accrues before June 1, 1978.

§ 34–20–2–1. Grounds for action. Except as provided in section 3 of this chapter, a person who sells, leases, or otherwise puts into the stream of commerce any product in a defective condition unreasonably dangerous to any user or consumer or to the user's or consumer's property is subject to liability for physical harm caused by that product to the user or consumer or to the user's or consumer's property if:

(1) that user or consumer is in the class of persons that the seller should reasonably foresee as being subject to the harm caused by the defective condition;

(2) the seller is engaged in the business of selling the product; and

(3) the product is expected to and does reach the user or consumer without substantial alteration in the condition in which the product is sold by the person sought to be held liable under this article.

§ 34–20–2–2. Exercise of reasonable care; privacy. The rule stated in section 1 of this chapter applies although:

(1) the seller has exercised all reasonable care in the manufacture and preparation of the product; and

(2) the user or consumer has not bought the product from or entered into any contractual relation with the seller.

However, in an action based on an alleged design defect in the product or based on an alleged failure to provide adequate warnings or instructions regarding the use of the product, the party making the claim must establish that the manufacturer or seller failed to exercise reasonable care under the circumstances in designing the product or in providing the warnings or instructions.

§ 34-20-2-3. **Strict liability of manufacturer.** A product liability action based on the doctrine of strict liability in tort may not be commenced or maintained against a seller of a product that is alleged to contain or possess a defective condition unreasonably dangerous to the user or consumer unless the seller is a manufacturer of the product or of the part of the product alleged to be defective.

§ 34-20-2-4. **Principal distributor, seller deemed manufacturer.** If a court is unable to hold jurisdiction over a particular manufacturer of a product or part of a product alleged to be defective, then that manufacturer's principal distributor or seller over whom a court may hold jurisdiction shall be considered, for the purposes of this chapter, the manufacturer of the product.

34-20-3-1. **Statute of limitations. Negligence and strict liability in tort action.** (a) This section applies to all persons regardless of minority or legal disability. Notwithstanding IC 34-11-6-1, this section applies in any product liability action in which the theory of liability is negligence or strict liability in tort.

(b) Except as provided in section 2 of this chapter, a product liability action must be commenced:

(1) within two (2) years after the cause of action accrues; or

(2) within ten (10) years after the delivery of the product to the initial user or consumer.

However, if the cause of action accrues at least eight (8) years but less than ten (10) years after that initial delivery, the action may be commenced at any time within two (2) years after the cause of action accrues.

§ 34-20-3-2. **Asbestos-related actions.** (a) A product liability action that is based on:

(1) property damage resulting from asbestos; or

(2) personal injury, disability, disease, or death resulting from exposure to asbestos;

must be commenced within two (2) years after the cause of action accrues. The subsequent development of an additional asbestos related disease or injury is a new injury and is a separate cause of action.

(b) A product liability action for personal injury, disability, disease, or death resulting from exposure to asbestos accrues on the date when the injured person knows that the person has an asbestos related disease or injury.

(c) A product liability action for property damage accrues on the date when the injured person knows that the property damage has resulted from asbestos.

(d) This section applies only to product liability actions against:

(1) persons who mined and sold commercial asbestos; and

(2) funds that have, as a result of bankruptcy proceedings or to avoid bankruptcy proceedings, been created for the payment of asbestos related disease claims or asbestos related property damage claims.

(e) For the purposes of IC 1–1–1–8, if any part of this section is held invalid, the entire section is void.

(f) Except for the cause of action expressly recognized in this section, this section does not otherwise modify the limitation of action or repose period contained in section 1 of this chapter.

34–20–4–1. Products which are considered defective. A product is in a defective condition under this article if, at the time it is conveyed by the seller to another party, it is in a condition:

(1) not contemplated by reasonable persons among those considered expected users or consumers of the product; and

(2) that will be unreasonably dangerous to the expected user or consumer when used in reasonably expectable ways of handling or consumption.

§ 34–20–4–2. Failure to provide adequate instructions or warnings. A product is defective under this article if the seller fails to:

(1) properly package or label the product to give reasonable warnings of danger about the product; or

(2) give reasonably complete instructions on proper use of the product; when the seller, by exercising reasonable diligence, could have made such warnings or instructions available to the user or consumer.

§ 34–20–4–3. Products made safe for reasonably expectable handling and consumption not deemed defective. A product is not defective under this article if it is safe for reasonably expectable handling and consumption. If an injury results from handling, preparation for use, or consumption that is not reasonably expectable, the seller is not liable under this article.

§ 34–20–4–4. Products incapable of being made safe not deemed defective. A product is not defective under this article if the product is incapable of being made safe for its reasonably expectable use, when manufactured, sold, handled, and packaged properly.

§ 34–20–5–1. Rebuttable presumption. In a product liability action, there is a rebuttable presumption that the product that caused the physical harm was not defective and that the manufacturer or seller of the product was not negligent if, before the sale by the manufacturer, the product:

(1) was in conformity with the generally recognized state of the art applicable to the safety of the product at the time the product was designed, manufactured, packaged, and labeled; or

(2) complied with applicable codes, standards, regulations, or specifications established, adopted, promulgated, or approved by the United States or by Indiana, or by an agency of the United States or Indiana.

§ 34–20–6–1. Applicability of defenses. The defenses in this chapter are defenses to an action brought under this article (or IC 33–1–1.5 before its repeal).

§ 34–20–6–2. Burden of proof. The burden of proof of any defense raised in an action under this article (or IC 33–1–1.5 before its repeal) is on the party raising the defense.

§§ 34–20–6–3. Use of product with knowledge of defect or danger. It is a defense to an action under this article (or IC 33–1–1.5 before its repeal) that the user or consumer bringing the action:

(1) knew of the defect;

(2) was aware of the danger in the product; and

(3) nevertheless proceeded to make use of the product and was injured.

§ 34–20–6–4. Misuse of product. It is a defense to an action under this article (or IC 33–1–1.5 before its repeal) that a cause of the physical harm is a misuse of the product by the claimant or any other person not reasonably expected by the seller at the time the seller sold or otherwise conveyed the product to another party.

§ 34–20–6–5. Modification or alteration of product. It is a defense to an action under this article (or IC 33–1–1.5 before its repeal) that a cause of the physical harm is a modification or alteration of the product made by any person after the product's delivery to the initial user or consumer if the modification or alteration is the proximate cause of physical harm where the modification or alteration is not reasonably expectable to the seller.

§ 34–20–7–1. Assessment of liability. In a product liability action where liability is assessed against more than one (1) defendant, a defendant is not liable for more than the amount of fault, as determined under IC 34–20–8, directly attributable to that defendant. A defendant in a product liability action may not be held jointly liable for damages attributable to the fault of another defendant.

§ 34–20–8–1. Assessment of percentage of fault. (a) In a product liability action, the fault of the person suffering the physical harm, as well as the fault of all others who caused or contributed to cause the harm, shall be compared by the trier of fact in accordance with IC 34–51–2–7, IC 34–51–2–8, or IC 34–51–2–9.

(b) In assessing percentage of fault, the jury shall consider the fault of all persons who contributed to the physical harm, regardless of whether the person was or could have been named as a party, as long as the nonparty was alleged to have caused or contributed to cause the physical harm.

§ 34–20–9–1. **Indemnification from person actually at fault for defect.** This article does not affect the right of any person who is found liable to seek and obtain indemnity from any other person whose actual fault caused a product to be defective.

IOWA CODE ANNOTATED

(1986, 2004)

§ 613.18. Limitation on products liability of nonmanufacturers. 1. A person who is not the assembler, designer, or manufacturer, and who wholesales, retails, distributes, or otherwise sells a product is:

a. Immune from any suit based upon strict liability in tort or breach of implied warranty of merchantability which arises solely from an alleged defect in the original design or manufacture of the product.

b. Not liable for damages based upon strict liability in tort or breach of implied warranty of merchantability for the product upon proof that the manufacturer is subject to the jurisdiction of the courts of this state and has not been judicially declared insolvent.

2. A person who is a retailer of a product and who assembles a product, such assembly having no causal relationship to the injury from which the claim arises, is not liable for damages based upon strict liability in tort or breach of implied warranty of merchantability which arises from an alleged defect in the original design or manufacture of the product upon proof that the manufacturer is subject to the jurisdiction of the courts of this state and has not been judicially declared insolvent.

3. An action brought pursuant to this section, where the claimant certifies that the manufacturer of the product is not yet identifiable, tolls the statute of limitations against such manufacturer until such time as discovery in the case has identified the manufacturer.

§ 614.1. Period. Actions may be brought within the times herein limited, respectively, after their causes accrue, and not afterwards, except when otherwise specially declared: 2A. With respect to products.

a. Those founded on the death of a person or injuries to the person or property brought against the manufacturer, assembler, designer, supplier of specifications, seller, lessor, or distributor of a product based upon an alleged defect in the design, inspection, testing, manufacturing, formulation, marketing, packaging, warning, labeling of the product, or any other alleged defect or failure of whatever nature or kind, based on the theories of strict liability in tort, negligence, or breach of an implied warranty shall not be commenced more than fifteen years after the product was first purchased, leased, bailed, or installed for use or consumption unless expressly warranted for a longer period of time by the manufacturer, assembler, designer, supplier of specifications, seller, lessor, or distributor of the product. This subsection shall not affect the time during which a person found liable may seek and obtain contribution or indemnity from another person whose actual fault caused a product to be defective. This subsection shall not apply if the manufacturer, assembler, designer, supplier of specifications, seller, lessor, or distributor of the product intentionally misrepresents facts about the product or fraudulently conceals information about the product and that conduct was a substantial cause of the claimant's harm.

b.(1) The fifteen-year limitation in paragraph "a" shall not apply to the time period in which to discover a disease that is latent and caused by exposure to a harmful material, in which event the cause of action shall be deemed to have accrued when the disease and such disease's cause have been made known to the person or at the point the person should have been aware of the disease and such disease's cause. This subsection shall not apply to cases governed by subsection 11 of this section.

(2) As used in this paragraph, "harmful material" means silicone gel breast implants, which were implanted prior to July 12, 1992; and chemical substances commonly known as asbestos, dioxins, tobacco, or polychlorinated biphenyls, whether alone or as part of any product; or any substance which is determined to present an unreasonable risk of injury to health or the environment by the United States environmental protection agency pursuant to the federal Toxic Substance Control Act, 15 U.S.C. § 2601 et seq., or by this state, if that risk is regulated by the United States environmental protection agency or this state.

§ 668.12. Liability for products—defenses. 1. In any action brought pursuant to this chapter against an assembler, designer, supplier of specifications, distributor, manufacturer, or seller for damages arising from an alleged defect in the design, testing, manufacturing, formulation, packaging, warning, or labeling of a product, a percentage of fault shall not be assigned to such persons if they plead and prove that the product conformed to the state of the art in existence at the time the product was designed, tested, manufactured, formulated, packaged, provided with a warning, or labeled.

2. Nothing contained in subsection 1 shall diminish the duty of an assembler, designer, supplier of specifications, distributor, manufacturer or seller to warn concerning subsequently acquired knowledge of a defect or dangerous condition that would render the product unreasonably dangerous for its foreseeable use or diminish the liability for failure to so warn.

3. An assembler, designer, supplier of specifications, distributor, manufacturer, or seller shall not be subject to liability for failure to warn regarding risks and risk-avoidance measures that should be obvious to, or generally known by, foreseeable product users. When reasonable minds may differ as to whether the risk or risk-avoidance measure was obvious or generally known, the issues shall be decided by the trier of fact.

4. In any action brought pursuant to this chapter against an assembler, designer, supplier of specifications, distributor, manufacturer, or seller for damages arising from an alleged defect in packaging, warning, or labeling of a product, a product bearing or accompanied by a reasonable and visible warning or instruction that is reasonably safe for use if the warning or instruction is followed shall not be deemed defective or unreasonably dangerous on the basis of failure to warn or instruct. When reasonable minds may differ as to whether the warning or instruction is reasonable and visible, the issues shall be decided by the trier of fact.

KANSAS REVISED STATUTES ANNOTATED

(1981–92)

§ 60–3301. Short title. The act shall be known and may be cited as the "Kansas Product Liability Act."

§ 60–3302. Definitions. (a) "Product seller" means any person or entity that is engaged in the business of selling products, whether the sale is for resale, or for use or consumption. The term includes a manufacturer, wholesaler, distributor or retailer of the relevant product, but does not include a health care provider, as defined in subsection (f) of K.S.A. 40–3401 and amendments thereto, who utilizes a product in the course of rendering professional services.

(b) "Manufacturer" includes a product seller who designs, produces, makes, fabricates, constructs, or remanufactures the relevant product or component part of a product before its sale to a user or consumer. It includes a product seller or entity not otherwise a manufacturer that holds itself out as a manufacturer, or that is owned in whole or in part by the manufacturer.

(c) "Product liability claim" includes any claim or action brought for harm caused by the manufacture, production, making, construction, fabrication, design, formula, preparation, assembly, installation, testing, warnings, instructions, marketing, packaging, storage or labeling of the relevant product. It includes, but is not limited to, any action based on strict liability in tort, negligence, breach of express or implied warranty, breach of, or failure to discharge a duty to warn or instruct, whether negligent or innocent, misrepresentation, concealment or nondisclosure, whether negligent or innocent, or under any other substantive legal theory.

(d) "Harm" includes: 1. damage to property; 2. personal physical injuries, illness and death; 3. mental anguish or emotional harm attendant to such personal physical injuries, illness or death. The term "harm" does not include direct or consequential economic loss.

§ 60–3303. Useful safe life, ten-year period of repose, evidence; latent disease exception; reviving certain causes of action. (a)(1) Except as provided in paragraph 2 of this subsection, a product seller shall not be subject to liability in a product liability claim if the product seller proves by a preponderance of the evidence that the harm was caused after the product's "useful safe life" had expired. "Useful safe life" begins at the time of delivery of the product and extends for the time during which the product would normally be likely to perform or be stored in a safe manner. For the purposes of this section, "time of delivery" means the time of delivery of a product to its first purchaser or lessee who was not engaged in the business of either selling such products or using them as component parts of another product to be sold.

Examples of evidence that is especially probative in determining whether a product's useful safe life had expired include:

(A) The amount of wear and tear to which the product had been subject;

(B) the effect of deterioration from natural causes, and from climate and other conditions under which the product was used or stored;

(C) the normal practices of the user, similar users and the product seller with respect to the circumstances, frequency and purposes of the product's use, and with respect to repairs, renewals and replacements;

(D) any representations, instructions or warnings made by the product seller concerning proper maintenance, storage and use of the product or the expected useful safe life of the product; and

(E) any modification or alteration of the product by a user or third party.

(2) A product seller may be subject to liability for harm caused by a product used beyond its useful safe life to the extent that the product seller has expressly warranted the product for a longer period.

(b)(1) In claims that involve harm caused more than 10 years after time of delivery, a presumption arises that the harm was caused after the useful safe life had expired. This presumption may only be rebutted by clear and convincing evidence.

(2)(A) If a product seller expressly warrants that its product can be utilized safely for a period longer than 10 years, the period of repose, after which the presumption created in paragraph 1. of this subsection arises, shall be extended according to that warranty or promise.

(B) The ten-year period of repose established in paragraph 1. of this subsection does not apply if the product seller intentionally misrepresents facts about its product, or fraudulently conceals information about it, and that conduct was a substantial cause of the claimant's harm.

(C) Nothing contained in this subsection shall affect the right of any person liable under a product liability claim to seek and obtain indemnity from any other person who is responsible for the harm which gave rise to the product liability claim.

(D) The ten-year period of repose established in paragraph 1. of this subsection shall not apply if the harm was caused by prolonged exposure to a defective product, or if the injury-causing aspect of the product that existed at the time of delivery was not discoverable by a reasonably prudent person until more than 10 years after the time of delivery, or if the harm caused within 10 years after the time of delivery did not manifest itself until after that time.

(c) Except as provided in subsections (d) and (e), nothing contained in subsections (a) and (b) above shall modify the application of K.S.A. 60–513, and amendments thereto.

(d)(1) In a product liability claim against the product seller, the ten-year limitation, as defined in K.S.A. 60–513, and amendments thereto, shall not apply to the time to discover a disease which is latent caused by exposure to a harmful material, in which event the action shall be deemed to have accrued when the disease and such disease's cause have been made known to the person or at the point the person should have been aware of the disease and such disease's cause.

(2) The term "harmful material" means silicone gel breast implants, which were implanted prior to July 1, 1992; any chemical substances commonly known as asbestos, dioxins, or polychlorinated biphenyls, whether alone or as part of any product, or any substance which is determined to present an unreasonable risk of injury to health or the environment by the United States Environmental Protection Agency pursuant to the Federal Toxic Substances Control Act, 15 U.S.C. § 2601 et seq., or the state of Kansas, and because of such risk is regulated by the state or the Environmental Protection Agency.

(e) Upon the effective date of this act through July 1, 1991, the provisions of this subsection shall revive such causes of action for latent diseases caused by exposure to a harmful material for: (1) Any person whose cause of action had accrued, as defined in subsection (d) on or after March 3, 1987; or (2) any person who had an action pending in any court on March 3, 1989, and because of the judicial interpretation of the ten-year limitation contained in subsection (b) of K.S.A. 60–513, and amendments thereto, as applied to latent disease caused by exposure to a harmful material the: (A) action was dismissed; (B) dismissal of the action was affirmed; or (C) action was subject to dismissal. The intent of this subsection is to revive causes of action for latent diseases caused by exposure to a harmful material which were barred by interpretation of K.S.A. 60–513, and amendments thereto, in effect prior to this enactment.

§ 60–3304. Legislative regulatory standards or administrative regulatory safety standards or mandatory government contract specifications—Defenses.

(a) When the injury-causing aspect of the product was, at the time of manufacture, in compliance with legislative regulatory standards or administrative regulatory safety standards relating to design or performance, the product shall be deemed not defective by reason of design or performance, or, if the standard addressed warnings or instructions, the product shall be deemed not defective by reason of warnings or instructions, unless the claimant proves by a preponderance of the evidence that a reasonably prudent product seller could and would have taken additional precautions.

(b) When the injury-causing aspect of the product was not, at the time of manufacture, in compliance with legislative regulatory standards or administrative regulatory safety standards relating to design, performance, warnings or instructions, the product shall be deemed defective unless the product seller proves by a preponderance of the evidence that its failure to comply was a reasonably prudent course of conduct under the circumstances.

(c) When the injury-causing aspect of the product was, at the time of manufacture, in compliance with a mandatory government contract specification relating to design, this shall be an absolute defense and the product shall be deemed not defective for that reason, or, if the specification related to warnings or instructions, then the product shall be deemed not defective for that reason.

(d) When the injury-causing aspect of the product was not, at the time of manufacture, in compliance with a mandatory government contract specification relating to design, the product shall be deemed defective for that reason, or if the specification related to warnings or instructions, the product shall be deemed defective for that reason.

§ 60–3305. Manufacturer's or seller's duty to warn or protect against danger, when. In any product liability claim any duty on the part of the manufacturer or seller of the product to warn or protect against a danger or hazard which could or did arise in the use or misuse of such product, and any duty to have properly instructed in the use of such product shall not extend: (a) To warnings, protecting against or instructing with regard to those safeguards, precautions and actions which a reasonable user or consumer of the product, with the training, experience, education and any special knowledge the user or consumer did, should or was required to possess, could and should have taken for such user or consumer or others, under all the facts and circumstances;

(b) to situations where the safeguards, precautions and actions would or should have been taken by a reasonable user or consumer of the product similarly situated exercising reasonable care, caution and procedure; or

(c) to warnings, protecting against or instructing with regard to dangers, hazards or risks which are patent, open or obvious and which should have been realized by a reasonable user or consumer of the product.

§ 60–3306. Seller not subject to liability. A product seller shall not be subject to liability in a product liability claim arising from an alleged defect in a product, if the product seller establishes that: (a) Such seller had no knowledge of the defect;

(b) such seller in the performance of any duties the seller performed, or was required to perform, could not have discovered the defect while exercising reasonable care;

(c) the seller was not a manufacturer of the defective product or product component;

(d) the manufacturer of the defective product or product component is subject to service of process either under the laws of the state of Kansas or the domicile of the person making the product liability claim; and

(e) any judgment against the manufacturer obtained by the person making the product liability claim would be reasonably certain of being satisfied.

§ 60–3307. Inadmissible evidence. (a) In a product liability claim, the following evidence shall not be admissible for any purpose:

(1) Evidence of any advancements or changes in technical or other knowledge or techniques, in design theory or philosophy, in manufacturing or testing knowledge, techniques or processes in labeling, warning of risks or hazards, instructions for the use of such product, if such advancements or changes have been made, learned or placed into common use subsequent to the time the product in issue was designed, formulated, tested, manufactured or sold by the manufacturer; and

(2) evidence of any changes made in the designing, planning, formulating, testing, preparing, manufacturing, packaging, warnings, labeling or instructing for use of, or with regard to, the product in issue, or any similar product, which changes were made subsequent to the time the product in issue was designed, formulated, tested, manufactured or sold by the manufacturer.

(b) This section does not require the exclusion of evidence of a subsequent measure if offered to impeach a witness for the manufacturer or seller of a product who has expressly denied the feasibility of such a measure.

KENTUCKY (REVISED) STATUTES ANNOTATED

(1979)

§ 411.300.   **Definitions.** (1) As used in KRS 411.310 to 411.340, a "product liability action" shall include any action brought for or on account of personal injury, death or property damage caused by or resulting from the manufacture, construction, design, formulation, development of standards, preparation, processing, assembly, testing, listing, certifying, warning, instructing, marketing, advertising, packaging or labeling of any product.

(2) As used in KRS 411.310 to 411.340, a "plaintiff" shall mean a person asserting a claim and, if said claim is asserted on behalf of an estate, "plaintiff" shall include plaintiff's decedent.

§ **411.310.   Presumptions in product liability actions.** (1) In any product liability action, it shall be presumed, until rebutted by a preponderance of the evidence to the contrary, that the subject product was not defective if the injury, death or property damage occurred either more than five (5) years after the date of sale to the first consumer or more than eight (8) years after the date of manufacture.

(2) In any product liability action, it shall be presumed, until rebutted by a preponderance of the evidence to the contrary, that the product was not defective if the design, methods of manufacture, and testing conformed to the generally recognized and prevailing standards or the state of the art in existence at the time the design was prepared, and the product was manufactured.

§ **411.320.   Circumstances under which defendant is liable.** (1) In any product liability action, a manufacturer shall be liable only for the personal injury, death or property damage that would have occurred if the product had been used in its original, unaltered and unmodified condition. For the purpose of this section, product alteration or modification shall include failure to observe routine care and maintenance, but shall not include ordinary wear and tear. This section shall apply to alterations or modifications made by any person or entity, except those made in accordance with specifications or instructions furnished by the manufacturer.

(2) In any product liability action, if the plaintiff performed an unauthorized alteration or an unauthorized modification, and such alteration or modification was a substantial cause of the occurrence that caused injury or damage to the plaintiff, the defendant shall not be liable whether or not said defendant was at fault or the product was defective.

(3) In any product liability action, if the plaintiff failed to exercise ordinary care in the circumstances in his use of the product, and such failure was a substantial cause of the occurrence that caused injury or damage to the plaintiff, the defendant shall not be liable whether or not said defendant was at fault or the product was defective.

§ 411.340.   When wholesaler, distributor, or retailer to be held liable. In any product liability action, if the manufacturer is identified and subject to the jurisdiction of the court, a wholesaler, distributor, or retailer who distributes or sells a product, upon his showing by a preponderance of the evidence that said product was sold by him in its original manufactured condition or package, or in the same condition such product was in when received by said wholesaler, distributor or retailer, shall not be liable to the plaintiff for damages arising solely from the distribution or sale of such product, unless such wholesaler, distributor or retailer, breached an express warranty or knew or should have known at the time of distribution or sale of such product that the product was in a defective condition, unreasonably dangerous to the user or consumer.

§ 411.350.   Short Title. KRS 411.300 to 411.340 shall be known as the "Product Liability Act of Kentucky."

LOUISIANA REVISED STATUTES ANNOTATED

(1988)

§ 2800.51. **Short title.** This Chapter shall be known and may be cited as the "Louisiana Products Liability Act."

§ 2800.52. **Scope of this chapter.** This Chapter establishes the exclusive theories of liability for manufacturers for damage caused by their products. A claimant may not recover from a manufacturer for damage caused by a product on the basis of any theory of liability that is not set forth in this Chapter. Conduct or circumstances that result in liability under this Chapter are "fault" within the meaning of Civil Code Article 2315. This Chapter does not apply to the rights of an employee or his personal representatives, dependents or relations against a manufacturer who is the employee's employer or against any principal or any officer, director, stockholder, partner or employee of such manufacturer or principal as limited by R.S. 23:1032, or to the rights of a claimant against the following, unless they assume the status of a manufacturer as defined in R.S. 9:2800.53(1):

(1) Providers of professional services, even if the service results in a product.

(2) Providers of nonprofessional services where the essence of the service is the furnishing of judgment or skill, even if the service results in a product.

(3) Producers of natural fruits and other raw products in their natural state that are derived from animals, fowl, aquatic life or invertebrates, including but not limited to milk, eggs, honey and wool.

(4) Farmers and other producers of agricultural plants in their natural state.

(5) Ranchers and other producers of animals, fowl, aquatic life or invertebrates in their natural state.

(6) Harvesters and other producers of fish, crawfish, oysters, crabs, mollusks or other aquatic animals in their natural state.

§ 2800.53. **Definitions.** The following terms have the following meanings for the purpose of this Chapter:

(1) "Manufacturer" means a person or entity who is in the business of manufacturing a product for placement into trade or commerce. "Manufacturing a product" means producing, making, fabricating, constructing, designing, remanufacturing, reconditioning or refurbishing a product. "Manufacturer" also means:

(a) A person or entity who labels a product as his own or who otherwise holds himself out to be the manufacturer of the product.

(b) A seller of a product who exercises control over or influences a characteristic of the design, construction or quality of the product that causes damage.

(c) A manufacturer of a product who incorporates into the product a component or part manufactured by another manufacturer.

(d) A seller of a product of an alien manufacturer if the seller is in the business of importing or distributing the product for resale and the seller is the alter ego of the alien manufacturer. The court shall take into consideration the following in determining whether the seller is the alien manufacturer's alter ego: whether the seller is affiliated with the alien manufacturer by way of common ownership or control; whether the seller assumes or administers product warranty obligations of the alien manufacturer; whether the seller prepares or modifies the product for distribution; or any other relevant evidence. A "product of an alien manufacturer" is a product that is manufactured outside the United States by a manufacturer who is a citizen of another country or who is organized under the laws of another country.

(2) "Seller" means a person or entity who is not a manufacturer and who is in the business of conveying title to or possession of a product to another person or entity in exchange for anything of value.

(3) "Product" means a corporeal movable that is manufactured for placement into trade or commerce, including a product that forms a component part of or that is subsequently incorporated into another product or an immovable. "Product" does not mean human blood, blood components, human organs, human tissue or approved animal tissue to the extent such are governed by R.S. 9:2797.

(4) "Claimant" means a person or entity who asserts a claim under this Chapter against the manufacturer of a product or his insurer for damage caused by the product.

(5) "Damage" means all damage caused by a product, including survival and wrongful death damages, for which Civil Code Articles 2315, 2315.1 and 2315.2 allow recovery. "Damage" includes damage to the product itself and economic loss arising from a deficiency in or loss of use of the product only to the extent that Section 3 of Chapter 6 of Title VII of Book III of the Civil Code, entitled "Of the Vices of the Thing Sold," does not allow recovery for such damage or economic loss. Attorneys' fees are not recoverable under this Chapter.

(6) "Express warranty" means a representation, statement of alleged fact or promise about a product or its nature, material or workmanship that represents, affirms or promises that the product or its nature, material or workmanship possesses specified characteristics or qualities or will meet a specified level of performance. "Express warranty" does not mean a general opinion about or general praise of a product. A sample or model of a product is an express warranty.

(7) "Reasonably anticipated use" means a use or handling of a product that the product's manufacturer should reasonably expect of an ordinary person in the same or similar circumstances.

(8) "Reasonably anticipated alteration or modification" means a change in a product that the product's manufacturer should reasonably expect to be made by an ordinary person in the same or similar circumstances, and also means a change arising from ordinary wear and tear. "Reasonably anticipated alteration or modification" does not mean the following:

(a) Alteration, modification or removal of an otherwise adequate warning provided about a product.

(b) The failure of a person or entity, other than the manufacturer of a product, reasonably to provide to the product user or handler an adequate warning that the manufacturer provided about the product, when the manufacturer has satisfied his obligation to use reasonable care to provide the adequate warning by providing it to such person or entity rather than to the product user or handler.

(c) Changes to or in a product or its operation because the product does not receive reasonable care and maintenance.

(9) "Adequate warning" means a warning or instruction that would lead an ordinary reasonable user or handler of a product to contemplate the danger in using or handling the product and either to decline to use or handle the product or, if possible, to use or handle the product in such a manner as to avoid the damage for which the claim is made.

§ 2800.54. Manufacturer responsibility and burden of proof. A. The manufacturer of a product shall be liable to a claimant for damage proximately caused by a characteristic of the product that renders the product unreasonably dangerous when such damage arose from a reasonably anticipated use of the product by the claimant or another person or entity.

B.   A product is unreasonably dangerous if and only if:

(1) The product is unreasonably dangerous in construction or composition as provided in R.S. 9:2800.55;

(2) The product is unreasonably dangerous in design as provided in R.S. 9:2800.56;

(3) The product is unreasonably dangerous because an adequate warning about the product has not been provided as provided in R.S. 9:2800.57; or

(4) The product is unreasonably dangerous because it does not conform to an express warranty of the manufacturer about the product as provided in R.S. 9:2800.58.

C.   The characteristic of the product that renders it unreasonably dangerous under R.S. 9:2800.55 must exist at the time the product left the control of its manufacturer. The characteristic of the product that renders it unreasonably dangerous under R.S. 9:2800.56 or 9:2800.57 must exist at the time the product left the control of its manufacturer or result from a reasonably anticipated alteration or modification of the product.

D. The claimant has the burden of proving the elements of Subsections A, B and C of this Section.

§ 2800.55. Unreasonably dangerous in construction or composition. A product is unreasonably dangerous in construction or composition if, at the time the product left its manufacturer's control, the product deviated in a material way from the manufacturer's specifications or performance standards for the product or from otherwise identical products manufactured by the same manufacturer.

§ 2800.56. Unreasonably dangerous in design. A product is unreasonably dangerous in design if, at the time the product left its manufacturer's control:

(1) There existed an alternative design for the product that was capable of preventing the claimant's damage; and

(2) The likelihood that the product's design would cause the claimant's damage and the gravity of that damage outweighed the burden on the manufacturer of adopting such alternative design and the adverse effect, if any, of such alternative design on the utility of the product. An adequate warning about a product shall be considered in evaluating the likelihood of damage when the manufacturer has used reasonable care to provide the adequate warning to users and handlers of the product.

§ 2800.57. Unreasonably dangerous because of inadequate warning. A. A product is unreasonably dangerous because an adequate warning about the product has not been provided if, at the time the product left its manufacturer's control, the product possessed a characteristic that may cause damage and the manufacturer failed to use reasonable care to provide an adequate warning of such characteristic and its danger to users and handlers of the product.

B. A manufacturer is not required to provide an adequate warning about his product when:

(1) The product is not dangerous to an extent beyond that which would be contemplated by the ordinary user or handler of the product, with the ordinary knowledge common to the community as to the product's characteristics; or

(2) The user or handler of the product already knows or reasonably should be expected to know of the characteristic of the product that may cause damage and the danger of such characteristic.

C. A manufacturer of a product who, after the product has left his control, acquires knowledge of a characteristic of the product that may cause damage and the danger of such characteristic, or who would have acquired such knowledge had he acted as a reasonably prudent manufacturer, is liable for damage caused by his subsequent failure to use reasonable care to provide an adequate warning of such characteristic and its danger to users and handlers of the product.

§ 2800.58. Unreasonably dangerous because of nonconformity to express warranty. A product is unreasonably dangerous when it does not conform to an express warranty made at any time by the manufacturer about the product if the express warranty has induced the claimant or another person or entity to use the product and the claimant's damage was proximately caused because the express warranty was untrue.

§ 2800.59. Manufacturer knowledge, design feasibility and burden of proof. A. Notwithstanding R.S. 9:2800.56, a manufacturer of a product shall not be liable for damage proximately caused by a characteristic of the product's design if the manufacturer proves that, at the time the product left his control:

(1) He did not know and, in light of then-existing reasonably available scientific and technological knowledge, could not have known of the design characteristic that caused the damage or the danger of such characteristic; or

(2) He did not know and, in light of then-existing reasonably available scientific and technological knowledge, could not have known of the alternative design identified by the claimant under R.S. 9:2800.56(1); or

(3) The alternative design identified by the claimant under R.S. 9:2800.56(1) was not feasible, in light of then-existing reasonably available scientific and technological knowledge or then-existing economic practicality.

B. Notwithstanding R.S. 9:2800.57(A) or (B), a manufacturer of a product shall not be liable for damage proximately caused by a characteristic of the product if the manufacturer proves that, at the time the product left his control, he did not know and, in light of then-existing reasonably available scientific and technological knowledge, could not have known of the characteristic that caused the damage or the danger of such characteristic.

MICHIGAN STATUTES ANNOTATED

(1995)

§ **600.2945.** As used in this section and sections 1629, 2945 to 2949a, and 5805:

(a) "Alteration" means a material change in a product after the product leaves the control of the manufacturer or seller. Alteration includes a change in the product's design, packaging, or labeling; a change to or removal of a safety feature, warning, or instruction; deterioration or damage caused by failure to observe routine care and maintenance or failure to observe an installation, preparation, or storage procedure; or a change resulting from repair, renovation, reconditioning, recycling, or reclamation of the product.

(b) "Drug" means that term as defined in section 201 of the federal food, drug, and cosmetic act, chapter 675, 52.1040, 21 U.S.C. 321. However, drug does not include a medical appliance or device.

(c) "Economic loss" means objectively verifiable pecuniary damages arising from medical expenses or medical care, rehabilitation services, custodial care, loss of wages, loss of future earnings, burial costs, loss of use of property, costs of repair or replacement of property, costs of obtaining substitute domestic services, loss of employment, or other objectively verifiable monetary losses.

(d) "Gross negligence" means conduct so reckless as to demonstrate a substantial lack of concern for whether injury results.

(e) "Misuse" means use of a product in a materially different manner than the product's intended use. Misuse includes uses inconsistent with the specifications and standards applicable to the product, uses contrary to a warning or instruction provided by the manufacturer, seller, or another person possessing knowledge or training regarding the use or maintenance of the product, and uses other than those for which the product would be considered suitable by a reasonably prudent person in the same or similar circumstances.

(f) "Noneconomic loss" means any type of pain, suffering, inconvenience, physical impairment, mental anguish, emotional distress, loss of society and companionship, loss of consortium injury to reputation, humiliation, or other nonpecuniary damages.

(g) "Product" includes any and all component parts to a product.

(h) "Product liability action" means an action based on a legal or equitable, theory of liability brought for the death of a person or for injury to a person or damage to property caused by or resulting from the production of a product.

(i) "Production" means manufacture, construction, design, formulation, development of standards, preparation, processing, assembly, inspection, testing, listing, certifying, warning, instructing, marketing, selling, advertising, packaging, or labeling.

(j) "Sophisticated user" means a person or entity that, by virtue of training, experience, a profession, or legal obligations, is or is generally expected to be knowledgeable about a product's properties, including a potential hazard or adverse effect. An employee who does not have actual knowledge of the product's potential hazard or adverse effect that caused the injury is not a sophisticated user.

§ 600.2946. Products Liability action; admissible evidence. (1) It shall be admissible as evidence in a product liability action that the production of the product was in accordance with the generally recognized and prevailing nongovernmental standards in existence at the time the specific unit of the product was sold or delivered by the defendant to the initial purchaser or user.

(2) In a product liability action brought against a manufacturer or seller for harm allegedly caused by a production defect, the manufacturer or seller is not liable unless the plaintiff establishes that the product was not reasonably safe at the time the specific unit of the product left the control of the manufacturer or seller and that, according to generally accepted production practices at the time the specific unit of the product left the control of the manufacturer or seller, a practical and technically feasible alternative production practice was available that would have prevented the harm without significantly impairing the usefulness or desirability of the product to users and without creating equal or greater risk of harm to others. An alternative production practice is practical and feasible only if the technical, medical, or scientific knowledge relating to production of the product, at the time the specific unit of the product left the control of the manufacturer or seller, was developed, available and capable of use in the production of the product and was economically feasible for use by the manufacturer. Technical, medical, or scientific knowledge is not economically feasible for use by the manufacturer if use of that knowledge in production of the product would significantly compromise the product's usefulness or desirability.

(3) With regard to the production of a product that is the subject of a product liability action, evidence of a philosophy, theory, knowledge, technique, or procedure that is learned, placed in use, or discontinued after the event resulting in the death of the person or injury to the person or property, which if learned, placed in use, or discontinued before the event would have made the event less likely to occur, is admissible only for the purpose of providing the feasibility of precautions, if controverted, or for impeachment.

(4) In a product liability action brought against a manufacturer or seller for harm allegedly caused by a product, there is a rebuttable presumption that the manufacturer or seller is not liable if; at the time the specific unit of the product was sold or delivered to the initial purchaser or

user, the aspect of the product that allegedly caused the harm was in compliance with standards relevant to the event causing the death or injury set forth in a federal or state statute or was approved by, or was in compliance with regulations or standards relevant to the event causing the death or injury promulgated by, a federal or state agency responsible for reviewing the safety of the product. Noncompliance with a standard relevant to the event causing the death or injury set forth in a federal or state statute or lack of approval by, or noncompliance with regulations or standards relevant to the event causing the death or injury promulgated by, a federal or state agency does not raise a presumption of negligence on the part of a manufacturer or seller. Evidence of compliance or noncompliance with a regulation or standard not relevant to the event causing the death or injury is not admissible.

§ 600.2946a. **Determination of damages; limitation.** (1) In an action for product liability, the total amount of damages for noneconomic loss shall not exceed $280,000.00, unless the defect in the product caused either the person's death or permanent loss of a vital bodily function, in which case the total amount of damages for noneconomic loss shall not exceed $500,000.00. On the effective date of the amendatory act that added this section, the state treasurer shall adjust the limitations set forth in this subsection so that the limitations are equal to the limitations provided in section 1483. After that date, the state treasurer shall adjust the limitations set forth in this subsection at the end of each calendar year so that they continue to be equal to the limitations provided in section 1483.

(2) In awarding damages in a product liability action, the trier of fact shall itemize damages into economic and noneconomic losses. Neither the court nor counsel for a party shall inform the jury of the limitations under subsection (1). The court shall adjust an award of noneconomic loss to conform to the limitations under subsection (1).

(3) The limitation on damages under subsection (1) for death or permanent loss of a vital bodily function does not apply to a defendant if the trier of fact determines by a preponderance of the evidence that the death or loss was the result of the defendant's gross negligence, or if the court finds that the matters stated in section 2949a are true.

(4) If damages for economic loss cannot readily be ascertained by the trier of fact, then the trier fact shall calculate damages for economic loss based on an amount that is equal to the state average median family income as reported in the immediately preceding federal decennial census and adjusted by the state treasurer in the same manner as provided in subsection (1).

§ 600.2947. **Product liability action; liability of manufacturer or seller.** (1) A manufacturer or seller is not liable in a product liability action for harm caused by an alteration of the product unless the alteration was reasonably foreseeable. Whether there was an alteration of a product and whether an alteration was reasonably foreseeable are legal issues to be resolved by the court.

(2) A manufacturer or seller is not liable in a product liability action for harm caused by misuse of a product unless the misuse was reasonably foreseeable. Whether there was misuse of a product and whether misuse was reasonably foreseeable are legal issues to be resolved by the court.

(3) A manufacturer or seller is not liable in a product liability action if the purchaser or user of the product was aware that use of the product created an unreasonable risk of personal injury and voluntarily exposed himself or herself to that risk and the risk that he or she exposed himself or herself to was the proximate cause of the injury. This subsection does not relieve a manufacturer or seller from a duty to use reasonable care in a product's production.

(4) Except to the extent a state or federal statute or regulation requires a manufacturer to warn, a manufacturer or seller is not liable in a product liability action for failure to provide an adequate warning if the product is provided for use by a sophisticated user.

(5) A manufacturer or seller is not liable in a product liability action if the alleged harm was caused by an inherent characteristic of the product that cannot be eliminated without substantially compromising the product's usefulness or desirability, and that is recognized by a person with the ordinary knowledge common to the community.

(6) In a product liability action, a seller other than a manufacturer is not liable for harm allegedly caused by the product unless either of the following is true:

(a) The seller failed to exercise reasonable care, including breach of any implied warranty, with respect to the product and that failure was a proximate cause of the person's injuries.

(b) The seller made an express warranty as to the product, the product failed to conform to the warranty, and the failure to conform to the warranty was a proximate cause of the person's harm.

§ 600.2948. Written warnings; failure to warn of material risks; burden of proof; duty of care. (1) Evidence is admissible in a product liability action that, before the death of the person or injury to the person or damage to property, pamphlets, booklets, labels, or other written warnings were provided that gave notice to foreseeable users of the material risk of injury, death, or damage connected with the foreseeable use of the product or provided instructions as to the foreseeable uses, applications, or limitations of the product that the defendant knew or should have known.

(2) A defendant is not liable for failure to warn of a material risk that is or should be obvious to a reasonably prudent product user or a material risk that is or should be a matter of common knowledge to persons in the same or similar position as the person upon whose injury or death the claim is based in a product liability action.

(3) In a product liability action brought against a manufacturer or seller for harm allegedly caused by a failure to provide adequate warnings or instructions, a manufacturer or seller is not liable unless the plaintiff proves that the manufacturer knew or should have known about the risk of harm based on the scientific, technical, or medical information reasonably available at the time the specific unit of the product left the control of the manufacturer.

(4) This section does not limit a manufacturer's or seller's duty to use reasonable care in relation to a product after the product has left the manufacturer's or seller's control.

§ 600.2949a. Defendant's actual knowledge; willful disregard of defects. In a product liability action, if the court determines that at the time of manufacture or distribution the defendant had actual knowledge that the product was defective and that there was a substantial likelihood that the defect would cause the injury that is the basis of the action, and the defendant willfully disregarded that knowledge in the manufacture or distribution of the product, then sections 2946(4), 2946a, 2947(1) to (4), and 2948(2) do not apply.

MISSISSIPPI CODE ANNOTATED

(1993, 2003, and 2004)

§ 11–1–63. Product liability suits. Subject to the provisions of § 11–1–64, in any action for damages caused by a product except for commercial damage to the product itself:

(a) The manufacturer or seller of the product shall not be liable if the claimant does not prove by the preponderance of the evidence that at the time the product left the control of the manufacturer or seller:

(i)1.   The product was defective because it deviated in a material way from the manufacturer's specifications or from otherwise identical units manufactured to the same manufacturing specifications, or

2.   The product was defective because it failed to contain adequate warnings or instructions, or

3.   The product was designed in a defective manner, or

4.   The product breached an express warranty or failed to conform to other express factual representations upon which the claimant justifiably relied in electing to use the product; and

(ii) The defective condition rendered the product unreasonably dangerous to the user or consumer; and

(iii) The defective and unreasonably dangerous condition of the product proximately caused the damages for which recovery is sought.

(b) A product is not defective in design or formulation if the harm for which the claimant seeks to recover compensatory damages was caused by an inherent characteristic of the product which is a generic aspect of the product that cannot be eliminated without substantially compromising the product's usefulness or desirability and which is recognized by the ordinary person with the ordinary knowledge common to the community.

(c)(i) In any action alleging that a product is defective because it failed to contain adequate warnings or instructions pursuant to paragraph (a)(i)2 of this section, the manufacturer or seller shall not be liable if the claimant does not prove by the preponderance of the evidence that at the time the product left the control of the manufacturer or seller, the manufacturer or seller knew or in light of reasonably available knowledge should have known about the danger that caused the damage for which recovery is sought and that the ordinary user or consumer would not realize its dangerous condition.

(ii) An adequate product warning or instruction is one that a reasonably prudent person in the same or similar circumstances would have provided with respect to the danger and that communicates sufficient information on the dangers and safe use of the product, taking into account the characteristics of, and the ordinary knowledge common to an ordinary consumer who purchases the product; or in the case of a prescription drug, medical device or other product that is intended to be used only under the supervision of a physician or other licensed professional person, taking into account the characteristics of, and the ordinary knowledge common to, a physician or other licensed professional who prescribes the drug, device or other product.

(d) In any action alleging that a product is defective pursuant to paragraph (a) of this section, the manufacturer or seller shall not be liable if the claimant (i) had knowledge of a condition of the product that was inconsistent with his safety; (ii) appreciated the danger in the condition; and (iii) deliberately and voluntarily chose to expose himself to the danger in such a manner to register assent on the continuance of the dangerous condition.

(e) In any action alleging that a product is defective pursuant to paragraph (a)(i)2 of this section, the manufacturer or seller shall not be liable if the danger posed by the product is known or is open and obvious to the user or consumer of the product, or should have been known or open and obvious to the user or consumer of the product, taking into account the characteristics of, and the ordinary knowledge common to, the persons who ordinarily use or consume the product.

(f) In any action alleging that a product is defective because of its design pursuant to paragraph (a)(i)3 of this section, the manufacturer or product seller shall not be liable if the claimant does not prove by the preponderance of the evidence that at the time the product left the control of the manufacturer or seller:

(i) The manufacturer or seller knew, or in light of reasonably available knowledge or in the exercise of reasonable care should have known, about the danger that caused the damage for which recovery is sought; and

(ii) The product failed to function as expected and there existed a feasible design alternative that would have to a reasonable probability prevented the harm. A feasible design alternative is a design that would have to a reasonable probability prevented the harm without impairing the utility, usefulness, practicality or desirability of the product to users or consumers.

(g)(i) The manufacturer of a product who is found liable for a defective product pursuant to Section 1(a) shall indemnify a product seller for the costs of litigation, any reasonable expenses, reasonable attorney's fees and any damages awarded by the trier of fact unless the seller exercised substantial control over that aspect of the design, testing, manufacture, packaging or labeling of the product that caused the harm for which recovery of damages is sought; the seller altered or modified the product, and the alteration or modification was a substantial factor in causing the harm for which recovery of damages is sought; the seller had actual knowledge of the defective condition of the product at the time he supplied same; or the seller made an express factual representation about the aspect of the product which caused the harm for which recovery of damages is sought.

(ii) Subparagraph (i) shall not apply unless the seller has given prompt notice of the suit to the manufacturer within ninety (90) days of the service of the complaint against the seller.

(h) In any action alleging that a product is defective pursuant to paragraph (a) of this section, the seller of a product other than the manufacturer shall not be liable unless the seller exercised substantial control over that aspect of the design, testing, manufacture, packaging or labeling of the product that caused the harm for which recovery of damages is sought; or the seller altered or modified the product, and the alteration or modification was a substantial factor in causing the harm for which recovery of damages is sought; or the seller had actual or constructive knowledge of the defective condition of the product at the time he supplied the product. It is the intent of this section to immunize innocent sellers who are not actively negligent, but instead are mere conduits of a product.

(i) Nothing in this section shall be construed to eliminate any common law defense to an action for damages caused by a product.

§ 11–1–64. Sellers in stream of commerce; dismissal of products liability claim; application; procedure. [Repealed by 2004 H.B. 13, §§ 6, 7].

§ 11–1–65. Punitive Damages. (1) In any action in which punitive damages are sought:

(a) Punitive damages may not be awarded if the claimant does not prove by clear and convincing evidence that the defendant against whom punitive damages are sought acted with actual malice, gross negligence which evidences a willful, wanton or reckless disregard for the safety of others, or committed actual fraud.

(b) In any action in which the claimant seeks an award of punitive damages, the trier of fact shall first determine whether compensatory damages are to be awarded and in what amount, before addressing any issues related to punitive damages.

(c) If, but only if, an award of compensatory damages has been made against a party, the court shall promptly commence an evidentiary hearing before the same trier of fact to determine whether punitive damages may be considered.

(d) The court shall determine whether the issue of punitive damages may be submitted to the trier of fact; and, if so, the trier of fact shall determine whether to award punitive damages and in what amount.

(e) In all cases involving an award of punitive damages, the fact finder, in determining the amount of punitive damages, shall consider, to the extent relevant, the following: the defendant's financial condition and net worth; the nature and reprehensibility of the defendant's wrongdoing, for example, the impact of the defendant's conduct on the plaintiff, or the relationship of the defendant to the plaintiff; the defendant's awareness of the amount of harm being caused and the defendant's motivation in causing such harm; the duration of the defendant's misconduct and whether the defendant attempted to conceal such misconduct; and any other circumstances shown by the evidence that bear on determining a proper amount of punitive damages. The trier of fact shall be instructed that the primary purpose of punitive damages is to punish the wrongdoer and deter similar misconduct in the future by the defendant and others while the purpose of compensatory damages is to make the plaintiff whole.

(f)(i) Before entering judgment for an award of punitive damages the trial court shall ascertain that the award is reasonable in its amount and rationally related to the purpose to punish what occurred giving rise to the award and to deter its repetition by the defendant and others.

(ii) In determining whether the award is excessive, the court shall take into consideration the following factors:

1. Whether there is a reasonable relationship between the punitive damage award and the harm likely to result from the defendant's conduct as well as the harm that actually occurred;

2. The degree of reprehensibility of the defendant's conduct, the duration of that conduct, the defendant's awareness, any concealment, and the existence and frequency of similar past conduct;

3. The financial condition and net worth of the defendant; and

4. In mitigation, the imposition of criminal sanctions on the defendant for its conduct and the existence of other civil awards against the defendant for the same conduct.

(2) The seller of a product other than the manufacturer shall not be liable for punitive damages unless the seller exercised substantial control over that aspect of the design, testing, manufacture, packaging or labeling of the product that caused the harm for which recovery of damages is sought; the seller altered or modified the product, and the alteration or modification was a substantial factor in causing the harm for which recovery of damages is sought; the seller had actual knowledge of the defective condition of the product at the time he supplied same.

(3)(a) In any civil action where an entitlement to punitive damages shall have been established under applicable laws, no award of punitive damages shall exceed the following:

(i) Twenty Million Dollars ($20,000,000.00) for a defendant with a net worth of more than One Billion Dollars ($1,000,000,000.00);

(ii) Fifteen Million Dollars ($15,000,000.00) for a defendant with a net worth of more than Seven Hundred Fifty Million Dollars ($750,000,000.00) but not more than One Billion Dollars ($1,000,000,000.00);

(iii) Ten Million Dollars ($10,000,000.00) for a defendant with a net worth of more than Five Hundred Million Dollars ($500,000,000.00) but not more than Seven Hundred Fifty Million Dollars ($750,000,000.00);

(iv) Seven Million Five Hundred Thousand Dollars ($7,500,000.00) for a defendant with a net worth of more than One Hundred Million Dollars ($100,000,000.00) but not more than Five Hundred Million Dollars ($500,-000,000.00);

(v) Five Million Dollars ($5,000,000.00) for a defendant with a net worth of more than Fifty Million Dollars ($50,000,000.00) but not more than One Hundred Million Dollars ($100,000,000.00); or

(vi) Four percent (4%) of the defendant's net worth for a defendant with a net worth of Fifty Million Dollars ($50,000,000.00) or less.

(b) For the purposes of determining the defendant's net worth in paragraph (a), the amount of the net worth shall be determined in accordance with Generally Accepted Accounting Principles.

(c) The limitation on the amount of punitive damages imposed by this subsection (3) shall not be disclosed to the trier of fact, but shall be applied by the court to any punitive damages verdict.

(d) The limitation on the amount of punitive damages imposed by this subsection (3) shall not apply to actions brought for damages or an injury resulting from an act or failure to act by the defendant:

(i) If the defendant was convicted of a felony under the laws of this state or under federal law which caused the damages or injury; or

(ii) While the defendant was under the influence of alcohol or under the influence of drugs other than lawfully prescribed drugs administered in accordance with a prescription.

(e) The exceptions provided in paragraph (d) shall not apply to an employer of a person acting outside the scope of such person's employment or responsibility as an agent or employee.

(4) Nothing in this section shall be construed as creating a right to an award of punitive damages or to limit the duty of the court, or the appellate courts, to scrutinize all punitive damage awards, ensure that all punitive damage awards comply with applicable procedural, evidentiary and constitutional requirements, and to order remittitur where appropriate.

(5) Subsections (1) and (2) of this section shall not apply to:

(a) Contracts;

(b) Libel and slander; or

(c) Causes of action for persons and property arising out of asbestos.

MISSOURI REVISED STATUTES

(1987)

§ 537.760. Products liability claim defined. As used in sections 33 to 36 of this act, the term "products liability claim" means a claim or portion of a claim in which the plaintiff seeks relief in the form of damages on a theory that the defendant is strictly liable for such damages because:

(1) The defendant, wherever situated in the chain of commerce, transferred a product in the course of his business; and

(2) The product was used in a manner reasonably anticipated; and

(3) Either or both of the following:

(a) The product was then in a defective condition unreasonably dangerous when put to a reasonably anticipated use, and the plaintiff was damaged as a direct result of such defective condition as existed when the product was sold; or

(b) The product was then unreasonably dangerous when put to a reasonably anticipated use without knowledge of its characteristics, and the plaintiff was damaged as a direct result of the product being sold without an adequate warning.

§ 537.762. Motion to dismiss, defendant whose only liability is as seller in stream of commerce. 1. A defendant whose liability is based solely on his status as a seller in the stream of commerce may be dismissed from a products liability claim as provided in this section.

2. This section shall apply to any products liability claim in which another defendant, including the manufacturer, is properly before the court and from whom total recovery may be had for plaintiff's claim.

3. A defendant may move for dismissal under this section within the time for filing an answer or other responsive pleading unless permitted by the court at a later time for good cause shown. The motion shall be accompanied by an affidavit which shall be made under oath and shall state that the defendant is aware of no facts or circumstances upon which a verdict might be reached against him, other than his status as a seller in the stream of commerce.

4. The parties shall have sixty days in which to conduct discovery on the issues raised in the motion and affidavit. The court for good cause shown, may extend the time for discovery, and may enter a protective order pursuant to the rules of civil procedure regarding the scope of discovery on other issues.

5. Any party may move for a hearing on a motion to dismiss under this section. If the requirements of subsections 2 and 3 of this section are met, and no party comes forward at such a hearing with evidence of facts which would render the defendant seeking dismissal under this section liable on some basis other than his status as a seller in the stream of

commerce, the court shall dismiss without prejudice the claim as to that defendant.

6. No order of dismissal under this section shall operate to divest a court of venue or jurisdiction otherwise proper at the time the action was commenced. A defendant dismissed pursuant to this section shall be considered to remain a party to such action only for such purposes.

7. An order of dismissal under this section shall be interlocutory until final disposition of plaintiff's claim by settlement or judgment and may be set aside for good cause shown at anytime prior to such disposition.

§ 537.764. State of the art, defined—affirmative defense in cases of strict liability for failure to warn. 1. As used in this section, "state of the art" means that the dangerous nature of the product was not known and could not reasonably be discovered at the time the product was placed into the stream of commerce.

2. The state of the art shall be a complete defense and relevant evidence only in an action based upon strict liability for failure to warn of the dangerous condition of a product. This defense shall be pleaded as an affirmative defense and the party asserting it shall have the burden of proof.

3. Nothing in this section shall be construed as limiting the rights of an injured party to maintain an action for negligence whenever such a cause of action would otherwise exist.

4. This section shall not be construed to permit or prohibit evidence of feasibility in products liability claims.

§ 537.765. Contributory fault as complete bar to plaintiff's recovery abolished. 1. Contributory fault, as a complete bar to plaintiff's recovery in a products liability claim, is abolished. The doctrine of pure comparative fault shall apply to products liability claims as provided in this section.

2. Defendant may plead and prove the fault of the plaintiff as an affirmative defense. Any fault chargeable to the plaintiff shall diminish proportionately the amount awarded as compensatory damages but shall not bar recovery.

3. For purposes of this section, "fault" is limited to:

(1) The failure to use the product as reasonably anticipated by the manufacturer;

(2) Use of the product for a purpose not intended by the manufacturer;

(3) Use of the product with knowledge of a danger involved in such use with reasonable appreciation of the consequences and the voluntary and unreasonable exposure to said danger;

(4) Unreasonable failure to appreciate the danger involved in use of the product or the consequences thereof and the unreasonable exposure to said danger;

(5) The failure to undertake the precautions a reasonably careful user of the product would take to protect himself against dangers which he would reasonably appreciate under the same or similar circumstances; or

(6) The failure to mitigate damages.

MONTANA CODE ANNOTATED

(1987, 1997)

§ 27–1–719. Liability of seller of product for physical harm to user or consumer. (1) As used in this section, "seller" means a manufacturer, wholesaler, or retailer.

(2) A person who sells a product in a defective condition unreasonably dangerous to a user or consumer or to the property of a user or consumer is liable for physical harm caused by the product to the ultimate user or consumer or to the user's or consumer's property if:

(a) the seller is engaged in the business of selling such a product; and

(b) the product is expected to and does reach the user or consumer without substantial change in the condition in which it is sold.

(3) The provisions of subsection (2) apply even if:

(a) the seller exercised all possible care in the preparation and sale of the product; and

(b) the user or consumer did not buy the product from or enter into any contractual relation with the seller.

(4) Subsection (2)(b) does not apply to a claim for relief based upon improper product design.

(5) Contributory fault is a defense to the liability of a seller, based on strict liability in tort, for personal injury or property damage caused by a defectively manufactured or defectively designed product. A seller named as a defendant in an action based on strict liability in tort for damages to a person or property caused by a defectively designed or defectively manufactured product may assert the following affirmative defenses against the user or consumer, the legal representative of the user or consumer, or any person claiming damages by reason of injury to the user or consumer:

(a) The user or consumer of the product discovered the defect or the defect was open and obvious and the user or consumer unreasonably made use of the product and was injured by it.

(b) The product was unreasonably misused by the user or consumer and the misuse caused or contributed to the injury.

(6) The affirmative defenses referred to in subsection (5) mitigate or bar recovery and must be applied in accordance with the principles of comparative fault set forth in 27–1–702 and 27–1–705.

NEBRASKA REVISED STATUTES

(1978, 1981, 1998)

§ 25–21,180. Terms, defined. As used in sections 25–224 and 25–21,180 to 25–21,182, unless the context otherwise requires: Product liability action shall mean any action brought against a manufacturer, seller, or lessor of a product, regardless of the substantive legal theory or theories upon which the action is brought, for or on account of personal injury, death, or property damage caused by or resulting from the manufacture, construction, design, formulation, installation, preparation, assembly, testing, packaging, or labeling of any product, or the failure to warn or protect against a danger or hazard in the use, misuse, or intended use of any product, or the failure to provide proper instructions for the use of any product.

§ 25–21,181. Action based on strict liability in tort; brought against seller or lessor; when. No product liability action based on the doctrine of strict liability in tort shall be commenced or maintained against any seller or lessor of a product which is alleged to contain or possess a defective condition unreasonably dangerous to the buyer, user, or consumer unless the seller or lessor is also the manufacturer of the product or the part thereof claimed to be defective.

§ 25–21,182. Product liability action; based upon negligent or defective design, testing, or labeling; defense. In any product liability action based upon negligent or defective design, testing, or labeling, proof establishing that such design, testing, or labeling was in conformity with the generally recognized and prevailing state of the art in the industry at the time the specific product involved in the action was first sold to any person not engaged in the business of selling such product shall be a defense. State of the art as used in this section shall be defined as the best technology reasonably available at the time.

§ 25–224. Actions on product liability. (1) All product liability actions, except one governed by subsection (5) of this section, shall be commenced within four years next after the date on which the death, injury, or damage complained of occurs.

(2)(a) Notwithstanding subsection (1) of this section or any other statutory provision to the contrary, any product liability action, except one governed by section 2–725, Uniform Commercial Code or by subsection (5) of this section, shall be commenced as follows:

(i) For products manufactured in Nebraska, within ten years after the date the product which allegedly caused the personal injury, death, or damage was first sold or leased for use or consumption; or

(ii) For products manufactured outside Nebraska, within the time allowed by the applicable statute of repose, if any, of the state or country where the product was manufactured, but in no event less than ten years. If the state or country where the product was manufactured does not have an applicable statute of repose, then the only limitation upon the commencement of an action for product liability shall be as set forth in subsection (1) of this section.

(b) If the changes made to this subsection by Laws 2001, LB 489, are declared invalid or unconstitutional, this subsection as it existed prior to September 1, 2001, shall be deemed in full force and effect and shall apply to all claims in which a final order has not been entered.

(3) The limitations contained in subsection (1), (2), or (5) of this section shall not be applicable to indemnity or contribution actions brought by a manufacturer or seller of a product against a person who is or may be liable to such manufacturer or seller for all or any portion of any judgment rendered against a manufacturer or seller.

(4) Notwithstanding the provisions of subsections (1) and (2) of this section, any cause of action or claim which any person may have on July 22, 1978, may be brought not later than two years following such date.

(5) Any action to recover damages based on injury allegedly resulting from exposure to asbestos composed of chrysotile, amosite, crocidolite, tremolite, anthrophyllite, actinolite, or any combination thereof, shall be commenced within four years after the injured person has been informed of discovery of the injury by competent medical authority and that such injury was caused by exposure to asbestos as described herein, or within four years after the discovery of facts which would reasonably lead to such discovery, whichever is earlier. No action commenced under this subsection based on the doctrine of strict liability in tort shall be commenced or maintained against any seller of a product which is alleged to contain or possess a defective condition unreasonably dangerous to the buyer, user, or consumer unless such seller is also the manufacturer of such product or the manufacturer of the part thereof claimed to be defective. Nothing in this subsection shall be construed to permit an action to be brought based on an injury described in this subsection discovered more than two years prior to August 30, 1981.

NEW JERSEY REVISED STATUTES

(1987 and 1995)

§ 2A:58C–1. **Legislative findings; definitions.** a. Legislative findings; definitions. a. The Legislature finds that there is an urgent need for remedial legislation to establish clear rules with respect to certain matters relating to actions for damages for harm caused by products, including certain principles under which liability is imposed and the standards and procedures for the award of punitive damages. This act is not intended to codify all issues relating to product liability, but only to deal with matters that require clarification. The Legislature further finds that such sponsors' or committee statements that may be adopted or included in the legislative history of this act shall be consulted in the interpretation and construction of this act.

b. As used in this Act:

(1) "Claimant" means any person who brings a product liability action, and if such an action is brought through or on behalf of an estate, the term includes the person's decedent, or if an action is brought through or on behalf of a minor, the term includes the person's parent or guardian.

(2) "Harm" means (a) physical damage to property, other than to the product itself; (b) personal physical illness, injury or death; (c) pain and suffering, mental anguish or emotional harm; and (d) any loss of consortium or services or other loss deriving from any type of harm described in subparagraphs (a) through (c) of this paragraph.

(3) "Product liability action" means any claim or action brought by a claimant for harm caused by a product, irrespective of the theory underlying the claim, except actions for harm caused by breach of an express warranty.

(4) "Environmental tort action" means a civil action seeking damages for harm where the cause of the harm is exposure to toxic chemicals or substances, but does not mean actions involving drugs or products intended for personal consumption or use.

§ 2A:58C–2. **Liability of manufacturer or seller.** A manufacturer or seller of a product shall be liable in a product liability action only if the claimant proves by a preponderance of the evidence that the product causing the harm was not reasonably fit, suitable or safe for its intended purpose because it: a. deviated from the design specifications, formulae, or performance standards of the manufacturer or from otherwise identical units manufactured to the same manufacturing specifications or formulae, or b. failed to contain adequate warnings or instructions, or c. was designed in a defective manner.

§ 2A:58C–3. **Defenses.** a. In any product liability action against a manufacturer or seller for harm allegedly caused by a product that was

247

designed in a defective manner, the manufacturer or seller shall not be liable if:

(1) At the time the product left the control of the manufacturer, there was not a practical and technically feasible alternative design that would have prevented the harm without substantially impairing the reasonably anticipated or intended function of the product; or

(2) The characteristics of the product are known to the ordinary consumer or user, and the harm was caused by an unsafe aspect of the product that is an inherent characteristic of the product and that would be recognized by the ordinary person who uses or consumes the product with the ordinary knowledge common to the class of persons for whom the product is intended, except that this paragraph shall not apply to industrial machinery or other equipment used in the workplace and it is not intended to apply to dangers posed by products such as machinery or equipment that can feasibly be eliminated without impairing the usefulness of the product; or

(3) The harm was caused by an unavoidably unsafe aspect of the product and the product was accompanied by an adequate warning or instruction as defined in section 4 of this act.

b.   The provisions of paragraph (1) of subsection a. of this section shall not apply if the court, on the basis of clear and convincing evidence, makes all of the following determinations:

(1) The product is egregiously unsafe or ultra-hazardous;

(2) The ordinary user or consumer of the product cannot reasonably be expected to have knowledge of the product's risks, or the product poses a risk of serious injury to persons other than the user or consumer; and

(3) The product has little or no usefulness.

c.   No provision of subsection a. of this section is intended to establish any rule, or alter any existing rule, with respect to the burden of proof.

§ 2A:58C–4. Adequate product warning or instruction. In any product liability action the manufacturer or seller shall not be liable for harm caused by a failure to warn if the product contains an adequate warning or instruction or, in the case of dangers a manufacturer or seller discovers or reasonably should discover after the product leaves its control, if the manufacturer or seller provides an adequate warning or instruction. An adequate product warning or instruction is one that a reasonably prudent person in the same or similar circumstances would have provided with respect to the danger and that communicates adequate information on the dangers and safe use of the product, taking into account the characteristics of, and the ordinary knowledge common to, the persons by whom the product is intended to be used, or in the case of prescription drugs, taking into account the characteristics of, and the ordinary knowledge common to, the prescribing physician. If the warning or instruction given in connection with a drug or device or food or food additive has been approved or prescribed by the federal Food and Drug Administration under the "Federal Food, Drug, and Cosmetic Act," 52 Stat. 1040, 21 U.S.C. § 301 et seq. or the "Public Health Service Act," 58 Stat. 682, 42 U.S.C. § 201 et seq., a rebuttable presumption shall arise that the warning or instruction is adequate. For purposes of this section, the terms "drug", "device", "food", and "food additive" have the meanings defined in the "Federal Food, Drug, and Cosmetic Act."

§ 2A:58C–5. Punitive damages. Punitive damages shall not be awarded if a drug or device or food or food additive which caused the claimant's harm was subject to premarket approval or licensure by the federal Food and Drug Administration under the "Federal Food, Drug, and Cosmetic Act," 52 Stat. 1040, 21 U.S.C. § 301 et seq. or the "Public Health Service Act," 58 Stat. 682, 42 U.S.C. § 201 et seq. and was approved or licensed; or is generally recognized as safe and effective pursuant to conditions established by the federal Food and Drug Administration and applicable regulations, including packaging and labeling regulations. However, where the product manufacturer knowingly withheld or misrepresented information required to be submitted under the agency's regulations, which information was material and relevant to the harm in question, punitive damages may be awarded. For purposes of this subsection, the terms "drug", "device", "food", and "food additive" have the meanings defined in the "Federal Food, Drug, and Cosmetic Act."

§ 2A:58C–6. Environmental tort action—Inapplicability of Act. The provisions of this act shall not apply to any environmental tort action.

§ 2A:58C–7. Burden of proof rules unaltered. Except as otherwise expressly provided in this act, no provision of this act is intended to establish any rule, or alter any existing rule, with respect to the burden of proof in a product liability action.

§ 2A:58C–8. Additional definitions. (1) As used in this act:

"Manufacturer" means (1) any person who designs, formulates, produces, creates, makes, packages, labels or constructs any product or component of a product; (2) a product seller with respect to a given product to the extent the product seller designs, formulates, produces, creates, makes, packages, labels or constructs the product before its sale; (3) any product seller not described in paragraph (2) which holds itself out as a manufacturer to the user of the product; or (4) a United States domestic sales subsidiary of a foreign manufacturer if the foreign manufacturer has a controlling interest in the domestic sales subsidiary.

"Product liability action" means any claim or action brought by a claimant for harm caused by a product, irrespective of the theory underlying the claim, except actions for harm caused by breach of an express warranty.

"Product seller" means any person who, in the course of a business conducted for that purpose: sells; distributes; leases; installs; prepares or assembles a manufacturer's product according to the manufacturer's plan, intention, design, specifications or formulations; blends; packages; labels; markets; repairs; maintains or otherwise is involved in placing a product in the line if commerce. The term "product seller" does not include:

(1) A seller of real property; or

(2) A provider of professional services in any case in which the sale or use of a product is incidental to the transaction and the essence of the transaction is the furnishing of judgment, skill or services; or

(3) Any person who acts in only a financial capacity with respect to the sale of a product.

§ 2A:58C–9. Identification of manufacturer; strict liability of supplier. a. In any product liability action against a product seller where the manufacturer has not been named a defendant, the product seller may file an affidavit certifying the correct identity of the manufacturer of the product which allegedly caused the injury, death or damage.

b. Upon filing the affidavit pursuant to subsection a. of this section, the product seller shall be relieved of all strict liability claims, subject to the provisions set forth in subsection d. Of this section. Due diligence shall be exercised in providing the plaintiff with the correct identity of the manufacturer or manufacturers.

c. The product seller shall be subject to strict liability if:

(1) The identity of the manufacturer given to the plaintiff by the product seller was incorrect. Once the correct identity of the manufacturer has been provided, the product seller shall again be relieved of all strict liability claims, subject to subsection d. of this section; or

(2) The manufacturer has no known agents, facility, or other presence within the United States; or

(3) The manufacturer has no attachable assets or has been adjudicated bankrupt and a judgment is not otherwise recoverable from the assets of the bankruptcy estate.

d. A product seller shall be liable if:

(1) The product seller has exercised some significant control over the design, manufacture, packaging or labeling of the product relative to the alleged defect in the product which caused the injury, death or damage; or

(2) The product seller knew or should have known of the defect in the product which caused the injury, death or damage or the plaintiff can affirmatively demonstrate that the product seller was in possession of facts from which a reasonable person would conclude that the product seller had or should have had knowledge of the alleged defect in the product which caused the injury, death or damage; or

(3) The product seller created the defect in the product which caused the injury, death or damage.

e. The commencement of a product liability action based in whole or in part on the doctrine of strict liability against a product seller shall toll the applicable statute of limitations with respect to manufacturers who have been identified pursuant to the provisions of subsection a of this section.

2. This act shall take effect immediately and shall apply to causes of action which occur on or after the effective date of this act.

§ 2A:58C–10. Definitions relative to health care providers. As used in this act:

"Health care provider" or "provider" means a provider of health care services and includes, but is not limited to, health care professionals, hospitals, nursing homes and other health care facilities.

"Health care service" means a service or product sold by a health care provider and includes, but is not limited to, hospital, medical, surgical, dental, hearing and vision services or products.

"Medical device" or "device" means a "device" as defined in subsection (h) of section 201 of the "Federal Food, Drug and Cosmetic Act," 52 Stat. 1040, (21 U.S.C. § 321).

§ 2A:58C–11. Liability of health care providers for medical devices. In any product liability action against a health care provider for harm allegedly caused by a medical device that was manufactured or designed in a defective manner, or for harm caused by a failure to warn of a danger related to the use of a medical device, the provider shall not be liable unless:

(1) the provider has exercised some significant control over the design, manufacture, packaging or labeling of the medical device relative to the alleged defect in the device which caused the injury, death or damage; or

(2) the provider knew or should have known of the defect in the medical device which caused the injury, death or damage, or the plaintiff can affirmatively demonstrate that the provider was in possession of facts from which a reasonable person would conclude that the provider had or should have had knowledge of the alleged defect in the medical device which caused the injury, death or damage; or

(3) the provider created the defect in the medical device which caused the injury, death or damage.

NORTH CAROLINA GENERAL STATUTES

(1979, 1987 and 1995)

§ **99B-1. Definitions.** When used in this Chapter, unless the context otherwise requires:

(1) "Claimant" means a person or other entity asserting a claim and, if said claim is asserted on behalf of an estate, an incompetent or a minor, "claimant" includes plaintiff's decedent, guardian, or guardian ad litem.

(2) "Manufacturer" means a person or entity who designs, assembles, fabricates, produces, constructs or otherwise prepares a product or component part of a product prior to its sale to a user or consumer, including a seller owned in whole or significant part by the manufacturer or a seller owning the manufacturer in whole or significant part.

(3) "Product liability action" includes any action brought for or on account of personal injury, death or property damage caused by or resulting from the manufacture, construction, design, formulation, development of standards, preparation, processing, assembly, testing, listing, certifying, warning, instructing, marketing, selling, advertising, packaging, or labeling of any product.

(4) "Seller" includes a retailer, wholesaler, or distributor, and means any individual or entity engaged in the business of selling a product, whether such sale is for resale or for use or consumption. "Seller" also includes a lessor or bailor engaged in the business of leasing or bailment of a product.

§ **99B-1.1. Strict liability.** There shall be no strict liability in tort in product liability actions.

§ **99B-1.2. Breach of warranty.** Nothing in this act shall preclude a product liability action that otherwise exists against a manufacturer or seller for breach of warranty. The defenses provided for in this Chapter shall apply to claims for breach of warranty unless expressly excluded under this Chapter.

§ **99B-2. Seller's opportunity to inspect; privity requirements for warranty claims.** (a) No product liability action, except an action for breach of express warranty, shall be commenced or maintained against any seller when the product was acquired and sold by the seller in a sealed container or when the product was acquired and sold by the seller under circumstances in which the seller was afforded no reasonable opportunity to inspect the product in such a manner that would have or should have, in the exercise of reasonable care, revealed the existence of the condition complained of, unless the seller damaged or mishandled the product while in his possession; provided, that the provisions of this section shall not apply if the manufacturer of the product is not subject to the jurisdiction of the courts of this State or if such manufacturer has been judicially declared insolvent.

(b) A claimant who is a buyer, as defined in the Uniform Commercial Code, of the product involved, or who is a member or a guest of a member of the family of the buyer, a guest of the buyer, or an employee of the buyer may bring a product liability action directly against the manufacturer of the product involved for breach of implied warranty; and the lack of privity of contract shall not be grounds for the dismissal of such action.

§ 99B–3. Alteration or modification of product.

(a) No manufacturer or seller of a product shall be held liable in any product liability action where a proximate cause of the personal injury, death, or damage to property was either an alteration or modification of the product by a party other than the manufacturer or seller, which alteration or modification occurred after the product left the control of such manufacturer or such seller unless:

(1) The alteration or modification was in accordance with the instructions or specifications of such manufacturer or such seller; or

(2) The alteration or modification was made with the express consent of such manufacturer or such seller.

(b) For the purposes of this section, alteration or modification includes changes in the design, formula, function, or use of the product from that originally designed, tested, or intended by the manufacturer. It includes failure to observe routine care and maintenance, but does not include ordinary wear and tear.

§ 99B–4. Knowledge or reasonable care.

No manufacturer or seller shall be held liable in any product liability action if:

(1) The use of the product giving rise to the product liability action was contrary to any express and adequate instructions or warnings delivered with, appearing on, or attached to the product or on its original container or wrapping, if the user knew or with the exercise of reasonable and diligent care should have known of such instructions or warnings; or

(2) The user knew of or discovered a defect or dangerous condition of the product that was inconsistent with the safe use of the product, and then unreasonably and voluntarily exposed himself or herself to the danger, and was injured by or caused injury with that product; or

(3) The claimant failed to exercise reasonable care under the circumstances in the use of the product, and such failure was a proximate cause of the occurrence that caused the injury or damage complained of.

§ 99B–5. Claims based on inadequate warning or instruction.

(a) No manufacturer or seller of a product shall be held liable in any product liability action for a claim based upon inadequate warning or instruction unless the claimant proves that the manufacturer or seller acted unreasonably in failing to provide such warning or instruction, that the failure to provide adequate warning or instruction was a proximate cause of the harm for which damages are sought, and also proves one of the following:

(1) At the time the product left the control of the manufacturer or seller, the product, without an adequate warning or instruction, created an unreasonably dangerous condition that the manufacturer or seller knew, or in the exercise of ordinary care should have known, posed a substantial risk of harm to a reasonably foreseeable claimant.

(2) After the product left the control of the manufacturer or seller, the manufacturer or seller became aware of or in the exercise of ordinary care should have known that the product posed a substantial risk of harm to a reasonably foreseeable user or consumer and failed to take reasonable steps to give adequate warning or instruction or to take other reasonable action under the circumstances.

(b) Notwithstanding subsection (a) of this section, no manufacturer or seller of a product shall be held liable in any product liability action for failing to warn about an open and obvious risk or a risk that is a matter of common knowledge.

(c) Notwithstanding subsection (a) of this section, no manufacturer or seller of a prescription drug shall be liable in a products liability action for failing to provide a warning or instruction directly to a consumer if an adequate warning or instruction has been provided to the physician or other legally authorized person who prescribes or dispenses that prescription drug for the claimant unless the United States Food and Drug Administration requires such direct consumer warning or instruction to accompany the product.

§ 99B–6. Claims based on inadequate design or formulation. (a) No manufacturer of a product shall be held liable in any product liability action for the inadequate design or formulation of the product unless the claimant proves that at the time of its manufacture the manufacturer acted unreasonably in designing or formulating the product, that this conduct was a proximate cause of the harm for which damages are sought, and also proves one of the following:

(1) At the time the product left the control of the manufacturer, the manufacturer unreasonably failed to adopt a safer, practical, feasible, and otherwise reasonable alternative design or formulation that could then have been reasonably adopted and that would have prevented or substantially reduced the risk of harm without substantially impairing the usefulness, practicality, or desirability of the product.

(2) At the time the product left the control of the manufacturer, the design or formulation of the product was so unreasonable that a reasonable person, aware of the relevant facts, would not use or consume a product of this design.

(b) In determining whether the manufacturer acted unreasonably under subsection (a) of this section, the factors to be considered shall include, but are not limited to, the following:

(1) The nature and magnitude of the risks of harm associated with the design or formulation in light of the intended and reasonably foreseeable uses, modifications, or alterations of the product.

(2) The likely awareness of product users, whether based on warnings, general knowledge, or otherwise, of those risks of harm.

(3) The extent to which the design or formulation conformed to any applicable government standard that was in effect when the product left the control of its manufacturer.

(4) The extent to which the labeling for a prescription or nonprescription drug approved by the United States Food and Drug Administration conformed to any applicable government or private standard that was in effect when the product left the control of its manufacturer.

(5) The utility of the product, including the performance, safety, and other advantages associated with that design or formulation.

(6) The technical, economic, and practical feasibility of using an alternative design or formulation at the time of manufacture.

(7) The nature and magnitude of any foreseeable risks associated with the alternative design or formulation.

(c) No manufacturer of a product shall be held liable in any product liability action for a claim under this section to the extent that it is based upon an inherent characteristic of the product that cannot be eliminated without substantially compromising the product's usefulness or desirability and that is recognized by the ordinary person with the ordinary knowledge common to the community.

(d) No manufacturer of a prescription drug shall be liable in a product liability action on account of some aspect of the prescription drug that is unavoidably unsafe, if an adequate warning and instruction has been provided pursuant to G.S. 99B–5(c). As used in this subsection, "unavoidably unsafe" means that, in the state of technical, scientific, and medical knowledge generally prevailing at the time the product left the control of its manufacturer, an aspect of that product that caused the claimant's harm was not reasonably capable of being made safe.

(e) Nothing in this section precludes an action against a manufacturer in accordance with the provisions of G.S. 99B–5.

NORTH DAKOTA CENTURY CODE

(1993, 1995)

§ 28–01.3–01. Definitions. As used in this chapter: 1. "Manufacturer" means a person or entity who designs, assembles, fabricates, produces, constructs, or otherwise prepares a product or a component part of a product prior to the sale of the product to a user or consumer. The term includes any seller of a product who is owned in whole or significant part by the manufacturer or who owns, in whole or significant part, the manufacturer.

2. "Product liability action" means any action brought against a manufacturer or seller of a product, regardless of the substantive legal theory or theories upon which the action is brought, for or on account of personal injury, death, or property damage caused by or resulting from the manufacture, construction, design, formula, installation, preparation, assembly, testing, packaging, labeling, or sale of any product, or the failure to warn or protect against a danger or hazard in the use, misuse, or unintended use of any product, or the failure to provide proper instructions for the use of any product.

3. "Seller" means any individual or entity, including a manufacturer, wholesaler, distributor, or retailer, who is engaged in the business of selling or leasing any product for resale, use, or consumption.

4. "Unreasonably dangerous" means that the product is dangerous to an extent beyond which would be contemplated by the ordinary and prudent buyer, consumer, or user of that product in that community considering the product's characteristics, propensities, risks, dangers, and uses, together with any actual knowledge, training, or experience possessed by that particular buyer, user, or consumer.

§ 28–01.3–02. Limitation on ad damnum clause. If a complaint filed in a products liability action prays for a recovery of money in an amount equal to or less than fifty thousand dollars, the amount must be stated. If a recovery of money in an amount greater than fifty thousand dollars is demanded, the pleading must state merely that recovery of reasonable damages in an amount greater than fifty thousand dollars is demanded. This action may be superseded by an amendment to the North Dakota Rules of Civil Procedure.

§ 28–01.3–03. Alteration or modification of product is defense to action. No manufacturer or seller of a product may be held liable in any products liability action where a substantial contributing cause of the injury, death, or damage to property was an alteration or modification of the product, which occurred subsequent to the sale by the manufacturer or seller to the initial user or consumer, and which changed the purpose, use, function, design, or intended use or manner of use of the product from that for which the product was originally designed, tested, or intended.

§ 28–01.3–04. Liability of nonmanufacturing sellers. 1. In any products liability action maintained against a seller of a product who did not manufacture the product, the seller shall upon answering or otherwise pleading file an affidavit certifying the correct identity of the manufacturer of the product allegedly causing the personal injury, death, or damage to property.

2. After the plaintiff has filed a complaint against the manufacturer and the manufacturer has or is required to have answered or otherwise pleaded, the court shall order the dismissal of the claim against the certifying seller, unless the plaintiff can show any of the following:

a. That the certifying seller exercised some significant control over the design or manufacture of the product, or provided instructions or warnings to the manufacturer relative to the alleged defect in the product which caused the personal injury, death, or damage to property.

b. That the certifying seller had actual knowledge of the defect in the product which caused the personal injury, death, or damage to property.

c. That the certifying seller created the defect in the product which caused the personal injury, death, or damage to property.

3. The plaintiff may at any time prior to the beginning of the trial move to vacate the order of dismissal and reinstate the certifying seller if the plaintiff can show any of the following:

a. That the applicable statute of limitation bars a product liability action against the manufacturer of the product allegedly causing the injury, death, or damage.

b. That the identity of the manufacturer given to the plaintiff by the certifying defendant was incorrect.

§ 28–01.3–05. Indemnity of seller. If a product liability action is commenced against a seller, and it is alleged that a product was defectively designed, contained defectively manufactured parts, had insufficient safety guards, or had inaccurate or insufficient warning; that such condition existed when the product left the control of the manufacturer; that the seller has not substantially altered the product; and that the defective condition or lack of safety guards or adequate warnings caused the injury or damage complained of; the manufacturer from whom the product was acquired by the seller must be required to assume the cost of defense of the action, and any liability that may be imposed on the seller. The obligation to assume the seller's cost of defense should also extend to an action in which the manufacturer and seller are ultimately found not liable.

§ 28–01.3–06. Determination of defective product. No product may be considered to have a defect or to be in a defective condition, unless at the time the product was sold by the manufacturer or other initial seller, there was a defect or defective condition in the product which made the product unreasonably dangerous to the user or consumer.

§ 28–01.3–07. Declaration of legislative findings and intent. 1. The legislative assembly finds that products liability reforms enacted in 1979, 1987, and 1993 have provided a needed degree of certainty in the laws governing civil actions against product manufacturers and sellers.

2. In recent years it has become increasingly evident that there are still serious problems with the current civil justice system. As a result, there is an urgent need for additional legislation to establish clear and predictable rules with respect to certain matters relating to products liability actions.

3. The purpose of sections 28–01.3–08 and 28–01.3–09 is to clarify and improve the method of determining responsibility for the payment of damages in products liability litigation; to restore balance and predictability between the consumer and the manufacturer or seller in product liability litigation; to bring about a more fair and equitable resolution of controversies in products liability litigation; to reenact a statute of repose to provide a reasonable period of time for the commencement of products liability litigation after a manufacturer or seller has parted with possession of its product; to address problems that have been created by judicial interpretation of our previous enactments; to enact, with minor changes, several provisions of former chapter 28–01.1; and to simplify and provide an increased degree of certainty and predictability to our products liability laws.

§ 28–01.3–08. Statute of limitation and repose. 1. Except as provided in subsections 4 and 5, there may be no recovery of damages in a products liability action unless the injury, death, or property damage occurs within ten years of the date of initial purchase for use or consumption, or within eleven years of the date of manufacture of a product.

2. This section applies to all persons, regardless of minority or other legal disability.

3. If a manufacturer, wholesaler, or retailer issues a recall of a product in any state or becomes aware of any defect in a product at any time and fails to take reasonable steps to warn users of the product defect, the provisions of subsection 1 do not bar a products liability action against the manufacturer or seller by a user of the product who is subsequently injured or damaged as a result of the defect.

4. An action to recover damages based on injury allegedly resulting from exposure to asbestos composed of chrysotile, amosite, crocidolite, tremolite, anthrophyllite, actinolite, or any combination thereof, must be commenced within three years after the injured person has been informed of discovery of the injury by competent medical authority and that the injury was caused by exposure to asbestos as described in this subsection, or within three years after the discovery of facts that would reasonably lead to the discovery, whichever is earlier. No action commenced under this subsection based on the doctrine of strict liability in tort may be commenced or maintained against any seller of a product that is alleged to

contain or possess a defective condition unreasonably dangerous to the buyer, user, or consumer unless the seller is also the manufacturer of the product or the manufacturer of the part of the product claimed to be defective.

5.   An action to recover damages based on injury to property allegedly resulting from the presence of products containing asbestos fibers of any type must be commenced within six years of the date upon which the owner of that property knew or should have known of facts giving rise to the cause of action.

§ 28–01.3–09. Rebuttable presumption against defects. There is a rebuttable presumption that a product is free from any defect or defective condition where the plans, designs, warnings, or instructions for the product or the methods and techniques of manufacturing, inspecting, and testing the product were in conformity with government standards established for that industry or where no government standards exist then with applicable industry standards, which were in existence at the time the plans, designs, warnings, or instructions for the product or the methods and techniques of manufacturing, inspecting, and testing the product were adopted.

OHIO REVISED CODE ANNOTATED

(2001, 2004)

§ 2307.71 Definitions. (A) As used in sections 2307.71 to 2307.80 of the Revised Code:

(1) "Claimant" means either of the following:

(a) A person who asserts a product liability claim or on whose behalf a product liability claim is asserted;

(b) If a product liability claim is asserted on behalf of the surviving spouse, children, parents, or other next of kin of a decedent or on behalf of the estate of a decedent, whether as a claim in an action for wrongful death under Chapter 2125. of the Revised Code or as a survivorship claim, whichever of the following is appropriate:

(i) The decedent, if the reference is to the person who allegedly sustained harm or economic loss for which, or in connection with which, compensatory damages or punitive or exemplary damages are sought to be recovered;

(ii) The personal representative of the decedent or the estate of the decedent, if the reference is to the person who is asserting or has asserted the product liability claim.

(2) "Economic loss" means direct, incidental, or consequential pecuniary loss, including, but not limited to, damage to the product involved and nonphysical damage to property other than that product. Harm is not "economic loss."

(3) "Environment" means navigable waters, surface water, ground water, drinking water supplies, land surface, subsurface strata, and air.

(4) "Ethical drug" means a prescription drug that is prescribed or dispensed by a physician or any other person who is legally authorized to prescribe or dispense a prescription drug.

(5) "Ethical medical device" means a medical device that is prescribed, dispensed, or implanted by a physician or any other person who is legally authorized to prescribe, dispense, or implant a medical device and that is regulated under the "Federal Food, Drug, and Cosmetic Act," 52 Stat. 1040, 21 U.S.C. 301–392, as amended.

(6) "Foreseeable risk" means a risk of harm that satisfies both of the following:

(a) It is associated with an intended or reasonably foreseeable use, modification, or alteration of a product.

(b) It is a risk that the manufacturer of the product should recognize while exercising both of the following:

(i) The attention, perception, memory, knowledge, and intelligence that a reasonable manufacturer should possess;

(ii) Any superior attention, perception, memory, knowledge, or intelligence that the manufacturer possesses.

(7) "Harm" means death, physical injury to person, serious emotional distress, or physical damage to property other than the product involved. Economic loss is not "harm."

(8) "Hazardous or toxic substances" include, but are not limited to, hazardous waste as defined in section 3734.01 of the Revised Code, hazardous waste as specified in the rules of the director of environmental protection pursuant to division (A) of section 3734.12 of the Revised Code, hazardous substances as defined in section 3716.01 of the Revised Code, and hazardous substances, pollutants, and contaminants as defined in or by regulations adopted pursuant to the "Comprehensive Environmental Response, Compensation, and Liability Act of 1980," 94 Stat. 2767, 42 U.S.C. 9601, as amended.

(9) "Manufacturer" means a person engaged in a business to design, formulate, produce, create, make, construct, assemble, or rebuild a product or a component of a product.

(10) "Person" has the same meaning as in division (C) of section 1.59 of the Revised Code and also includes governmental entities.

(11) "Physician" means a person who is licensed to practice medicine and surgery or osteopathic medicine and surgery by the state medical board.

(12)(a) "Product" means, subject to division (A)(12)(b) of this section, any object, substance, mixture, or raw material that constitutes tangible personal property and that satisfies all of the following:

(i) It is capable of delivery itself, or as an assembled whole in a mixed or combined state, or as a component or ingredient.

(ii) It is produced, manufactured, or supplied for introduction into trade or commerce.

(iii) It is intended for sale or lease to persons for commercial or personal use.

(b) "Product" does not include human tissue, blood, or organs.

(13) "Product liability claim" means a claim that is asserted in a civil action pursuant to sections 2307.71 to 2307.80 of the Revised Code and that seeks to recover compensatory damages from a manufacturer or supplier for death, physical injury to person, emotional distress, or physical damage to property other than the product in question, that allegedly arose from any of the following:

(a) The design, formulation, production, construction, creation, assembly, rebuilding, testing, or marketing of that product;

(b) Any warning or instruction, or lack of warning or instruction, associated with that product;

(c) Any failure of that product to conform to any relevant representation or warranty.

(14) "Representation" means an express representation of a material fact concerning the character, quality, or safety of a product.

(15)(a) "Supplier" means, subject to division (O)(2) of this section, either of the following:

(i) A person that, in the course of a business conducted for the purpose, sells, distributes, leases, prepares, blends, packages, labels, or otherwise participates in the placing of a product in the stream of commerce;

(ii) A person that, in the course of a business conducted for the purpose, installs, repairs, or maintains any aspect of a product that allegedly causes harm.

(b) "Supplier" does not include any of the following:

(i) A manufacturer;

(ii) A seller of real property;

(iii) A provider of professional services who, incidental to a professional transaction the essence of which is the furnishing of judgment, skill, or services, sells or uses a product;

(iv) Any person who acts only in a financial capacity with respect to the sale of a product, or who leases a product under a lease arrangement in which the selection, possession, maintenance, and operation of the product are controlled by a person other than the lessor.

(16) "Unavoidably unsafe" means that, in the state of technical, scientific, and medical knowledge at the time a product left the control of its manufacturer, an aspect of that product was incapable of being made safe.

(B) Sections 2307.71 to 2307.80 of the Revised Code are intended to abrogate all all common law product liability causes of action.

§ 2307.711. Assumption of risk as affirmative defense to claim.

(A) Subject to divisions (B)(1), (2), and (3) of this section, sections 2315.32 to 2315.36 of the Revised Code apply to a product liability claim that is asserted pursuant to sections 2307.71 to 2307.80 of the Revised Code.

(B)(1) Express or implied assumption of the risk may be asserted as an affirmative defense to a product liability claim under sections 2307.71 to 2307.80 of the Revised Code, except that express or implied assumption of the risk may not be asserted as an affirmative defense to an intentional tort claim.

(2) Subject to division (B)(3) of this section, if express or implied assumption of the risk is asserted as an affirmative defense to a product

liability claim under sections 2307.71 to 2307.80 of the Revised Code and if it is determined that the claimant expressly or impliedly assumed a risk and that the express or implied assumption of the risk was a direct and proximate cause of harm for which the claimant seeks to recover damages, the express or implied assumption of the risk is a complete bar to the recovery of those damages.

(3) If implied assumption of the risk is asserted as an affirmative defense to a product liability claim against a supplier under division (A)(1) of section 2307.78 of the Revised Code, sections 2315.32 to 2315.36 of the Revised Code are applicable to that affirmative defense and shall be used to determine whether the claimant is entitled to recover compensatory damages based on that claim and the amount of any recoverable compensatory damages.

§ 2307.72. **Damage claims; contamination or pollution claims; multiple claims asserted in one civil action.** (A) Any recovery of compensatory damages based on a product liability claim is subject to sections 2307.71 to 2307.79 of the Revised Code.

(B) Any recovery of punitive or exemplary damages in connection with a product liability claim is subject to sections 2307.71 to 2307.80 of the Revised Code.

(C) Any recovery of compensatory damages for economic loss based on a claim that is asserted in a civil action, other than a product liability claim, is not subject to sections 2307.71 to 2307.79 of the Revised Code but may occur under the common law of this state or other applicable sections of the Revised Code.

(D)(1) Sections 2307.71 to 2307.80 of the Revised Code do not supersede, modify, or otherwise affect any statute, regulation, or rule of this state or of the United States, or the common law of this state or of the United States, that relates to liability in compensatory damages or punitive or exemplary damages for injury, death, or loss to person or property, or to relief in the form of the abatement of a nuisance, civil penalties, cleanup costs, cost recovery, an injunction or temporary restraining order, or restitution, that arises, in whole or in part, from contamination or pollution of the environment or a threat of contamination or pollution of the environment, including contamination or pollution or a threat of contamination or pollution from hazardous or toxic substances.

(2) Consistent with the Rules of Civil Procedure, in the same civil action against the same defendant or different defendants, a claimant may assert both of the following:

(a) A product liability claim, including a claim for the recovery of punitive or exemplary damages in connection with a product liability claim;

(b) A claim for the recovery of compensatory damages or punitive or exemplary damages for injury, death, or loss to person or property, or for relief in the form of the abatement of a nuisance, civil penalties, cleanup costs, cost recovery, an injunction or temporary restraining order, or restitution, that arises, in whole or in part, from contamination or pollution of the environment or a threat of contamination or pollution of the environment, including contamination or pollution or a threat of contamination or pollution from hazardous or toxic substances.

§ 2307.73. Standard of proof for manufacturer's liability for compensatory damages; evidence of subsequent remedial measures.
(A) A manufacturer is subject to liability for compensatory damages based on a product liability claim only if the claimant establishes, by a preponderance of the evidence, both of the following:

(1) Subject to division (B) of this section, the product was defective in manufacture or construction as described in section 2307.74 of the Revised Code, was defective in design or formulation as described in section 2307.75 of the Revised Code, was defective due to inadequate warning or instruction as described in section 2307.76 of the Revised Code, or was defective because it did not conform to a representation made by the manufacturer as described in section 2307.77 of the Revised Code;

(2) A defective aspect of the product as described in division (A)(1) of this section was a proximate cause of harm for which the claimant seeks to recover compensatory damages.

(B) If a claimant is unable because a product was destroyed to establish by direct evidence that the product was defective or if a claimant otherwise is unable to establish by direct evidence that a product was defective, it shall be sufficient for the claimant to present, consistent with the Rules of Evidence, circumstantial or other competent evidence that establishes, by a preponderance of the evidence, that the product was defective in any one of the four respects specified in division (A)(1) of this section.

§ 2307.74. Products defective in manufacture or construction.
A product is defective in manufacture or construction if, when it left the control of its manufacturer, it deviated in a material way from the design specifications, formula, or performance standards of the manufacturer, or from otherwise identical units manufactured to the same design specifications, formula, or performance standards. A product may be defective in manufacture or construction as described in this section even though its manufacturer exercised all possible care in its manufacture or construction.

§ 2307.75. Products defective in design or formulation; foreseeable risks; benefits; drug or medical device.
(A) Subject to divisions (D), (E), and (F) of this section, a product is defective in design or formulation if at the time it left the control of its manufacturer, the foreseeable risks associated with its design or formulation as determined pursuant to division (B) of this section exceeded the benefits associated with that design or formulation as determined pursuant to division (C) of this section.

(B) The foreseeable risks associated with the design or formulation of a product shall be determined by considering factors including, but not limited to, the following:

(1) The nature and magnitude of the risks of harm associated with that design or formulation in light of the intended and reasonably foreseeable uses, modifications, or alterations of the product;

(2) The likely awareness of product users, whether based on warnings, general knowledge, or otherwise, of those risks of harm;

(3) The likelihood that that design or formulation would cause harm in light of the intended and reasonably foreseeable uses, modifications, or alterations of the product;

(4) The extent to which that design or formulation conformed to any applicable public or private product standard that was in effect when the product left the control of its manufacturer;

(5) The extent to which the design or formulation is more dangerous than a reasonably prudent consumer would expect when used in an intended or reasonably foreseeable manner.

(C) The benefits associated with the design or formulation of a product shall be determined by considering factors including, but not limited to, the following:

(1) The intended or actual utility of the product, including any performance or safety advantages associated with that design or formulation;

(2) The technical and economic feasibility, when the product left the control of its manufacturer, of using an alternative design or formulation;

(3) The nature and magnitude of any foreseeable risks associated with an alternative design or formulation.

(D) An ethical drug or ethical medical device is not defective in design or formulation because some aspect of it is unavoidably unsafe, if the manufacturer of the ethical drug or ethical medical device provides adequate warning and instruction under section 2307.76 of the Revised Code concerning that unavoidably unsafe aspect.

(E) A product is not defective in design or formulation if the harm for which the claimant seeks to recover compensatory damages was caused by an inherent characteristic of the product which is a generic aspect of the product that cannot be eliminated without substantially compromising the product's usefulness or desirability and which is recognized by the ordinary person with the ordinary knowledge common to the community.

(F) A product is not defective in design or formulation if, at the time the product left the control of its manufacturer, a practical and technically feasible alternative design or formulation was not available that would have prevented the harm for which the claimant seeks to recover compensatory damages without substantially impairing the usefulness or intended purpose of the product.

§ 2307.76. Products defective due to inadequate warning or instruction. (A) Subject to divisions (B) and (C) of this section, a product is defective due to inadequate warning or instruction if either of the following applies:

(1) it is defective due to inadequate warning or instruction at the time of marketing if, when it left the control of its manufacturer, both of the following applied:

(a) the manufacturer knew or, in the exercise of reasonable care, should have known about a risk that is associated with the product and that allegedly caused harm for which the claimant seeks to recover compensatory damages;

(b) the manufacturer failed to provide the warning or instruction that a manufacturer exercising reasonable care would have provided concerning that risk, in light of the likelihood that the product would cause harm of the type for which the claimant seeks to recover compensatory damages and in light of the likely seriousness of that harm.

(2) It is defective due to inadequate post-marketing warning or instruction if, at a relevant time after it left the control of its manufacturer, both of the following applied:

(a) the manufacturer knew or, in the exercise of reasonable care, should have known about a risk that is associated with the product and that allegedly caused harm for which the claimant seeks to recover compensatory damages;

(b) the manufacturer failed to provide the post-marketing warning or instruction that a manufacturer exercising reasonable care would have provided concerning that risk, in light of the likelihood that the product would cause harm of the type for which the claimant seeks to recover compensatory damages and in light of the likely seriousness of that harm.

(B) A product is not defective due to lack of warning or instruction or inadequate warning or instruction as a result of the failure of its manufacturer to warn or instruct about an open and obvious risk or a risk that is a matter of common knowledge.

(C) An ethical drug is not defective due to inadequate warning or instruction if its manufacturer provides otherwise adequate warning and instruction to the physician or other legally authorized person who prescribes or dispenses that ethical drug for a claimant in question and if the federal Food and Drug Administration has not provided that warning or instruction relative to that ethical drug is to be given directly to the ultimate user of it.

§ 2307.77. Products defective due to nonconformance with manufacturer's representations. A product is defective if it did not conform, when it left the control of its manufacturer, to a representation made by that manufacturer. A product may be defective because it did not conform to a representation even though its manufacturer did not act fraudulently, recklessly, or negligently in making the representation.

§ 2307.78. Liability of supplier. (A) Subject to division (B) of this section, a supplier is subject to liability for compensatory damages based on a product liability claim only if the claimant establishes, by a preponderance of the evidence, that either of the following applies:

(1) The supplier was negligent, and, the negligence was a proximate cause of harm for which the claimant seeks to recover compensatory damages.

(2) The product did not conform, when it left the control of the supplier, to a representation made by the supplier, and the representation and the failure to conform to it were a proximate cause of harm for which the claimant seeks to recover compensatory damages. A supplier is subject to liability for the representation and the failure to conform to it even though the supplier did not act fraudulently, recklessly, or negligently in making the representation.

(B) A supplier of a product is subject to liability for compensatory damages based on a product liability claim under sections 2307.71 to 2307.77 of the Revised Code, as if it were the manufacturer of that product, if the manufacturer of that product is or would be subject to liability for compensatory damages based on a product liability claim under sections 2307.71 to 2307.77 of the Revised Code and any of the following applies:

(1) The manufacturer of that product is not subject to judicial process in this state.

(2) The claimant will be unable to enforce a judgment against the manufacturer of that product due to actual or asserted insolvency of the manufacturer.

(3) The supplier owns or, when it supplied that product, owned, in whole or in part, the manufacturer of that product.

(4) The supplier is owned or, when it supplied that product, was owned, in whole or in part, by the manufacturer of that product.

(5) The supplier created or furnished a manufacturer with the design or formulation that was used to produce, create, make, construct, assemble, or rebuild that product or a component of that product.

(6) The supplier altered, modified, or failed to maintain that product after it came into the possession of, and before it left the possession of, the supplier, and the alteration, modification, or failure to maintain that product rendered it defective.

(7) The supplier marketed that product under its own label or trade name.

(8) The supplier failed to respond timely and reasonably to a written request by or on behalf of the claimant to disclose to the claimant the name and address of the manufacturer of that product.

§ 2307.79. Compensatory damages. (A) If a claimant is entitled to recover compensatory damages for harm from a manufacturer in accordance with section 2307.73 of the Revised Code or from a supplier in accordance with division (B) of section 2307.78 of the Revised Code, the claimant may recover from the manufacturer or supplier in question, in that action, compensatory damages for any economic loss that proximately resulted from the defective aspect of the product in question.

(B) If a claimant is entitled to recover compensatory damages for harm from a supplier in accordance with division (A) of section 2307.78 of the Revised Code, the claimant may recover from the supplier in question, in that action, compensatory damages for any economic loss that proximately resulted from the negligence of that supplier or from the representation made by that supplier and the failure of the product in question to conform to that representation.

§ 2307.80. Effect of recall notification. (A) Subject to divisions (C) and (D) of this section, punitive or exemplary damages shall not be awarded against a manufacturer or supplier in question in connection with a product liability claim unless the claimant establishes, by clear and convincing evidence, that harm for which the claimant is entitled to recover compensatory damages in accordance with section 2307.73 or 2307.78 of the Revised Code was the result of misconduct of the manufacturer or supplier in question that manifested a flagrant disregard of the safety of persons who might be harmed by the product in question. The fact by itself that a product is defective does not establish a flagrant disregard of the safety of persons who might be harmed by that product.

(B) Whether the trier of fact is a jury or the court, if the trier of fact determines that a manufacturer or supplier in question is liable for punitive or exemplary damages in connection with a product liability claim, the amount of those damages shall be determined by the court. In determining the amount of punitive or exemplary damages, the court shall consider factors including, but not limited to, the following:

(1) The likelihood that serious harm would arise from the misconduct of the manufacturer or supplier in question;

(2) The degree of the awareness of the manufacturer or supplier in question of that likelihood;

(3) The profitability of the misconduct to the manufacturer or supplier in question;

(4) The duration of the misconduct and any concealment of it by the manufacturer or supplier in question;

(5) The attitude and conduct of the manufacturer or supplier in question upon the discovery of the misconduct and whether the misconduct has terminated;

(6) The financial condition of the manufacturer or supplier in question;

(7) The total effect of other punishment imposed or likely to be imposed upon the manufacturer or supplier in question as a result of the misconduct, including awards of punitive or exemplary damages to persons similarly situated to the claimant and the severity of criminal penalties to which the manufacturer or supplier in question has been or is likely to be subjected.

(C)(1) Except as provided in division (C)(2) of this section, if a claimant alleges in a product liability claim that a drug or device caused harm to the claimant, the manufacturer of the drug or device shall not be liable for punitive or exemplary damages in connection with that product liability claim if the drug or device that allegedly caused the harm satisfies either of the following:

(a) It was manufactured and labeled in relevant and material respects in accordance with the terms of an approval or license issued by the federal food and drug administration under the "Federal Food, Drug, and Cosmetic Act," 52 Stat. 1040 (1938), 21 U.S.C. 301–392, as amended, or the "Public Health Service Act," 58 Stat. 682 (1944), 42 U.S.C. 201–300cc–15, as amended.

(b) It was an over-the-counter drug marketed pursuant to federal regulations, was generally recognized as safe and effective and as not being misbranded pursuant to the applicable federal regulations, and satisfied in relevant and material respects each of the conditions contained in the applicable regulations and each of the conditions contained in an applicable monograph.

(2) Division (C)(1) of this section does not apply if the claimant establishes, by a preponderance of the evidence, that the manufacturer fraudulently and in violation of applicable regulations of the food and drug administration withheld from the food and drug administration information known to be material and relevant to the harm that the claimant allegedly suffered or misrepresented to the food and drug administration information of that type.

(3) For purposes of divisions (C) and (D) of this section:

(a) "Drug" has the same meaning as in the "Federal Food, Drug, and Cosmetic Act," 52 Stat. 1040, 1041 (1938), 21 U.S.C. 321(g)(1), as amended.

(b) "Device" has the same meaning as in the "Federal Food, Drug, and Cosmetic Act," 52 Stat. 1040, 1041 (1938), 21 U.S.C. 321(h), as amended.

(D)(1) If a claimant alleges in a product liability claim that a product other than a drug or device caused harm to the claimant, the manufacturer or supplier of the product shall not be liable for punitive or exemplary damages in connection with the claim if the manufacturer or supplier fully complied with all applicable government safety and performance standards, whether or not designated as such by the government, relative to the product's manufacture or construction, the product's design or formulation, adequate warnings or instructions, and representations when the product left the control of the manufacturer or supplier, and the claimant's injury results from an alleged defect of a product's manufacture or construction, the product's design or formulation, adequate warnings or instructions, and representations for which there is an applicable government safety or performance standard.

(2) Division (D)(1) of this section does not apply if the claimant establishes, by a preponderance of the evidence, that the manufacturer or supplier of the product other than a drug or device fraudulently and in violation of applicable government safety and performance standards, whether or not designated as such by the government, withheld from an applicable government agency information known to be material and relevant to the harm that the claimant allegedly suffered or misrepresented to an applicable government agency information of that type.

(E) The bifurcated trial provisions of division (B) of section 2315.21 of the Revised Code, the ceiling on recoverable punitive or exemplary damages specified in division (D)(1) of that section, and the provisions of division (D)(3) of that section apply to awards of punitive or exemplary damages under this section.

OREGON REVISED STATUTES

(1977, 1979, 1989, 1995, 2003, 2005)

§ 30.900. "Product liability civil action" defined. As used in ORS 30.900 to 30.920 "product liability civil action" means a civil action brought against a manufacturer, distributor, seller or lessor of a product for damages for personal injury, death or property damage arising out of:

(1) Any design, inspection, testing, manufacturing or other defect in a product;

(2) Any failure to warn regarding a product; or

(3) Any failure to properly instruct in the use of a product.

§ 30.905. Time for commencement of action. (1) Except as provided in ORS 30.907 and 30.908 (1) to (4), a product liability civil action may not be brought for any death, personal injury or property damage that is caused by a product and that occurs more than eight years after the date on which the product was first purchased for use or consumption.

(2) Except as provided in ORS 30.907 and 30.908 (1) to (4), a product liability civil action for personal injury or property damage must be commenced not later than the earlier of:

(a) Two years after the date on which the plaintiff discovers, or reasonably should have discovered, the personal injury or property damage and the causal relationship between the injury or damage and the product, or the causal relationship between the injury or damage and the conduct of the defendant; or

(b) Ten years after the date on which the product was first purchased for use or consumption.

(3) Except as provided in ORS 30.907 and 30.908 (1) to (4), a product liability civil action for death must be commenced not later than the earlier of:

(a) The limitation provided by ORS 30.020; or

(b) Ten years after the date on which the product was first purchased for use or consumption.

§ 30.907. Asbestos-related disease damages; limitations. (1) A product liability civil action for damages resulting from asbestos-related disease shall be commenced not later than two years after the date on which the plaintiff first discovered, or in the exercise of reasonable care should have discovered, the disease and the cause thereof.

(2) A product liability civil action may not be brought against a contractor, as defined in ORS 701.005, for damages resulting from asbestos-related disease if the contractor:

(a) Used or installed products containing asbestos pursuant to plans, specifications or directions prepared for a project by or on behalf of the owner of the project;

(b) Is not the manufacturer or distributor of the products containing asbestos; and

(c) Did not furnish the products containing asbestos independent of the provision of labor.

(3) Subsection (2) of this section does not affect a plaintiff's ability to bring a product liability civil action against a contractor if:

(a) The contractor substituted a product containing asbestos on a project when the plans, specifications or directions for the project prepared by or on behalf of the owner did not specify the use or installation of a product containing asbestos; and

(b) The owner or the owner's representative did not expressly direct or consent to the substitution of the product containing asbestos.

§ 30.908. Action arising out of injury from breast implants; limitations. (1) Notwithstanding ORS 30.020, a product liability civil action for death, injury or damage resulting from breast implants containing silicone, silica or silicon as a component must be commenced not later than two years after the date on which the plaintiff first discovered, or in the exercise of reasonable care should have discovered:

(a) The death or specific injury, disease or damage for which the plaintiff seeks recovery;

(b) The tortious nature of the act or omission of the defendant that gives rise to a claim for relief against the defendant; and

(c) All other elements required to establish plaintiff's claim for relief.

(2) A product liability civil action for death, injury or damage resulting from breast implants containing silicone, silica or silicon as a component is not subject to ORS 30.905 or any other statute of repose in Oregon Revised Statutes.

(3) For the purposes of subsection (1) of this section, an action for wrongful death must be commenced not later than two years after the earliest date that the discoveries required by subsection (1) of this section are made by any of the following persons:

(a) The decedent;

(b) The personal representative for the decedent; or

(c) Any person for whose benefit the action could be brought.

(4) Subsections (1) to (4) of this section do not apply to a person that supplied component parts or raw materials to manufacturers of breast implants containing silicone, silica or silicon as a component, and the person shall remain subject to the limitations on actions imposed by ORS 30.020 and 30.905, if:

(a) The person did not manufacture breast implants containing silicone, silica or silicon as a component at any time; and

(b) The person was not owned by and did not own a business that manufactured breast implants containing silicone, silica or silicon as a component at any time.

(5) A physician licensed pursuant to ORS chapter 677 is not a manufacturer, distributor, seller or lessor of a breast implant for the purposes of ORS 30.900 to 30.920 if the implant is provided by the physician to a patient as part of a medical implant procedure.

(6) A health care facility licensed under ORS chapter 442 is not a manufacturer, distributor, seller or lessor of a breast implant for the purposes of ORS 30.900 to 30.920 if the implant is provided by the facility to a patient as part of a medical implant procedure.

§ 30.910. Product disputably presumed not unreasonably dangerous. It is a disputable presumption in a products liability civil action that a product as manufactured and sold or leased is not unreasonably dangerous for its intended use.

§ 30.915. Defenses. It shall be a defense to a product liability civil action that an alteration or modification of a product occurred under the following circumstances:

(1) The alteration or modification was made without the consent of or was made not in accordance with the instructions or specifications of the manufacturer, distributor, seller or lessor;

(2) The alteration or modification was a substantial contributing factor to the personal injury, death or property damage; and

(3) If the alteration or modification was reasonably foreseeable, the manufacturer, distributor, seller or lessor gave adequate warning.

§ 30.920. When seller or lessor of product liable—Effect of liability rule. (1) One who sells or leases any product in a defective condition unreasonably dangerous to the user or consumer or to his property is subject to liability for physical harm or damage to property caused by that condition, if:

(a) The seller or lessor is engaged in the business of selling or leasing such a product; and

(b) The product is expected to and does reach the user or consumer without substantial change in the condition in which it is sold or leased.

(2) The rule stated in subsection (1) of this section shall apply, even though:

(a) The seller or lessor has exercised all possible care in the preparation and sale or lease of the product; and

(b) The user, consumer or injured party has not purchased or leased the product from or entered into any contractual relations with the seller or lessor.

(3) It is the intent of the Legislative Assembly that the rule stated in subsections (1) and (2) of this section shall be construed in accordance with the *Restatement (Second) of Torts* § 402A, Comments *a* to *m* (1965). All references in these comments to sale, sell, selling or seller shall be construed to include lease, leases, leasing or lessor.

(4) Nothing in this section shall be construed to limit the rights and liabilities of sellers and lessors under principles of common law negligence or under ORS chapter 72.

§ 30.925. Punitive damages. (1) In a product liability civil action, punitive damages shall not be recoverable except as provided in ORS 31.730.

(2) Punitive damages, if any, shall be determined and awarded based upon the following criteria:

(a) The likelihood at the time that serious harm would arise from the defendant's misconduct;

(b) The degree of the defendant's awareness of that likelihood;

(c) The profitability of the defendant's misconduct;

(d) The duration of the misconduct and any concealment of it;

(e) The attitude and conduct of the defendant upon discovery of the misconduct;

(f) The financial condition of the defendant; and

(g) The total deterrent effect of other punishment imposed upon the defendant as a result of the misconduct, including, but not limited to, punitive damage awards to persons in situations similar to the claimant's and the severity of criminal penalties to which the defendant has been or may be subjected.

§ 30.927. When manufacturer of drug not liable for punitive damages; exceptions. (1) Where a drug allegedly caused the plaintiff harm, the manufacturer of the drug shall not be liable for punitive damages if the drug product alleged to have caused the harm:

(a) Was manufactured and labeled in relevant and material respects in accordance with the terms of an approval or license issued by the Federal Food and Drug Administration under the Federal Food, Drug and Cosmetic Act or the Public Health Service Act; or

(b) Is generally recognized as safe and effective pursuant to conditions established by the Federal Food and Drug Administration and applicable regulations, including packaging and labeling regulations.

(2) Subsection (1) of this section does not apply if the plaintiff proves, in accordance with the standard of proof set forth in ORS 30.925 (1), that

the defendant, either before or after making the drug available for public use, knowingly in violation of applicable Federal Food and Drug Administration regulations withheld from or misrepresented to the agency or prescribing physician information known to be material and relevant to the harm which the plaintiff allegedly suffered.

(3) Nothing contained in this section bars an award of punitive damages where a manufacturer of a drug intentionally fails to conduct a recall required by a valid order of a federal or state agency authorized by statute to require such a recall.

(4) For the purposes of this section, the term "drug" has the meaning given to the term in section 1201 (g)(1) of the Federal Food, Drug and Cosmetic Act, 21 U.S.C. 321 (g)(1).

§ 31.730. Standards for award of punitive damages; required review of award by court; additional reduction of award for remedial measures. (1) Punitive damages are not recoverable in a civil action unless it is proven by clear and convincing evidence that the party against whom punitive damages are sought has acted with malice or has shown a reckless and outrageous indifference to a highly unreasonable risk of harm and has acted with a conscious indifference to the health, safety and welfare of others.

(2) If an award of punitive damages is made by a jury, the court shall review the award to determine whether the award is within the range of damages that a rational juror would be entitled to award based on the record as a whole, viewing the statutory and common-law factors that allow an award of punitive damages for the specific type of claim at issue in the proceeding.

(3) In addition to any reduction that may be made under subsection (2) of this section, upon the motion of a defendant the court may reduce the amount of any judgment requiring the payment of punitive damages entered against the defendant if the defendant establishes that the defendant has taken remedial measures that are reasonable under the circumstances to prevent reoccurrence of the conduct that gave rise to the claim for punitive damages. In reducing awards of punitive damages under the provisions of this subsection, the court shall consider the amount of any previous judgment for punitive damages entered against the same defendant for the same conduct giving rise to a claim for punitive damages.

RHODE ISLAND GENERAL LAWS

(1965, 1978, 1985)

§ 9–1–13. Limitation of actions generally—Product liability. (a) Except as otherwise specially provided, all civil actions shall be commenced within ten (10) years next after the cause of action shall accrue, and not after.

(b) Notwithstanding the provisions of subsection (a) of this section, an action for the recovery of damages for personal injury, death, or damage to real or personal property, including any action based upon implied warranties arising out of an alleged design, inspection, listing, or manufacturing defect, or any other alleged defect of whatsoever kind or nature in a product, or arising out of any alleged failure to warn regarding a product, or arising out of any alleged failure to properly instruct in the use of a product, shall be commenced within ten (10) years after the date the product was first purchased for use or consumption.

§ 9–1–32. Effect of alteration of product after sale. (a) As used in this section:

(1) "Product liability damages" means damages because of personal injury, death, or property damage sustained by reason of an alleged defect in a product, or an alleged failure to warn or protect against a danger or hazard in the use or misuse of the product, or an alleged failure to instruct properly in the use of a product.

(2) "Subsequent alteration or modification" means an alteration or modification of a product made subsequent to the manufacture or sale by the manufacturer or seller which altered, modified, or changed the purpose, use, function, design, or manner of use of the product from that originally designed, tested, or intended by the manufacturer, or the purpose, use, function, design, or manner of use or intended use for which the product was originally designed, tested, or manufactured.

(b) No manufacturer or seller of a product shall be liable for product liability damages where a substantial cause of the injury, death, or damage was a subsequent alteration or modification.

SOUTH CAROLINA CODE ANNOTATED

(1974)

§ 15–73–10. Liability of seller for defective product. (1) One who sells any product in a defective condition unreasonably dangerous to the user or consumer or to his property is subject to liability for physical harm caused to the ultimate user or consumer, or to his property, if

a. The seller is engaged in the business of selling such a product, and

b. It is expected to and does reach the user or consumer without substantial change in the condition in which it is sold.

2. The rule stated in subsection (1) shall apply although

a. The seller has exercised all possible care in the preparation and sale of his product, and

b. The user or consumer has not brought the product from or entered into any contractual relation with the seller.

§ 15–73–20. Situation in which recovery shall be barred. If the user or consumer discovers the defect and is aware of the danger, and nevertheless proceeds unreasonably to make use of the product and is injured by it, he is barred from recovery.

§ 15–73–30. Intent of chapter. Comments to § 402A of the Restatement of Torts, 2d, are incorporated herein by reference thereto as the legislative intent of this chapter.

SOUTH DAKOTA CODIFIED LAWS

(1985, 1979, 1995)

§ 15–2–12.2. Product liability actions—Prospective application. An action against a manufacturer, lessor, or seller of a product, regardless of the substantive legal theory upon which the action is brought, for or on account of personal injury, death, or property damage caused by or resulting from the manufacture, construction, design, formula, installation, inspection, preparation, assembly, testing, packaging, labeling, or sale of any product or failure to warn or protect against a danger or hazard in the use, misuse, or unintended use of any product, or the failure to provide proper instructions for the use of any product may be commenced only within three years of the date when the personal injury, death, or property damage occurred, became known or should have become known to the injured party. This section is prospective in application.

§ 20–9–9. Product's dealers and sellers immune from strict liability except for manufacturers or those who knew of defect— Other causes of action against seller not limited. No cause of action based on the doctrine of strict liability in tort may be asserted or maintained against any distributor, wholesaler, dealer, or retail seller of a product which is alleged to contain or possess a latent defective condition unreasonably dangerous to the buyer, user, or consumer unless said distributor, wholesaler, dealer, or retail seller is also the manufacturer or assembler of said product or the maker of a component part of the final product, or unless said dealer, wholesaler, or retail seller knew, or, in the exercise of ordinary care, should have known, of the defective condition of the final product. Nothing in this section shall be construed to limit any other cause of action from being brought against any seller of a product.

§ 20–9–10. Product's manufacturer, assembler, or seller immune from strict liability for injury caused by certain alterations or modifications. No manufacturer, assembler, or seller of a product may be held liable for damages for personal injury, death, or property damage sustained by reason of the doctrine of strict liability in tort based on a defect in a product, or failure to warn or protect against a danger or hazard in the use or misuse of such a product, or failure to properly instruct in the use or misuse of such product, where a proximate cause of the injury, death, or damage was an alteration or modification of such product made under all of the following circumstances:

(1) The alteration or modification was made subsequent to the manufacture, assembly, or sale of the product;

(2) The alteration or modification altered or modified the purpose, use, function, design, or manner of use of the product from that originally designed, tested, or intended by the manufacturer, assembler, or seller; and

(3) It was not foreseeable by the manufacturer, assembler, or seller of the product that the alteration or modification would be made, and, if made, that it would render the product unsafe.

§ 20–9–10.1. State of the art defense in product liability actions. In any product liability action based upon negligence or strict liability, whether the design, manufacture, inspection, testing, packaging, warning, or labeling was in conformity with the generally recognized and prevailing state of the art existing at the time the specific product involved was first sold to any person not engaged in the business of selling such a product, may be considered in determining the standard of care, whether the standard of care was breached or whether the product was in a defective condition or unreasonably dangerous to the user.

TENNESSEE CODE ANNOTATED

(1978)

§ 29–28–101. Short title. This chapter shall be known and may be cited as the "Tennessee Products Liability Act of 1978."

§ 29–28–102. Definitions. As used in this chapter unless the context otherwise requires:

(1) "Anticipated life." The anticipated life of a product shall be determined by the expiration date placed on the product by the manufacturer when required by law but shall not commence until the date the product was first purchased for use or consumption;

(2) "Defective condition" means a condition of a product that renders it unsafe for normal or anticipatable handling and consumption;

(3) "Employer" means any person exercising legal supervisory control or guidance of users or consumers of products;

(4) "Manufacturer" means the designer, fabricator, producer, compounder, processor or assembler of any product or its component parts;

(5) "Product" means any tangible object or goods produced;

(6) "Product liability action" for purposes of this chapter includes all actions brought for or on account of personal injury, death or property damage caused by or resulting from the manufacture, construction, design, formula, preparation, assembly, testing, service, warning, instruction, marketing, packaging or labeling of any product. "Product liability action" includes, but is not limited to, all actions based upon the following theories: strict liability in tort; negligence; breach of warranty, express or implied; breach of or failure to discharge a duty to warn or instruct, whether negligent, or innocent; misrepresentation, concealment, or nondisclosure, whether negligent, or innocent; or under any other substantive legal theory in tort or contract whatsoever;

(7) "Seller" includes a retailer, wholesaler, or distributor, and means any individual or entity engaged in the business of selling a product, whether such sale is for resale, or for use or consumption. "Seller" also includes a lessor or bailor engaged in the business of leasing or bailment of a product; and.

(8) "Unreasonably dangerous" means that a product is dangerous to an extent beyond that which would be contemplated by the ordinary consumer who purchases it, with the ordinary knowledge common to the community as to its characteristics, or that the product because of its dangerous condition would not be put on the market by a reasonably prudent manufacturer or seller, assuming that the manufacturer or seller knew of its dangerous condition.

§ 29–28–103. Limitation of actions. (a) Any action against a manufacturer or seller of a product for injury to person or property caused by its defective or unreasonably dangerous condition must be brought within the period fixed by §§ 28–3–104, 28–3–105, 28–3–202 and 47–2–725, but notwithstanding any exceptions to these provisions, it must be brought within six (6) years of the date of injury, in any event, the action must be brought within ten (10) years from the date on which the product was first purchased for use or consumption, or within one (1) year after the expiration of the anticipated life of the product, whichever is the shorter, except in the case of injury to minors whose action must be brought within a period of one (1) year after attaining the age of majority, whichever occurs sooner.

(b) The foregoing limitation of actions shall not apply to any action resulting from exposure to asbestos or to the human implantation of silicone gel breast implants.

(c)(1) Any action against a manufacturer or seller for injury to a person caused by a silicone gel breast implant must be brought within a period not to exceed twenty-five (25) years from the date such product was implanted; provided, that such action must be brought within four (4) years from the date the plaintiff knew or should have known of the injury.

(2) For purposes of this subsection only, "seller" does not include a hospital or other medical facility where the procedure took place, nor does "seller" include the physician or other medical personnel involved in the procedure.

(3) The provisions of this subsection only apply to causes of action not pending or decided on or before May 26, 1993. For the purposes of this subsection, a "pending case" is defined as a case actually filed by a silicone gel-filled breast implant recipient.

§ 29–28–104. Government standard; compliance; presumptions.
Compliance by a manufacturer or seller with any federal or state statute or administrative regulation existing at the time a product was manufactured and prescribing standards for design, inspection, testing, manufacture, labeling, warning or instructions for use of a product, shall raise a rebuttable presumption that the product is not in an unreasonably dangerous condition in regard to matters covered by these standards.

§ 29–28–105. Defective or dangerous conditions; determination.
(a) A manufacturer or seller of a product shall not be liable for any injury to a person or property caused by the product unless the product is determined to be in a defective condition or unreasonably dangerous at the time it left the control of the manufacturer or seller.

(b) In making this determination, the state of scientific and technological knowledge available to the manufacturer or seller at the time the product was placed on the market, rather than at the time of injury, is applicable. Consideration is given also to the customary designs, methods, standards and techniques of manufacturing, inspecting and testing by other manufacturers or sellers of similar products.

(c) The provisions of this section do not apply to an action based on express warranty or misrepresentation regarding the chattel.

(d) A product is not unreasonably dangerous because of a failure to adequately warn of a danger or hazard that is apparent to the ordinary user.

§ 29–28–106. Sellers. (a) No "product liability action," as defined in § 29–28–102(6), shall be commenced or maintained against any seller when the product is acquired and sold by the seller in a sealed container and/or when the product is acquired and sold by the seller under circumstances in which the seller is afforded no reasonable opportunity to inspect the product in such a manner which would or should, in the exercise of reasonable care, reveal the existence of the defective condition. The provisions of the first sentence of this subsection shall not apply to:

(1) Actions based upon a breach of warranty, express or implied, as defined by title 47, chapter 2; or

(2) Actions where the manufacturer of the product or part in question shall not be subject to service of process in the state of Tennessee and where service cannot be secured by the long-arm statutes of Tennessee; or

(3) Actions where the manufacturer has been judicially declared insolvent.

(b) No "product liability action," as defined in § 29–28–102(6), when based on the doctrine of strict liability in tort, shall be commenced or maintained against any seller of a product which is alleged to contain or possess a defective condition unreasonably dangerous to the buyer, user or consumer unless the seller is also the manufacturer of the product or the manufacturer of the part thereof claimed to be defective, or unless the manufacturer of the product or part in question shall not be subject to service of process in the state of Tennessee or service cannot be secured by the long-arm statutes of Tennessee or unless such manufacturer has been judicially declared insolvent.

§ 29–28–107. Complaint; damages. Any complaint filed in a products liability action shall state an amount of said suit sought to be recovered from any defendant.

§ 29–28–108. Alteration or improper use. If a product is not unreasonably dangerous at the time it leaves the control of the manufacturer or seller but was made unreasonably dangerous by subsequent unforeseeable alteration, change, improper maintenance or abnormal use, the manufacturer or seller is not liable.

TEXAS CIVIL PRACTICE AND REMEDIES CODE ANNOTATED

(1993, 2003, 2005)

§ 82.001. **Definitions.** In this chapter:

(1) "Claimant" means a party seeking relief, including a plaintiff, counterclaimant, or cross-claimant.

(2) "Products liability action" means any action against a manufacturer or seller for recovery of damages arising out of personal injury, death, or property damage allegedly caused by a defective product whether the action is based in strict tort liability, strict products liability, negligence, misrepresentation, breach of express or implied warranty, or any other theory or combination of theories.

(3) "Seller" means a person who is engaged in the business of distributing or otherwise placing, for any commercial purpose, in the stream of commerce for use or consumption a product or any component part thereof.

(4) "Manufacturer" means a person who is a designer, formulator, constructor, rebuilder, fabricator, producer, compounder, processor, or assembler of any product or any component part thereof and who places the product or any component part thereof in the stream of commerce.

§ 82.002. **Manufacturer's Duty to Indemnify.** (a) A manufacturer shall indemnify and hold harmless a seller against loss arising out of a products liability action, except for any loss caused by the seller's negligence, intentional misconduct, or other act or omission, such as negligently modifying or altering the product, for which the seller is independently liable.

(b) For purposes of this section, "loss" includes court costs and other reasonable expenses, reasonable attorney fees, and any reasonable damages.

(c) Damages awarded by the trier of fact shall, on final judgment, be deemed reasonable for purposes of this section.

(d) For purposes of this section, a wholesale distributor or retail seller who completely or partially assembles a product in accordance with the manufacturer's instructions shall be considered a seller.

(e) The duty to indemnify under this section:

(1) applies without regard to the manner in which the action is concluded; and

(2) is in addition to any duty to indemnify established by law, contract, or otherwise.

(f) A seller eligible for indemnification under this section shall give reasonable notice to the manufacturer of a product claimed in a petition or complaint to be defective, unless the manufacturer has been served as a party or otherwise has actual notice of the action.

(g) A seller is entitled to recover from the manufacturer court costs and other reasonable expenses, reasonable attorney fees, and any reasonable damages incurred by the seller to enforce the seller's right to indemnification under this section.

§ 82.003. Liability of nonmanufacturing sellers. (a) A seller that did not manufacture a product is not liable for harm caused to the claimant by that product unless the claimant proves:

(1) that the seller participated in the design of the product;

(2) that the seller altered or modified the product and the claimant's harm resulted from that alteration or modification;

(3) that the seller installed the product, or had the product installed, on another product and the claimant's harm resulted from the product's installation onto the assembled product;

(4) that:

(A) the seller exercised substantial control over the content of a warning or instruction that accompanied the product;

(B) the warning or instruction was inadequate; and

(C) the claimant's harm resulted from the inadequacy of the warning or instruction;

(5) that:

(A) the seller made an express factual representation about an aspect of the product;

(B) the representation was incorrect;

(C) the claimant relied on the representation in obtaining or using the product; and

(D) if the aspect of the product had been as represented, the claimant would not have been harmed by the product or would not have suffered the same degree of harm;

(6) that:

(A) the seller actually knew of a defect to the product at the time the seller supplied the product; and

(B) the claimant's harm resulted from the defect; or

(7) that the manufacturer of the product is:

(A) insolvent; or

(B) not subject to the jurisdiction of the court.

(b) This section does not apply to a manufacturer or seller whose liability in a products liability action is governed by Chapter 2301, Occupations Code. In the event of a conflict, Chapter 2301, Occupations Code, prevails over this section.

§ 82.004. Inherently Unsafe Products. (a) In a products liability action, a manufacturer or seller shall not be liable if:

(1) the product is inherently unsafe and the product is known to be unsafe by the ordinary consumer who consumes the product with the ordinary knowledge common to the community; and

(2) the product is a common consumer product intended for personal consumption, such as sugar, castor oil, alcohol, tobacco, and butter, as identified in Comment i to Section 402A of the Restatement (Second) of Torts.

(b) For purposes of this section, the term "products liability action" does not include an action based on manufacturing defect or breach of an express warranty.

§ 82.005 Design Defects. (a) In a products liability action in which a claimant alleges a design defect, the burden is on the claimant to prove by a preponderance of the evidence that:

(1) there was a safer alternative design; and

(2) the defect was a producing cause of the personal injury, property damage, or death for which the claimant seeks recovery.

(b) In this section, "safer alternative design" means a product design other than the one actually used that in reasonable probability:

(1) would have prevented or significantly reduced the risk of the claimant's personal injury, property damage, or death without substantially impairing the product's utility; and

(2) was economically and technologically feasible at the time the product left the control of the manufacturer or seller by the application of existing or reasonably achievable scientific knowledge.

(c) This section does not supersede or modify any statute, regulation, or other law of this state or of the United States that relates to liability for, or to relief in the form of, abatement of nuisance, civil penalties, cleanup costs, cost recovery, an injunction, or restitution that arises from contamination or pollution of the environment.

(d) This section does not apply to:

(1) a cause of action based on a toxic or environmental tort as defined by Sections 33.013(c)(2) and (3); or

(2) a drug or device, as those terms are defined in the federal Food, Drug, and Cosmetic Act (21 U.S.C. Section 321).

(e) This section is not declarative, by implication or otherwise, of the common law with respect to any product and shall not be construed to restrict the courts of this state in developing the common law with respect to any product which is not subject to this section.

§ 82.006. Firearms and Ammunition. (a) In a products liability action brought against a manufacturer or seller of a firearm or ammunition that alleges a design defect in the firearm or ammunition, the burden is on the claimant to prove, in addition to any other elements that the claimant must prove, that:

(1) the actual design of the firearm or ammunition was defective, causing the firearm or ammunition not to function in a manner reasonably expected by an ordinary consumer of firearms or ammunition; and

(2) the defective design was a producing cause of the personal injury, property damage, or death.

(b) The claimant may not prove the existence of the defective design by a comparison or weighing of the benefits of the firearm or ammunition against the risk of personal injury, property damage, or death posed by its potential to cause such injury, damage, or death when discharged.

§ 82.007. **Medicines.** (a) In a products liability action alleging that an injury was caused by a failure to provide adequate warnings or information with regard to a pharmaceutical product, there is a rebuttable presumption that the defendant or defendants, including a health care provider, manufacturer, distributor, and prescriber, are not liable with respect to the allegations involving failure to provide adequate warnings or information if:

(1) the warnings or information that accompanied the product in its distribution were those approved by the United States Food and Drug Administration for a product approved under the Federal Food, Drug, and Cosmetic Act (21 U.S.C. Section 301 et seq.), as amended, or Section 351, Public Health Service Act (42 U.S.C. Section 262), as amended; or

(2) the warnings provided were those stated in monographs developed by the United States Food and Drug Administration for pharmaceutical products that may be distributed without an approved new drug application.

(b) The claimant may rebut the presumption in Subsection (a) as to each defendant by establishing that:

(1) the defendant, before or after pre-market approval or licensing of the product, withheld from or misrepresented to the United States Food and Drug Administration required information that was material and relevant to the performance of the product and was causally related to the claimant's injury;

(2) the pharmaceutical product was sold or prescribed in the United States by the defendant after the effective date of an order of the United States Food and Drug Administration to remove the product from the market or to withdraw its approval of the product;

(3)(A) the defendant recommended, promoted, or advertised the pharmaceutical product for an indication not approved by the United States Food and Drug Administration;

(B) the product was used as recommended, promoted, or advertised; and

(C) the claimant's injury was causally related to the recommended, promoted, or advertised use of the product;

(4)(A) the defendant prescribed the pharmaceutical product for an indication not approved by the United States Food and Drug Administration;

(B) the product was used as prescribed; and

(C) the claimant's injury was causally related to the prescribed use of the product; or

(5) the defendant, before or after pre-market approval or licensing of the product, engaged in conduct that would constitute a violation of 18 U.S.C. Section 201 and that conduct caused the warnings or instructions approved for the product by the United States Food and Drug Administration to be inadequate.

§ 82.008. Compliance With Government Standards. (a) In a products liability action brought against a product manufacturer or seller, there is a rebuttable presumption that the product manufacturer or seller is not liable for any injury to a claimant caused by some aspect of the formulation, labeling, or design of a product if the product manufacturer or seller establishes that the product's formula, labeling, or design complied with mandatory safety standards or regulations adopted and promulgated by the federal government, or an agency of the federal government, that were applicable to the product at the time of manufacture and that governed the product risk that allegedly caused harm.

(b) The claimant may rebut the presumption in Subsection (a) by establishing that:

(1) the mandatory federal safety standards or regulations applicable to the product were inadequate to protect the public from unreasonable risks of injury or damage; or

(2) the manufacturer, before or after marketing the product, withheld or misrepresented information or material relevant to the federal government's or agency's determination of adequacy of the safety standards or regulations at issue in the action.

(c) In a products liability action brought against a product manufacturer or seller, there is a rebuttable presumption that the product manufacturer or seller is not liable for any injury to a claimant allegedly caused by some aspect of the formulation, labeling, or design of a product if the product manufacturer or seller establishes that the product was subject to pre-market licensing or approval by the federal government, or an agency of the federal government, that the manufacturer complied with all of the government's or agency's procedures and requirements with respect to pre-market licensing or approval, and that after full consideration of the product's risks and benefits the product was approved or licensed for sale by the government or agency. The claimant may rebut this presumption by establishing that:

(1) the standards or procedures used in the particular pre-market approval or licensing process were inadequate to protect the public from unreasonable risks of injury or damage; or

(2) the manufacturer, before or after pre-market approval or licensing of the product, withheld from or misrepresented to the government or agency information that was material and relevant to the performance of the product and was causally related to the claimant's injury.

(d) This section does not extend to manufacturing flaws or defects even though the product manufacturer has complied with all quality control and manufacturing practices mandated by the federal government or an agency of the federal government.

(e) This section does not extend to products covered by Section 82.007.

§ 16.012.   Products Liability. (a) In this section:

(1) "Claimant," "seller," and "manufacturer" have the meanings assigned by Section 82.001.

(2) "Products liability action" means any action against a manufacturer or seller for recovery of damages or other relief for harm allegedly caused by a defective product, whether the action is based in strict tort liability, strict products liability, negligence, misrepresentation, breach of express or implied warranty, or any other theory or combination of theories, and whether the relief sought is recovery of damages or any other legal or equitable relief, including a suit for:

(A) injury or damage to or loss of real or personal property;

(B) personal injury;

(C) wrongful death;

(D) economic loss; or

(E) declaratory, injunctive, or other equitable relief.

(b) Except as provided by Subsections (c), (d), and (d–1), a claimant must commence a products liability action against a manufacturer or seller of a product before the end of 15 years after the date of the sale of the product by the defendant.

(c) If a manufacturer or seller expressly warrants in writing that the product has a useful safe life of longer than 15 years, a claimant must commence a products liability action against that manufacturer or seller of the product before the end of the number of years warranted after the date of the sale of the product by that seller.

(d) This section does not apply to a products liability action seeking damages for personal injury or wrongful death in which the claimant alleges:

(1) the claimant was exposed to the product that is the subject of the action before the end of 15 years after the date the product was first sold;

(2) the claimant's exposure to the product caused the claimant's disease that is the basis of the action; and

(3) the symptoms of the claimant's disease did not, before the end of 15 years after the date of the first sale of the product by the defendant, manifest themselves to a degree and for a duration that would put a reasonable person on notice that the person suffered some injury.

(d–1) This section does not reduce a limitations period for a cause of action described by Subsection (d) that accrues before the end of the limitations period under this section.

(e) This section does not extend the limitations period within which a products liability action involving the product may be commenced under any other law.

(f) This section applies only to the sale and not to the lease of a product.

§ 90.001. Definitions—Asbestos and Silica-related Claims.

In this chapter:

(1) "Asbestos" means chrysotile, amosite, crocidolite, tremolite asbestos, anthophyllite asbestos, actinolite asbestos, and any of these minerals that have been chemically treated or altered.

(2) "Asbestos-related injury" means personal injury or death allegedly caused, in whole or in part, by inhalation or ingestion of asbestos.

(3) "Asbestosis" means bilateral diffuse interstitial fibrosis of the lungs caused by inhalation of asbestos fibers.

(4) "Certified B-reader" means a person who has successfully completed the x-ray interpretation course sponsored by the National Institute for Occupational Safety and Health (NIOSH) and passed the B-reader certification examination for x-ray interpretation and whose NIOSH certification is current at the time of any readings required by this chapter.

(5) "Chest x-ray" means chest films that are taken in accordance with all applicable state and federal regulatory standards and in the posterior-anterior view.

(6) "Claimant" means an exposed person and any person who is seeking recovery of damages for or arising from the injury or death of an exposed person.

(7) "Defendant" means a person against whom a claim arising from an asbestos-related injury or a silica-related injury is made.

(8) "Exposed person" means a person who is alleged to have suffered an asbestos-related injury or a silica-related injury.

(9) "FEV1" means forced expiratory volume in the first second, which is the maximal volume of air expelled in one second during performance of simple spirometric tests.

(10) "FVC" means forced vital capacity, which is the maximal volume of air expired with maximum effort from a position of full inspiration.

(11) "ILO system of classification" means the radiological rating system of the International Labor Office in "Guidelines for the Use of ILO International Classification of Radiographs of Pneumoconioses" (2000), as amended.

(12) "MDL pretrial court" means the district court to which related cases are transferred for consolidated or coordinated pretrial proceedings under Rule 13, Texas Rules of Judicial Administration.

(13) "MDL rules" means the rules adopted by the supreme court under Subchapter H, Chapter 74, Government Code.

(14) "Mesothelioma" means a rare form of cancer allegedly caused in some instances by exposure to asbestos in which the cancer invades cells in the membrane lining:

(A) the lungs and chest cavity (the pleural region);

(B) the abdominal cavity (the peritoneal region); or

(C) the heart (the pericardial region).

(15) "Nonmalignant asbestos-related injury" means an asbestos-related injury other than mesothelioma or other cancer.

(16) "Nonmalignant silica-related injury" means a silica-related injury other than cancer.

(17) "Physician board certified in internal medicine" means a physician who is certified by the American Board of Internal Medicine or the American Osteopathic Board of Internal Medicine.

(18) "Physician board certified in occupational medicine" means a physician who is certified in the subspecialty of occupational medicine by the American Board of Preventive Medicine or the American Osteopathic Board of Preventive Medicine.

(19) "Physician board certified in oncology" means a physician who is certified in the subspecialty of medical oncology by the American Board of Internal Medicine or the American Osteopathic Board of Internal Medicine.

(20) "Physician board certified in pathology" means a physician who holds primary certification in anatomic pathology or clinical pathology from the American Board of Pathology or the American Osteopathic Board of Internal Medicine and whose professional practice:

(A) is principally in the field of pathology; and

(B) involves regular evaluation of pathology materials obtained from surgical or postmortem specimens.

(21) "Physician board certified in pulmonary medicine" means a physician who is certified in the subspecialty of pulmonary medicine by the American Board of Internal Medicine or the American Osteopathic Board of Internal Medicine.

(22) "Plethysmography" means the test for determining lung volume, also known as "body plethysmography," in which the subject of the test is enclosed in a chamber that is equipped to measure pressure, flow, or volume change.

(23) "Pulmonary function testing" means spirometry, lung volume, and diffusion capacity testing performed in accordance with Section 90.002 using equipment, methods of calibration, and techniques that meet:

(A) the criteria incorporated in the American Medical Association Guides to the Evaluation of Permanent Impairment and reported in 20 C.F.R. Part 404, Subpart P, Appendix 1, Part (A), Sections 3.00(E) and (F)(2003); and

(B) the interpretative standards in the Official Statement of the American Thoracic Society entitled "Lung Function Testing: Selection of Reference Values and Interpretative Strategies," as published in 144 American Review of Respiratory Disease 1202-1218 (1991).

(24) "Report" means a report required by Section 90.003, 90.004, or 90.010(f)(1).

(25) "Respirable," with respect to silica, means particles that are less than 10 microns in diameter.

(26) "Serve" means to serve notice on a party in compliance with Rule 21a, Texas Rules of Civil Procedure.

(27) "Silica" means a respirable form of crystalline silicon dioxide, including alpha quartz, cristobalite, and tridymite.

(28) "Silica-related injury" means personal injury or death allegedly caused, in whole or in part, by inhalation of silica.

(29) "Silicosis" means interstitial fibrosis of the lungs caused by inhalation of silica, including:

(A) acute silicosis, which may occur after exposure to very high levels of silica within a period of months to five years after the initial exposure;

(B) accelerated silicosis; and

(C) chronic silicosis.

§ 90.002. Pulmonary Function Testing.

Pulmonary function testing required by this chapter must be interpreted by a physician:

(1) who is licensed in this state or another state of the United States;

(2) who is board certified in pulmonary medicine, internal medicine, or occupational medicine; and

(3) whose license and certification were not on inactive status at the time the testing was interpreted.

§ 90.003. Reports Required for Claims Involving Asbestos–Related Injury.

(a) A claimant asserting an asbestos-related injury must serve on each defendant the following information:

(1) a report by a physician who is board certified in pulmonary medicine, occupational medicine, internal medicine, oncology, or pathology and whose license and certification were not on inactive status at the time the report was made stating that:

(A) the exposed person has been diagnosed with malignant mesothelioma or other malignant asbestos-related cancer; and

(B) to a reasonable degree of medical probability, exposure to asbestos was a cause of the diagnosed mesothelioma or other cancer in the exposed person; or

(2) a report by a physician who is board certified in pulmonary medicine, internal medicine, or occupational medicine and whose license and certification were not on inactive status at the time the report was made that:

(A) verifies that the physician or a medical professional employed by and under the direct supervision and control of the physician:

(i) performed a physical examination of the exposed person, or if the exposed person is deceased, reviewed available records relating to the exposed person's medical condition;

(ii) took a detailed occupational and exposure history from the exposed person or, if the exposed person is deceased, from a person knowledgeable about the alleged exposure or exposures that form the basis of the action; and

(iii) took a detailed medical and smoking history that includes a thorough review of the exposed person's past and present medical problems and their most probable cause;

(B) sets out the details of the exposed person's occupational, exposure, medical, and smoking history and verifies that at least 10 years have elapsed between the exposed person's first exposure to asbestos and the date of diagnosis;

(C) verifies that the exposed person has:

(i) a quality 1 or 2 chest x-ray that has been read by a certified B-reader according to the ILO system of classification as showing:

(a) bilateral small irregular opacities (s, t, or u) with a profusion grading of 1/1 or higher, for an action filed on or after May 1, 2005;

(b) bilateral small irregular opacities (s, t, or u) with a profusion grading of 1/0 or higher, for an action filed before May 1, 2005; or

(c) bilateral diffuse pleural thickening graded b2 or higher including blunting of the costophrenic angle; or

(ii) pathological asbestosis graded 1(B) or higher under the criteria published in "Asbestos–Associated Diseases," 106 Archives of Pathology and Laboratory Medicine 11, Appendix 3 (October 8, 1982);

(D) verifies that the exposed person has asbestos-related pulmonary impairment as demonstrated by pulmonary function testing showing:

(i) forced vital capacity below the lower limit of normal or below 80 percent of predicted and FEV1/FVC ratio (using actual values) at or above the lower limit of normal or at or above 65 percent; or

(ii) total lung capacity, by plethysmography or timed gas dilution, below the lower limit of normal or below 80 percent of predicted;

(E) verifies that the physician has concluded that the exposed person's medical findings and impairment were not more probably the result of causes other than asbestos exposure revealed by the exposed person's occupational, exposure, medical, and smoking history; and

(F) is accompanied by copies of all ILO classifications, pulmonary function tests, including printouts of all data, flow volume loops, and other information demonstrating compliance with the equipment, quality, interpretation, and reporting standards set out in this chapter, lung volume tests, diagnostic imaging of the chest, pathology reports, or other testing reviewed by the physician in reaching the physician's conclusions.

(b) The detailed occupational and exposure history required by Subsection (a)(2)(A)(ii) must describe:

(1) the exposed person's principal employments and state whether the exposed person was exposed to airborne contaminants, including asbestos fibers and other dusts that can cause pulmonary impairment; and

(2) the nature, duration, and frequency of the exposed person's exposure to airborne contaminants, including asbestos fibers and other dusts that can cause pulmonary impairment.

(c) If a claimant's pulmonary function test results do not meet the requirements of Subsection (a)(2)(D)(i) or (ii), the claimant may serve on each defendant a report by a physician who is board certified in pulmonary medicine, internal medicine, or occupational medicine and whose license and certification were not on inactive status at the time the report was made that:

(1) verifies that the physician has a physician-patient relationship with the exposed person;

(2) verifies that the exposed person has a quality 1 or 2 chest x-ray that has been read by a certified B-reader according to the ILO system of classification as showing bilateral small irregular opacities (s, t, or u) with a profusion grading of 2/1 or higher;

(3) verifies that the exposed person has restrictive impairment from asbestosis and includes the specific pulmonary function test findings on which the physician relies to establish that the exposed person has restrictive impairment;

(4) verifies that the physician has concluded that the exposed person's medical findings and impairment were not more probably the result of causes other than asbestos exposure revealed by the exposed person's occupational, exposure, medical, and smoking history; and

(5) is accompanied by copies of all ILO classifications, pulmonary function tests, including printouts of all data, flow volume loops, and other information demonstrating compliance with the equipment, quality, interpretation, and reporting standards set out in this chapter, lung volume tests, diagnostic imaging of the chest, pathology reports, or other testing reviewed by the physician in reaching the physician's conclusions.

(d) If a claimant's radiologic findings do not meet the requirements of Subsection (a)(2)(C)(i), the claimant may serve on each defendant a report by a physician who is board certified in pulmonary medicine, internal medicine, or occupational medicine and whose license and certification were not on inactive status at the time the report was made that:

(1) verifies that the physician has a physician-patient relationship with the exposed person;

(2) verifies that the exposed person has asbestos-related pulmonary impairment as demonstrated by pulmonary function testing showing:

(A) either:

(i) forced vital capacity below the lower limit of normal or below 80 percent of predicted and total lung capacity, by plethysmography, below the lower limit of normal or below 80 percent of predicted; or

(ii) forced vital capacity below the lower limit of normal or below 80 percent of predicted and FEV1/FVC ratio (using actual values) at or above the lower limit of normal or at or above 65 percent; and

(B) diffusing capacity of carbon monoxide below the lower limit of normal or below 80 percent of predicted;

(3) verifies that the exposed person has a computed tomography scan or high-resolution computed tomography scan showing either bilateral pleural disease or bilateral parenchymal disease consistent with asbestos exposure;

(4) verifies that the physician has concluded that the exposed person's medical findings and impairment were not more probably the result of causes other than asbestos exposure as revealed by the exposed person's occupational, exposure, medical, and smoking history; and

(5) is accompanied by copies of all computed tomography scans, ILO classifications, pulmonary function tests, including printouts of all data, flow volume loops, and other information demonstrating compliance with the equipment, quality, interpretation, and reporting standards set out in this chapter, lung volume tests, diagnostic imaging of the chest, pathology reports, or other testing reviewed by the physician in reaching the physician's conclusions.

§ 90.004. Reports Required for Claims Involving Silica-related Injury.

(a) A claimant asserting a silica-related injury must serve on each defendant a report by a physician who is board certified in pulmonary medicine, internal medicine, oncology, pathology, or, with respect to a claim for silicosis, occupational medicine and whose license and certification were not on inactive status at the time the report was made that:

(1) verifies that the physician or a medical professional employed by and under the direct supervision and control of the physician:

(A) performed a physical examination of the exposed person, or if the exposed person is deceased, reviewed available records relating to the exposed person's medical condition;

(B) took a detailed occupational and exposure history from the exposed person or, if the exposed person is deceased, from a person knowledgeable about the alleged exposure or exposures that form the basis of the action; and

(C) took a detailed medical and smoking history that includes a thorough review of the exposed person's past and present medical problems and their most probable cause;

(2) sets out the details of the exposed person's occupational, exposure, medical, and smoking history;

(3) verifies that the exposed person has one or more of the following:

(A) a quality 1 or 2 chest x-ray that has been read by a certified B-reader according to the ILO system of classification as showing:

(i) bilateral predominantly nodular opacities (p, q, or r) occurring primarily in the upper lung fields, with a profusion grading of 1/1 or higher, for an action filed on or after May 1, 2005; or

(ii) bilateral predominantly nodular opacities (p, q, or r) occurring primarily in the upper lung fields, with a profusion grading of 1/0 or higher, for an action filed before May 1, 2005;

(B) pathological demonstration of classic silicotic nodules exceeding one centimeter in diameter as published in "Diseases Associated with Exposure to Silica and Nonfibrous Silicate Minerals," 112 Archives of Pathology and Laboratory Medicine 7 (July 1988);

(C) progressive massive fibrosis radiologically established by large opacities greater than one centimeter in diameter; or

(D) acute silicosis; and

(4) is accompanied by copies of all ILO classifications, pulmonary function tests, including printouts of all data, flow volume loops, and other information demonstrating compliance with the equipment, quality, interpretation, and reporting standards set out in this chapter, lung volume tests, diagnostic imaging of the chest, pathology reports, or other testing reviewed by the physician in reaching the physician's conclusions.

(b) If the claimant is asserting a claim for silicosis, the report required by Subsection (a) must also verify that:

(1) there has been a sufficient latency period for the applicable type of silicosis;

(2) the exposed person has at least Class 2 or higher impairment due to silicosis, according to the American Medical Association Guides to the Evaluation of Permanent Impairment and reported in 20 C.F.R. Part 404, Subpart P, Appendix 1, Part (A), Sections 3.00(E) and (F)(2003); and

(3) the physician has concluded that the exposed person's medical findings and impairment were not more probably the result of causes other than silica exposure revealed by the exposed person's occupational, exposure, medical, and smoking history.

(c) If the claimant is asserting a claim for silica-related lung cancer, the report required by Subsection (a) must also:

(1) include a diagnosis that the exposed person has primary lung cancer and that inhalation of silica was a substantial contributing factor to that cancer; and

(2) verify that at least 15 years have elapsed from the date of the exposed person's first exposure to silica until the date of diagnosis of the exposed person's primary lung cancer.

(d) If the claimant is asserting a claim for any disease other than silicosis and lung cancer alleged to be related to exposure to silica, the report required by Subsection (a) must also verify that the physician has diagnosed the exposed person with a disease other than silicosis or silica-related lung cancer and has concluded that the exposed person's disease is not more probably the result of causes other than silica exposure.

(e) The detailed occupational and exposure history required by Subsection (a)(1)(B) must describe:

(1) the exposed person's principal employments and state whether the exposed person was exposed to airborne contaminants, including silica and other dusts that can cause pulmonary impairment; and

(2) the nature, duration, and frequency of the exposed person's exposure to airborne contaminants, including silica and other dusts that can cause pulmonary impairment.

§ 90.005. Prohibited Basis for Diagnosis.

(a) For purposes of this chapter, a physician may not, as the basis for a diagnosis, rely on the reports or opinions of any doctor, clinic, laboratory, or testing company that performed an examination, test, or screening of the exposed person's medical condition that was conducted in violation of any law, regulation, licensing requirement, or medical code of practice of the state in which the examination, test, or screening was conducted.

(b) If a physician relies on any information in violation of Subsection (a), the physician's opinion or report does not comply with the requirements of this chapter.

§ 90.006. Serving Reports.

(a) In an action filed on or after the date this chapter becomes law, a report prescribed by Section 90.003 or 90.004 must be served on each defendant not later than the 30th day after the date that defendant answers or otherwise enters an appearance in the action.

(b) In an action pending on the date this chapter becomes law and in which the trial, or any new trial or retrial following motion, appeal, or otherwise, commences on or before the 90th day after the date this chapter becomes law, a claimant is not required to serve a report on any defendant unless a mistrial, new trial, or retrial is subsequently granted or ordered.

(c) In an action pending on the date this chapter becomes law and in which the trial, or any new trial or retrial following motion, appeal, or otherwise, commences after the 90th day after the date this chapter becomes law, a report must be served on each defendant on or before the earlier of the following dates:

(1) the 60th day before trial commences; or

(2) the 180th day after the date this chapter becomes law.

§ 90.007. Motion to Dismiss.

(a) In an action filed on or after the date this chapter becomes law, if a claimant fails to timely serve a report on a defendant, or serves on the defendant a report that does not comply with the requirements of Section 90.003 or 90.004, the defendant may file a motion to dismiss the claimant's asbestos-related claims or silica-related claims. The motion must be filed on or before the 30th day after the date the report is served on the defendant. If a claimant fails to serve a report on the defendant, the motion must be filed on or before the 30th day after the date the report was required to be served on the defendant under Section 90.006. If the basis of the motion is that the claimant has served on the defendant a report that does not comply with Section 90.003 or 90.004, the motion must include the reasons why the report does not comply with that section.

(b) A claimant may file a response to a motion to dismiss on or before the 15th day after the date the motion to dismiss is served. A report required by Section 90.003 or 90.004 may be filed, amended, or supplemented within the time required for responding to a motion to dismiss. The service of an amended or supplemental report does not require the filing of an additional motion to dismiss if the reasons stated in the original motion to dismiss are sufficient to require dismissal under this chapter.

(c) Except as provided by Section 90.010(d) or (e), if the court is of the opinion that a motion to dismiss is meritorious, the court shall, by written order, grant the motion and dismiss all of the claimant's asbestos-related claims or silica-related claims, as appropriate, against the defendant. A dismissal under this section is without prejudice to the claimant's right, if any, to assert claims for an asbestos-related injury or a silica-related injury in a subsequent action.

(d) On the filing of a motion to dismiss under this section, all further proceedings in the action are stayed until the motion is heard and determined by the court.

(e) On the motion of a party showing good cause, the court may shorten or extend the time limits provided in this section for filing or serving motions, responses, or reports.

§ 90.008. Voluntary Dismissal.

Before serving a report required by Section 90.003 or 90.004, a claimant seeking damages arising from an asbestos-related injury or silica-related injury may voluntarily dismiss the claimant's action. If a claimant files a voluntary dismissal under this section, the claimant's voluntary dismissal is without prejudice to the claimant's right to file a subsequent action seeking damages arising from an asbestos-related injury or a silica-related injury.

§ 90.009. Joinder of Claimants.

Unless all parties agree otherwise, claims relating to more than one exposed person may not be joined for a single trial.

§ 90.010. Multidistrict Litigation Proceedings.

(a) The MDL rules apply to any action pending on the date this chapter becomes law in which the claimant alleges personal injury or death from exposure to asbestos or silica unless:

(1) the action was filed before September 1, 2003, and trial has commenced or is set to commence on or before the 90th day after the date this chapter becomes law, except that the MDL rules shall apply to the action if the trial does not commence on or before the 90th day after the date this chapter becomes law;

(2) the action was filed before September 1, 2003, and the claimant serves a report that complies with Section 90.003 or 90.004 on or before the 90th day after the date this chapter becomes law; or

(3) the action was filed before September 1, 2003, and the exposed person has been diagnosed with malignant mesothelioma, other malignant asbestos-related cancer, or malignant silica-related cancer.

(b) If the claimant fails to serve a report complying with Section 90.003 or 90.004 on or before the 90th day after the date this chapter becomes law under Subsection (a)(2), the defendant may file a notice of transfer to the MDL pretrial court. If the MDL pretrial court determines that the claimant served a report that complies with Section 90.003 or 90.004 on or before the 90th day after the date this chapter becomes law, the MDL pretrial court shall remand the action to the court in which the action was filed. If the MDL pretrial court determines that the report was not served on or before the 90th day after the date this chapter becomes law or that the report served does not comply with Section 90.003 or 90.004, the MDL pretrial court shall retain jurisdiction over the action pursuant to the MDL rules.

(c) In an action transferred to an MDL pretrial court in which the exposed person is living and has been diagnosed with malignant mesothelioma, other malignant asbestos-related cancer, malignant silica-related cancer, or acute silicosis, the MDL pretrial court shall expedite the action in a manner calculated to provide the exposed person with a trial or other disposition in the shortest period that is fair to all parties and consistent with the principles of due process. The MDL pretrial court should, as far as reasonably possible, ensure that such action is brought to trial or final disposition within six months from the date the action is transferred to the MDL pretrial court, provided that all discovery and case management requirements of the MDL pretrial court have been satisfied.

(d) In an action pending on the date this chapter becomes law that is transferred to or pending in an MDL pretrial court and in which the claimant does not serve a report that complies with Section 90.003 or 90.004, the MDL pretrial court shall not dismiss the action pursuant to this chapter but shall retain jurisdiction over the action under the MDL rules. The MDL pretrial court shall not remand such action for trial unless:

(1) the claimant serves a report complying with Section 90.003 or 90.004; or

(2)(A) the claimant does not serve a report that complies with Section 90.003 or 90.004;

(B) the claimant serves a report complying with Subsection (f)(1); and

(C) the court, on motion and hearing, makes the findings required by Subsection (f)(2).

(e) In an action filed on or after the date this chapter becomes law that is transferred to an MDL pretrial court and in which the claimant does not serve on a defendant a report that complies with Section 90.003 or 90.004, the MDL pretrial court shall, on motion by a defendant, dismiss the action under Section 90.007 unless:

(1) the claimant serves a report that complies with Subsection (f)(1); and

(2) the court, on motion and hearing, makes the findings required by Subsection (f)(2).

(f) In an action in which the claimant seeks remand for trial under Subsection (d)(2) or denial of a motion to dismiss under Subsection (e):

(1) the claimant shall serve on each defendant a report that:

(A) complies with the requirements of Sections 90.003(a)(2)(A), (B), (E), and (F) and 90.003(b) or Sections 90.004(a)(1), (2), and (4) and 90.004(e); and

(B) verifies that:

(i) the physician making the report has a physician-patient relationship with the exposed person;

(ii) pulmonary function testing has been performed on the exposed person and the physician making the report has interpreted the pulmonary function testing;

(iii) the physician making the report has concluded, to a reasonable degree of medical probability, that the exposed person has radiographic, pathologic, or computed tomography evidence establishing bilateral pleural disease or bilateral parenchymal disease caused by exposure to asbestos or silica; and

(iv) the physician has concluded that the exposed person has asbestos-related or silica-related physical impairment comparable to the impairment the exposed person would have had if the exposed person met the criteria set forth in Section 90.003 or 90.004; and

(2) the MDL pretrial court shall determine whether:

(A) the report and medical opinions offered by the claimant are reliable and credible;

(B) due to unique or extraordinary physical or medical characteristics of the exposed person, the medical criteria set forth in Sections 90.003 and 90.004 do not adequately assess the exposed person's physical impairment caused by exposure to asbestos or silica; and

(C) the claimant has produced sufficient credible evidence for a finder of fact to reasonably find that the exposed person is physically impaired as the result of exposure to asbestos or silica to a degree comparable to the impairment the exposed person would have had if the exposed person met the criteria set forth in Section 90.003 or 90.004.

(g) A court's determination under Subsection (f) shall be made after conducting an evidentiary hearing at which the claimant and any defendant to the action may offer supporting or controverting evidence. The parties shall be permitted a reasonable opportunity to conduct discovery before the evidentiary hearing.

(h) The court shall state its findings under Subsection (f)(2) in writing and shall address in its findings:

(1) the unique or extraordinary physical or medical characteristics of the exposed person that justify the application of this section; and

(2) the reasons the criteria set forth in Sections 90.003 and 90.004 do not adequately assess the exposed person's physical impairment caused by exposure to asbestos or silica.

(i) Any findings made by a court under Subsection (f) are not admissible for any purpose at a trial on the merits.

(j) Subsections (d)(2) and (e)–(i) apply only in exceptional and limited circumstances in which the exposed person does not satisfy the medical criteria of Section 90.003 or 90.004 but can demonstrate meaningful asbestos-related or silica-related physical impairment that satisfies the requirements of Subsection (f). Subsections (d)(2) and (e)–(i) have limited application and shall not be used to negate the requirements of this chapter.

(k) On or before September 1, 2010, each MDL pretrial court having jurisdiction over cases to which this chapter applies shall deliver a report to the governor, lieutenant governor, and the speaker of the house of representatives stating:

(1) the number of cases on the court's multidistrict litigation docket as of August 1, 2010;

(2) the number of cases on the court's multidistrict litigation docket as of August 1, 2010, that do not meet the criteria of Section 90.003 or 90.004, to the extent known;

(3) the court's evaluation of the effectiveness of the medical criteria established by Sections 90.003 and 90.004;

(4) the court's recommendation, if any, as to how medical criteria should be applied to the cases on the court's multidistrict litigation docket as of August 1, 2010; and

(5) any other information regarding the administration of cases in the MDL pretrial courts that the court deems appropriate.

§ 90.011. Bankruptcy.

Nothing in this chapter is intended to affect the rights of any party in a bankruptcy proceeding or affect the ability of any person to satisfy the claim criteria for compensable claims or demands under a trust established pursuant to a plan of reorganization under Chapter 11 of the United States Bankruptcy Code (11 U.S.C. Section 1101 et seq.).

§ 90.012. Supreme Court Rulemaking.

The supreme court may promulgate amendments to the Texas Rules of Civil Procedure regarding the joinder of claimants in asbestos-related actions or silica-related actions if the rules are consistent with Section 90.009.

UTAH CODE ANNOTATED

(1989, 2000)

§ 78–15–1. Short title of act. This act shall be known and may be cited as the "Utah Product Liability Act."

§ 78–15–3. Statute of limitations. A civil action under this chapter shall be brought within two years from the time the individual who would be the claimant in such action discovered, or in the exercise of due diligence should have discovered, both the harm and its cause.

§ 78–15–4. Prayer for damages. No dollar amount shall be specified in the prayer of a complaint filed in a product liability action against a product manufacturer, wholesaler or retailer. The complaint shall merely pray for such damages as are reasonable in the premises.

§ 78–15–5. Alteration or modification of product after sale as substantial contributing cause—Manufacturer or seller not liable. For purposes of Section 78–27–38, fault shall include an alteration or modification of the product, which occurred subsequent to the sale by the manufacturer or seller to the initial user or consumer, and which changed the purpose, use, function, design, or intended use or manner of use of the product from that for which the product was originally designed, tested, or intended.

§ 78–15–6. Defect or defective condition making product unreasonably dangerous—Rebuttable presumption. In any action for damages for personal injury, death, or property damage allegedly caused by a defect in a product:

(1) No product shall be considered to have a defect or to be in a defective condition, unless at the time the product was sold by the manufacturer or other initial seller, there was a defect or defective condition in the product which made the product unreasonably dangerous to the user or consumer.

(2) As used in this act, "unreasonably dangerous" means that the product was dangerous to an extent beyond which would be contemplated by the ordinary and prudent buyer, consumer or user of that product in that community considering the product's characteristics, propensities, risks, dangers and uses together with any actual knowledge, training, or experience possessed by that particular buyer, user or consumer.

(3) There is a rebuttable presumption that a product is free from any defect or defective condition where the alleged defect in the plans or designs for the product or the methods and techniques of manufacturing, inspecting and testing the product were in conformity with government standards established for that industry which were in existence at the time the plans or designs for the product or the methods and techniques of manufacturing, inspecting and testing the product were adopted.

§ 78–15–7. Indemnification provisions void and unenforceable.

Any clause in a sales contract or collateral document that requires a purchaser or end user of a product to indemnify, hold harmless, or defend a manufacturer of a product shall be contrary to public policy and is void and unenforceable if a defect in the design or manufacturing of the product causes an injury or death.

WASHINGTON REVISED CODE ANNOTATED

(1981–91, 2004)

§ 7.72.010. **Definitions.** For the purposes of this chapter, unless the context clearly indicates to the contrary:

(1) Product seller. "Product seller" means any person or entity that is engaged in the business of selling products, whether the sale is for resale, or for use or consumption. The term includes a manufacturer, wholesaler, distributor, or retailer of the relevant product. The term also includes a party who is in the business of leasing or bailing such products. The term "product seller" does not include:

(a) A seller of real property, unless that person is engaged in the mass production and sale of standardized dwellings or is otherwise a product seller;

(b) A provider of professional services who utilizes or sells products within the legally authorized scope of the professional practice of the provider;

(c) A commercial seller of used products who resells a product after use by a consumer or other product user: Provided, That when it is resold, the used product is in essentially the same condition as when it was acquired for resale;

(d) A finance lessor who is not otherwise a product seller. A "finance lessor" is one who acts in a financial capacity, who is not a manufacturer, wholesaler, distributor, or retailer, and who leases a product without having a reasonable opportunity to inspect and discover defects in the product, under a lease arrangement in which the selection, possession, maintenance, and operation of the product are controlled by a person other than the lessor; and

(e) A licensed pharmacist who dispenses a prescription product in the form manufactured by a commercial manufacturer pursuant to a prescription issued by a licensed prescribing practitioner if the claim against the pharmacist is based upon strict liability in tort or the implied warranty provisions under the uniform commercial code, Title 62A RCW, and if the pharmacist complies with recordkeeping requirements pursuant to chapters 18.64, 69.41, and 69.50 RCW, and related administrative rules as provided in RCW 7.72.040. Nothing in this subsection (1)(e) affects a pharmacist's liability under RCW 7.72.040(1).

(2) Manufacturer. "Manufacturer" includes a product seller who designs, produces, makes, fabricates, constructs, or remanufactures the relevant product or component part of a product before its sale to a user or consumer. The term also includes a product seller or entity not otherwise a manufacturer that holds itself out as a manufacturer.

A product seller acting primarily as a wholesaler, distributor, or retailer of a product may be a "manufacturer" but only to the extent that it designs, produces, makes, fabricates, constructs, or remanufactures the product for its sale. A product seller who performs minor assembly of a product in accordance with the instructions of the manufacturer shall not be deemed a manufacturer. A product seller that did not participate in the design of a product and that constructed the product in accordance with the design specifications of the claimant or another product seller shall not be deemed a manufacturer for the purposes of RCW 7.72.030(1)(a).

(3) Product. "Product" means any object possessing intrinsic value, capable of delivery either as an assembled whole or as a component part or parts, and produced for introduction into trade or commerce. Human tissue and organs, including human blood and its components, are excluded from this term.

The "relevant product" under this chapter is that product or its component part or parts, which gave rise to the product liability claim.

(4) Product liability claim. "Product liability claim" includes any claim or action brought for harm caused by the manufacture, production, making, construction, fabrication, design, formula, preparation, assembly, installation, testing, warnings, instructions, marketing, packaging, storage or labeling of the relevant product. It includes, but is not limited to, any claim or action previously based on: Strict liability in tort; negligence; breach of express or implied warranty; breach of, or failure to, discharge a duty to warn or instruct, whether negligent or innocent; misrepresentation, concealment, or nondisclosure, whether negligent or innocent; or other claim or action previously based on any other substantive legal theory except fraud, intentionally caused harm or a claim or action under the consumer protection act, chapter 19.86 RCW.

(5) Claimant. "Claimant" means a person or entity asserting a product liability claim, including a wrongful death action, and, if the claim is asserted through or on behalf of an estate, the term includes claimant's decedent. "Claimant" includes any person or entity that suffers harm. A claim may be asserted under this chapter even though the claimant did not buy the product from, or enter into any contractual relationship with, the product seller.

(6) Harm. "Harm" includes any damages recognized by the courts of this state: Provided, That the term "harm" does not include direct or consequential economic loss under Title 62A RCW [Uniform Commercial Code].

§ 7.72.020. Scope. (1) The previous existing applicable law of this state on product liability is modified only to the extent set forth in this chapter.

(2) Nothing in [this] chapter shall prevent the recovery of direct or consequential economic loss under Title 62A RCW [Uniform Commercial Code].

§ 7.72.030. Liability of manufacturers. (1) A product manufacturer is subject to liability to a claimant if the claimant's harm was proximately caused by the negligence of the manufacturer in that the product was not reasonably safe as designed or not reasonably safe because adequate warnings or instructions were not provided.

(a) A product is not reasonably safe as designed, if, at the time of manufacture, the likelihood that the product would cause the claimant's harm or similar harms, and the seriousness of those harms, outweighed the burden on the manufacturer to design a product that would have prevented those harms and the adverse effect that an alternative design that was practical and feasible would have on the usefulness of the product: Provided, That a firearm or ammunition shall not be deemed defective in design on the basis that the benefits of the product do not outweigh the risk of injury posed by its potential to cause serious injury, damage, or death when discharged.

(b) A product that is not reasonably safe because adequate warnings or instructions were not provided with the product, if, at the time of manufacture, the likelihood that the product would cause the claimant's harm or similar harms, and the seriousness of those harms, rendered the warnings or instructions of the manufacturer inadequate and the manufacturer could have provided the warnings or instructions which the claimant alleges would have been adequate.

(c) A product is not reasonably safe because adequate warnings or instructions were not provided after the product was manufactured where a manufacturer learned or where a reasonably prudent manufacturer should have learned about a danger connected with the product after it was manufactured. In such a case, the manufacturer is under a duty to act with regard to issuing warnings or instructions concerning the danger in the manner that a reasonably prudent manufacturer would act in the same or similar circumstances. This duty is satisfied if the manufacturer exercises reasonable care to inform product users.

(2) A product manufacturer is subject to strict liability to a claimant if the claimant's harm was proximately caused by the fact that the product was not reasonably safe in construction or not reasonably safe because it did not conform to the manufacturer's express warranty or to the implied warranties under Title 62A RCW [Uniform Commercial Code].

(a) A product is not reasonably safe in construction if, when the product left the control of the manufacturer, the product deviated in some material way from the design specifications or performance standards of the manufacturer, or deviated in some material way from otherwise identical units of the same product line.

(b) A product does not conform to the express warranty of the manufacturer if it is made part of the basis of the bargain and relates to a material fact or facts concerning the product and the express warranty proved to be untrue.

(c) Whether or not a product conforms to an implied warranty created under Title 62A RCW [Uniform Commercial Code] shall be determined under that title.

(3) In determining whether a product was not reasonably safe under this section, the trier of fact shall consider whether the product was unsafe to an extent beyond that which would be contemplated by the ordinary consumer.

§ **7.72.040. Liability of product sellers other than manufacturers.** (1) Except as provided in subsection (2) of this section, a product seller other than a manufacturer is liable to the claimant only if the claimant's harm was proximately caused by:

(a) The negligence of such product seller; or

(b) Breach of an express warranty made by such product seller; or

(c) The intentional misrepresentation of facts about the product by such product seller or the intentional concealment of information about the product by such product seller.

(2) A product seller, other than a manufacturer, shall have the liability of a manufacturer to the claimant if:

(a) No solvent manufacturer who would be liable to the claimant is subject to service of process under the laws of the claimant's domicile or the state of Washington; or

(b) The court determines that it is highly probable that the claimant would be unable to enforce a judgment against any manufacturer; or

(c) The product seller is a controlled subsidiary of a manufacturer, or the manufacturer is a controlled subsidiary of the product seller; or

(d) The product seller provided the plans or specifications for the manufacture or preparation of the product and such plans or specifications were a proximate cause of the defect in the product; or

(e) The product was marketed under a trade name or brand name of the product seller.

(3) Subsection (2) of this section does not apply to a pharmacist who dispenses a prescription product in the form manufactured by a commercial manufacturer pursuant to a prescription issued by a licensed practitioner if the pharmacist complies with recordkeeping requirements pursuant to chapters 18.64, 69.41, and 69.50 RCW, and related administrative rules.

§ **7.72.050. Relevance of industry custom, technological feasibility, and nongovernmental, legislative or administrative regulatory standards.** (1) Evidence of custom in the product seller's industry, technological feasibility or that the product was or was not, in compliance with nongovernmental standards or with legislative regulatory standards or administrative regulatory standards, whether relating to design, construction or performance of the product or to warnings or instructions as to its use may be considered by the trier of fact.

(2) When the injury-causing aspect of the product was, at the time of manufacture, in compliance with a specific mandatory government contract specification relating to design or warnings, this compliance shall be an absolute defense. When the injury-causing aspect of the product was not, at the time of manufacture, in compliance with a specific mandatory government specification relating to design or warnings, the product shall be deemed not reasonably safe under RCW 7.72.030(1).

§ 7.72.060. Length of time product sellers are subject to liability. (1) *Useful safe life.* (a) Except as provided in subsection (1)(b) hereof, a product seller shall not be subject to liability to a claimant for harm under this chapter if the product seller proves by a preponderance of the evidence that the harm was caused after the product's "useful safe life" had expired.

"Useful safe life" begins at the time of delivery of the product and extends for the time during which the product would normally be likely to perform or be stored in a safe manner. For the purposes of this chapter, "time of delivery" means the time of delivery of a product to its first purchaser or lessee who was not engaged in the business of either selling such products or using them as component parts of another product to be sold. In the case of a product which has been remanufactured by a manufacturer, "time of delivery" means the time of delivery of the remanufactured product to its first purchaser or lessee who was not engaged in the business of either selling such products or using them as component parts of another product to be sold.

(b) A product seller may be subject to liability for harm caused by a product used beyond its useful safe life, if:

(i) The product seller has warranted that the product may be utilized safely for such longer period; or

(ii) The product seller intentionally misrepresents facts about its product, or intentionally conceals information about it, and that conduct was a proximate cause of the claimant's harm; or

(iii) The harm was caused by exposure to a defective product, which exposure first occurred within the useful safe life of the product, even though the harm did not manifest itself until after the useful safe life had expired.

(2) *Presumption regarding useful safe life.* If the harm was caused more than twelve years after the time of delivery, a presumption arises that the harm was caused after the useful safe life had expired. This presumption may only be rebutted by a preponderance of the evidence.

(3) *Statute of limitation.* Subject to the applicable provisions of chapter 4.16 RCW pertaining to the tolling and extension of any statute of limitation, no claim under this chapter may be brought more than three years

from the time the claimant discovered or in the exercise of due diligence should have discovered the harm and its cause.

§ **7.72.070. Food and beverage consumption.** (1) Any manufacturer, packer, distributor, carrier, holder, marketer, or seller of a food or nonalcoholic beverage intended for human consumption, or an association of one or more such entities, shall not be subject to civil liability in an action brought by a private party based on an individual's purchase or consumption of food or nonalcoholic beverages in cases where liability is premised upon the individual's weight gain, obesity, or a health condition associated with the individual's weight gain or obesity and resulting from the individual's long-term purchase or consumption of a food or nonalcoholic beverage.

(2) For the purposes of this section, the term "long-term consumption" means the cumulative effect of the consumption of food or nonalcoholic beverages, and not the effect of a single instance of consumption.

CONSUMER PRODUCT SAFETY ACT*

Selected Sections

* 15 U.S.C.A. § 2051–82; Act of October 27, 1972, Pub.L. 92–573, 86 Stat. 1207–33; as amended by Consumer Product Safety Improvement Act of 1990, Pub.L. 101–608, 104 Stat. 3110; Consumer Product Safety Amendments of 1981, Pub.L. 97–35, 95 Stat. 724, Emergency Interim Consumer Product Safety Standard Act of 1978, Pub.L. 95–319, 92 Stat. 386, and Consumer Product Safety Commission Improvements Act of 1976, Pub.L. 94–284, 90 Stat. 503.

311

---

§ 2051. Congressional findings and declaration of purpose

(a) The Congress finds that—

(1) an unacceptable number of consumer products which present unreasonable risks of injury are distributed in commerce;

(2) complexities of consumer products and the diverse nature and abilities of consumers using them frequently result in an inability of users to anticipate risks and to safeguard themselves adequately;

(3) the public should be protected against unreasonable risks of injury associated with consumer products;

(4) control by State and local governments of unreasonable risks of injury associated with consumer products is inadequate and may be burdensome to manufacturers;

(5) existing Federal authority to protect consumers from exposure to consumer products presenting unreasonable risks of injury is inadequate; and

(6) regulation of consumer products the distribution or use of which affects interstate or foreign commerce is necessary to carry out this chapter.

(b) The purposes of this chapter are—

(1) to protect the public against unreasonable risks of injury associated with consumer products;

(2) to assist consumers in evaluating the comparative safety of consumer products;

(3) to develop uniform safety standards for consumer products and to minimize conflicting State and local regulations; and

(4) to promote research and investigation into the causes and prevention of product-related deaths, illnesses, and injuries.

Pub.L. 92–573, § 2, Oct. 27, 1972, 86 Stat. 1207.

§ 2052. Definitions

(a) For purposes of this chapter:

(1) The term "consumer product" means any article, or component part thereof, produced or distributed (i) for sale to a consumer for use in or around a permanent or temporary household or residence, a school, in recreation, or otherwise, or (ii) for the personal use, consumption or enjoyment of a consumer in or around a permanent or temporary household or residence, a school, in recreation, or otherwise; but such term does not include—

(A) any article which is not customarily produced or distributed for sale to, or use or consumption by, or enjoyment of, a consumer,

(B) tobacco and tobacco products,

(C) motor vehicles or motor vehicle equipment (as defined by sections 102(3) and (4) of the National Traffic and Motor Vehicle Safety Act of 1966),

(D) pesticides (as defined by the Federal Insecticide, Fungicide, and Rodenticide Act),

(E) any article which, if sold by the manufacturer, producer, or importer, would be subject to the tax imposed by section 4181 of the Internal Revenue Code of 1954 (determined without regard to any exemptions from such tax provided by section 4182 or 4221, or any other provision of such Code), or any component of any such article,

(F) aircraft, aircraft engines, propellers, or appliances (as defined in section 101 of the Federal Aviation Act of 1958),

(G) boats which could be subjected to safety regulation under the Federal Boat Safety Act of 1971; vessels, and appurtenances to vessels (other than such boats), which could be subjected to safety regulation under title 52 of the Revised Statutes or other marine safety statutes administered by the department in which the Coast Guard is operating; and equipment (including associated equipment, as defined in section 3(8) of the Federal Boat Safety Act of 1971) to the extent that a risk of injury associated with the use of such equipment on boats or vessels could be eliminated or reduced by actions taken under any statute referred to in this subparagraph,

(H) drugs, devices, or cosmetics (as such terms are defined in sections 201(g), (h), and (i) of the Federal Food, Drug, and Cosmetic Act), or

(I) food. The term "food", as used in this subparagraph means all "food", as defined in section 201(f) of the Federal Food, Drug, and Cosmetic Act, including poultry and poultry products (as defined in sections 4(e) and (f) of the Poultry Products Inspection Act), meat, meat food products (as defined in section 1(j) of the Federal Meat Inspection Act), and eggs and egg products (as defined in section 4 of the Egg Products Inspection Act).

Such term includes any mechanical device which carries or conveys passengers along, around, or over a fixed or restricted route or course or within a defined area for the purpose of giving its passengers amusement, which is customarily controlled or directed by an individual who is employed for that purpose and who is not a consumer with respect to such device, and which is not permanently fixed to a site. Such term does not include such a device which is permanently fixed to a site. Except for the regulation under this chapter or the Federal Hazardous Substances Act of fireworks devices or any substance intended for use as a component of any such device, the Commission shall have no authority under the functions transferred pursuant to section 2079 of this title to regulate any product or article described in subparagraph (E) of this paragraph or described, without regard to quantity, in section 845(a)(5) of Title 18. See sections 2079(d) and 2080 of this title, for other limitations on Commission's authority to regulate certain consumer products.

(2) The term "consumer product safety rule" means a consumer products safety standard described in section 2056(a) of this title, or a rule under this chapter declaring a consumer product a banned hazardous product.

(3) The term "risk of injury" means a risk of death, personal injury, or serious or frequent illness.

(4) The term "manufacturer" means any person who manufactures or imports a consumer product.

(5) The term "distributor" means a person to whom a consumer product is delivered or sold for purposes of distribution in commerce, except that such term does not include a manufacturer or retailer of such product.

(6) The term "retailer" means a person to whom a consumer product is delivered or sold for purposes of sale or distribution by such person to a consumer.

(7)(A) The term "private labeler" means an owner of a brand or trademark on the label of a consumer product which bears a private label.

(B) A consumer product bears a private label if (i) the product (or its container) is labeled with the brand or trademark of a person other than a manufacturer of the product, (ii) the person with whose brand or trademark the product (or container) is labeled has authorized or caused the product to be so labeled, and (iii) the brand or trademark of a manufacturer of such product does not appear on such label.

(8) The term "manufactured" means to manufacture, produce, or assemble.

(9) The term "Commission" means the Consumer Product Safety Commission, established by section 2053 of this title.

(10) The term "State" means a State, the District of Columbia, the Commonwealth of Puerto Rico, the Virgin Islands, Guam, Wake Island, Midway Island, Kingman Reef, Johnston Island, the Canal Zone, American Samoa, or the Trust Territory of the Pacific Islands.

(11) The terms "to distribute in commerce" and "distribution in commerce" mean to sell in commerce, to introduce or deliver for introduction into commerce, or to hold for sale or distribution after introduction into commerce.

(12) The term "commerce" means trade, traffic, commerce, or transportation—

    (A) between a place in a State and any place outside thereof, or

    (B) which affects trade, traffic, commerce, or transportation described in subparagraph (A).

(13) The terms "import" and "importation" include reimporting a consumer product manufactured or processed, in whole or in part, in the United States.

(14) The term "United States", when used in the geographic sense, means all of the States (as defined in paragraph (10)).

(b) A common carrier, contract carrier, or freight forwarder shall not, for purposes of this chapter, be deemed to be a manufacturer, distributor, or retailer of a consumer product solely by reason of receiving or transporting a consumer product in the ordinary course of its business as such a carrier or forwarder.

As amended Pub.L. 94–284, § 3(b), (d), May 11, 1976, 90 Stat. 503; Pub.L. 97–35, Title XII, § 1213, Aug. 13, 1981, 95 Stat. 724.

§ 2053.   Consumer Product Safety Commission

(a) Establishment; Chairman

(a) An independent regulatory commission is hereby established, to be known as the Consumer Product Safety Commission, consisting of five

Commissioners who shall be appointed by the President, by and with the advice and consent of the Senate. In making such appointments, the President shall consider individuals who, by reason of their background and expertise in areas related to consumer products and protection of the public from risks to safety, are qualified to serve as members of the Commission. The Chairman shall be appointed by the President, by and with the advice and consent of the Senate, from among the members of the Commission. An individual may be appointed as a member of the Commission and as Chairman at the same time. Any member of the Commission may be removed by the President for neglect of duty or malfeasance in office but for no other cause.

(b) Term; vacancies

(b)(1) Except as provided in paragraph (2), (A) the Commissioners first appointed under this section shall be appointed for terms ending three, four, five, six, and seven years, respectively, after October 27, 1972, the term of each to be designated by the President at the time of nomination; and (B) each of their successors shall be appointed for a term of seven years from the date of the expiration of the term for which his predecessor was appointed.

(2) Any Commissioner appointed to fill a vacancy occurring prior to the expiration of the term for which his predecessor was appointed shall be appointed only for the remainder of such term. A Commissioner may continue to serve after the expiration of his term until his successor has taken office, except that he may not so continue to serve more than one year after the date on which his term would otherwise expire under this subsection.

(c) Restrictions on Commissioners' outside activities

(c) Not more than three of the Commissioners shall be affiliated with the same political party. No individual (1) in the employ of, or holding any official relation to, any person engaged in selling or manufacturing consumer products, or (2) owning stock or bonds of substantial value in a person so engaged, or (3) who is in any other manner pecuniarily interested in such a person, or in a substantial supplier of such a person, shall hold the office of Commissioner. A Commissioner may not engage in any other business, vocation, or employment.

(d) Quorum; seal; Vice Chairman

(d) No vacancy in the Commission shall impair the right of the remaining Commissioners to exercise all the powers of the Commission, but three members of the Commission shall constitute a quorum for the transaction of business, except that if there are only three members serving on the Commission because of vacancies in the Commission, two members of the Commission shall constitute a quorum for the transaction of business, and if there are only two members serving on the Commission because of vacancies in the Commission, two members shall constitute a quorum for the six month period beginning on the date of the vacancy which caused the number on the Commission to decline to two. The Commission shall have an official seal of which judicial notice shall be taken. The Commission shall annually elect a Vice Chairman to act in the absence or disability of the Chairman or in case of a vacancy in the office of the Chairman.

(e) Offices

(e) The Commission shall maintain a principal office and such field offices as it deems necessary and may meet and exercise any of its powers at any other place.

(f) Functions of Chairman

(f)(1) The Chairman of the Commission shall be the principal executive officer of the Commission, and he shall exercise all of the executive and administrative functions of the Commission, including functions of the Commission with respect to (A) the appointment and supervision of personnel employed under the Commission (other than personnel employed regularly and full time in the immediate offices of commissioners other than the Chairman), (B) the distribution of business among personnel appointed and supervised by the Chairman and among administrative units of the Commission, and (C) the use and expenditure of funds.

(2) In carrying out any of his functions under the provisions of this subsection the Chairman shall be governed by general policies of the Commission and by such regulatory decisions, findings, and determinations as the Commission may by law be authorized to make.

(3) Requests or estimates for regular, supplemental, or deficiency appropriations on behalf of the Commission may not be submitted by the Chairman without the prior approval of the Commission.

(g) Executive Director; officers and employees

(g)(1)(A) The Chairman, subject to the approval of the Commission, shall appoint as officers of the Commission an Executive Director, a General Counsel, an Associate Executive Director for Engineering Sciences, an Associate Executive Director for Epidemiology, an Associate Director for Compliance and Administrative Litigation, an Associate Executive Director for Health Sciences, an Associate Executive Director for Economic Analysis, an Associate Executive Director for Administration, an Associate Executive Director for Field Operations, a Director for Office of Program, Management and Budget, and a Director for Office of Information and Public

Affairs. Any other individual appointed to a position designated as an Associate Executive Director shall be appointed by the Chairman subject to the removal of the Commission. The Chairman may only appoint an attorney to the position of Associate Executive Director of Compliance and Administrative Litigation except the position of Acting Associate Executive Director of Compliance and Administrative Litigation.

(B)(i) No individual may be appointed to such a position on an acting basis for a period longer than 90 days unless such appointment is approved by the Commission.

(ii) The Chairman, with the approval of the Commission, may remove any individual serving in a position appointed under subparagraph (A).

(C) Subparagraph (A) shall not be construed to prohibit appropriate reorganizations or changes in classifications.

(2) The Chairman, subject to subsection (f)(2), of this section, may employ such other officers and employees (including attorneys) as are necessary in the execution of the Commission's functions. No regular officer or employee of the Commission who was at any time during the 12 months preceding the termination of his employment with the Commission compensated at a rate in excess of the annual rate of basic pay in effect for grade GS-14 of the General Schedule, shall accept employment or compensation from any manufacturer subject to this chapter, for a period of 12 months after terminating employment with the Commission.

(3) In addition to the number of positions authorized by section 5108(a) of Title 5, the Chairman, subject to the approval of the Commission, and subject to the standards and procedures prescribed by chapter 51 of Title 5, may place a total of twelve positions in grades GS-16, GS-17, and GS-18.

(4) The appointment of any officer (other than a Commissioner) or employee of the Commission shall not be subject, directly or indirectly, to review or approval by any officer or entity within the Executive Office of the President.

(h) Civil action against the United States

(h) Subsections (a) and (h) of section 2680 of Title 28 do not prohibit the bringing of a civil action on a claim against the United States which—

(1) is based upon—

(A) misrepresentation or deceit on the part of the Commission or any employee thereof, or

(B) any exercise or performance, or failure to exercise or perform, a discretionary function on the part of the Commission or any employee thereof, which exercise, performance, or failure was grossly negligent; and

(2) is not made with respect to any agency action (as defined in section 551(13) of Title 5).

In the case of a civil action on a claim based upon the exercise or performance of, or failure to exercise or perform, a discretionary function, no judgment may be entered against the United States unless the court in which such action was brought determines (based upon consideration of all the relevant circumstances, including the statutory responsibility of the Commission and the public interest in encouraging rather than inhibiting the exercise of discretion) that such exercise, performance, or failure to exercise or perform was unreasonable.

(i) Agenda; establishment and comments

At least 30 days before the beginning of each fiscal year, the Commission shall establish an agenda for Commission action under the Acts under its jurisdiction and, to the extent feasible, shall establish priorities for such actions. Before establishing such agenda and priorities, the Commission shall conduct a public hearing on the agenda and priorities and shall provide reasonable opportunity for the submission of comments.

As amended Pub.L. 94–284, §§ 4, 5(a), May 11, 1976, 90 Stat. 504; Pub.L. 95–631, § 2, Nov. 10, 1978, 92 Stat. 3742; Pub.L. 96–373, Oct. 3, 1980, 94 Stat. 1366; Pub.L. 101–608, Title I §§ 102–104, 105(a), Nov. 16, 1990, 104 Stat. 3110, 3111.

§ 2054. Product safety information and research

(a) Injury Information Clearinghouse; duties

(a) The Commission shall—

(1) maintain an Injury Information Clearinghouse to collect, investigate, analyze, and disseminate injury data, and information, relating to the causes and prevention of death, injury, and illness associated with consumer products;

(2) conduct such continuing studies and investigations of deaths, injuries, diseases, other health impairments, and economic losses resulting from accidents involving consumer products as it deems necessary;

(3) following publication of an advance notice of proposed rulemaking or a notice of proposed rulemaking for a product safety rule under any rulemaking authority administered by the Commission, assist public and private organizations or groups of manufacturers, administratively and technically, in the development of safety standards addressing the risk of injury identified in such notice; and

(4) to the extent practicable and appropriate (taking into account the resources and priorities of the Commission), assist public and

private organizations or groups of manufacturers, administratively and technically, in the development of product safety standards and test methods.

(b) Research, investigation and testing of consumer products

(b) The Commission may—

(1) conduct research, studies, and investigations on the safety of consumer products and on improving the safety of such products;

(2) test consumer products and develop product safety test methods and testing devices; and

(3) offer training in product safety investigation and test methods.

(c) Grants and contracts for conduct of functions

(c) In carrying out its functions under this section, the Commission may make grants or enter into contracts for the conduct of such functions with any person (including a governmental entity).

(d) Availability to public of information

(d) Whenever the Federal contribution for any information, research, or development activity authorized by this chapter is more than minimal, the Commission shall include in any contract, grant, or other arrangement for such activity, provisions effective to insure that the rights to all information, uses, processes, patents, and other developments resulting from that activity will be made available to the public without charge on a nonexclusive basis. Nothing in this subsection shall be construed to deprive any person of any right which he may have had, prior to entering into any arrangement referred to in this subsection, to any patent, patent application, or invention.

As amended Pub.L. 97–35, Title XII, § 1209(a), (b), Aug. 13, 1981, 95 Stat. 720.

§ 2055.   Public disclosure of information

(a) Disclosure requirements for manufacturers or private labelers; procedures applicable

(a)(1) Nothing contained in this Act shall be construed to require the release of any information described by subsection (b) of section 552 of Title 5 or which is otherwise protected by law from disclosure to the public.

(2) All information reported to or otherwise obtained by the Commission or its representative under this Act which information contains or relates to a trade secret or other matter referred to in section 1905 of Title 18 or subject to section 552(b)(4) of Title 5 shall be considered confidential and shall not be disclosed.

(3) The Commission shall, prior to the disclosure of any information which will permit the public to ascertain readily the identity of a manufacturer or private labeler of a consumer product, offer such manufacturer or private labeler an opportunity to mark such information as confidential and therefore barred from disclosure under paragraph (2).

(4) All information that a manufacturer or private labeler has marked to be confidential and barred from disclosure under paragraph (2), either at the time of submission or pursuant to paragraph (3), shall not be disclosed, except in accordance with the procedures established in paragraphs (5) and (6).

(5) If the Commission determines that a document marked as confidential by a manufacturer or private labeler to be barred from disclosure under paragraph (2) may be disclosed because it is not confidential information as provided in paragraph (2), the Commission shall notify such person in writing that the Commission intends to disclose such document at a date not less than 10 days after the date of receipt of notification.

(6) Any person receiving such notification may, if he believes such disclosure is barred by paragraph (2), before the date set for release of the document, bring an action in the district court of the United States in the district in which the complainant resides, or has his principal place of business, or in which the documents are located, or in the United States District Court for the District of Columbia to restrain disclosure of the document. Any person receiving such notification may file with the appropriate district court or court of appeals of the United States, as appropriate, an application for a stay of disclosure. The documents shall not be disclosed until the court has ruled on the application for a stay.

(7) Nothing in this Act shall authorize the withholding of information by the Commission or any officer or employee under its control from the duly authorized committees or subcommittees of the Congress, and the provisions of paragraphs (2) through (6) shall not apply to such disclosures, except that the Commission shall immediately notify the manufacturer or private labeler of any such request for information designated as confidential by the manufacturer or private labeler.

(8) The provisions of paragraphs (2) through (6) shall not prohibit the disclosure of information to other officers or employees, or other representatives of the Commission (including contractors) concerned with carrying out this chapter or when relevant to any administrative proceeding under this chapter or in judicial proceedings to which the Commission is a party. Any disclosure of relevant information—

(A) in Commission administrative proceedings or in judicial proceedings to which the Commission is a party, or

(B) to representatives of the Commission (including contractors),

shall be governed by the rules of the Commission (including in camera review rules for confidential material) for such proceedings or for disclosures to such representatives or by court rules or orders, except that the rules of the Commission shall not be amended in a manner inconsistent with the purposes of this section.

(b) Additional disclosure requirements for manufacturers or private labelers; procedures applicable

(b)(1) Except as provided by paragraph (4) of this subsection, not less than 30 days prior to its public disclosure of any information obtained under this Act, or to be disclosed to the public in connection therewith (unless the Commission finds that the public health and safety requires a lesser period of notice and publishes such a finding in the Federal Register), the Commission shall, to the extent practicable, notify and provide a summary of the information to, each manufacturer or private labeler of any consumer product to which such information pertains, if the manner in which such consumer product is to be designated or described in such information will permit the public to ascertain readily the identity of such manufacturer or private labeler, and shall provide such manufacturer or private labeler with a reasonable opportunity to submit comments to the Commission in regard to such information. The Commission shall take reasonable steps to assure, prior to its public disclosure thereof, that information from which the identity of such manufacturer or private labeler may be readily ascertained is accurate, and that such disclosure is fair in the circumstances and reasonably related to effectuating the purposes of this Act. In disclosing any information under this subsection, the Commission may, and upon the request of the manufacturer or private labeler shall, include with the disclosure any comments or other information or a summary thereof submitted by such manufacturer or private labeler to the extent permitted by and subject to the requirements of this section.

(2) If the Commission determines that a document claimed to be inaccurate by a manufacturer or private labeler under paragraph (1) should be disclosed because the Commission believes it has complied with paragraph (1), the Commission shall notify the manufacturer or private labeler that the Commission intends to disclose such document at a date not less than 10 days after the date of the receipt of notification. The Commission may provide a lesser period of notice of intent to disclose if the Commission finds that the public health and safety requires a lesser period of notice and publishes such finding in the Federal Register.

(3) Prior to the date set for release of the document, the manufacturer or private labeler receiving the notice described in paragraph (2) may bring an action in the district court of the United States in the district in which the complainant resides, or has his principal place of business, or in which the documents are located or in the United States District Court for the District of Columbia to enjoin disclosure of the document. The district

court may enjoin such disclosure if the Commission has failed to take the reasonable steps prescribed in paragraph (1).

(4) Paragraphs (1) through (3) of this subsection shall not apply to the public disclosure of (A) information about any consumer product with respect to which product the Commission has filed an action under section 2061 of this title (relating to imminently hazardous products), or which the Commission has reasonable cause to believe is in violation of section 2068 of this title (relating to prohibited acts); or (B) information in the course of or concerning a rulemaking proceeding (which shall commence upon the publication of an advance notice of proposed rulemaking or a notice of proposed rulemaking), an adjudicatory proceeding (which shall commence upon the issuance of a complaint) or other administrative or judicial proceeding under this Act.

(5) In addition to the requirements of paragraph (1), the Commission shall not disclose to the public information submitted pursuant to section 2064(b) of this title respecting a consumer product unless—

(A) the Commission has issued a complaint under section 2064(c) or (d) of this title alleging that such product presents a substantial product hazard;

(B) in lieu of proceeding against such product under section 2064(c) or (d) of this title, the Commission has accepted in writing a remedial settlement agreement dealing with such product; or

(C) the person who submitted the information under section 2064(b) of this title agrees to its public disclosure.

The provisions of this paragraph shall not apply to the public disclosure of information with respect to a consumer product which is the subject of an action brought under section 2061 of this title, or which the Commission has reasonable cause to believe is in violation of section 2068(a) of this title, or information in the course of or concerning a judicial proceeding.

(6) Where the Commission initiates the public disclosure of information that reflects on the safety of a consumer product or class of consumer products, whether or not such information would enable the public to ascertain readily the identity of a manufacturer or private labeler, the Commission shall establish procedures designed to ensure that such information is accurate and not misleading.

(7) If the Commission finds that, in the administration of this Act, it has made public disclosure of inaccurate or misleading information which reflects adversely upon the safety of any consumer product or class of consumer products, or the practices of any manufacturer, private labeler, distributor, or retailer of consumer products, it shall, in a manner equivalent to that in which such disclosure was made, take reasonable steps to publish a retraction of such inaccurate or misleading information.

(8) If, after the commencement of a rulemaking or the initiation of an adjudicatory proceeding, the Commission decides to terminate the proceed-

ing before taking final action, the Commission shall, in a manner equivalent to that in which such commencement or initiation was publicized, take reasonable steps to make known the decision to terminate.

(c) Communications with manufacturers

(c) The Commission shall communicate to each manufacturer of a consumer product, insofar as may be practicable, information as to any significant risk of injury associated with such product.

(d) Definition; coverage

(d)(1) For purposes of this section, the term "Act" means the Consumer Product Safety Act, the Flammable Fabrics Act, the Poison Prevention Packaging Act, and the Federal Hazardous Substances Act.

(2) The provisions of this section shall apply whenever information is to be disclosed by the Commission, any member of the Commission, or any employee, agent, or representative of the Commission in an official capacity. Commission shall include in any contract, grant, or other arrangement for such activity, provisions effective to insure that the rights to all information, uses, processes, patents, and other developments resulting from that activity will be made available to the public without charge on a nonexclusive basis. Nothing in this subsection shall be construed to deprive any person of any right which he may have had, prior to entering into any arrangement referred to in this subsection, to any patent, patent application, or invention.

(e) Disclosure of information

(e)(1) Notwithstanding the provisions of section 552 of Title 5, subsection (a)(7) of this section, or of any other law, except as provided in paragraphs (2), (3), and (4), no member of the Commission, no officer or employee of the Commission, and no officer or employee of the Department of Justice may—

    (A) publicly disclose information furnished under subsection (c)(1) or (c)(2)(A) of section 2084 of this title;

    (B) use such information for any purpose other than to carry out the Commission's responsibilities; or

    (C) permit anyone (other than the members, officers and employees of the Commission or officers or employees of the Department of Justice who require such information for an action filed on behalf of the Commission) to examine such information.

(2) Any report furnished under subsection (c)(1) or (c)(2)(A) of section 2084 of this title shall be immune from legal process and shall not be subject to subpoena or other discovery in any civil action in a State or

Federal court or in any administrative proceeding, except in an action against such manufacturer under section 2069, 2070 or 2071 of this title for failure to furnish information required by section 2084 of this title.

(3) The Commission may, upon written request, furnish to any manufacturer or to the authorized agent of such manufacturer authenticated copies of reports furnished by or on behalf of such manufacturer in accordance with section 2084 of this title, upon payment of the actual or estimated cost of searching the records and furnishing the copies.

(4) Upon written request of the Chairman or Ranking Minority Member of the Committee on Commerce, Science and Transportation of the Senate or the Committee on Energy and Commerce of the House of Representatives or any subcommittee of such committee, the Commission shall provide to the Chairman or Ranking Minority Member any information furnished to the Commission under section 2084 of this title for purposes that are related to the jurisdiction of such committee or subcommittee.

(5) Any officer or employee of the Commission or other officer or employee of the Federal Government who receives information provided under section 2084 of this title, who willfully violates the requirements of this subsection shall be subject to dismissal or other appropriate disciplinary action consistent with procedures and requirements established by the Office of Personnel Management.

As amended Pub.L. 97–35, Title XII, § 1204(a), (b), Aug. 13, 1981, 95 Stat. 713, Pub.L. 97–414, § 9(j)(1), Jan. 4, 1983, 96 Stat. 2064; Pub.L. 101–608, Title I, § 106, 112(c), Nov. 16, 1990, 104 Stat. 3111, 3116.

§ 2056. Consumer product safety standards

(a) Types of requirements

(a) The Commission may promulgate consumer product safety standards in accordance with the provisions of section 2058 of this title. A consumer product safety standard shall consist of one or more of any of the following types of requirements:

(1) Requirements expressed in terms of performance requirements.

(2) Requirements that a consumer product be marked with or accompanied by clear and adequate warnings or instructions, or requirements respecting the form of warnings or instructions.

Any requirement of such a standard shall be reasonably necessary to prevent or reduce an unreasonable risk of injury associated with such product.

(b) Reliance of Commission upon voluntary standards

(b)(1) The Commission shall rely upon voluntary consumer product safety standards rather than promulgate a consumer product safety standard prescribing requirements described in subsection (a) of this section whenever compliance with such voluntary standards would eliminate or adequately reduce the risk of injury addressed and it is likely that there will be substantial compliance with such voluntary standards.

(2) The Commission shall devise procedures to monitor compliance with any voluntary standards—

> (A) upon which the Commission has relied under paragraph (1);

> (B) which were developed with the participation of the Commission; or

> (C) whose development the Commission has monitored.

(c) Contribution of Commission to development cost

(c) If any person participates with the Commission in the development of a consumer product safety standard, the Commission may agree to contribute to the person's cost with respect to such participation, in any case in which the Commission determines that such contribution is likely to result in a more satisfactory standard than would be developed without such contribution, and that the person is financially responsible. Regulations of the Commission shall set forth the items of cost in which it may participate, and shall exclude any contribution to the acquisition of land or buildings. Payments under agreements entered into under this subsection may be made without regard to section 3324(a) and (b) of Title 31.

As amended Pub.L. 94–284, §§ 6–8(a), May 11, 1976, 90 Stat. 505, 506; Pub.L. 95–631, §§ 3, 4(a)–(c), 5, Nov. 10, 1978, 92 Stat. 3742–3744; Pub.L. 97–35, Title XII, § 1202, Aug. 13, 1981, 95 Stat. 703, 97–258, § 4(b), Sept. 13, 1982, 96 Stat. 1067; Pub.L. 101–608, Title I, § 107(a), Nov. 16, 1990, 104 Stat. 3111.

§ 2057.   Banned hazardous products

Whenever the Commission finds that—

> (1) a consumer product is being, or will be, distributed in commerce and such consumer product presents an unreasonable risk of injury; and

> (2) no feasible consumer product safety standard under this chapter would adequately protect the public from the unreasonable risk of injury associated with such product,

the Commission may, in accordance with section 2058 of this title, promulgate a rule declaring such product a banned hazardous product.

As amended Pub.L. 97–35, Title XII, § 1203(c), Aug. 13, 1981, 95 Stat. 713.

§ 2058. Procedure for consumer product safety rules

(a) Commencement of proceeding; publication of prescribed notice of proposed rulemaking; transmittal of notice

(a) A proceeding for the development of a consumer product safety rule shall be commenced by the publication in the Federal Register of an advance notice of proposed rulemaking which shall—

(1) identify the product and the nature of the risk of injury associated with the product;

(2) include a summary of each of the regulatory alternatives under consideration by the Commission (including voluntary consumer product safety standards);

(3) include information with respect to any existing standard known to the Commission which may be relevant to the proceedings, together with a summary of the reasons why the Commission believes preliminarily that such standard does not eliminate or adequately reduce the risk of injury identified in paragraph (1);

(4) invite interested persons to submit to the Commission, within such period as the Commission shall specify in the notice (which period shall not be less than 30 days or more than 60 days after the date of publication of the notice), comments with respect to the risk of injury identified by the Commission, the regulatory alternatives being considered, and other possible alternatives for addressing the risk;

(5) invite any person (other than the Commission) to submit to the Commission, within such period as the Commission shall specify in the notice (which period shall not be less than 30 days after the date of publication of the notice), an existing standard or a portion of a standard as a proposed consumer product safety standard; and

(6) invite any person (other than the Commission) to submit to the Commission, within such period as the Commission shall specify in the notice (which period shall not be less than 30 days after the date of publication of the notice), a statement of intention to modify or develop a voluntary consumer product safety standard to address the risk of injury identified in paragraph (1) together with a description of a plan to modify or develop the standard.

The Commission shall transmit such notice within 10 calendar days to the Committee on Commerce, Science, and Transportation of the Senate and the Committee on Energy and Commerce of the House of Representatives.

(b) Voluntary standard; publication as proposed rule; notice of reliance of Commission on standard

(b)(1) If the Commission determines that any standard submitted to it in response to an invitation in a notice published under subsection (a)(5) of this section if promulgated (in whole, in part, or in combination with any other standard submitted to the Commission or any part of such a standard) as a consumer product safety standard, would eliminate or adequately reduce the risk of injury identified in the notice under subsection (a)(1), of this section, the Commission may publish such standard, in whole, in part, or in such combination and with nonmaterial modifications, as a proposed consumer product safety rule.

(2) If the Commission determines that—

(A) compliance with any standard submitted to it in response to an invitation in a notice published under subsection (a)(6) of this section is likely to result in the elimination or adequate reduction of the risk of injury identified in the notice, and

(B) it is likely that there will be substantial compliance with such standard,

the Commission shall terminate any proceeding to promulgate a consumer product safety rule respecting such risk of injury and shall publish in the Federal Register a notice which includes the determination of the Commission and which notifies the public that the Commission will rely on the voluntary standard to eliminate or reduce the risk of injury, except that the Commission shall terminate any such proceeding and rely on a voluntary standard only if such voluntary standard is in existence. For purposes of this section, a voluntary standard shall be considered to be in existence when it is finally approved by the organization or other person which developed such standard, irrespective of the effective date of the standard. Before relying on any voluntary consumer product safety standard, the Commission shall afford interested persons (including manufacturers, consumers and consumer organizations) a reasonable opportunity to submit written comments regarding such standard. The Commission shall consider such comments in making any determination regarding reliance on the involved voluntary standard under this subsection.

(c) Publication of proposed rule; preliminary regulatory analysis; contents; transmittal of notice

(c) No consumer product safety rule may be proposed by the Commission unless, not less than 60 days after publication of the notice required in subsection (a) of this section, the Commission publishes in the Federal Register the text of the proposed rule, including any alternatives, which the Commission proposes to promulgate, together with a preliminary regulatory analysis containing—

(1) a preliminary description of the potential benefits and potential costs of the proposed rule, including any benefits or costs that

cannot be quantified in monetary terms, and an identification of those likely to receive the benefits and bear the costs;

(2) a discussion of the reasons any standard or portion of a standard submitted to the Commission under subsection (a)(5) of this section was not published by the Commission as the proposed rule or part of the proposed rule;

(3) a discussion of the reasons for the Commission's preliminary determination that efforts proposed under subsection (a)(6) of this section and assisted by the Commission as required by section 2054(a)(3) of this title would not, within a reasonable period of time, be likely to result in the development of a voluntary consumer product safety standard that would eliminate or adequately reduce the risk of injury addressed by the proposed rule; and

(4) a description of any reasonable alternatives to the proposed rule, together with a summary description of their potential costs and benefits, and a brief explanation of why such alternatives should not be published as a proposed rule.

The Commission shall transmit such notice within 10 calendar days to the Committee on Commerce, Science, and Transportation of the Senate and the Committee on Energy and Commerce of the House of Representatives. Any proposed consumer product safety rule shall be issued within twelve months after the date of publication of an advance notice of proposed rulemaking under subsection (a) of this section relating to the product involved, unless the Commission determines that such proposed rule is not in the public interest. The Commission may extend the twelve-month period for good cause. If the Commission extends such period, it shall immediately transmit notice of such an extension to the Committee on Commerce, Science, and Transportation of the Senate and the Committee on Energy and Commerce of the House of Representatives. Such notice shall include an explanation for the reasons for such extension, together with an estimate of the date by which the Commission anticipates such rulemaking will be completed. The Commission shall publish notice of such an extension and the information submitted to the Congress in the Federal Register.

(d) Promulgation of rule; time

(d)(1) Within 60 days after the publication under subsection (c) of this section of a proposed consumer product safety rule respecting a risk of injury associated with a consumer product, the Commission shall—

(A) promulgate a consumer product safety rule respecting the risk of injury associated with such product, if it makes the findings required under subsection (f) of this section, or

(B) withdraw the applicable notice of proposed rulemaking if it determines that such rule is not (i) reasonably necessary to eliminate or reduce an unreasonable risk of injury associated with the product, or (ii) in the public interest;

except that the Commission may extend such 60–day period for good cause shown (if it publishes its reasons therefor in the Federal Register).

(2) Consumer product safety rules shall be promulgated in accordance with section 553 of Title 5 except that the Commission shall give interested persons an opportunity for the oral presentation of data, views, or arguments, in addition to an opportunity to make written submissions. A transcript shall be kept of any oral presentation.

(e) Expression of risk of injury; consideration of available product data; needs of elderly and handicapped

(e) A consumer product safety rule shall express in the rule itself the risk of injury which the standard is designed to eliminate or reduce. In promulgating such a rule the Commission shall consider relevant available product data including the results of research, development, testing, and investigation activities conducted generally and pursuant to this chapter. In the promulgation of such a rule the Commission shall also consider and take into account the special needs of elderly and handicapped persons to determine the extent to which such persons may be adversely affected by such rule.

(f) Findings; final regulatory analysis; judicial review of rule

(f)(1) Prior to promulgating a consumer product safety rule, the Commission shall consider, and shall make appropriate findings for inclusion in such rule with respect to—

(A) the degree and nature of the risk of injury the rule is designed to eliminate or reduce;

(B) the approximate number of consumer products, or types or classes thereof, subject to such rule;

(C) the need of the public for the consumer products subject to such rule, and the probable effect of such rule upon the utility, cost, or availability of such products to meet such need; and

(D) any means of achieving the objective of the order while minimizing adverse effects on competition or disruption or dislocation of manufacturing and other commercial practices consistent with the public health and safety.

(2) The Commission shall not promulgate a consumer product safety rule unless it has prepared, on the basis of the findings of the Commission under paragraph (1) and on other information before the Commission, a final regulatory analysis of the rule containing the following information:

(A) A description of the potential benefits and potential costs of the rule, including costs and benefits that cannot be quantified in monetary terms, and the identification of those likely to receive the benefits and bear the costs.

(B) A description of any alternatives to the final rule which were considered by the Commission, together with a summary description of their potential benefits and costs and a brief explanation of the reasons why these alternatives were not chosen.

(C) A summary of any significant issues raised by the comments submitted during the public comment period in response to the preliminary regulatory analysis, and a summary of the assessment by the Commission of such issues.

The Commission shall publish its final regulatory analysis with the rule.

(3) The Commission shall not promulgate a consumer product safety rule unless it finds (and includes such finding in the rule)—

(A) that the rule (including its effective date) is reasonably necessary to eliminate or reduce an unreasonable risk of injury associated with such product;

(B) that the promulgation of the rule is in the public interest;

(C) in the case of a rule declaring the product a banned hazardous product, that no feasible consumer product safety standard under this chapter would adequately protect the public from the unreasonable risk of injury associated with such product;

(D) in the case of a rule which relates to a risk of injury with respect to which persons who would be subject to such rule have adopted and implemented a voluntary consumer product safety standard, that—

(i) compliance with such voluntary consumer product safety standard is not likely to result in the elimination or adequate reduction of such risk of injury; or

(ii) it is unlikely that there will be substantial compliance with such voluntary consumer product safety standard;

(E) that the benefits expected from the rule bear a reasonable relationship to its costs; and

(F) that the rule imposes the least burdensome requirement which prevents or adequately reduces the risk of injury for which the rule is being promulgated.

(4)(A) Any preliminary or final regulatory analysis prepared under subsection (c) or (f)(2) of this section shall not be subject to independent judicial review, except that when an action for judicial review of a rule is instituted, the contents of any such regulatory analysis shall constitute part of the whole rulemaking record of agency action in connection with such review.

(B) The provisions of subparagraph (A) shall not be construed to alter the substantive or procedural standards otherwise applicable to judicial review of any action by the Commission.

(g) Effective date of rule or standard; stockpiling of product

(g)(1) Each consumer product safety rule shall specify the date such rule is to take effect not exceeding 180 days from the date promulgated, unless the Commission finds, for good cause shown, that a later effective date is in the public interest and publishes its reasons for such finding. The effective date of a consumer product safety standard under this chapter shall be set at a date at least 30 days after the date of promulgation unless the Commission for good cause shown determines that an earlier effective date is in the public interest. In no case may the effective date be set at a date which is earlier than the date of promulgation. A consumer product safety standard shall be applicable only to consumer products manufactured after the effective date.

(2) The Commission may by rule prohibit a manufacturer of a consumer product from stockpiling any product to which a consumer product safety rule applies, so as to prevent such manufacturer from circumventing the purpose of such consumer product safety rule. For purposes of this paragraph, the term "stockpiling" means manufacturing or importing a product between the date of promulgation of such consumer product safety rule and its effective date at a rate which is significantly greater (as determined under the rule under this paragraph) than the rate at which such product was produced or imported during a base period (prescribed in the rule under this paragraph) ending before the date of promulgation of the consumer product safety rule.

(h) Amendment or revocation of rule

(h) The Commission may by rule amend or revoke any consumer product safety rule. Such amendment or revocation shall specify the date on which it is to take effect which shall not exceed 180 days from the date the amendment or revocation is published unless the Commission finds for good cause shown that a later effective date is in the public interest and publishes its reasons for such finding. Where an amendment involves a material change in a consumer product safety rule, sections 2056 and 2057 of this title, and subsections (a) through (g) of this section shall apply. In order to revoke a consumer product safety rule, the Commission shall publish a proposal to revoke such rule in the Federal Register, and allow oral and written presentations in accordance with subsection (d)(2) of this section. It may revoke such rule only if it determines that the rule is not reasonably necessary to eliminate or reduce an unreasonable risk of injury associated with the product. Section 2060 of this title shall apply to any amendment of a consumer product safety rule which involves a material change and to any revocation of a consumer product safety rule, in the same manner and to the same extent as such section applies to the Commission's action in promulgating such a rule.

(i) Petition to initiate rulemaking

(i) The Commission shall grant, in whole or in part, or deny any petition under section 553(e) of Title 5, requesting the Commission to initiate a rulemaking, within a reasonable time after the date on which such petition is field. The Commission shall state the reasons for granting or denying such petition. The Commission may not deny any such petition on the basis of a voluntary standard unless the voluntary standard is in existence at the time of the denial of the petition, the Commission has determined that the voluntary standard is likely to result in the elimination or adequate reduction of the risk of injury identified with the petition, and it is likely that there will be substantial compliance with the standard.

As amended Pub.L. 94–284, § 9, May 11, 1976, 90 Stat. 506; Pub.L. 95–631, § 4(d), Nov. 10, 1978, 92 Stat. 3744; Pub.L. 97–35, Title XII, § 1203(a), Aug. 13, 1981, 95 Stat. 704; Pub.L. 101–608, Title I, § 108(a), 109, 110(a), Nov. 16, 1990, 104 Stat. 3112, 3113.

§ 2060. Judicial review of consumer product safety rules

(a) Petition by persons adversely affected, consumers, or consumer organizations

(a) Not later than 60 days after a consumer product safety rule is promulgated by the Commission, any person adversely affected by such rule, or any consumer or consumer organization, may file a petition with the United States court of appeals for the District of Columbia or for the circuit in which such person, consumer, or organization resides or has his principal place of business for judicial review of such rule. Copies of the petition shall be forthwith transmitted by the clerk of the court to the Commission or other officer designated by it for that purpose and to the Attorney General. The record of the proceedings on which the Commission based its rule shall be filed in the court as provided for in section 2112 of Title 28. For purposes of this section, the term "record" means such consumer product safety rule; any notice or proposal published pursuant to section 2056, 2057, or 2058 of this title; the transcript required by section 2058(d)(2) of this title of any oral presentation; any written submission of interested parties; and any other information which the Commission considers relevant to such rule.

(b) Additional data, views, or arguments

(b) If the petitioner applies to the court for leave to adduce additional data, views, or arguments and shows to the satisfaction of the court that such additional data, views, or arguments are material and that there were reasonable grounds for the petitioner's failure to adduce such data, views, or arguments in the proceeding before the Commission, the court may order the Commission to provide additional opportunity for the oral presentation of data, views, or arguments and for written submissions. The Commission may modify its findings, or make new findings by reason of the additional data, views, or arguments so taken and shall file such modified or new findings, and its recommendation, if any, for the modification or setting aside of its original rule, with the return of such additional data, views, or arguments.

(c) Jurisdiction; costs and attorneys' fees; substantial evidence to support administrative findings

(c) Upon the filing of the petition under subsection (a) of this section the court shall have jurisdiction to review the consumer product safety rule in accordance with chapter 7 of Title 5, and to grant appropriate relief, including interim relief, as provided in such chapter. A court may in the interest of justice include in such relief an award of the costs of suit, including reasonable attorneys' fees (determined in accordance with subsection (f) of this section) and reasonable expert witnesses' fees. Attorneys' fees may be awarded against the United States (or any agency or official of the United States) without regard to section 2412 of Title 28 or any other provision of law. The consumer product safety rule shall not be affirmed unless the Commission's findings under sections 2058(f)(1) and 2058(f)(3) of this title are supported by substantial evidence on the record taken as a whole.

(d) Supreme Court review

(d) The judgment of the court affirming or setting aside, in whole or in part, any consumer product safety rule shall be final, subject to review by the Supreme Court of the United States upon certiorari or certification, as provided in section 1254 of Title 28.

(e) Availability of other remedies

(e) The remedies provided for in this section shall be in addition to and not in lieu of any other remedies provided by law.

(f) Computation of reasonable fee for attorney

(f) For purposes of this section and sections 2072(a) and 2073 of this title, a reasonable attorney's fee is a fee (1) which is based upon (A) the actual time expended by an attorney in providing advice and other legal services in connection with representing a person in an action brought under this section, and (B) such reasonable expenses as may be incurred by the attorney in the provision of such services, and (2) which is computed at the rate prevailing for the provision of similar services with respect to actions brought in the court which is awarding such fee.

As amended Pub.L. 94–284, §§ 10(b), 11(a), May 11, 1976, 90 Stat. 507; Pub.L. 97–35, Title XII, § 1211(h)(1)–(3)(A), Aug. 13, 1981, 95 Stat. 723; Pub.L. 97–414, § 9(j)(2), Jan. 4, 1983, 96 Stat. 2064.

§ 2061. Imminent hazards

(a) Filing of action

(a) The Commission may file in a United States district court an action (1) against an imminently hazardous consumer product for seizure of such product under subsection (b)(2) of this section, or (2) against any person who is a manufacturer, distributor, or retailer of such product, or (3) against both. Such an action may be filed notwithstanding the existence of a consumer product safety rule applicable to such product, or the pendency of any administrative or judicial proceedings under any other provision of this chapter. As used in this section, and hereinafter in this chapter, the term "imminently hazardous consumer product" means a consumer product which presents imminent and unreasonable risk of death, serious illness, or severe personal injury.

(b) Relief; product condemnation and seizure

(b)(1) The district court in which such action is filed shall have jurisdiction to declare such product an imminently hazardous consumer product, and (in the case of an action under subsection (a)(2) of this section) to grant (as ancillary to such declaration or in lieu thereof) such temporary or permanent relief as may be necessary to protect the public from such risk. Such relief may include a mandatory order requiring the notification of such risk to purchasers of such product known to the defendant, public notice, the recall, the repair or the replacement of, or refund for, such product.

(2) In the case of an action under subsection (a)(1) of this section, the consumer product may be proceeded against by process of libel for the seizure and condemnation of such product in any United States district court within the jurisdiction of which such consumer product is found. Proceedings and cases instituted under the authority of the preceding sentence shall conform as nearly as possible to proceedings in rem in admiralty.

(c) Consumer product safety rule

(c) Where appropriate, concurrently with the filing of such action or as soon thereafter as may be practicable, the Commission shall initiate a proceeding to promulgate a consumer product safety rule applicable to the consumer product with respect to which such action is filed.

(d) Jurisdiction and venue; process; subpoena

(d)(1) An action under subsection (a)(2) of this section may be brought in the United States district court for the District of Columbia or in any judicial district in which any of the defendants is found, is an inhabitant or transacts business; and process in such an action may be served on a defendant in any other district in which such defendant resides or may be found. Subpenas requiring attendance of witnesses in such an action may run into any other district. In determining the judicial district in which an action may be brought under this section in instances in which such action may be brought in more than one judicial district, the Commission shall take into account the convenience of the parties.

(2) Whenever proceedings under this section involving substantially similar consumer products are pending in courts in two or more judicial districts, they shall be consolidated for trial by order of any such court upon application reasonably made by any party in interest, upon notice to all other parties in interest.

(e) Employment of attorneys by Commission

(e) Notwithstanding any other provision of law, in any action under this section, the Commission may direct attorneys employed by it to appear and represent it.

(g)* Consideration of cost of compliance

(g) Nothing in this section shall be construed to require the Commission, in determining whether to bring an action against a consumer product or a person under this section, to prepare a comparison of the costs that would be incurred in complying with the relief that may be ordered in such action with the benefits to the public from such relief. [Note: this subsection was added at the end, notwithstanding the fact that no subsection (f) has been enacted.]

As amended Pub.L. 97–35, Title XII, § 1205(a)(2), Aug. 13, 1981, 95 Stat. 716; Pub.L. 101–608, Title I, § 111(a)(1), Nov. 16, 1990, 104 Stat. 3114.

§ 2063. Product certification and labeling

(a)(1) Every manufacturer of a product which is subject to a consumer product safety standard under this chapter and which is distributed in commerce (and the private labeler of such product if it bears a private label) shall issue a certificate which shall certify that such product conforms to all applicable consumer product safety standards, and shall specify any standard which is applicable. Such certificate shall accompany the product or shall otherwise be furnished to any distributor or retailer to

---

* So in original. Probably should be "(f)".

whom the product is delivered. Any certificate under this subsection shall be based on a test of each product or upon a reasonable testing program; shall state the name of the manufacturer or private labeler issuing the certificate; and shall include the date and place of manufacture.

(2) In the case of a consumer product for which there is more than one manufacturer or more than one private labeler, the Commission may by rule designate one or more of such manufacturers or one or more of such private labelers (as the case may be) as the persons who shall issue the certificate required by paragraph (1) of this subsection, and may exempt all other manufacturers of such product or all other private labelers of the product (as the case may be) from the requirement under paragraph (1) to issue a certificate with respect to such product.

(b) The Commission may by rule prescribe reasonable testing programs for consumer products which are subject to consumer product safety standards under this chapter and for which a certificate is required under subsection (a) of this section. Any test or testing program on the basis of which a certificate is issued under subsection (a) of this section may, at the option of the person required to certify the product, be conducted by an independent third party qualified to perform such tests or testing programs.

(c) The Commission may by rule require the use and prescribe the form and content of labels which contain the following information (or that portion of it specified in the rule)—

(1) The date and place of manufacture of any consumer product.

(2) A suitable identification of the manufacturer of the consumer product, unless the product bears a private label in which case it shall identify the private labeler and shall also contain a code mark which will permit the seller of such product to identify the manufacturer thereof to the purchaser upon his request.

(3) In the case of a consumer product subject to a consumer product safety rule, a certification that the product meets all applicable consumer product safety standards and a specification of the standards which are applicable.

Such labels, where practicable, may be required by the Commission to be permanently marked on or affixed to any such consumer product. The Commission may, in appropriate cases, permit information required under paragraphs (1) and (2) of this subsection to be coded.

Pub.L. 92–573, § 14, Oct. 27, 1972, 86 Stat. 1220.

§ 2064.   Substantial product hazards

(a) Definition

(a) For purposes of this section, the term "substantial product hazard" means—

(1) a failure to comply with an applicable consumer product safety rule which creates a substantial risk of injury to the public, or

(2) a product defect which (because of the pattern of defect, the number of defective products distributed in commerce, the severity of the risk, or otherwise) creates a substantial risk of injury to the public.

(b) Noncompliance with applicable consumer product safety rules; product defects; notice to Commission by manufacturer, distributor, or retailer

Every manufacturer of a consumer product distributed in commerce, and every distributor and retailer of such product, who obtains information which reasonably supports the conclusion that such product—

(1) fails to comply with an applicable consumer product safety rule or with a voluntary consumer product safety standard upon which the Commission has relied under section 2058 of this title;

(2) contains a defect which could create a substantial product hazard described in subsection (a)(2) of this section; or

(3) creates an unreasonable risk of serious injury or death, shall immediately inform the Commission of such failure to comply, of such defect, or of such risk, unless such manufacturer, distributor, or retailer has actual knowledge that the Commission has been adequately informed of such defect, failure to comply, or such risk.

(c) Public notice of defect or failure to comply; mail notice

(c) If the Commission determines (after affording interested persons, including consumers and consumer organizations, an opportunity for a hearing in accordance with subsection (f) of this section) that a product distributed in commerce presents a substantial product hazard and that notification is required in order to adequately protect the public from such substantial product hazard, the Commission may order the manufacturer or any distributor or retailer of the product to take any one or more of the following actions:

(1) To give public notice of the defect or failure to comply.

(2) To mail notice to each person who is a manufacturer, distributor, or retailer of such product.

(3) To mail notice to every person to whom the person required to give notice knows such product was delivered or sold.

Any such order shall specify the form and content of any notice required to be given under such order.

(d) Repair; replacement; refunds; action plan

(d) If the Commission determines (after affording interested parties, including consumers and consumer organizations, an opportunity for a hearing in accordance with subsection (f) of this section) that a product distributed in commerce presents a substantial product hazard and that action under this subsection is in the public interest, it may order the manufacturer or any distributor or retailer of such product to take whichever of the following actions the person to whom the order is directed elects:

(1) To bring such product into conformity with the requirements of the applicable consumer product safety rule or to repair the defect in such product.

(2) To replace such product with a like or equivalent product which complies with the applicable consumer product safety rule or which does not contain the defect.

(3) To refund the purchase price of such product (less a reasonable allowance for use, if such product has been in the possession of a consumer for one year or more (A) at the time of public notice under subsection (c) of this section, or (B) at the time the consumer receives actual notice of the defect or noncompliance, whichever first occurs).

An order under this subsection may also require the person to whom it applies to submit a plan, satisfactory to the Commission, for taking action under whichever of the preceding paragraphs of this subsection under which such person has elected to act. The Commission shall specify in the order the persons to whom refunds must be made if the person to whom the order is directed elects to take the action described in paragraph (3). If an order under this subsection is directed to more than one person, the Commission shall specify which person has the election under this subsection. An order under this subsection may prohibit the person to whom it applies from manufacturing for sale, offering for sale, distributing in commerce, or importing into the customs territory of the United States (as defined in general note 2 to the Harmonized Tariff Schedule of the United States), or from doing any combination of such actions, the product with respect to which the order was issued.

(e) Reimbursement

(e)(1) No charge shall be made to any person (other than a manufacturer, distributor, or retailer) who avails himself of any remedy provided under an order issued under subsection (d) of this section, and the person subject to the order shall reimburse each person (other than a manufacturer, distributor, or retailer) who is entitled to such a remedy for any reasonable and foreseeable expenses incurred by such person in availing himself of such remedy.

(2) An order issued under subsection (c) or (d) of this section with respect to a product may require any person who is a manufacturer, distributor, or retailer of the product to reimburse any other person who is a manufacturer, distributor, or retailer of such product for such other person's expenses in connection with carrying out the order, if the Commission determines such reimbursement to be in the public interest.

(f) Hearing

(f) An order under subsection (c) or (d) of this section may be issued only after an opportunity for a hearing in accordance with section 554 of Title 5, except that, if the Commission determines that any person who wishes to participate in such hearing is a part of a class of participants who share an identity of interest, the Commission may limit such person's participation in such hearing to participation through a single representative designated by such class (or by the Commission if such class fails to designate such a representative). Any settlement offer which is submitted to the presiding officer at a hearing under this subsection shall be transmitted by the officer to the Commission for its consideration unless the settlement offer is clearly frivolous or duplicative of offers previously made.

(g) Preliminary injunction

(g)(1) If the Commission has initiated a proceeding under this section for the issuance of an order under subsection (d) of this section with respect to a product which the Commission has reason to believe presents a substantial product hazard, the Commission (without regard to section 2076(b)(7) of this title) or the Attorney General may, in accordance with section 2061(d)(1) of this title, apply to a district court of the United States for the issuance of a preliminary injunction to restrain the distribution in commerce of such product pending the completion of such proceeding. If such a preliminary injunction has been issued, the Commission (or Attorney General if the preliminary injunction was issued upon an application of the Attorney General) may apply to the issuing court for extensions of such preliminary injunction.

(2) Any preliminary injunction, and any extension of a preliminary injunction, issued under this subsection with respect to a product shall be in effect for such period as the issuing court prescribes not to exceed a period which extends beyond the thirtieth day from the date of the issuance of the preliminary injunction (or, in the case of a preliminary injunction which has been extended, the date of its extension) or the date of the completion or termination of the proceeding under this section respecting such product, whichever date occurs first.

(3) The amount in controversy requirement of section 1331 of Title 28, does not apply with respect to the jurisdiction of a district court of the United States to issue or exend[1] a preliminary injunction under this subsection.

(h) Consideration of cost of notification

(h) Nothing in this section shall be construed to require the Commission, in determining that a product distributed in commerce presents a substantial product hazard and that notification or other action under this section should be taken, to prepare a comparison of the costs that would be incurred in providing notification or taking other action under this section with the benefits from such notification or action.

Pub.L. 92–573, § 15, Oct. 27, 1972, 86 Stat. 1221; Pub.L. 94–284, § 12(a), May 11, 1976, 90 Stat. 508; Pub.L. 97–35, Title XII, § 1211(h)(4), Aug. 13, 1981, 95 Stat. 723, as amended Pub.L. 97–414, § 9(j)(3), Jan. 4, 1983, 96 Stat. 2064; Pub.L. 97–35, Title XII, § 1211(h)(4), as amended Pub.L. 97–414, § 9(m), Jan. 4, 1983, 96 Stat. 2065; Pub.L. 100–418, Title I, § 1214(d), Aug. 23, 1988, 102 Stat. 1156; Pub.L. 101–608, Title I, §§ 111(a)(2), 112(a), 113, Nov. 16, 1990, 104 Stat. 3114, 3115, 3117.

§ 2065. Inspection and recordkeeping

(a) For purposes of implementing this chapter, or rules or orders prescribed under this chapter, officers or employees duly designated by the Commission, upon presenting appropriate credentials and a written notice from the Commission to the owner, operator, or agent in charge, are authorized—

(1) to enter, at reasonable times, (A) any factory, warehouse, or establishment in which consumer products are manufactured or held, in connection with distribution in commerce, or (B) any conveyance being used to transport consumer products in connection with distribution in commerce; and

(2) to inspect, at reasonable times and in a reasonable manner such conveyance or those areas of such factory, warehouse, or establishment where such products are manufactured, held, or transported and which may relate to the safety of such products. Each such inspection shall be commenced and completed with reasonable promptness.

(b) Every person who is a manufacturer, private labeler, or distributor of a consumer product shall establish and maintain such records, make such reports, and provide such information as the Commission may, by rule, reasonably require for the purposes of implementing this chapter, or to determine compliance with rules or orders prescribed under this chapter.

---

1. So in original. Probably should read "extend".

Upon request of an officer or employee duly designated by the Commission, every such manufacturer, private labeler, or distributor shall permit the inspection of appropriate books, records, and papers relevant to determining whether such manufacturer, private labeler, or distributor has acted or is acting in compliance with this chapter and rules under this chapter.

Pub.L. 92–573, § 16, Oct. 27, 1972, 86 Stat. 1222.

§ 2066. Imported products

(a) Refusal of admission

(a) Any consumer product offered for importation into the customs territory of the United States (as defined in general note 2 to the Harmonized Tariff Schedule of the United States) shall be refused admission into such customs territory if such product—

(1) fails to comply with an applicable consumer product safety rule;

(2) is not accompanied by a certificate required by section 2063 of this title, or is not labeled in accordance with regulations under section 2063(c) of this title;

(3) is or has been determined to be an imminently hazardous consumer product in a proceeding brought under section 2061 of this title;

(4) has a product defect which constitutes a substantial product hazard (within the meaning of section 2064(a)(2) of this title); or

(5) is a product which was manufactured by a person who the Commission has informed the Secretary of the Treasury is in violation of subsection (g) of this section.

(b) Samples

(b) The Secretary of the Treasury shall obtain without charge and deliver to the Commission, upon the latter's request, a reasonable number of samples of consumer products being offered for import. Except for those owners or consignees who are or have been afforded an opportunity for a hearing in a proceeding under section 2061 of this title with respect to an imminently hazardous product, the owner or consignee of the product shall be afforded an opportunity by the Commission for a hearing in accordance with section 554 of Title 5 with respect to the importation of such products into the customs territory of the United States. If it appears from examination of such samples or otherwise that a product must be refused admission under the terms of subsection (a) of this section, such product shall be refused admission, unless subsection (c) of this section applies and is complied with.

(c) Modification

(c) If it appears to the Commission that any consumer product which may be refused admission pursuant to subsection (a) of this section can be so modified that it need not (under the terms of paragraphs (1) through (4) of subsection (a) of this section) be refused admission, the Commission may defer final determination as to the admission of such product and, in accordance with such regulations as the Commission and the Secretary of the Treasury shall jointly agree to, permit such product to be delivered from customs custody under bond for the purpose of permitting the owner or consignee an opportunity to so modify such product.

(d) Supervision of modifications

(d) All actions taken by an owner or consignee to modify such product under subsection (c) of this section shall be subject to the supervision of an officer or employee of the Commission and of the Department of the Treasury. If it appears to the Commission that the product cannot be so modified or that the owner or consignee is not proceeding satisfactorily to modify such product, it shall be refused admission into the customs territory of the United States, and the Commission may direct the Secretary to demand redelivery of the product into customs custody, and to seize the product in accordance with section 2071(b) of this title if it is not so redelivered.

(e) Product destruction

(e) Products refused admission into the customs territory of the United States under this section must be exported, except that upon application, the Secretary of the Treasury may permit the destruction of the product in lieu of exportation. If the owner or consignee does not export the product within a reasonable time, the Department of the Treasury may destroy the product.

(f) Payment of expenses occasioned by refusal of admission

(f) All expenses (including travel, per diem or subsistence, and salaries of officers or employees of the United States) in connection with the destruction provided for in this section (the amount of such expenses to be determined in accordance with regulations of the Secretary of the Treasury) and all expenses in connection with the storage, cartage, or labor with respect to any consumer product refused admission under this section, shall be paid by the owner or consignee and, in default of such payment, shall constitute a lien against any future importations made by such owner or consignee.

(g) Importation conditioned upon manufacturer's compliance

(g) The Commission may, by rule, condition the importation of a consumer product on the manufacturer's compliance with the inspection and recordkeeping requirements of this chapter and the Commission's rules with respect to such requirements.

(h) Product surveillance program

(h)(1) The Commission shall establish and maintain a permanent product surveillance program, in cooperation with other appropriate Federal agencies, for the purpose of carrying out the Commission's responsibilities under this chapter and the other Acts administered by the Commission and preventing the entry of unsafe consumer products into the commerce of the United States.

(2) The Commission may provide to the agencies with which it is cooperating under paragraph (1) such information, data, violator lists, test results, and other support, guidance and documents as may be necessary or helpful for such agencies to cooperate with the Commission to carry out the product surveillance program under paragraph (1).

(3) The Commission shall periodically report to the Congress the results of the surveillance program under paragraph (1).

Pub.L. 92–573, § 17, Oct. 27, 1972, 86 Stat. 1223; as amended Pub.L. 100–418, Title I, § 1214(d), Aug. 23, 1988, 103 Stat. 1156; Pub.L. 101–608, Title I, § 114, Nov. 16, 1990, 104 Stat. 3118.

§ 2067. Exemption of exports

(a) Risk of injury to consumers within United States

(a) This chapter shall not apply to any consumer product if (1) it can be shown that such product is manufactured, sold, or held for sale for export from the United States (or that such product was imported for export), unless (A) such consumer product is in fact distributed in commerce for use in the United States, or (B) the Commission determines that exportation of such product presents an unreasonable risk of injury to consumers within the United States, and (2) such consumer product when distributed in commerce, or any container in which it is enclosed when so distributed, bears a stamp or label stating that such consumer product is intended for export; except that this chapter shall apply to any consumer product manufactured for sale, offered for sale, or sold for shipment to any installation of the United States located outside of the United States.

(b) Statement of exportation: filing period, information; notification of foreign country; petition for minimum filing period: good cause

(b) Not less than thirty days before any person exports to a foreign country any product—

(1) which is not in conformity with an applicable consumer product safety standard in effect under this chapter, or

(2) which is declared to be a banned hazardous substance by a rule promulgated under section 2058 of this title,

such person shall file a statement with the Commission notifying the Commission of such exportation, and the Commission, upon receipt of such statement, shall promptly notify the government of such country of such exportation and the basis for such safety standard or rule. Any statement filed with the Commission under the preceding sentence shall specify the anticipated date of shipment of such product, the country and port of destination of such product, and the quantity of such product that will be exported, and shall contain such other information as the Commission may by regulation require. Upon petition filed with the Commission by any person required to file a statement under this subsection respecting an exportation, the Commission may, for good cause shown, exempt such person from the requirement of this subsection that such a statement be filed no less than thirty days before the date of the exportation, except that in no case shall the Commission permit such a statement to be filed later than the tenth day before such date.

As amended Pub.L. 95–631, § 6(a), Nov. 10, 1978, 92 Stat. 3745.

§ 2068. Prohibited acts

(a) It shall be unlawful for any person to—

(1) manufacture for sale, offer for sale, distribute in commerce, or import into the United States any consumer product which is not in conformity with an applicable consumer product safety standard under this chapter;

(2) manufacture for sale, offer for sale, distribute in commerce, or import into the United States any consumer product which has been declared a banned hazardous product by a rule under this chapter;

(3) fail or refuse to permit access to or copying of records, or fail or refuse to establish or maintain records, or fail or refuse to make reports or provide information, or fail or refuse to permit entry or inspection, as required under this chapter or rule thereunder;

(4) fail to furnish information required by section 2064(b) of this title;

(5) fail to comply with an order issued under section 2064(c) or (d) of this title (relating to notification, to repair, replacement, and refund, and to prohibited acts);

(6) fail to furnish a certificate required by section 2063 of this title or issue a false certificate if such person in the exercise of due care has reason to know that such certificate is false or misleading in any material respect; or to fail to comply with any rule under section 2063(c) of this title (relating to labeling);

(7) fail to comply with any rule under section 2058(g)(2) of this title (relating to stockpiling); or

(8) fail to comply with any rule under section 2076(e) of this title (relating to provision of performance and technical data); and

(9) fail to comply with any rule or requirement under section 2082 of this title (relating to labeling and testing of cellulose insulation).

(10) fail to file a statement with the Commission pursuant to section 2067(b) of this title.

(11) fail to furnish information required by section 2084 of this title.

(b) Paragraphs (1) and (2) of subsection (a) of this section shall not apply to any person (1) who holds a certificate issued in accordance with section 2063(a) of this title to the effect that such consumer product conforms to all applicable consumer product safety rules, unless such person knows that such consumer product does not conform, or (2) who relies in good faith on the representation of the manufacturer or a distributor of such product that the product is not subject to an applicable product safety rule.

As amended Pub.L. 97–414, § 9(j)(4), Jan. 4, 1983, 96 Stat. 2064; Pub.L. 101–608, Title I, § 112(d), Nov. 16, 1990, 104 Stat. 3117.

§ 2069. Civil penalties

(a) Amount of penalty

(a)(1) Any person who knowingly violates section 2068 of this title shall be subject to a civil penalty not to exceed $5,000 for each such violation. Subject to paragraph (2), a violation of section 2068(a)(1), (2), (4), (5), (6), (7), (8), (9), (10), or (11) of this title shall constitute a separate offense with respect to each consumer product involved, except that the maximum civil penalty shall not exceed $1,250,000 for any related series of violations. A violation of section 2068(a)(3) of this title shall constitute a separate violation with respect to each failure or refusal to allow or perform an act required thereby; and, if such violation is a continuing one, each day of such violation shall constitute a separate offense, except that the maximum civil penalty shall not exceed $1,250,000 for any related series of violations.

(2) The second sentence of paragraph (1) of this subsection shall not apply to violations of paragraph (1) or (2) of section 2068(a) of this title—

(A) if the person who violated such paragraphs is not the manufacturer or private labeler or a distributor of the products involved, and

(B) if such person did not have either (i) actual knowledge that his distribution or sale of the product violated such paragraphs or (ii) notice from the Commission that such distribution or sale would be a violation of such paragraphs.

(3)(A) The maximum penalty amounts authorized in paragraph (1) shall be adjusted for inflation as provided in this paragraph.

(B) Not later than December 1, 1994, and December 1 of each fifth calendar year thereafter, the Commission shall prescribe and publish in the Federal Register a schedule of maximum authorized penalties that shall apply for violations that occur after January 1 of the year immediately following such publication.

(C) The schedule of maximum authorized penalties shall be prescribed by increasing each of the amounts referred to in paragraph (1) by the cost-of-living adjustment for the preceding five years. Any increase determined under the preceding sentence shall be rounded to—

(i) in the case of penalties greater than $1,000 but less than or equal to $10,000, the nearest multiple of $1,000;

(ii) in the case of penalties greater than $10,000 but less than or equal to $100,000, the nearest multiple of $5,000;

(iii) in the case of penalties greater than $100,000, but less than or equal to $200,000, the nearest multiple of $10,000; and

(iv) in the case of penalties greater than $200,000, the nearest multiple of $25,000.

(D) For purposes of this subsection:

(i) The term "Consumer Price Index" means the Consumer Price Index for all urban consumers published by the Department of Labor.

(ii) The term "cost-of-living adjustment for the preceding five years" means the percentage by which—

(I) the Consumer Price Index for the month of June of the calendar year preceding the adjustment; exceeds

(II) the Consumer Price Index for the month of June preceding the date on which the maximum authorized penalty was last adjusted.

(b) Relevant factors in assessment of penalty

(b) In determining the amount of any penalty to be sought upon commencing an action seeking to assess a penalty for a violation of section 2068(a) of this title, the Commission shall consider the nature of the product defect, the severity of the risk of injury, the occurrence or absence of injury, the number of defective products distributed, and the appropriateness of such penalty in relation to the size of the business of the person charged.

(c) Compromise of penalty; deductions from penalty

(c) Any civil penalty under this section may be compromised by the Commission. In determining the amount of such penalty or whether it should be remitted or mitigated and in what amount, the Commission shall consider the appropriateness of such penalty to the size of the business of the person charged, the nature of the product defect, the severity of the risk of injury, the occurrence or absence of injury, and the number of defective products distributed. The amount of such penalty when finally determined, or the amount agreed on compromise, may be deducted from any sums owing by the United States to the person charged.

(d) "Knowingly" defined

(d) As used in the first sentence of subsection (a)(1) of this section, the term "knowingly" means (1) the having of actual knowledge, or (2) the presumed having of knowledge deemed to be possessed by a reasonable man who acts in the circumstances, including knowledge obtainable upon the exercise of due care to ascertain the truth of representations.

As amended Pub.L. 94–284, § 13(b), May 11, 1976, 90 Stat. 509; Pub.L. 95–631, § 6(c), Nov. 10, 1978, 92 Stat. 3745; Pub.L. 97–35, Title XII, § 1211(c), Aug. 13, 1981, 95 Stat. 721; As amended Pub.L. 101–608, Title I, §§ 112(e), 115(a), Nov. 16, 1990, 104 Stat. 3117, 3118.

§ 2070. Criminal penalties

(a) Any person who knowingly and willfully violates section 2068 of this title after having received notice of noncompliance from the Commission shall be fined not more than $50,000 or be imprisoned not more than one year, or both.

(b) Any individual director, officer, or agent of a corporation who knowingly and willfully authorizes, orders, or performs any of the acts or practices constituting in whole or in part a violation of section 2068 of this title, and who has knowledge of notice of noncompliance received by the corporation from the Commission, shall be subject to penalties under this section without regard to any penalties to which that corporation may be subject under subsection (a) of this section.

Pub.L. 92–573, § 21, Oct. 27, 1972, 86 Stat. 1225.

§ 2071. Injunctive enforcement and seizure

(a) The United States district courts shall have jurisdiction to take the following action:

(1) Restrain any violation of section 2068 of this title.

(2) Restrain any person from manufacturing for sale, offering for sale, distributing in commerce, or importing into the United States a product in violation of an order in effect under section 2064(d) of this title.

(3) Restrain any person from distributing in commerce a product which does not comply with a consumer product safety rule.

Such actions may be brought by the Commission (without regard to section 2076(b)(7)(A) of this title) or by the Attorney General in any United States district court for a district wherein any act, omission, or transaction constituting the violation occurred, or in such court for the district wherein the defendant is found or transacts business. In any action under this section process may be served on a defendant in any other district in which the defendant resides or may be found.

(b) Any consumer product—

(1) which fails to conform with an applicable consumer product safety rule, or

(2) the manufacture for sale, offering for sale, distribution in commerce, or the importation into the United States of which has been prohibited by an order in effect under section 2064(d) of this title, when introduced into or while in commerce or while held for sale after shipment in commerce shall be liable to be proceeded against on libel of information and condemned in any district court of the United States within the jurisdiction of which such consumer product is found. Proceedings in cases instituted under the authority of this subsection shall conform as nearly as possible to proceedings in rem in admiralty. Whenever such proceedings involving substantially similar consumer products are pending in courts of two or more judicial districts they shall be consolidated for trial by order of any such court upon application reasonably made by any party in interest upon notice to all other parties in interest.

As amended Pub.L. 94–284, §§ 11(b), 12(c), May 11, 1976, 90 Stat. 507, 508.

§ 2072. Suits for damages

(a) Persons injured; costs; amount in controversy

(a) Any person who shall sustain injury by reason of any knowing (including willful) violation of a consumer product safety rule, or any other rule or order issued by the Commission may sue any person who knowingly (including willfully) violated any such rule or order in any district court of the United States in the district in which the defendant resides or is found or has an agent, shall recover damages sustained, and may, if the court determines it to be in the interest of justice, recover the costs of suit, including reasonable attorneys' fees (determined in accordance with section 2060(f) of this title) and reasonable expert witnesses' fees: Provided, That the matter in controversy exceeds the sum or value of $10,000, exclusive of interest and costs, unless such action is brought against the United States, any agency thereof, or any officer or employee thereof in his official capacity.

(b) Denial and imposition of costs

(b) Except when express provision is made in a statute of the United States, in any case in which the plaintiff is finally adjudged to be entitled to recover less than the sum or value of $10,000, computed without regard to any setoff or counterclaim to which the defendant may be adjudged to be entitled, and exclusive of interests and costs, the district court may deny costs to the plaintiff and, in addition, may impose costs on the plaintiff.

(c) Remedies available

(c) The remedies provided for in this section shall be in addition to and not in lieu of any other remedies provided by common law or under Federal or State law.

As amended Pub.L. 94–284, § 10(c), May 11, 1976, 90 Stat. 507; Pub.L. 96–486, § 3, Dec. 1, 1980, 94 Stat. 2369; Pub.L. 97–35, Title XII, § 1211(h)(3)(B), Aug. 13, 1981, 95 Stat. 723.

§ 2073.   Private enforcement

Any interested person (including any individual or nonprofit, business, or other entity) may bring an action in any United States district court for the district in which the defendant is found or transacts business to enforce a consumer product safety rule or an order under section 2064 of this title, and to obtain appropriate injunctive relief. Not less than thirty days prior to the commencement of such action, such interested person shall give notice by registered mail to the Commission, to the Attorney General, and to the person against whom such action is directed. Such notice shall state the nature of the alleged violation of any such standard or order, the relief to be requested, and the court in which the action will be brought. No separate suit shall be brought under this section if at the time the suit is brought the same alleged violation is the subject of a pending civil or criminal action by the United States under this chapter. In any action under this section the court may in the interest of justice award the costs of suit, including reasonable attorneys' fees (determined in accordance with section 2060(f) of this title) and reasonable expert witnesses' fees.

As amended Pub.L. 94–284, § 10(d), May 11, 1976, 90 Stat. 507; Pub.L. 97–35, Title XII, § 1211(a), (h)(3)(C), Aug. 13, 1981, 95 Stat. 721, 723.

§ 2074. Private remedies

(a) Liability at common law or under State statute not relieved by compliance

(a) Compliance with consumer product safety rules or other rules or orders under this chapter shall not relieve any person from liability at common law or under State statutory law to any other person.

(b) Evidence of Commission's inaction inadmissible in actions relating to consumer products

(b) The failure of the Commission to take any action or commence a proceeding with respect to the safety of a consumer product shall not be admissible in evidence in litigation at common law or under State statutory law relating to such consumer product.

(c) Public information

(c) Subject to sections 2055(a)(2) and 2055(b) of this title but notwithstanding section 2055(a)(1) of this title, (1) any accident or investigation report made under this chapter by an officer or employee of the Commission shall be made available to the public in a manner which will not identify any injured person or any person treating him, without the consent of the person so identified, and (2) all reports on research projects, demonstration projects, and other related activities shall be public information.

Pub.L. 92–573, § 25, Oct. 27, 1972, 86 Stat. 1227.

§ 2075. State standards

(a) State compliance to Federal standards

(a) Whenever a consumer product safety standard under this chapter is in effect and applies to a risk of injury associated with a consumer product, no State or political subdivision of a State shall have any authority either to establish or to continue in effect any provision of a safety standard or regulation which prescribes any requirements as to the performance, composition, contents, design, finish, construction, packaging, or labeling of such product which are designed to deal with the same risk of injury associated with such consumer product, unless such requirements are identical to the requirements of the Federal standard.

(b) Consumer product safety requirements which impose performance standards more stringent than Federal standards

(b) Subsection (a) of this section does not prevent the Federal Government or the government of any State or political subdivision of a State from establishing or continuing in effect a safety requirement applicable to a consumer product for its own use which requirement is designed to protect against a risk of injury associated with the product and which is not identical to the consumer product safety standard applicable to the product under this chapter if the Federal, State, or political subdivision requirement provides a higher degree of protection from such risk of injury than the standard applicable under this chapter.

(c) Exemptions

(c) Upon application of a State or political subdivision of a State, the Commission may by rule, after notice and opportunity for oral presentation of views, exempt from the provisions of subsection (a) of this section (under such conditions as it may impose in the rule) any proposed safety standard or regulation which is described in such application and which is designed to protect against a risk of injury associated with a consumer product subject to a consumer product safety standard under this chapter if the State or political subdivision standard or regulation—

(1) provides a significantly higher degree of protection from such risk of injury than the consumer product safety standard under this chapter, and

(2) does not unduly burden interstate commerce.

In determining the burden, if any, of a State or political subdivision standard or regulation on interstate commerce, the Commission shall consider and make appropriate (as determined by the Commission in its discretion) findings on the technological and economic feasibility of complying with such standard or regulation, the cost of complying with such standard or regulation, the geographic distribution of the consumer product to which the standard or regulation would apply, the probability of other States or political subdivisions applying for an exemption under this subsection for a similar standard or regulation, and the need for a national, uniform standard under this chapter for such consumer product.

As amended Pub.L. 94–284, § 17(d), May 11, 1976, 90 Stat. 514.

§ 2076. Additional functions of Consumer Product Safety Commission

(a) Authority to conduct hearings or other inquiries

(a) The Commission may, by one or more of its members or by such agents or agency as it may designate, conduct any hearing or other inquiry necessary or appropriate to its functions anywhere in the United States. A Commissioner who participates in such a hearing or other inquiry shall not be disqualified solely by reason of such participation from subsequently participating in a decision of the Commission in the same matter. The Commission shall publish notice of any proposed hearing in the Federal

Register and shall afford a reasonable opportunity for interested persons to present relevant testimony and data.

(b) Commission powers; orders

(b) The commission shall also have the power—

(1) to require, by special or general orders, any person to submit in writing such reports and answers to questions as the Commission may prescribe to carry out a specific regulatory or enforcement function of the Commission; and such submission shall be made within such reasonable period and under oath or otherwise as the Commission may determine;

(2) to administer oaths;

(3) to require by subpena the attendance and testimony of witnesses and the production of all documentary evidence relating to the execution of its duties;

(4) in any proceeding or investigation to order testimony to be taken by deposition before any person who is designated by the Commission and has the power to administer oaths and, in such instances, to compel testimony and the production of evidence in the same manner as authorized under paragraph (3) of this subsection;

(5) to pay witnesses the same fees and mileage as are paid in like circumstances in the courts of the United States;

(6) to accept gifts and voluntary and uncompensated services, notwithstanding the provisions of section 1342 of Title 31;

(7) to—

(A) initiate, prosecute, defend, or appeal (other than to the Supreme Court of the United States), through its own legal representative and in the name of the Commission, any civil action if the Commission makes a written request to the Attorney General for representation in such civil action and the Attorney General does not within the 45–day period beginning on the date such request was made notify the Commission in writing that the Attorney General will represent the Commission in such civil action, and

(B) initiate, prosecute, or appeal, through its own legal representative, with the concurrence of the Attorney General or through the Attorney General, any criminal action, for the purpose of enforcing the laws subject to its jurisdiction;

(8) to lease buildings or parts of buildings in the District of Columbia, without regard to the Act of March 3, 1877 (section 34 of Title 40), for the use of the Commission; and

(9) to delegate any of its functions or powers, other than the power to issue subpenas under paragraph (3), to any officer or employee of the Commission.

An order issued under paragraph (1) shall contain a complete statement of the reason the Commission requires the report or answers specified in the order to carry out a specific regulatory or enforcement function of the Commission. Such an order shall be designed to place the least burden on the person subject to the order as is practicable taking into account the purpose for which the order was issued.

(c) Noncompliance with subpoena or Commission order; contempt

(c) Any United States district court within the jurisdiction of which any inquiry is carried on, may, upon petition by the Commission (subject to subsection (b)(7) of this section) or by the Attorney General, in case of refusal to obey a subpena or order of the Commission issued under subsection (b) of this section, issue an order requiring compliance therewith; and any failure to obey the order of the court may be punished by the court as a contempt thereof.

(d) Disclosure of information

(d) No person shall be subject to civil liability to any person (other than the Commission or the United States) for disclosing information at the request of the Commission.

(e) Performance and technical data

(e) The Commission may by rule require any manufacturer of consumer products to provide to the Commission such performance and technical data related to performance and safety as may be required to carry out the purposes of this chapter, and to give such notification of such performance and technical data at the time of original purchase to prospective purchasers and to the first purchaser of such product for purposes other than resale, as it determines necessary to carry out the purposes of this chapter.

(f) Purchase of consumer products by Commission

(f) For purposes of carrying out this chapter, the Commission may purchase any consumer product and it may require any manufacturer, distributor, or retailer of a consumer product to sell the product to the Commission at manufacturer's, distributor's, or retailer's cost.

(g) Contract authority

(g) The Commission is authorized to enter into contracts with governmental entities, private organizations, or individuals for the conduct of activities authorized by this chapter.

(h) Research, development, and testing facilities

(h) The Commission may plan, construct, and operate a facility or facilities suitable for research, development, and testing of consumer products in order to carry out this chapter.

(i) Recordkeeping; audit

(i)(1) Each recipient of assistance under this chapter pursuant to grants or contracts entered into under other than competitive bidding procedures shall keep such records as the Commission by rule shall prescribe, including records which fully disclose the amount and disposition by such recipient of the proceeds of such assistance, the total cost of the project undertaken in connection with which such assistance is given or used, and the amount of that portion of the cost of the project or undertaking supplied by other sources, and such other records as will facilitate an effective audit.

(2) The Commission and the Comptroller General of the United States, or their duly authorized representatives, shall have access for the purpose of audit and examination to any books, documents, papers, and records of the recipients that are pertinent to the grants or contracts entered into under this chapter under other than competitive bidding procedures.

(j) Report to President and Congress

(j) The Commission shall prepare and submit to the President and the Congress at the beginning of each regular session of Congress a comprehensive report on the administration of this chapter for the preceding fiscal year. Such report shall include—

(1) a thorough appraisal, including statistical analyses, estimates, and long-term projections, of the incidence of injury and effects to the population resulting from consumer products, with a breakdown, insofar as practicable, among the various sources of such injury;

(2) a list of consumer product safety rules prescribed or in effect during such year;

(3) an evaluation of the degree of observance of consumer product safety rules, including a list of enforcement actions, court decisions, and compromises of alleged violations, by location and company name;

(4) a summary of outstanding problems confronting the administration of this chapter in order of priority;

(5) an analysis and evaluation of public and private consumer product safety research activities;

(6) a list, with a brief statement of the issues, of completed or pending judicial actions under this chapter;

(7) the extent to which technical information was disseminated to the scientific and commercial communities and consumer information was made available to the public;

(8) the extent of cooperation between Commission officials and representatives of industry and other interested parties in the implementation of this chapter, including a log or summary of meetings held between Commission officials and representatives of industry and other interested parties;

(9) an appraisal of significant actions of State and local governments relating to the responsibilities of the Commission;

(10) with respect to voluntary consumer product safety standards for which the Commission has participated in the development through monitoring or offering of assistance and with respect to voluntary consumer product safety standards relating to risks of injury that are the subject of regulatory action by the Commission, a description of—

(A) the number of such standards adopted;

(B) the nature and number of the products which are the subject of such standards;

(C) the effectiveness of such standards in reducing potential harm from consumer products;

(D) the degree to which staff members of the Commission participate in the development of such standards;

(E) the amount of resources of the Commission devoted to encouraging development of such standards; and

(F) such other information as the Commission determines appropriate or necessary to inform the Congress on the current status of the voluntary consumer product safety standard program; and

(11) such recommendations for additional legislation as the Commission deems necessary to carry out the purposes of this chapter.

(k) Budget estimates and requests; legislative recommendations; testimony; comments on legislation

(k)(1) Whenever the Commission submits any budget estimate or request to the President or the Office of Management and Budget, it shall concurrently transmit a copy of that estimate or request to the Congress.

(2) Whenever the Commission submits any legislative recommendations, or testimony, or comments on legislation to the President or the Office of Management and Budget, it shall concurrently transmit a copy thereof to the Congress. No officer or agency of the United States shall have any authority to require the Commission to submit its legislative recommendations, or testimony, or comments on legislation, to any officer

or agency of the United States for approval, comments, or review, prior to the submission of such recommendations, testimony, or comments to the Congress.

Pub.L. 94–273, § 31, Apr. 21, 1976, 90 Stat. 380; Pub.L. 94–284, §§ 8(b), 11(c), (d), 14, May 11, 1976, 90 Stat. 506–509; Pub.L. 95–631, § 11, Nov. 10, 1978, 92 Stat. 3748; Pub.L. 97–35, Title XII, §§ 1207(b), 1208, 1209(c), 1211(d), Aug. 13, 1981, 95 Stat. 718, 720, 721, Pub.L. 97–258, § 4(b), Sept. 13, 1982, 96 Stat. 1067.

§ 2076a. Report on civil penalties

(1) Beginning 1 year after Nov. 16, 1990, and every year thereafter, the Consumer Product Safety Commission shall submit to the Committee on Commerce, Science, and Transportation of the Senate and the Committee on Energy and Commerce of the House of Representatives the information specified in paragraph (2) of this subsection. Such information may be included in the annual report to the Congress submitted by the Commission.

(2) The Commission shall submit information with respect to the imposition of civil penalties under the statutes which it administers. The information shall included the number of civil penalties imposed, an identification of the violations that led to the imposition of such penalties, and the amount of revenue recovered from the imposition of such penalties.

Pub.L. 101–608, Title I, § 115(d), Nov. 16, 1990, 104 Stat. 3121.

§ 2077. Chronic Hazard Advisory Panels

(a) Appointment; purposes

(a) The Commission shall appoint Chronic Hazard Advisory Panels (hereinafter referred to as the Panel or Panels) to advise the Commission in accordance with the provisions of section 2080(b) of this title respecting the chronic hazards of cancer, birth defects, and gene mutations associated with consumer products.

(b) Composition; membership

(b) Each Panel shall consist of 7 members appointed by the Commission from a list of nominees who shall be nominated by the President of the National Academy of Sciences from scientists—

(1) who are not officers or employees of the United States, (other than employees of the National Institutes of Health, the National Toxicology Program, or the National Center for Toxicological Research) and who do not receive compensation from or have any substantial financial interest in any manufacturer, distributor, or retailer of a consumer product; and

(2) who have demonstrated the ability to critically assess chronic hazards and risks to human health presented by the exposure of humans to toxic substances or as demonstrated by the exposure of animals to such substances.

The President of the National Academy of Sciences shall nominate for each Panel a number of individuals equal to three times the number of members to be appointed to the Panel.

(c) Chairman and Vice Chairman; election; term

(c) The Chairman and Vice Chairman of the Panel shall be elected from among the members and shall serve for the duration of the Panel.

(d) Majority vote

(d) Decisions of the Panel shall be made by a majority of the Panel.

(e) Administrative support services

(e) The Commission shall provide each Panel with such administrative support services as it may require to carry out its duties under section 2080 of this title.

(f) Compensation

(f) A member of a Panel appointed under subsection (a) of this section shall be paid at a rate not to exceed the daily equivalent of the annual rate of basic pay in effect for grade GS–18 of the General Schedule for each day (including travel time) during which the member is engaged in the actual performance of the duties of the Panel.

(g) Requests for and disclosures of information

(g) Each Panel shall request information and disclose information to the public, as provided in subsection (h) of this section, only through the Commission.

(h) Information from other Federal departments and agencies

(h)(1) Notwithstanding any statutory restriction on the authority of agencies and departments of the Federal Government to share information, such agencies and departments shall provide the Panel with such information and data as each Panel, through the Commission, may request to carry out its duties under section 2080 of this title. Each Panel may request information, through the Commission, from States, industry and other private sources as it may require to carry out its responsibilities.

(2) Section 2055 of this title shall apply to the disclosure of information by the Panel but shall not apply to the disclosure of information to the Panel.

Pub.L. 92–573, § 28, as added Pub.L. 97–35, Title XII, § 1206(a), Aug. 13, 1981, 95 Stat. 716; as amended Pub.L. 101–608, Title I § 116, Nov. 16, 1990, 104 Stat. 3121.

§ 2078. Cooperation with States and other Federal agencies

(a) The Commission shall establish a program to promote Federal–State cooperation for the purposes of carrying out this chapter. In implementing such program the Commission may—

(1) accept from any State or local authorities engaged in activities relating to health, safety, or consumer protection assistance in such functions as injury data collection, investigation, and educational programs, as well as other assistance in the administration and enforcement of this chapter which such States or localities may be able and willing to provide and, if so agreed, may pay in advance or otherwise for the reasonable cost of such assistance, and

(2) commission any qualified officer or employee of any State or local agency as an officer of the Commission for the purpose of conducting examinations, investigations, and inspections.

(b) In determining whether such proposed State and local programs are appropriate in implementing the purposes of this chapter, the Commission shall give favorable consideration to programs which establish separate State and local agencies to consolidate functions relating to product safety and other consumer protection activities.

(c) The Commission may obtain from any Federal department or agency such statistics, data, program reports, and other materials as it may deem necessary to carry out its functions under this chapter. Each such department or agency may cooperate with the Commission and, to the extent permitted by law, furnish such materials to it. The Commission and the heads of other departments and agencies engaged in administering programs related to product safety shall, to the maximum extent practicable, cooperate and consult in order to insure fully coordinated efforts.

(d) The Commission shall, to the maximum extent practicable, utilize the resources and facilities of the National Institute of Standards and Technology, on a reimbursable basis, to perform research and analyses related to risks of injury associated with consumer products (including fire and flammability risks), to develop test methods, to conduct studies and investigations, and to provide technical advice and assistance in connection with the functions of the Commission.

(e) The Commission may provide to another Federal agency or a State or local agency or authority engaged in activities relating to health, safety, or consumer protection, copies of any accident or investigation report made under this chapter by any officer, employee or agent of the Commission only if (1) information which under section 2055(a)(2) of this title is to be considered confidential and is not included in any copy of such report which is provided under this subsection; and (2) each Federal agency and State and local agency and authority which is to receive under this subsection a copy of such report provided assurances satisfactory to the Commission that the identity of any injured person will not, without the consent of the person identified, be included in—

   (A) any copy of such report, or

   (B) any information contained in any such report,

which the agency or authority makes available to any member of the public. No Federal agency or State or local agency or authority may disclose to the public any information contained in a report received by the agency or authority under this subsection unless with respect to such information the Commission has complied with the applicable requirements of section 2055(b) of this title.

Pub.L. 92–573, § 29, Oct. 27, 1972, 86 Stat. 1230; Pub.L. 94–284, § 15, May 11, 1976, 90 Stat. 510; as amended Pub.L. 100–418, Title V, § 5115(c), Aug. 23, 1988, 102 Stat. 1433.

§ 2079. Transfers of functions

(a) Hazardous substances and poisons

   (a) The functions of the Secretary of Health, Education, and Welfare under the Federal Hazardous Substances Act and the Poison Prevention Packaging Act of 1970 are transferred to the Commission. The functions of the Secretary of Health, Education, and Welfare under the Federal Food, Drug, and Cosmetic Act (15 U.S.C. 301 et seq.[2]), to the extent such functions relate to the administration and enforcement of the Poison Prevention Packaging Act of 1970, are transferred to the Commission.

(b) Flammable fabrics

   (b) The functions of the Secretary of Health, Education, and Welfare, the Secretary of Commerce, and the Federal Trade Commission under the Flammable Fabrics Act are transferred to the Commission. The functions of the Federal Trade Commission under the Federal Trade Commission Act, to the extent such functions relate to the administration and enforcement of the Flammable Fabrics Act, are transferred to the Commission.

(c) Household refrigerators

   (c) The functions of the Secretary of Commerce and the Federal Trade Commission under the Act of August 2, 1956, are transferred to the Commission.

   2. So in original. Probably should be "21 U.S.C. 301 et seq.".

**(d) Regulation by Commission of consumer products
in accordance with other provisions of law**

(d) A risk of injury which is associated with a consumer product and which could be eliminated or reduced to a sufficient extent by action under the Federal Hazardous Substances Act, the Poison Prevention Packaging Act of 1970, or the Flammable Fabrics Act may be regulated under this chapter only if the Commission by rule finds that it is in the public interest to regulate such risk of injury under this chapter. Such a rule shall identify the risk of injury proposed to be regulated under this chapter and shall be promulgated in accordance with section 553 of Title 5; except that the period to be provided by the Commission pursuant to subsection (c) of such section for the submission of data, views, and arguments respecting the rule shall not exceed thirty days from the date of publication pursuant to subsection (b) of such section of a notice respecting the rule.

**(e) Transfer of personnel, property, records, etc.;
continued application of orders, rules, etc.**

(e)(1)(A) All personnel, property, records, obligations, and commitments, which are used primarily with respect to any function transferred under the provisions of subsections (a), (b) and (c) of this section shall be transferred to the Commission, except those associated with fire and flammability research in the National Institute of Standards and Technology. The transfer of personnel pursuant to this paragraph shall be without reduction in classification or compensation for one year after such transfer, except that the Chairman of the Commission shall have full authority to assign personnel during such one-year period in order to efficiently carry out functions transferred to the Commission under this section.

(B) Any commissioned officer of the Public Health Service who upon the day before the effective date of this section, is serving as such officer primarily in the performance of functions transferred by this chapter to the Commission, may, if such officer so elects, acquire competitive status and be transferred to a competitive position in the Commission subject to subparagraph (A) of this paragraph, under the terms prescribed in paragraphs (3) through (8)(A) of section 15(b) of the Clean Air Amendments of 1970.

(2) All orders, determinations, rules, regulations, permits, contracts, certificates, licenses, and privileges (A) which have been issued, made, granted, or allowed to become effective in the exercise of functions which are transferred under this section by any department or agency, any functions of which are transferred by this section, and (B) which are in effect at the time this section takes effect, shall continue in effect according to their terms until modified, terminated, superseded, set aside, or repealed

by the Commission, by any court of competent jurisdiction, or by operation of law.

(3) The provisions of this section shall not affect any proceedings pending at the time this section takes effect before any department or agency, functions of which are transferred by this section; except that such proceedings, to the extent that they relate to functions so transferred, shall be continued before the Commission. Orders shall be issued in such proceedings, appeals shall be taken therefrom, and payments shall be made pursuant to such orders, as if this section had not been enacted; and orders issued in any such proceedings shall continue in effect until modified, terminated, superseded, or repealed by the Commission, by a court of competent jurisdiction, or by operation of law.

(4) The provisions of this section shall not affect suits commenced prior to the date this section takes effect and in all such suits proceedings shall be had, appeals taken, and judgments rendered, in the same manner and effect as if this section had not been enacted; except that if before the date on which this section takes effect, any department or agency (or officer thereof in his official capacity) is a party to a suit involving functions transferred to the Commission, then such suit shall be continued by the Commission. No cause of action, and no suit, action, or other proceeding, by or against any department or agency (or officer thereof in his official capacity) functions of which are transferred by this section, shall abate by reason of the enactment of this section. Causes of actions, suits, actions, or other proceedings may be asserted by or against the United States or the Commission as may be appropriate and, in any litigation pending when this section takes effect, the court may at any time, on its own motion or that of any party, enter an order which will give effect of the provisions of this paragraph.

(f) Definition of "function"

(f) For purposes of this section, (1) the term "function" includes power and duty, and (2) the transfer of a function, under any provision of law, of an agency or the head of a department shall also be a transfer of all functions under such law which are exercised by any office or officer of such agency or department.

As amended Pub.L. 94–284, §§ 3(f), 16, May 11, 1976, 90 Stat. 504, 510; as amended Pub.L. 100–418, Title V, § 5115(c), Aug. 23, 1988, 102 Stat. 1433.

§ 2080. Limitations on Jurisdiction of Consumer Product Safety Commission

(a) Authority to regulate

(a) The Commission shall have no authority under this chapter to regulate any risk of injury associated with a consumer product if such risk could be eliminated or reduced to a sufficient extent by actions taken under the Occupational Safety and Health Act of 1970; the Atomic Energy Act of 1954; or the Clean Air Act. The Commission shall have no authority under this chapter to regulate any risk of injury associated with electronic product radiation emitted from an electronic product (as such terms are defined by sections 355(1) and (2) of the Public Health Service Act) if such risk of injury may be subjected to regulation under subpart 3 of part F of title III of the Public Health Service Act.

(b) Certain notices of proposed rulemaking; duties of Chronic Hazard Advisory Panel

(1) The Commission may not issue—

(A) an advance notice of proposed rulemaking for a consumer product safety rule,

(B) a notice of proposed rulemaking for a rule under section 2076(e) of this title, or

(C) an advance notice of proposed rulemaking for regulations under section 1261(q)(1) of this title,

relating to a risk of cancer, birth defects, or gene mutations from a consumer product unless a Chronic Hazard Advisory Panel, established under section 2077 of this title, has, in accordance with paragraph (2), submitted a report to the Commission with respect to whether a substance contained in such product is a carcinogen, mutagen, or teratogen.

(2)(A) Before the Commission issues an advance notice of proposed rulemaking for—

(i) a consumer product safety rule,

(ii) a rule under section 2076(e) of this title, or

(iii) a regulation under section 1261(q)(1) of this title,

relating to a risk of cancer, birth defects, or gene mutations from a consumer product, the Commission shall request the Panel to review the scientific data and other relevant information relating to such risk to determine if any substance in the product is a carcinogen, mutagen, or a teratogen and to report its determination to the Commission.

(B) When the Commission appoints a Panel, the Panel shall convene within 30 days after the date the final appointment is made to the Panel. The Panel shall report its determination to the Commission not later than 120 days after the date the Panel is convened or, if the Panel requests additional time, within a time period specified by the Commission. If the determination reported to the Commission states that a substance in a product is a carcinogen, mutagen, or a teratogen, the Panel shall include in its report an estimate, if such an estimate is feasible, of the probable harm to human health that will result from exposure to the substance.

(C) A Panel appointed under section 2077 of this title shall terminate when it has submitted its report unless the Commission extends the existence of the Panel.

(D) The Federal Advisory Committee Act shall not apply with respect to any Panel established under this section.

(c) Panel report; incorporation into advance notice and final rule

(c) Each Panel's report shall contain a complete statement of the basis for the Panel's determination. The Commission shall consider the report of the Panel and incorporate such report into the advance notice of proposed rulemaking and final rule.

Pub.L. 97–35, Title XII, § 1206(b), Aug. 13, 1981, 95 Stat. 717, Pub.L. 97–414, § 9(j)(5), Jan. 4, 1983, 96 Stat. 2064.

§ 2081. Authorization of appropriations

(a) There are authorized to be appropriated for the purposes of carrying out the provisions of this chapter (other than the provisions of section 2076(h) of this title which authorize the planning and construction of research, development, and testing facilities) and for the purpose of carrying out the functions, powers, and duties transferred to the Commission under section 2079 of this title, not to exceed—

(1) $42,000,000 for fiscal year 1991, and

(2) $45,000,000 for fiscal year 1992.

For payment of accumulated and accrued leave under section 5551 of Title 5 severance pay under section 5595 under such title, and any other expense related to a reduction in force in the Commission, there are authorized to be appropriated such sums as may be necessary.

(b)(1) There are authorized to be appropriated such sums as may be necessary for the planning and construction of research, development and testing facilities described in section 2076(h) of this title; except that no appropriation shall be made for any such planning or construction involving an expenditure in excess of $100,000 if such planning or construction has not been approved by resolutions adopted in substantially the same form by the Committee on Energy and Commerce of the House of Representatives, and by the Committee on Commerce, Science, and Transportation of the Senate. For the purpose of securing consideration of such approval the Commission shall transmit to Congress a prospectus of the proposed facility including (but not limited to)—

(A) a brief description of the facility to be planned or constructed;

(B) the location of the facility, and an estimate of the maximum cost of the facility;

(C) a statement of those agencies, private and public, which will use such facility, together with the contribution to be made by each such agency toward the cost of such facility; and

(D) a statement of justification of the need for such facility.

(2) The estimated maximum cost of any facility approved under this subsection as set forth in the prospectus may be increased by the amount equal to the percentage increase, if any, as determined by the Commission, in construction costs, from the date of the transmittal of such prospectus to Congress, but in no event shall the increase authorized by this paragraph exceed 10 per centum of such estimated maximum cost.

(c) No funds appropriated under subsection (a) of this section may be used to pay any claim described in section 2053(h) of this title whether pursuant to a judgment of a court or under any award, compromise, or settlement of such claim made under section 2672 of Title 28, or under any other provision of law.

As amended Pub.L. 94–284, §§ 2, 5(b), May 11, 1976, 90 Stat. 503, 505; S.Res. 4, Feb. 4, 1977; Pub.L. 95–631, § 1, Nov. 10, 1978, 92 Stat. 3742; H.Res. 459, Mar. 25, 1980; Pub.L. 97–35, Title XII, § 1214, Aug. 13, 1981, 95 Stat. 724; as amended Pub.L. 101–608, § 117, Nov. 16, 1990, 104 Stat. 3121; Pub.L. 103–437, § 5(c)(1), Nov. 2, 1994, 108 Stat. 4582.

§ **2082.** Interim cellulose insulation safety standard

(a) Applicability of specification of General Services Administration; authority and effect of interim standard; modifications; criteria; labeling requirements

(a)(1) Subject to the provisions of paragraph (2), on and after the last day of the 60–day period beginning on the effective date of this section, the requirements for flame resistance and corrosiveness set forth in the General Services Administration's specification for cellulose insulation, HH–I–515C (as such specification was in effect on February 1, 1978), shall be deemed to be an interim consumer product safety standard which shall have all the authority and effect of any other consumer product safety standard promulgated by the Commission under this chapter. During the 45–day period beginning on the effective date of this section, the Commission may make, and shall publish in the Federal Register, such technical, nonsubstantive changes in such requirements as it deems appropriate to make such requirements suitable for promulgation as a consumer product safety standard. At the end of the 60–day period specified in the first sentence of this paragraph, the Commission shall publish in the Federal Register such interim consumer product safety standard, as altered by the Commission under this paragraph.

(2) The interim consumer product safety standard established in paragraph (1) shall provide that any cellulose insulation which is produced or

distributed for sale or use as a consumer product shall have a flame spread rating of 0 to 25, as such rating is set forth in the General Services Administration's specification for cellulose insulation, HH–I–515C.

(3) During the period for which the interim consumer product safety standard established in subsection (a) of this section is in effect, in addition to complying with any labeling requirement established by the Commission under this chapter, each manufacturer or private labeler of cellulose insulation shall include the following statement on any container of such cellulose insulation: "ATTENTION: This material meets the applicable minimum Federal flammability standard. This standard is based upon laboratory tests only, which do not represent actual conditions which may occur in the home". Such statement shall be located in a conspicuous place on such container and shall appear in conspicuous and legible type in contrast by typography, layout, and color with other printed matter on such container.

(b) Scope of judicial review

(b) Judicial review of the interim consumer product safety standard established in subsection (a) of this section, as such standard is in effect on and after the last day of the 60–day period specified in such subsection, shall be limited solely to the issue of whether any changes made by the Commission under paragraph (1) are technical, nonsubstantive changes. For purposes of such review, any change made by the Commission under paragraph (1) which requires that any test to determine the flame spread rating of cellulose insulation shall include a correction for variations in test results caused by equipment used in the test shall be considered a technical, nonsubstantive change.

(c) Enforcement; violations; promulgation of final standard; procedures applicable to promulgation; revision of interim standard; procedures applicable to revision

(c)(1)(A) Any interim consumer product safety standard established pursuant to this section shall be enforced in the same manner as any other consumer product safety standard until such time as there is in effect a final consumer product safety standard promulgated by the Commission, as provided in subparagraph (B), or until such time as it is revoked by the Commission under section 2058(e) of this title. A violation of the interim consumer product safety standard shall be deemed to be a violation of a consumer product safety standard promulgated by the Commission under section 2058 of this title.

(B) If the Commission determines that the interim consumer product safety standard does not adequately protect the public from the unreasonable risk of injury associated with flammable or corrosive cellulose insulation, it shall promulgate a final consumer product safety standard to protect against such risk. Such final standard shall be promulgated pursuant to section 553 of Title 5, except that the Commission shall give interested persons an opportunity for the oral presentation of data, views, or arguments, in addition to an opportunity to make written submissions. A transcript shall be kept of any oral presentation. The provisions of section 2058(b), (c), and (d) of this title shall apply to any proceeding to promulgate such final standard. In any judicial review of such final standard under section 2060 of this title, the court shall not require any demonstration that each particular finding made by the Commission under section 2058(c) of this title is supported by substantial evidence. The court shall affirm the action of the Commission unless the court determines that such action is not supported by substantial evidence on the record taken as a whole.

(2)(A) Until there is in effect such a final consumer product safety standard, the Commission shall incorporate into the interim consumer product safety standard, in accordance with the provisions of this paragraph, each revision superseding the requirements for flame resistance and corrosiveness referred to in subsection (a) of this section and promulgated by the General Services Administration.

(B) At least 45 days before any revision superseding such requirements is to become effective, the Administrator of the General Services Administration shall notify the Commission of such revision. In the case of any such revision which becomes effective during the period beginning on February 1, 1978, and ending on the effective date of this section, such notice from the Administrator of the General Services Administration shall be deemed to have been made on the effective date of this section.

(C)(i) No later than 45 days after receiving any notice under subparagraph (B), the Commission shall publish the revision, including such changes in the revision as it considers appropriate to make the revision suitable for promulgation as an amendment to the interim consumer product safety standard, in the Federal Register as a proposed amendment to the interim consumer product safety standard.

(ii) The Commission may extend the 45–day period specified in clause (i) for an additional period of not more than 150 days if the Commission determines that such extension is necessary to study the technical and scientific basis for the revision involved, or to study the safety and economic consequences of such revision.

(D)(i) Additional extensions of the 45–day period specified in subparagraph (C)(i) may be taken by the Commission if—

(I) the Commission makes the determination required in subparagraph (C)(ii) with respect to each such extension; and

(II) in the case of further extensions proposed by the Commission after an initial extension under this clause, such further extensions have not been disapproved under clause (iv).

(ii) Any extension made by the Commission under this subparagraph shall be for a period of not more than 45 days.

(iii) Prior notice of each extension made by the Commission under this subparagraph, together with a statement of the reasons for such extension and an estimate of the length of time required by the Commission to complete its action upon the revision involved, shall be published in the Federal Register and shall be submitted to the Committee on Commerce, Science, and Transportation of the Senate and the Committee on Interstate and Foreign Commerce of the House of Representatives.

(iv) In any case in which the Commission takes an initial 45–day extension under clause (i), the Commission may not take any further extensions under clause (i) if each committee referred to in clause (iii) disapproves by committee resolution any such further extensions before the end of the 15–day period following notice of such initial extension made by the Commission in accordance with clause (iii).

(E) The Commission shall give interested persons an opportunity to comment upon any proposed amendment to the interim consumer product safety standard during the 30–day period following any publication by the Commission under subparagraph (C).

(F) No later than 90 days after the end of the period specified in subparagraph (E), the Commission shall promulgate the amendment to the interim consumer product safety standard unless the Commission determines, after consultation with the Secretary of Energy, that—

(i) such amendment is not necessary for the protection of consumers from the unreasonable risk of injury associated with flammable or corrosive cellulose insulation; or

(ii) implementation of such amendment will create an undue burden upon persons who are subject to the interim consumer product safety standard.

(G) The provisions of section 2060 of this title shall not apply to any judicial review of any amendment to the interim product safety standard promulgated under this paragraph.

(d) Reporting requirements of other Federal departments, agencies, etc. of violations

(d) Any Federal department, agency, or instrumentality, or any Federal independent regulatory agency, which obtains information which reasonably indicates that cellulose insulation is being manufactured or distributed in violation of this chapter shall immediately inform the Commission of such information.

(e) Reporting requirements of Commission to Congressional committees; contents, time of submission, etc.

(e)(1) The Commission, no later than 45 days after the effective date of this section, shall submit a report to the Committee on Commerce, Science, and Transportation of the Senate and to the Committee on Interstate and Foreign Commerce of the House of Representatives which shall contain a detailed statement of the manner in which the Commission intends to carry out the enforcement of this section.

(2)(A) The Commission, no later than 6 months after the date upon which the report required in paragraph (1) is due (and no later than the end of each 6–month period thereafter), shall submit a report to each committee referred to in paragraph (1) which shall describe the enforcement activities of the Commission with respect to this section during the most recent 6–month period.

(B) The first report which the Commission submits under subparagraph (A) shall include the results of tests of cellulose insulation manufactured by at least 25 manufacturers which the Commission shall conduct to determine whether such cellulose insulation complies with the interim consumer product safety standard. The second such report shall include the results of such tests with respect to 50 manufacturers who were not included in testing conducted by the Commission for inclusion in the first report.

(f) Compliance with certification requirements; implementation; waiver; rules and regulations

(f)(1) The Commission shall have the authority to require that any person required to comply with the certification requirements of section 2063 of this title with respect to the manufacture of cellulose insulation shall provide for the performance of any test or testing program required for such certification through the use of an independent third party qualified to perform such test or testing program. The Commission may impose such requirement whether or not the Commission has established a testing program for cellulose insulation under section 2063(b) of this title.

(2) The Commission, upon petition by a manufacturer, may waive the requirements of paragraph (1) with respect to such manufacturer if the Commission determines that the use of an independent third party is not necessary in order for such manufacturer to comply with the certification requirements of section 2063 of this title.

(3) The Commission may prescribe such rules as it considers necessary to carry out the provisions of this subsection.

(g) Authorization of appropriations

(g) There are authorized to be appropriated, for each of the fiscal years 1978, 1979, 1980, and 1981, such sums as may be necessary to carry out the provisions of this section.

Pub.L. 92–573, § 35, as added Pub.L. 95–319, § 3(a), July 11, 1978, 92 Stat. 386; H.Res. 549, Mar. 25, 1980; as amended Pub.L. 104–437, § 5(c)(2), Nov. 2, 1994, 108 Stat. 4582.

§ 2083.   Congressional veto of consumer product safety rules

Unconstitutionality of Legislative Veto Provisions

The provisions of former section 1254(c)(2) of Title 8, Aliens and Nationality, which authorized a House of Congress, by resolution, to invalidate an action of the Executive Branch, were declared unconstitutional in Immigration and Naturalization Service v. Chadha, 1983, 462 U.S. 919, 103 S.Ct. 2764, 77 L.Ed.2d 317. See similar provisions in this section.

(a) Transmission to Congress

(a) The Commission shall transmit to the Secretary of the Senate and the Clerk of the House of Representatives a copy of any consumer product safety rule promulgated by the Commission under section 2058 of this title.

(b) Disapproval by concurrent resolution

(b) Any rule specified in subsection (a) of this section shall not take effect if—

(1) within the 90 calendar days of continuous session of the Congress which occur after the date of the promulgation of such rule, both Houses of the Congress adopt a concurrent resolution, the matter after the resolving clause of which is as follows (with the blank spaces appropriately filled): "That the Congress disapproves the consumer product safety rule which was promulgated by the Consumer Product Safety Commission with respect to _____ and which was transmitted to the Congress on _____ and disapproves the rule for the following reasons: _____."; or

(2) within the 60 calendar days of continuous session of the Congress which occur after the date of the promulgation of such rule, one House of the Congress adopts such concurrent resolution and transmits such resolution to the other House and such resolution is not disapproved by such other House within the 30 calendar days of continuous session of the Congress which occur after the date of such transmittal.

(c) Presumptions from Congressional action or inaction

(c) Congressional inaction on, or rejection of, a concurrent resolution of disapproval under this section shall not be construed as an expression of approval of the rule involved, and shall not be construed to create any presumption of validity with respect to such rule.

(d) Continuous session of Congress

(d) For purposes of this section—

(1) continuity of session is broken only by an adjournment of the Congress sine die; and

(2) the days on which either House is not in session because of an adjournment of more than 3 days to a day certain are excluded in the computation of the periods of continuous session of the Congress specified in subsection (b) of this section.

Pub.L. 92–573, § 36, as added Pub.L. 97–35, Title XII, § 1207(a), Aug. 13, 1981, 95 Stat. 718.

§ 2084. Information reporting

(a) Notification of settlements or judgments

(a) If a particular model of a consumer product is the subject of at least 3 civil actions that have been filed in Federal or State court for death or grievous bodily injury which in each of the 24–month periods defined in subsection (b) of this section result in either a final settlement involving the manufacturer or a court judgment in favor of the plaintiff, the manufacturer of said product shall, in accordance with subsection (c) of this section, report to the Commission each such civil action within 30 days after the final settlement or court judgment in the third of such civil actions, and, within 30 days after any subsequent settlement or judgment in that 24–month period, any other such action.

(b) Calculation of the 24 month period

(b) The 24–month periods referred to in subsection (a) of this section are in the 24–month period commencing on January 1, 1991, and subsequent 24–month periods beginning January 1 of the calendar year that is two years following the beginning of the previous 24–month period.

(c) Information required to be reported

(c)(1) The information required by subsection (a) of this section to be reported to the Commission with respect to each civil action described in subsection (a) of this section, shall include and in addition to any voluntary information provided under paragraph (2) shall be limited to the following:

(A) The name and address of the manufacturer.

(B) The model and model number or designation of the consumer product subject to the civil action.

(C) A statement as to whether the civil action alleged death or grievous bodily injury, and in the case of an allegation of grievous bodily injury, a statement of the category of such injury.

(D) A statement as to whether the civil action resulted in a final settlement or a judgment in favor of the plaintiff.

(E) in the case of a judgment in favor of the plaintiff, the name of the civil action, the number assigned the civil action, and the court in which the civil action was filed.

(2) A manufacturer furnishing the report required by paragraph (1) may include (A) a statement as to whether any judgment in favor of the plaintiff is under appeal or is expected to be appealed or (B) any other information which the manufacturer chooses to provide. A manufacturer reporting to the Commission under subsection (a) of this section need not admit or may specifically deny that the information it submits reasonably supports the conclusion that its consumer product caused a death or grievous bodily injury.

(3) No statement of the amount paid by the manufacturer in a final settlement shall bee required as part of the report furnished under subsection (a) of this section, nor shall such a statement of settlement amount be required under any other section of this chapter.

(d) Report not deemed an admission of liability

The reporting of a civil action described in subsection (a) of this section by a manufacturer shall not constitute an admission of—

(1) an unreasonable risk of injury,

(2) a defect in the consumer product which was the subject of this action,

(3) a substantial product hazard,

(4) an imminent hazard, or

(5) any other admission of liability under any statute or under any common law.

(e) Definitions

For purposes of this section:

(1) A grievous bodily injury includes any of the following categories of injury: mutilation, amputation, dismemberment, disfigurement, loss of important bodily functions, debilitating internal disorder, severe burn, severe electric shock, and injuries likely to require extended hospitalization.

(2) For purposes of this section, a particular model of a consumer product is one that is distinctive in functional design, construction, warnings or instructions related to safety, function, user population, or other characteristics which could affect the product's safety related performance.

Pub.L. 92–573, § 37, as added Pub.L. 101–608, § 112(b), Nov. 16, 1990, 104 Stat. 3115.

MAGNUSON–MOSS WARRANTY ACT*

Enacted as Title I of "Magnuson–Moss Warranty— Federal Trade Commission Improvement Act"

---

* Act of January 4, 1975, Public Law 93–637, 88 Stat. 2183–93; 15 U.S.C.A. §§ 2301–12.

Code of Federal Regulations

Rules, Regulations, Statements and Interpretations under the Magnuson–Moss Warranty Act, see 16 CFR 701.1 et seq.

§ 2301. Definitions

For the purposes of this chapter:

(1) The term "consumer product" means any tangible personal property which is distributed in commerce and which is normally used for personal, family, or household purposes (including any such property intended to be attached to or installed in any real property without regard to whether it is so attached or installed).

(2) The term "Commission" means the Federal Trade Commission.

(3) The term "consumer" means a buyer (other than for purposes of resale) of any consumer product, any person to whom such product is transferred during the duration of an implied or written warranty (or service contract) applicable to the product, and any other person who is entitled by the terms of such warranty (or service contract) or under applicable State law to enforce against the warrantor (or service contractor) the obligations of the (warranty or service contract).

(4) The term "supplier" means any person engaged in the business of making a consumer product directly or indirectly available to consumers.

(5) The term "warrantor" means any supplier or other person who gives or offers to give a written warranty or who is or may be obligated under an implied warranty.

(6) The term "written warranty" means—

    (A) any written affirmation of fact or written promise made in connection with the sale of a consumer product by a supplier to a buyer which relates to the nature of the material or workmanship and affirms or promises that such material or workmanship is defect free or will meet a specified level of performance over a specified period of time, or

    (B) any undertaking in writing in connection with the sale by a supplier of a consumer product to refund, repair, replace, or take other remedial action with respect to such product in the event that such product fails to meet the specifications set forth in the undertaking.

Which written affirmation, promise, or undertaking becomes part of the basis of the bargain between a supplier and a buyer for purposes other than resale of such product.

    (7) The term "implied warranty" means an implied warranty arising under State law (as modified by sections 2308 and 2304(a) of this title) in connection with the sale by a supplier of a consumer product.

    (8) The term "service contract" means a contract in writing to perform, over a fixed period of time or for a specified duration, services relating to the maintenance or repair (or both) of a consumer product.

    (9) The term "reasonable and necessary maintenance" consists of those operations (A) which the consumer reasonably can be expected to perform or have performed and (B) which are necessary to keep any consumer product performing its intended function and operating at a reasonable level of performance.

    (10) The term "remedy" means whichever of the following actions the warrantor elects:

    (A) repair,

    (B) replacement, or

    (C) refund;

except that the warrantor may not elect refund unless (i) the warrantor is unable to provide replacement and repair is not commercially practicable or cannot be timely made, or (ii) the consumer is willing to accept such refund.

    (11) The term "replacement" means furnishing a new consumer product which is identical or reasonably equivalent to the warranted consumer product.

    (12) The term "refund" means refunding the actual purchase price (less reasonable depreciation based on actual use where permitted by rules of the Commission).

    (13) The term "distributed in commerce" means sold in commerce, introduced or delivered for introduction into commerce, or held for sale or distribution after introduction into commerce.

    (14) The term "commerce" means trade, traffic, commerce, or transportation—

(A) between a place in a State and any place outside thereof, or

(B) which affects trade, traffic, commerce, or transportation described in subparagraph (A).

(15) The term "State" means a State, the District of Columbia, the Commonwealth of Puerto Rico, the Virgin Islands, Guam, the Canal Zone, or American Samoa. The term "State law" includes a law of the United States applicable only to the District of Columbia or only to a territory or possession of the United States; and the term "Federal law" excludes any State law.

Pub.L. 93–637, Title I, § 101, Jan. 4, 1975, 88 Stat. 2183.

§ 2302. Rules governing contents of warranties

(a) Full and conspicuous disclosure of terms and conditions; additional requirements for contents

(a) In order to improve the adequacy of information available to consumers, prevent deception, and improve competition in the marketing of consumer products any warrantor warranting a consumer product to a consumer by means of a written warranty shall, to the extent required by rules of the Commission, fully and conspicuously disclose in simple and readily understood language the terms and conditions of such warranty. Such rules may require inclusion in the written warranty of any of the following items among others:

(1) The clear identification of the names and addresses of the warrantors.

(2) The identity of the party or parties to whom the warranty is extended.

(3) The products or parts covered.

(4) A statement of what the warrantor will do in the event of a defect, malfunction, or failure to conform with such written warranty—at whose expense—and for what period of time.

(5) A statement of what the consumer must do and expenses he must bear.

(6) Exceptions and exclusions from the terms of the warranty.

(7) The step-by-step procedure which the consumer should take in order to obtain performance of any obligation under the warranty, including the identification of any person or class of persons authorized to perform the obligation set forth in the warranty.

(8) Information respecting the availability of any informal dispute settlement procedure offered by the warrantor and a recital, where the

warranty so provides, that the purchaser may be required to resort to such procedure before pursuing any legal remedies in the courts.

(9) A brief, general description of the legal remedies available to the consumer.

(10) The time at which the warrantor will perform any obligations under the warranty.

(11) The period of time within which, after notice of a defect, malfunction, or failure to conform with the warranty, the warrantor will perform any obligations under the warranty.

(12) The characteristics or properties of the products, or parts thereof, that are not covered by the warranty.

(13) The elements of the warranty in words or phrases which would not mislead a reasonable, average consumer as to the nature or scope of the warranty.

(b) Availability of terms to consumer; manner and form for presentation and display of information; duration; extension of period for written warranty or service contract

(b)(1)(A) The Commission shall prescribe rules requiring that the terms of any written warranty on a consumer product be made available to the consumer (or prospective consumer) prior to the sale of the product to him.

(B) The Commission may prescribe rules for determining the manner and form in which information with respect to any written warranty of a consumer product shall be clearly and conspicuously presented or displayed so as not to mislead the reasonable, average consumer, when such information is contained in advertising, labeling, point-of-sale material, or other representations in writing.

(2) Nothing in this chapter (other than paragraph (3) of this subsection) shall be deemed to authorize the Commission to prescribe the duration of written warranties given or to require that a consumer product or any of its components be warranted.

(3) The Commission may prescribe rules for extending the period of time a written warranty or service contract is in effect to correspond with any period of time in excess of a reasonable period (not less than 10 days) during which the consumer is deprived of the use of such consumer product by reason of failure of the product to conform with the written warranty or by reason of the failure of the warrantor (or service contractor) to carry out such warranty (or service contract) within the period specified in the warranty (or service contract).

(c) No warrantor of a consumer product may condition his written or implied warranty of such product on the consumer's using, in connection with such product, any article or service (other than article or service provided without charge under the terms of the warranty) which is identified by brand, trade, or corporate name; except that the prohibition of this subsection may be waived by the Commission if—

(1) the warrantor satisfies the Commission that the warranted product will function properly only if the article or service so identified is used in connection with the warranted product, and

(2) the Commission finds that such a waiver is in the public interest.

The Commission shall identify in the Federal Register, and permit public comment on, all applications for waiver of the prohibition of this subsection, and shall publish in the Federal Register its disposition of any such application, including the reasons therefor.

(d) Incorporation by reference of detailed substantive warranty provisions

(d) The Commission may by rule devise detailed substantive warranty provisions which warrantors may incorporate by reference in their warranties.

(e) Applicability to consumer products costing more than $5.00

(e) The provisions of this section apply only to warranties which pertain to consumer products actually costing the consumer more than $5.

Pub.L. 93–637, Title I, § 102, Jan. 4, 1975, 88 Stat. 2185.

§ 2303. Designation of written warranties

(a) Full (statement of duration) or limited warranty

(a) Any warrantor warranting a consumer product by means of a written warranty shall clearly and conspicuously designate such warranty in the following manner, unless exempted from doing so by the Commission pursuant to subsection (c) of this section:

(1) If the written warranty meets the Federal minimum standards for warranty set forth in section 2304 of this title, then it shall be conspicuously designated a "full (statement of duration) warranty".

(2) If the written warranty does not meet the Federal minimum standards for warranty set forth in section 2304 of this title, then it shall be conspicuously designated a "limited warranty".

(b) Applicability of requirements, standards, etc., to representations or statements of customer satisfaction

(b) This section and sections 2302 and 2304 of this title shall not apply to statements or representations which are similar to expressions of general policy concerning customer satisfaction and which are not subject to any specific limitations.

(c) Exemptions by Commission

(c) In addition to exercising the authority pertaining to disclosure granted in section 2302 of this title, the Commission may by rule determine when a written warranty does not have to be designated either "full (statement of duration)" or "limited" in accordance with this section.

(d) Applicability to consumer products costing more than $10.00 and not designated as full warranties

(d) The provisions of subsections (a) and (c) of this section apply only to warranties which pertain to consumer products actually costing the consumer more than $10 and which are not designated "full (statement of duration) warranties".

Pub.L. 93–637, Title I, § 103, Jan. 4, 1975, 88 Stat. 2187.

§ 2304. Federal minimum standards for warranties

(a) Remedies under written warranty; duration of implied warranty; exclusion or limitation on consequential damages for breach of written or implied warranty; election of refund or replacement

(a) In order for a warrantor warranting a consumer product by means of a written warranty to meet the Federal minimum standards for warranty—

(1) such warrantor must as a minimum remedy such consumer product within a reasonable time and without charge, in the case of a defect, malfunction, or failure to conform with such written warranty;

(2) notwithstanding section 2308(b) of this title, such warrantor may not impose any limitation on the duration of any implied warranty on the product;

(3) such warrantor may not exclude or limit consequential damages for breach of any written or implied warranty on such product, unless such exclusion or limitation conspicuously appears on the face of the warranty; and

(4) if the product (or a component part thereof) contains a defect or malfunction after a reasonable number of attempts by the warrantor to remedy defects or malfunctions in such product, such warrantor

must permit the consumer to elect either a refund for, or replacement without charge of, such product or part (as the case may be). The Commission may by rule specify for purposes of this paragraph, what constitutes a reasonable number of attempts to remedy particular kinds of defects or malfunctions under different circumstances. If the warrantor replaces a component part of a consumer product, such replacement shall include installing the part in the product without charge.

(b) Duties and conditions imposed on consumer by warrantor

(b)(1) In fulfilling the duties under subsection (a) of this section respecting a written warranty, the warrantor shall not impose any duty other than notification upon any consumer as a condition of securing remedy of any consumer product which malfunctions, is defective, or does not conform to the written warranty, unless the warrantor has demonstrated in a rulemaking proceeding, or can demonstrate in an administrative or judicial enforcement proceeding (including private enforcement), or in an informal dispute settlement proceeding, that such a duty is reasonable.

(2) Notwithstanding paragraph (1), a warrantor may require, as a condition to replacement of, or refund for, any consumer product under subsection (a) of this section, that such consumer product shall be made available to the warrantor free and clear of liens and other encumbrances, except as otherwise provided by rule or order of the Commission in cases in which such a requirement would not be practicable.

(3) The Commission may, by rule define in detail the duties set forth in subsection (a) of this section and the applicability of such duties to warrantors of different categories of consumer products with "full (statement of duration)" warranties.

(4) The duties under subsection (a) of this section extend from the warrantor to each person who is a consumer with respect to the consumer product.

(c) Waiver of standards

(c) The performance of the duties under subsection (a) of this section shall not be required of the warrantor if he can show that the defect, malfunction, or failure of any warranted consumer product to conform with a written warranty, was caused by damage (not resulting from defect or malfunction) while in the possession of the consumer, or unreasonable use (including failure to provide reasonable and necessary maintenance).

(d) Remedy without charge

(d) For purposes of this section and of section 2302(c) of this title, the term "without charge" means that the warrantor may not assess the

383

consumer for any costs the warrantor or his representatives incur in connection with the required remedy of a warranted consumer product. An obligation under subsection (a)(1)(A) of this section to remedy without charge does not necessarily require the warrantor to compensate the consumer for incidental expenses; however, if any incidental expenses are incurred because the remedy is not made within a reasonable time or because the warrantor imposed an unreasonable duty upon the consumer as a condition of securing remedy, then the consumer shall be entitled to recover reasonable incidental expenses which are so incurred in any action against the warrantor.

(e) Incorporation of standards to products designated with full warranty for purposes of judicial actions

(e) If a supplier designates a warranty applicable to a consumer product as a "full (statement of duration)" warranty, then the warranty on such product shall, for purposes of any action under section 2310(d) of this title or under any State law, be deemed to incorporate at least the minimum requirements of this section and rules prescribed under this section.

Pub.L. 93–637, Title I, § 104, Jan. 4, 1975, 88 Stat. 2187.

§ 2305. Full and limited warranting of a consumer product

Nothing in this chapter shall prohibit the selling of a consumer product which has both full and limited warranties if such warranties are clearly and conspicuously differentiated.

Pub.L. 93–637, Title I, § 105, Jan. 4, 1975, 88 Stat. 2188.

§ 2306. Service contracts; rules for full, clear and conspicuous disclosure of terms and conditions; addition to or in lieu of written warranty

(a) The Commission may prescribe by rule the manner and form in which the terms and conditions of service contracts shall be fully, clearly, and conspicuously disclosed.

(b) Nothing in this chapter shall be construed to prevent a supplier or warrantor from entering into a service contract with the consumer in addition to or in lieu of a written warranty if such contract fully, clearly, and conspicuously discloses its terms and conditions in simple and readily understood language.

Pub.L. 93–637, Title I, § 106, Jan. 4, 1975, 88 Stat. 2188.

§ 2307. Designation of representatives by warrantor to perform duties under written or implied warranty

Nothing in this chapter shall be construed to prevent any warrantor from designating representatives to perform duties under the written or implied warranty: *Provided,* That such warrantor shall make reasonable arrangements for compensation of such designated representatives, but no such designation shall relieve the warrantor of his direct responsibilities to the consumer or make the representative a cowarrantor.

Pub.L. 93–637, Title I, § 107, Jan. 4, 1975, 88 Stat. 2189.

§ 2308. Implied warranties

(a) Restrictions on disclaimers or modifications

(a) No supplier may disclaim or modify (except as provided in subsection (b) of this section) any implied warranty to a consumer with respect to such consumer product if (1) such supplier makes any written warranty to the consumer with respect to such consumer product, or (2) at the time of sale, or within 90 days thereafter, such supplier enters into a service contract with the consumer which applies to such consumer product.

(b) Limitation on duration

(b) For purposes of this chapter (other than section 2304(a)(2) of this title), implied warranties may be limited in duration to the duration of a written warranty of reasonable duration, if such limitation is conscionable and is set forth in clear and unmistakable language and prominently displayed on the face of the warranty.

(c) Effectiveness of disclaimers, modifications, or limitations

(c) A disclaimer, modification, or limitation made in violation of this section shall be ineffective for purposes of this chapter and State law.

Pub.L. 93–637, Title I, § 108, Jan. 4, 1975, 88 Stat. 2189.

§ 2309. Procedures applicable to promulgation of rules by Commission; rulemaking proceeding for warranty and warranty practices involved in sale of used motor vehicles

(a) Any rule prescribed under this chapter shall be prescribed in accordance with section 553 of Title 5; except that the Commission shall give interested persons an opportunity for oral presentations of data, views, and arguments, in addition to written submissions. A transcript shall be kept of any oral presentation. Any such rule shall be subject to judicial review under section 57a(e) of this title in the same manner as rules prescribed under section 57a(a)(1)(B) of this title, except that section 57a(e)(3)(B) of this title shall not apply.

(b) The Commission shall initiate within one year after January 4, 1975, a rulemaking proceeding dealing with warranties and warranty practices in connection with the sale of used motor vehicles; and, to the extent necessary to supplement the protections offered the consumer by this chapter, shall prescribe rules dealing with such warranties and practices. In prescribing rules under this subsection, the Commission may exercise any authority it may have under this chapter, or other law, and in addition it may require disclosure that a used motor vehicle is sold without any warranty and specify the form and content of such disclosure.

Pub.L. 93–637, Title I, § 109, Jan. 4, 1975, 88 Stat. 2189.

§ 2310. Remedies in consumer disputes

(a) Informal dispute settlement procedures; establishment; rules setting forth minimum requirements; effect of compliance by warrantor; review of informal procedures or implementation by Commission; application to existing informal procedures

(a)(1) Congress hereby declares it to be its policy to encourage warrantors to establish procedures whereby consumer disputes are fairly and expeditiously settled through informal dispute settlement mechanisms.

(2) The Commission shall prescribe rules setting forth minimum requirements for any informal dispute settlement procedure which is incorporated into the terms of a written warranty to which any provision of this chapter applies. Such rules shall provide for participation in such procedure by independent or governmental entities.

(3) One or more warrantors may establish an informal dispute settlement procedure which meets the requirements of the Commission's rules under paragraph (2). If—

(A) a warrantor establishes such a procedure,

(B) such procedure, and its implementation, meets the requirements of such rules, and

(C) he incorporates in a written warranty a requirement that the consumer resort to such procedure before pursuing any legal remedy under this section respecting such warranty,

then (i) the consumer may not commence a civil action (other than a class action) under subsection (d) of this section unless he initially resorts to such procedure; and (ii) a class of consumers may not proceed in a class action under subsection (d) of this section except to the extent the court determines necessary to establish the representative capacity of the named plaintiffs, unless the named plaintiffs (upon notifying the defendant that they are named plaintiffs in a class action with respect to a warranty obligation) initially resort to such procedure. In the case of such a class action which is brought in a district court of the United States, the representative capacity of the named plaintiffs shall be established in the application of rule 23 of the Federal Rules of Civil Procedure. In any civil action arising out of a warranty obligation and relating to a matter considered in such a procedure, any decision in such procedure shall be admissible in evidence.

(4) The Commission on its own initiative may, or upon written complaint filed by any interested person shall, review the bona fide operation of any dispute settlement procedure resort to which is stated in a written warranty to be a prerequisite to pursuing a legal remedy under this section. If the Commission finds that such procedure or its implementation fails to comply with the requirements of the rules under paragraph (2), the Commission may take appropriate remedial action under any authority it may have under this chapter or any other provision of law.

(5) Until rules under paragraph (2) take effect, this subsection shall not affect the validity of any informal dispute settlement procedure respecting consumer warranties, but in any action under subsection (d) of this section, the court may invalidate any such procedure if it finds that such procedure is unfair.

(b) Prohibited acts

(b) It shall be a violation of section 45(a)(1) of this title for any person to fail to comply with any requirement imposed on such person by this chapter (or a rule thereunder) or to violate any prohibition contained in this chapter (or a rule thereunder).

(c) Injunction proceedings by Attorney General or Commission for deceptive warranty, noncompliance with requirements, or violating prohibitions; procedures; definitions

(c)(1) The district courts of the United States shall have jurisdiction of any action brought by the Attorney General (in his capacity as such), or by the Commission by any of its attorneys designated by it for such purpose, to restrain (A) any warrantor from making a deceptive warranty with respect to a consumer product, or (B) any person from failing to comply with any requirement imposed on such person by or pursuant to this chapter or from violating any prohibition contained in this chapter. Upon proper showing that, weighing the equities and considering the Commission's or Attorney General's likelihood of ultimate success, such action would be in the public interest and after notice to the defendant, a temporary restraining order or preliminary injunction may be granted without bond. In the case of an action brought by the Commission, if a complaint under section 45 of Title 15 is not filed within such period (not exceeding 10 days) as may be specified by the court after the issuance of the temporary restraining order or preliminary injunction, the order or injunction shall be dissolved by the court and be of no further force and effect. Any suit shall be brought in the district in which such person resides or transacts business. Whenever it appears to the court that the ends of justice require that other persons should be parties in the action, the court may cause them to be summoned whether or not they reside in the district in which the court is held, and to that end process may be served in any district.

(2) For the purposes of this subsection, the term "deceptive warranty" means (A) a written warranty which (i) contains an affirmation, promise, deception, or representation which is either false or fraudulent, or which, in light of all the circumstances, would mislead a reasonable individual exercising due care; or (ii) fails to contain information which is necessary in light of all of the circumstances, to make the warranty not misleading to a reasonable individual exercising due care; or (B) a written warranty created by the use of such terms as "guaranty" or "warranty", if the terms and conditions of such warranty so limit its scope and application as to deceive a reasonable individual.

(d) Civil action by consumer for damages, etc.; jurisdiction; recovery of costs and expenses; cognizable claims

(d)(1) Subject to subsections (a)(3) and (e) of this section, a consumer who is damaged by the failure of a supplier, warrantor, or service contractor to comply with any obligation under this chapter, or under a written warranty, implied warranty, or service contract, may bring suit for damages and other legal and equitable relief—

(A) in any court of competent jurisdiction in any State or the District of Columbia; or

(B) in an appropriate district court of the United States, subject to paragraph (3) of this subsection.

(2) If a consumer finally prevails in any action brought under paragraph (1) of this subsection, he may be allowed by the court to recover as part of the judgment a sum equal to the aggregate amount of cost and expenses (including attorneys' fees based on actual time expended) determined by the court to have been reasonably incurred by the plaintiff for or in connection with the commencement and prosecution of such action, unless the court in its discretion shall determine that such an award of attorneys' fees would be inappropriate.

(3) No claim shall be cognizable in a suit brought under paragraph (1)(B) of this subsection—

(A) if the amount in controversy of any individual claim is less than the sum or value of $25;

(B) if the amount in controversy is less than the sum or value of $50,000 (exclusive of interests and costs) computed on the basis of all claims to be determined in this suit; or

(C) if the action is brought as a class action, and the number of named plaintiffs is less than one hundred.

(e) Class actions; conditions; procedures applicable

(e) No action (other than a class action or an action respecting a warranty to which subsection (a)(3) of this section applies) may be brought under subsection (d) of this section for failure to comply with any obligation under any written or implied warranty or service contract, and a class of consumers may not proceed in a class action under such subsection with respect to such a failure except to the extent the court determines necessary to establish the representative capacity of the named plaintiffs, unless the person obligated under the warranty or service contract is afforded a reasonable opportunity to cure such failure to comply. In the case of such a class action (other than a class action respecting a warranty to which subsection (a)(3) of this section applies) brought under subsection (d) of this section for breach of any written or implied warranty or service contract, such reasonable opportunity will be afforded by the named plaintiffs and they shall at that time notify the defendant that they are acting on behalf of the class. In the case of such a class action which is brought in a district court of the United States, the representative capacity of the named plaintiffs shall be established in the application of rule 23 of the Federal Rules of Civil Procedure.

(f) Warrantors subject to enforcement of remedies

(f) For purposes of this section, only the warrantor actually making a written affirmation of fact, promise, or undertaking shall be deemed to have created a written warranty, and any rights arising thereunder may be enforced under this section only against such warrantor and no other person.

Pub.L. 93–637, Title I, § 110, Jan. 4, 1975, 88 Stat. 2189.

§ 2311. Applicability of provisions to other Federal or State laws and requirements

(a)(1) Nothing contained in this chapter shall be construed to repeal, invalidate, or supersede the Federal Trade Commission Act or any statute defined therein as an Antitrust Act.

(2) Nothing in this chapter shall be construed to repeal, invalidate, or supersede the Federal Seed Act and nothing in this chapter shall apply to seed for planting.

(b)(1) Nothing in this chapter shall invalidate or restrict any right or remedy of any consumer under State law or any other Federal law.

(2) Nothing in this chapter (other than sections 2304(a)(2) and (4) and 2308 of this title) shall (A) affect the liability of, or impose liability on, any person for personal injury, or (B) supersede any provision of State law regarding consequential damages for injury to the person or other injury.

(c)(1) Except as provided in subsection (b) of this section and in paragraph (2) of this subsection, a State requirement—

(A) which relates to labeling or disclosure with respect to written warranties or performance thereunder;

(B) which is within the scope of an applicable requirement of sections 2302, 2303, and 2304 of this title (and rules implementing such sections), and

(C) which is not identical to a requirement of section 2302, 2303, or 2304 of this title (or a rule thereunder),

shall not be applicable to written warranties complying with such sections (or rules thereunder).

(2) If, upon application of an appropriate State agency, the Commission determines (pursuant to rules issued in accordance with section 2309 of this title) that any requirement of such State covering any transaction to which this chapter applies (A) affords protection to consumers greater than the requirements of this chapter and (B) does not unduly burden interstate commerce, then such State requirement shall be applicable (notwithstanding the provisions of paragraph (1) of this subsection) to the extent specified in such determination for so long as the State administers and enforces effectively any such greater requirement.

(d) This chapter (other than section 2302(c) of this title) shall be inapplicable to any written warranty the making or content of which is otherwise governed by Federal law. If only a portion of a written warranty is so governed by Federal law, the remaining portion shall be subject to this chapter.

Pub.L. 93–637, Title I, § 111, Jan. 4, 1975, 88 Stat. 2192.

§ 2312.　Effective dates; time for promulgation of rules by Commission

(a) Except as provided in subsection (b) of this section, this chapter shall take effect 6 months after January 4, 1975, but shall not apply to consumer products manufactured prior to such date.

(b) Section 2302(a) of this title shall take effect 6 months after the final publication of rules respecting such section; except that the Commission, for good cause shown, may postpone the applicability of such sections until one year after such final publication in order to permit any designated classes of suppliers to bring their written warranties into compliance with rules promulgated pursuant to this chapter.

(c) The Commission shall promulgate rules for initial implementation of this chapter as soon as possible after January 4, 1975, but in no event later than one year after such date.

Pub.L. 93–637, Title I, § 112, Jan. 4, 1975, 88 Stat. 2192.

PROTECTION OF LAWFUL COMMERCE IN ARMS ACT
15 U.S.C.A. §§ 7901-7903

---

§ 7901. Findings; purposes.

(a) Findings

Congress finds the following:

(1) The Second Amendment to the United States Constitution provides that the right of the people to keep and bear arms shall not be infringed.

(2) The Second Amendment to the United States Constitution protects the rights of individuals, including those who are not members of a militia or engaged in military service or training, to keep and bear arms.

(3) Lawsuits have been commenced against manufacturers, distributors, dealers, and importers of firearms that operate as designed and intended, which seek money damages and other relief for the harm caused by the misuse of firearms by third parties, including criminals.

(4) The manufacture, importation, possession, sale, and use of firearms and ammunition in the United States are heavily regulated by Federal, State, and local laws. Such Federal laws include the Gun Control Act of 1968, the National Firearms Act, and the Arms Export Control Act.

(5) Businesses in the United States that are engaged in interstate and foreign commerce through the lawful design, manufacture, marketing, distribution, importation, or sale to the public of firearms or ammunition products that have been shipped or transported in interstate or foreign commerce are not, and should not, be liable for the harm caused by those who criminally or unlawfully misuse firearm products or ammunition products that function as designed and intended.

(6) The possibility of imposing liability on an entire industry for harm that is solely caused by others is an abuse of the legal system, erodes public confidence in our Nation's laws, threatens the diminution of a basic

constitutional right and civil liberty, invites the disassembly and destabilization of other industries and economic sectors lawfully competing in the free enterprise system of the United States, and constitutes an unreasonable burden on interstate and foreign commerce of the United States.

(7) The liability actions commenced or contemplated by the Federal Government, States, municipalities, and private interest groups and others are based on theories without foundation in hundreds of years of the common law and jurisprudence of the United States and do not represent a bona fide expansion of the common law. The possible sustaining of these actions by a maverick judicial officer or petit jury would expand civil liability in a manner never contemplated by the framers of the Constitution, by Congress, or by the legislatures of the several States. Such an expansion of liability would constitute a deprivation of the rights, privileges, and immunities guaranteed to a citizen of the United States under the Fourteenth Amendment to the United States Constitution.

(8) The liability actions commenced or contemplated by the Federal Government, States, municipalities, private interest groups and others attempt to use the judicial branch to circumvent the Legislative branch of government to regulate interstate and foreign commerce through judgments and judicial decrees thereby threatening the Separation of Powers doctrine and weakening and undermining important principles of federalism, State sovereignty and comity between the sister States.

(b) Purposes

The purposes of this chapter are as follows:

(1) To prohibit causes of action against manufacturers, distributors, dealers, and importers of firearms or ammunition products, and their trade associations, for the harm solely caused by the criminal or unlawful misuse of firearm products or ammunition products by others when the product functioned as designed and intended.

(2) To preserve a citizen's access to a supply of firearms and ammunition for all lawful purposes, including hunting, self-defense, collecting, and competitive or recreational shooting.

(3) To guarantee a citizen's rights, privileges, and immunities, as applied to the States, under the Fourteenth Amendment to the United States Constitution, pursuant to section 5 of that Amendment.

(4) To prevent the use of such lawsuits to impose unreasonable burdens on interstate and foreign commerce.

(5) To protect the right, under the First Amendment to the Constitution, of manufacturers, distributors, dealers, and importers of firearms or ammunition products, and trade associations, to speak freely, to assemble peaceably, and to petition the Government for a redress of their grievances.

(6) To preserve and protect the Separation of Powers doctrine and important principles of federalism, State sovereignty and comity between sister States.

(7) To exercise congressional power under article IV, section 1 (the Full Faith and Credit Clause) of the United States Constitution.

(Pub. L. 109-92, § 2, Oct. 26, 2005, 119 Stat. 2095.)

§ 7902. Prohibition on bringing of qualified civil liability actions in Federal or State court.

(a) In general

A qualified civil liability action may not be brought in any Federal or State court.

(b) Dismissal of pending actions

A qualified civil liability action that is pending on October 26, 2005, shall be immediately dismissed by the court in which the action was brought or is currently pending.

(Pub. L. 109-92, § 3, Oct. 26, 2005, 119 Stat. 2096.)

§ 7903. Definitions.

In this chapter:

(1) Engaged in the business

The term "engaged in the business" has the meaning given that term in section 921(a)(21) of Title 18, and, as applied to a seller of ammunition, means a person who devotes time, attention, and labor to the sale of ammunition as a regular course of trade or business with the principal objective of livelihood and profit through the sale or distribution of ammunition.

(2) Manufacturer

The term "manufacturer" means, with respect to a qualified product, a person who is engaged in the business of manufacturing the product in interstate or foreign commerce and who is licensed to engage in business as such a manufacturer under chapter 44 of Title 18.

(3) Person

The term "person" means any individual, corporation, company, association, firm, partnership, society, joint stock company, or any other entity, including any governmental entity.

(4) Qualified product

The term "qualified product" means a firearm (as defined in subparagraph (A) or (B) of section 921(a)(3) of Title 18), including any antique firearm (as defined in section 921(a)(16) of such title), or ammunition (as defined in section 921(a)(17)(A) of such title), or a component part of a firearm or ammunition, that has been shipped or transported in interstate or foreign commerce.

(5) Qualified civil liability action

(A) In general

The term "qualified civil liability action" means a civil action or proceeding or an administrative proceeding brought by any person against a manufacturer or seller of a qualified product, or a trade association, for damages, punitive damages, injunctive or declaratory relief, abatement, restitution, fines, or penalties, or other relief, resulting from the criminal or unlawful misuse of a qualified product by the person or a third party, but shall not include—

(i) an action brought against a transferor convicted under section 924(h) of Title 18, or a comparable or identical State felony law, by a party directly harmed by the conduct of which the transferee is so convicted;

(ii) an action brought against a seller for negligent entrustment or negligence per se;

(iii) an action in which a manufacturer or seller of a qualified product knowingly violated a State or Federal statute applicable to the sale or marketing of the product, and the violation was a proximate cause of the harm for which relief is sought, including—

(I) any case in which the manufacturer or seller knowingly made any false entry in, or failed to make appropriate entry in, any record required to be kept under Federal or State law with respect to the qualified product, or aided, abetted, or conspired with any person in making any false or fictitious oral or written statement with respect to any fact material to the lawfulness of the sale or other disposition of a qualified product; or

(II) any case in which the manufacturer or seller aided, abetted, or conspired with any other person to sell or otherwise dispose of a qualified product, knowing, or having reasonable cause to believe, that the actual buyer of the qualified product was prohibited from possessing or receiving a firearm or ammunition under subsection (g) or (n) of section 922 of Title 18;

(iv) an action for breach of contract or warranty in connection with the purchase of the product;

(v) an action for death, physical injuries or property damage resulting directly from a defect in design or manufacture of the product, when used as intended or in a reasonably foreseeable manner, except that where the discharge of the product was caused by a volitional act that constituted a criminal offense, then such act shall be considered the sole proximate cause of any resulting death, personal injuries or property damage; or

(vi) an action or proceeding commenced by the Attorney General to enforce the provisions of chapter 44 of Title 18 or chapter 53 of Title 26.

(B) Negligent entrustment

As used in subparagraph (A)(ii), the term "negligent entrustment" means the supplying of a qualified product by a seller for use by another person when the seller knows, or reasonably should know, the person to whom the product is supplied is likely to, and does, use the product in a manner involving unreasonable risk of physical injury to the person or others.

(C) Rule of construction

The exceptions enumerated under clauses (i) through (v) of subparagraph (A) shall be construed so as not to be in conflict, and no provision of this chapter shall be construed to create a public or private cause of action or remedy.

(D) Minor child exception

Nothing in this chapter shall be construed to limit the right of a person under 17 years of age to recover damages authorized under Federal or State law in a civil action that meets 1 of the requirements under clauses (i) through (v) of subparagraph (A).

(6) Seller

The term "seller" means, with respect to a qualified product—

(A) an importer (as defined in section 921(a)(9) of Title 18) who is engaged in the business as such an importer in interstate or foreign commerce and who is licensed to engage in business as such an importer under chapter 44 of Title 18;

(B) a dealer (as defined in section 921(a)(11) of Title 18) who is engaged in the business as such a dealer in interstate or foreign commerce and who is licensed to engage in business as such a dealer under chapter 44 of Title 18; or

(C) a person engaged in the business of selling ammunition (as defined in section 921(a)(17)(A) of Title 18) in interstate or foreign commerce at the wholesale or retail level.

(7) State

The term "State" includes each of the several States of the United States, the District of Columbia, the Commonwealth of Puerto Rico, the Virgin Islands, Guam, American Samoa, and the Commonwealth of the Northern Mariana Islands, and any other territory or possession of the United States, and any political subdivision of any such place.

(8) Trade association

The term "trade association" means—

(A) any corporation, unincorporated association, federation, business league, professional or business organization not organized or operated for profit and no part of the net earnings of which inures to the benefit of any private shareholder or individual;

(B) that is an organization described in section 501(c)(6) of Title 26 and exempt from tax under section 501(a) of such title; and

(C) 2 or more members of which are manufacturers or sellers of a qualified product.

(9) Unlawful misuse

The term "unlawful misuse" means conduct that violates a statute, ordinance, or regulation as it relates to the use of a qualified product. (Pub. L. 109-92, § 4, Oct. 26, 2005, 119 Stat. 2097.)

EEC DIRECTIVE ON LIABILITY FOR DEFECTIVE PRODUCTS

COUNCIL DIRECTIVE

of

25 July 1985 on the approximation of the laws, regulations and administrative provisions of the Member States concerning liability for defective products

(85/374/EEC)

THE COUNCIL OF THE EUROPEAN COMMUNITIES,

Having regard to the Treaty establishing the European Economic Community, and in particular Article 100 thereof,

Having regard to the proposal from the Commission,

Having regard to the opinion of the European Parliament,

Having regard to the opinion of the Economic and Social Committee,

Whereas approximation of the laws of the Member States concerning the liability of the producer for damage caused by the defectiveness of his products is necessary because the existing divergences may distort competition and affect the movement of goods within the common market and entail a differing degree of protection of the consumer against damage caused by a defective product to his health or property;

Whereas liability without fault on the part of the producer is the sole means of adequately solving the problem, peculiar to our age of increasing technicality, of a fair apportionment of the risks inherent in modern technological production;

Whereas liability without fault should apply only to movables which have been industrially produced; whereas, as a result, it is appropriate to exclude liability for agricultural products and game, except where they have undergone a processing of an industrial nature which could cause a defect in these products; whereas the liability provided for in this Directive should also apply to movables which are used in the construction of immovables or are installed in immovables;

Whereas protection of the consumer requires that all producers involved in the production process should be made liable, in so far as their finished product, component part or any raw material supplied by them was defective; whereas, for the same reason, liability should extend to importers of products into the Community and to persons who present themselves as producers by affixing their name, trade mark or other distinguishing feature or who supply a product the producer of which cannot be identified;

Whereas, in situations where several persons are liable for the same damage, the protection of the consumer requires that the injured person should be able to claim full compensation for the damage from any one of them;

Whereas, to protect the physical well-being and property of the consumer, the defectiveness of the product should be determined by reference not to its fitness for use but to the lack of the safety which the public at large is entitled to expect; whereas the safety is assessed by excluding any misuse of the product not reasonable under the circumstances;

Whereas a fair apportionment of risk between the injured person and the producer implies that the producer should be able to free himself from liability if he furnishes proof as to the existence of certain exonerating circumstances;

Whereas the protection of the consumer requires that the liability of the producer remains unaffected by acts or omissions of other persons having contributed to cause the damage; whereas, however, the contributory negligence of the injured person may be taken into account to reduce or disallow such liability;

Whereas the protection of the consumer requires compensation for death and personal injury as well as compensation for damage to property; whereas the latter should nevertheless be limited to goods for private use or consumption and be subject to a deduction of a lower threshold of a fixed amount in order to avoid litigation in an excessive number of cases; whereas this Directive should not prejudice compensation for pain and suffering and other non-material damages payable, where appropriate, under the law applicable to the case;

Whereas a uniform period of limitation for the bringing of action for compensation is in the interests both of the injured person and of the producer;

Whereas products age in the course of time, higher safety standards are developed and the state of science and technology progresses; whereas, therefore, it would not be reasonable to make the producer liable for an unlimited period for the defectiveness of his product; whereas, therefore, liability should expire after a reasonable length of time, without prejudice to claims pending at law;

Whereas, to achieve effective protection of consumers, no contractual derogation should be permitted as regards the liability of the producer in relation to the injured person;

Whereas under the legal systems of the Member States an injured party may have a claim for damages based on grounds of contractual liability or on grounds of non-contractual liability other than that provided for in this Directive; in so far as these provisions also serve to attain the objective of effective protection of consumers, they should remain unaffected by this Directive; whereas, in so far as effective protection of consumers in the sector of pharmaceutical products is already also attained in a Member

State under a special liability system, claims based on this system should similarly remain possible;

Whereas, to the extent that liability for nuclear injury or damage is already covered in all Member States by adequate special rules, it has been possible to exclude damage of this type from the scope of this Directive;

Whereas, since the exclusion of primary agricultural products and game from the scope of this Directive may be felt, in certain Member States, in view of what is expected for the protection of consumers, to restrict unduly such protection, it should be possible for a Member State to extend liability to such products;

Whereas, for similar reasons, the possibility offered to a producer to free himself from liability if he proves that the state of scientific and technical knowledge at the time when he put the product into circulation was not such as to enable the existence of a defect to be discovered may be felt in certain Member States to restrict unduly the protection of the consumer; whereas it should therefore be possible for a Member State to maintain in its legislation or to provide by new legislation that this exonerating circumstance is not admitted; whereas, in the case of new legislation, making use of this derogation should, however, be subject to a Community stand-still procedure, in order to raise, if possible, the level of protection in a uniform manner throughout the Community;

Whereas, taking into account the legal traditions in most of the Member States, it is inappropriate to set any financial ceiling on the producer's liability without fault; whereas, in so far as there are, however, differing traditions, it seems possible to admit that a Member State may derogate from the principle of unlimited liability by providing a limit for the total liability of the producer for damage resulting from a death or personal injury and caused by identical items with the same defect, provided that this limit is established at a level sufficiently high to guarantee adequate protection of the consumer and the correct functioning of the common market;

Whereas the harmonization resulting from this cannot be total at the present stage, but opens the way towards greater harmonization; whereas it is therefore necessary that the Council receive at regular intervals, reports from the Commission on the application of this Directive, accompanied, as the case may be, by appropriate proposals;

Whereas it is particularly important in this respect that a re-examination be carried out of those parts of the Directive relating to the derogations open to the Member States, at the expiry of a period of sufficient length to gather practical experience on the effects of these derogations on the protection of consumers and on the functioning of the common market,

HAS ADOPTED THIS DIRECTIVE:

Article 1

The producer shall be liable for damage caused by a defect in his product.

Article 2

For the purpose of this Directive "product" means all movables, with the exception of primary agricultural products and game, even though incorporated into another movable or into an immovable. "Primary agricultural products" means the products of the soil, of stock-farming and of fisheries, excluding products which have undergone initial processing. "Product" includes electricity.

Article 3

1. "Producer" means the manufacturer of a finished product, the producer of any raw material or the manufacturer of a component part and any person who, by putting his name, trade mark or other distinguishing feature on the product presents himself as its producer.

2. Without prejudice to the liability of the producer, any person who imports into the Community a product for sale, hire, leasing or any form of distribution in the course of his business shall be deemed to be a producer within the meaning of this Directive and shall be responsible as a producer.

3. Where the producer of the product cannot be identified, each supplier of the product shall be treated as its producer unless he informs the injured person, within a reasonable time, of the identity of the producer or of the person who supplied him with the product. The same shall apply, in the case of an imported product, if this product does not indicate the identity of the importer referred to in paragraph 2, even if the name of the producer is indicated.

Article 4

The injured person shall be required to prove the damage, the defect and the causal relationship between defect and damage.

Article 5

Where, as a result of the provisions of this Directive, two or more persons are liable for the same damage, they shall be liable jointly and severally, without prejudice to the provisions of national law concerning the rights of contribution or recourse.

Article 6

1. A product is defective when it does not provide the safety which a person is entitled to expect, taking all circumstances into account, including:

(a) the presentation of the product;

(b) the use to which it could reasonably be expected that the product would be put;

(c) the time when the product was put into circulation.

2.   A product shall not be considered defective for the sole reason that a better product is subsequently put into circulation.

Article 7

The producer shall not be liable as a result of this Directive if he proves:

(a) that he did not put the product into circulation; or

(b) that, having regard to the circumstances, it is probable that the defect which caused the damage did not exist at the time when the product was put into circulation by him or that this defect came into being afterwards; or

(c) that the product was neither manufactured by him for sale or any form of distribution for economic purpose nor manufactured or distributed by him in the course of his business; or

(d) that the defect is due to compliance of the product with mandatory regulations issued by the public authorities; or

(e) that the state of scientific and technical knowledge at the time when he put the product into circulation was not such as to enable the existence of the defect to be discovered; or

(f) in the case of a manufacturer of a component, that the defect is attributable to the design of the product in which the component has been fitted or to the instructions given by the manufacturer of the product.

Article 8

1.   Without prejudice to the provisions of national law concerning the right of contribution or recourse, the liability of the producer shall not be reduced when the damage is caused both by a defect in product and by the act or omission of a third party.

2.   The liability of the producer may be reduced or disallowed when, having regard to all the circumstances, the damage is caused both by a defect in the product and by the fault of the injured person or any person for whom the injured person is responsible.

Article 9

For the purpose of Article 1, "damage" means:

(a) damage caused by death or by personal injuries;

(b) damage to, or destruction of, any item of property other than the defective product itself, with a lower threshold of 500 ECU, provided that the item of property:

　(i) is of a type ordinarily intended for private use or consumption, and

　(ii) was used by the injured person mainly for his own private use or consumption.

401

This Article shall be without prejudice to national provisions relating to non-material damage.

Article 10

1. Member States shall provide in their legislation that a limitation period of three years shall apply to proceedings for the recovery of damages as provided for in this Directive. The limitation period shall begin to run from the day on which the plaintiff became aware, or should reasonably have become aware, of the damage, the defect and the identity of the producer.

2. The laws of Member States regulating suspension or interruption of the limitation period shall not be affected by this Directive.

Article 11

Member States shall provide in their legislation that the rights conferred upon the injured person pursuant to this Directive shall be extinguished upon the expiry of a period of 10 years from the date on which the producer put into circulation the actual product which caused the damage, unless the injured person has in the meantime instituted proceedings against the producer.

Article 12

The liability of the producer arising from this Directive may not, in relation to the injured person, be limited or excluded by a provision limiting his liability or exempting him from liability.

Article 13

This Directive shall not affect any rights which an injured person may have according to the rules of the law of contractual or non-contractual liability or a special liability system existing at the moment when this Directive is notified.

Article 14

This Directive shall not apply to injury or damage arising from nuclear accidents and covered by international conventions ratified by the Member States.

Article 15

1. Each Member State may:

(a) by way of derogation from Article 2, provide in its legislation that within the meaning of Article 1 of this Directive "product" also means primary agricultural products and game;

(b) by way of derogation from Article 7(e), maintain or, subject to the procedure set out in paragraph 2 of this Article, provide in this legislation that the producer shall be liable even if he proves that the state of scientific and technical knowledge at the time when he put the product into circulation was not such as to enable the existence of a defect to be discovered.

2. A Member State wishing to introduce the measure specified in paragraph 1(b) shall communicate the text of the proposed measure to the Commission. The Commission shall inform the other Member States thereof.

The Member State concerned shall hold the proposed measure in abeyance for nine months after the Commission is informed and provided that in the meantime the Commission has not submitted to the Council a proposal amending this Directive on the relevant matter. However, if within three months of receiving the said information, the Commission does not advise the Member State concerned that it intends submitting such a proposal to the Council, the Member State may take the proposed measure immediately.

If the Commission does submit to the Council such a proposal amending this Directive within the aforementioned nine months, the Member State concerned shall hold the proposed measure in abeyance for a further period of 18 months from the date on which the proposal is submitted.

3. Ten years after the date of notification of this Directive, the Commission shall submit to the Council a report on the effect that rulings by the courts as to the application of Article 7(e) and of paragraph 1(b) of this Article have on consumer protection and the functioning of the common market. In the light of this report the Council, acting on a proposal from the Commission and pursuant to the terms of Article 100 of the Treaty, shall decide whether to repeal Article 7(e).

Article 16

1. Any Member State may provide that a producer's total liability for damage resulting from a death or personal injury and caused by identical items with the same defect shall be limited to an amount which may not be less than 70 million ECU.

2. Ten years after the date of notification of this Directive, the Commission shall submit to the Council a report on the effect on consumer protection and the functioning of the common market of the implementation of the financial limit on liability by those Member States which have used the option provided for in paragraph 1. In the light of this report the Council, acting on a proposal from the Commission and pursuant to the terms of Article 100 of the Treaty, shall decide whether to repeal paragraph 1.

Article 17

This Directive shall not apply to products put into circulation before the date on which the provisions referred to in Article 19 enter into force.

Article 18

1. For the purposes of this Directive, the ECU shall be that defined by Regulation (EEC) No 3180/78, as amended by Regulation (EEC) No 2626/84. The equivalent in national currency shall initially be calculated at the rate obtaining on the date of adoption of this Directive.

2. Every five years the Council, acting on a proposal from the Commission, shall examine and, if need be, revise the amounts in this Directive, in the light of economic and monetary trends in the Community.

Article 19

1. Member States shall bring into force, not later than three years from the date of notification of this Directive, the laws, regulations and administrative provisions necessary to comply with this Directive. They shall forthwith inform the Commission thereof.

2. The procedure set out in Article 15(2) shall apply from the date of notification of this Directive.

Article 20

Member States shall communicate to the Commission the texts of the main provisions of national law which they subsequently adopt in the field governed by this Directive.

Article 21

Every five years the Commission shall present a report to the Council on the application of this Directive and, if necessary, shall submit appropriate proposals to it.

Article 22

This Directive is addressed to the Member States.

Done at Brussels, 25 July 1985.

For the Council

The President

J. POOS

†